S0-BDA-715

Women's Basketball

Women's Basketball

Mildred J. Barnes

Central Missouri State University

ALLYN AND BACON, INC.

BOSTON · LONDON · SYDNEY · TORONTO

© Copyright 1972 by Allyn and Bacon, Inc., 470 Atlantic Avenue, Boston.

All rights reserved. Printed in the United States of America. No part of the material protected by this copyright notice may be reproduced or utilized in any form or by any means, electronic or mechanical, including photocopying, recording, or by any informational storage and retrieval system, without written permission from the copyright owner.

Library of Congress Catalog Number: 72–76472
ISBN: 0-205-03450-0

Seventh printing . . . August, 1976

To

Gretchen Schuyler and Helen McNaughton

who typify

the quality of leadership needed by youth today

Acknowledgements

The author wishes to express her gratitude to the players, coaches, umpires and friends who have made the game of basketball so enjoyable over the years. Particular gratitude is expressed to my former players who have provided me with considerable satisfaction and reward.

Special thanks is extended to all those coaches who have discussed tactics and offered suggestions for the book. Particular thanks is expressed to Norm Short, head basketball coach at Central Missouri State University and his assistants, Ron Heinrichs and Dan Wall; and to Ralph Miller, currently head coach at Oregon State University.

The author is particularly indebted to Gil D. Haynes, H. Gordon Gray and to the Tom Broderick Company, Inc. for providing the uniforms worn by players in the photographs. Numbers one and two are used on the uniforms for illustrative purposes although it is recognized that these single digits are illegal during competitive play.

The author is especially grateful to Don Fagg, Head, Production Photography Department at Central Missouri State University and to Robert Hammermeister and Kem McDaniels who took the photographs which appear throughout the book.

Thanks is also extended to the players who participated in the filming — Deborah Brown, Kay Byers, Diana Burrell, Mary Kaye Dooley, Ronda Miles, Debbie Schooling, Gay Steenbergen, Robin Turley, and Deborah Watson. Special thanks is given to Laurie Arrants and to Margaret Propst, a former international player.

The author would also like to express her appreciation to Dean Martin for her suggestions in the preparation of the manuscript, to Sue Boyd who so capably typed the manuscript, and to Marion Broer who granted permission to adapt diagrams from her book.

Contents

Preface

Women's basketball has undergone considerable change in the last ten years. The transition has been made from a six-player game with a divided court (three players remaining on each side of the division line) to a six-player game with two roving players who could move the full length of the court. Following two years of experimentation, the Joint DGWS-AAU Basketball Rules Committee, at its annual meeting in February, 1971, voted unanimously to adopt rules for a five-player game. At a subsequent meeting of a rules committee under the jurisdiction of the National Federation of State High School Associations, rules for the five-player game were also adopted. This assures that all colleges and naturally all public schools will be playing five-player basketball in the future. Only public schools in a few states will continue playing the six-player game.

Because of the significant change in rules, this text was written for the primary purpose of providing teachers, coaches, and players alike with basic fundamentals for the five-player game of basketball. Consideration was given to the knowledges needed by the beginning teacher, coach, and player as well as to those who are more experienced. An effort was made to provide information for the player and teacher in the physical education class situation, as well as information for players and coaches in the competitive situation.

The book is divided into four parts.

Part I *Offense* deals with the development of individual offensive skills: the use of two, three, and four players in developing offensive tactics and the coordination of five players into an offensive unit. Considerable attention is devoted to the proper technique for executing fundamental skills. Cutting, screening, and scissoring are discussed in detail with variations in the usual execution noted according to defensive deployment. In the chapter on Team Offense the fast break and offenses to use against man-to-man and zone defenses are suggested. Various offensive alignments are discussed to identify options for placement of players depending upon their qualifications. Means of attacking a pressing defense are also offered.

Part II *Defense* deals with individual defense: two-, three-, and four-player defense and team defense. Fundamental defensive body position and methods of guarding an opponent with and without the ball are discussed. Attention is also given to guarding a post player and defensive rebounding. The means by which defenders cope with offensive cuts, screens, scissor maneuvers, and a player advantage are reviewed. Different types of man-to-man, zone, and combination defenses are analyzed. Pressure defenses, defense against the fast break, and team rebounding are included.

Part III *Special Situations* is concerned with the offensive and defensive positioning and strategy involved in jump ball, out-of-bounds, free throw, and end of game situations.

Part IV *Teaching and Coaching* is designed to provide the physical education class instructor with suggestions for class organization, teaching aids, and progressions. It also provides the coach with suggestions for preparations for the season, individual games, and team statistics.

Scattered throughout the book are over 375 drills. Each chapter has many drills listed to provide the instructor or player with ideas for developing individual skills or team play. Sufficient time should be provided for beginning players to acquire some mastery in a few fundamentals rather than a cursory competency in a greater number of skills. In this way a solid foundation can be built and each year additional skills can be mastered. While fundamental skills are acquired, fundamental strategy can be introduced. The reader will note that in most instances the drills call for players to be positioned in their normal playing positions. Use of circles, double-line formations, and so forth, seems antiquated unless the primary purpose of the drill is the improvement of peripheral vision, speed of passing, and so forth. It appears far more sensible when developing passing skills, for example, to teach pass-and-cut or screening techniques simultaneously. By using this method the student can see the need for accuracy, acquire the timing necessary, and develop the correct speed and distance for the pass. At the same time, she is learning a tactic that can be used while playing. When defense players are added, she can understand the need for learning to pivot, to fake well, to release the ball at

varying levels, and so forth, so that a natural teaching progression is based on the student needs and is self-motivating.

Most skills should be learned individually and then attempted against an opponent. Other skills, passing for example, must be practiced with a partner and later with opponents. Additional players are added to the small groups until players are practicing in a five-on-five situation. Small groups provide considerably more practice and promote better learning than playing a full court game.

Throughout the book the reader will find approximately 400 photographs depicting individual and team play. Many of the illustrations demonstrate sequential action to provide both player and reader a better view of the action described.

Another feature of the text is the Glossary provided. Included are common terms that player, teacher, and coach should know. Beginning players and teachers may wish to consult the Glossary when unfamiliar terms are discovered in the text.

Symbols

Key To Diagrams

●	ball
– – – →	pass
⟶	path of player
∿∿∿∿	dribble
)	screen
══	hand-off
A, B, C, D, E	players on the offensive team (players A and B are guards, C is the pivot, and D and E are forwards)
1, 2, 3, 4, 5	players on the defensive team (players 1 and 2 are guards, 3 is the pivot, and 4 and 5 are forwards)

Formations For Drills

pairs	two opponents
partners	two teammates
columns	x x x x x ⟶ x x x x x ⟶
lines	x x x x x ↓ ↑ x x x x x
shuttle	x x x x x → ← x x x x x

I

Offense

1

Individual Offensive Skills

The primary purpose of the game of basketball is to score points and to score more of them than the opponents. Basic to the development of scoring opportunities is the ability to perform fundamental skills to get the ball into a position where shooting percentages are highest. In order to advance the ball to the scoring area, players must be skillful in rebounding, passing, receiving, cutting, feinting, pivoting, dribbling, and setting screens. All of these must be performed with the body under control.

Important to the development of any offensive system is the knowledge that most of the time players are performing without the ball. Since only one out of the five players may have the ball at any one time, the rest of the players must assist the offense by executing basic techniques to get free, assist a teammate in getting free, or simply keep an opponent occupied. These techniques consist of cutting, faking, pivoting, and setting screens. To get free, a player must know how to fake, pivot, cut, and use screens to her advantage. A player may also cut, without the primary intent of receiving a pass, to free a passing lane for her teammate or to set a screen to free her teammate. If a player is not involved in a particular offensive thrust, she must keep her opponent occupied so that she is less able to help her teammates. This is done by faking and cutting away from the desired passing lanes. In addition, a player must be alert to change from offense to defense, to adjust and react to any type of defense the opponents employ, to play her part in any fast break attempt, and to contribute to offensive rebounding.

The player with the ball must be skilled in passing, dribbling, shooting, and using screens. She must be able to adapt her style of play to that of the team offense. In so doing she must be able to find a free player in a more advantageous position as well as be able to work one on one when the situation arises.

PASSING AND RECEIVING

In order for any offense to be effective, there must be a combination of accurate and crisp passes that can be received easily. Two of the greatest nemeses to any offense are fumbled catches and inadvertent passes. They throw off the timing of a teammate's moves, allow time for the defense to adjust, and result in many turnovers.

Accuracy in passing is probably more important than speed, although soft and slow passes give the defense time to intercept or adjust their positions. The responsibility for a successful pass (interception) must rest with the passer. She must recognize her teammates' weaknesses in receiving passes and must pass the ball so they *can* catch it. Passing accuracy will improve if a player starts in a balanced position with her center of gravity over her base of support. Beginners should step or turn in the direction of the pass, but advanced players may use more deceptive techniques.

The ball should be thrown with little spin. This is particularly true of the long overarm, full court pass. The ball has a relatively large cross section and

3

air resistance will act more noticeably on it if there is sidespin. On some bounce passes, backspin and top-spin are desirable. These will be discussed under the description for bounce passes (page 6).

Passes should be snappy, crisp, and thrown to the side away from the opponent. Potential receivers who are closely guarded should extend an arm for a target away from the defender. Passes to loosely guarded teammates may be made directly to them. Passes should be received between waist and shoulder level, with the exception of bounce passes which should be received at waist level. Although generally the pass should be crisp, the speed and type should be adjusted according to the situation.

Passing in a skilled game should be fast and continuous. A deliberate type of passing attack gives the defense time to adjust their positions. Players should learn to catch and pass in one continuous motion and in the same plane. Before releasing the ball however, the passer must exercise judgment in determining whether the receiver is free. Automatic passing to a predetermined receiver can be extremely dangerous.

A passer will learn that her defender may take any of three defensive positions (or modifications of these) while guarding her—normal, sagging, or pressing. She should recognize that problems in passing differ according to whether the defender is guarding closely or loosely. In the former situation when an opponent is pressing or when she moves closer following the pickup of a dribble, the passer (if she has poise and body control) should find the passing lanes open. It becomes a matter of faking her opponent out of position before releasing the pass, so that her defender cannot deflect the pass or force her to make a badly thrown pass.

If an opponent guards loosely or sags after a dribbler picks up the ball, the ball handler finds it easy to pass well; but, she finds that the passing lanes are not as open. By dropping back, the defender places herself in a passing lane 6–8 ft. from the passer, which allows her more time to react and intercept the pass. Against a sagging defender it is important then for a player who dribbles to pass immediately after she catches her dribble. This does not allow the defender time to drop back and intercept. On the other hand if the defender plays loosely most of the time the ball handler may dribble toward the defense player so that she can pass around her more easily. If this does not seem desirable at the time, the ball handler should use some means of deception in order to insure that the passing lane is open. She may fake one kind of pass and alter the plane and/or the type of pass before releasing the ball. A player with good peripheral vision also can look in one direction and pass ac-

curately in another. Whatever technique she uses, she must not telegraph her pass.

A ball handler should understand that when she is guarded closely or in a normal position, she must maintain her poise and pass accurately so that her opponent's teammates cannot intercept the pass. When she is being guarded loosely, she must maneuver in such a way that her own opponent cannot intercept her pass.

If a passer is confronted by a taller opponent, she should not try to pass over her; similarly, a passer should not use bounce passes against a short player. Overhead passes should be used if the passer is taller than her opponent. If the opponent guards with a wide side stride, passes can be made between her legs; if she has a forward-backward stride with one arm up and one arm out, the pass should be made under the high arm or over the shoulder and by the ear on the side of the lower arm; and, if both arms are low and to the side, the pass should be made over either shoulder or above the head.

There is a suitable pass for every situation. This is the reason for learning a variety of passes. Two-hand passes should be used for relatively short distances, and only one-hand passes should be used for long passes—i.e., distances greater than 20 ft. Passes intended for a cutter should lead the player so that she does not have to slow down to make the reception. A player should always attempt to use simple passes rather than gain recognition as a "fancy Nan." Use of the cross court pass in both back court and front court is extremely dangerous and should be exercized with caution.

RECEIVING

To eliminate or reduce interceptions, a player should go to meet each pass. This may be done by cutting toward the ball against a pressing defense or by taking a step and reaching for the ball against a sagging defense. The receiver should concentrate on watching the ball until it is in her hands. Too many fumbles occur when a player concentrates on her next move before she actually has caught the ball. As the ball approaches, arms relax and reach for the ball. Fingers and thumbs are relaxed and cupped with fingers pointing up or down, depending upon the height of the ball. (Fingers never point toward the ball, as the ball may strike the tips and result in a jammed finger.) The ball is caught by the pads on the tips of the fingers. The ball's kinetic energy is reduced with the giving of hands and arms toward the body.

The ball should be caught with both hands whenever possible. In advanced play this may not be de-

a   b   c

Fig. 1.1 *Receiving. The player cuts and indicates that the pass should be made to the off-guard side (a). The catch is made with one hand, and the player guides the ball to the other hand as quickly as possible (b). Note that the right knee is well flexed to allow the weight to be lowered and remain over the base (c). The pivot is made so that the player is a threat to drive, shoot, or pass.*

sirable. If the ball is thrown to a spot away from a closely guarding defender, the catch may be made by raising one hand and letting the ball fall to rest against it. Then it should be covered or secured with the other hand, much like a first baseman in softball catches the ball (Fig. 1.1). This same technique may be used when catching a lob pass or a long, overarm down-court pass.

Players must make every attempt to catch a pass regardless of how poorly it is thrown. Turnovers are demoralizing and possession is too important to give the ball away without effort to retrieve it. Once the ball is caught, the fingers should remain spread along the sides of the ball in a cupped position so that the palms of the hands do not touch the ball. Fingertip control is necessary. If a pass is not made immediately, the ball should be held at chest level so that the player is a threat to pass, dribble, or shoot. Feet are comfortably spread, preferably in a side stride position, trunk and elbows slightly flexed to protect the ball (Fig. 1.2).

PASSING

In all types of passing, there is little time to increase the ball's acceleration. It must be practically in-

Fig. 1.2 *Holding the Ball. The ball is held close to the body at chest level to protect the ball before passing, dribbling, or shooting.*

5

stantaneous. In basketball the slower moving parts of the body are practically eliminated from the throwing movements, and the fast wrist snap is used almost exclusively for imparting force to the ball. Rotation of hips, trunk, and shoulders is all but eliminated except in the long, full court overarm throw.

Chest Pass

The chest pass is one of the most commonly used passes in the game. Hands are on the side of the ball, fingers well spread, and thumbs point toward each other. Elbows are flexed, bringing the ball close to the chest; force is given to the ball by a fast extension of the elbows followed by radial abduction and wrist and finger extension at release. The wrist snap thus derived will produce some backspin on the ball. A follow-through with the backs of the hands facing each other and palms outward will assist the beginner in attaining the desired results. Beginners often have

difficulty in keeping their elbows in and applying wrist snap. They derive most of their force from elbow extension only. This position of the back of the hands facing one another on the follow-through will insure the acquisition of proper wrist snap (Fig. 1.3).

Beginners also often start with the ball 10–12 in. or more from their chest. This means that they have relatively little distance over which to apply force. If the ball is brought back close to the chest on the ''backswing,'' there is greater distance over which force can be applied.

Bounce Pass

The bounce is an effective pass because defenders seem to try instinctively to prevent the ball from going over their head. While an opponent has her arms up, the ball may be bounced under them. But players must recognize that the bounce is one of the slowest of all passes since it must travel a long path to cover

a   b   c

Fig. 1.3 *Chest Pass. The player has her fingers well spread on the ball and has started to bring the ball downward* (a). *The ball is brought upward close to the body with elbows close to the side and hands radially flexed to provide additional force to the pass. A forward stride is taken as the ball is raised* (b). *Weight is transferred to the forward foot as the arms extend to provide force* (c).

DRILLS FOR CHEST PASS

1. Partners stand about 15 ft. apart with one ball between them. Pass ball back and forth. Emphasis should be on quick and crisp passes. Later, move players further apart.

2. Each player has a ball and stands about 6 ft. from a clear wall space. Players attempt to execute as many passes as possible in a short period. Emphasis is on passing quickly and sharply. Later, add a competitive flavor by providing a 30-sec. time period. Who can execute the greatest number of passes during the time limit? This is an excellent drill for developing the desired wrist snap.

3. Partners position themselves as either two guards or as guard and forward. Players face the basket in their positions and fake before passing to their teammate. Continue to pass ball back and forth. Caution must be exercised that players do not start to face one another. Before passing they must be facing the basket, but may take a step toward the receiver as the ball is released.

4. Same as drill 3 above, only add two defense players.

5. Partners position themselves as either two guards or as guard and forward. Using the chest pass, players use the give-and-go play. Player B passes to E, and E returns the pass to B as she cuts for the basket. Continue from the other side. Later, add defense players.

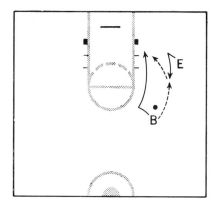

Fig. 1.4 *A guard and forward practice the chest pass while using a give-and-go pattern.*

a given distance. It is executed similar to the chest pass, except the force is exerted downward rather than forward (Fig. 1.5). The ball should strike the floor about two-thirds of the way to the receiver so that she may catch it at waist level. It is useful when attacking a zone defense, feeding a pivot, and climaxing a fast break.

Often the bounce pass needs to be preceded by a fake shot or high pass to raise the arms of the opponent. When a bounce pass is used for a "lead" pass, it may be desirable to use backspin to cause the ball to bounce higher and slower on the rebound. If the defense is playing "tight" and there is little opening through which the ball may be passed, topspin can be used to cause the ball to rebound lower and faster. This also makes it more difficult to receive, however. Backspin can be applied by rolling the thumbs sharply downward under the ball at release, and topspin is applied by rolling the thumbs over the top of the ball at release. Bounce passes with topspin should bounce further from the receiver than normal and those with backspin closer to the receiver. Use of spins probably should be delayed for advanced play.

One-Hand Bounce Pass

This pass is more difficult to disguise than the two-hand bounce pass and once started is difficult to stop. Generally it requires a longer backswing, but it can be protected by using a crossover step prior to release (Fig. 1.6). When the crossover step is not used, a short backswing should accompany the pass so as not to telegraph it. The pass can also be made while dribbling.

Two-Hand Overhead Pass

This pass is used extensively to feed the post player and in feeding cutters. Prior to the pass, some type

a   b   c

Fig. 1.5 *Two-Hand Bounce Pass. It is executed similarly to the chest pass. The ball is brought downward (a), raised to chest level (b), and the arms forcefully extend (c). Note the transfer of weight from the rear foot (a) to the forward foot (b and c).*

a   b   c

Fig. 1.6 *One-Hand Bounce Pass. The player is dribbling at full speed (a). She raises her trunk to slow her forward speed (b). The left foot moves forward to give added protection, and the ball is allowed to bounce higher than normal so that force can be applied over a longer distance (c).*

DRILLS FOR BOUNCE PASS

1. Partners stand about 8 ft. apart. Bounce pass back and forth. Emphasis should be on the crispness of the pass and it should be received at waist level.

2. Partners position themselves as two guards or as guard and forward. Practice the give-and-go play with the second pass as a bounce pass. Player A passes to B, and B gives a bounce pass to A as she cuts for the basket. Repeat from the other side. Later add two defense players.

3. Groups of three—the pivot player in a high post position (or a forward in her position), a guard, and her opponent. The guard fakes her opponent out of position and bounce passes into the pivot player. Repeat from various positions on the floor.

4. Partners position themselves as guard and forward. The guard has the ball and dribbles toward the edge of the circle. The forward cuts for the basket and receives a bounce pass.

5. Same as drill 4 above, only add defense players. Let the forward try a reverse cut if the defender presses.

6. Partners position themselves as guard and pivot player in a high post position. The guard dribbles toward the top of the circle but bounce passes to the pivot without first catching the ball. Later, add defense players.

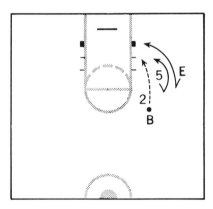

Fig. 1.7 *Player E is closely guarded by player 5. E fakes toward B and uses a reverse cut to become free and receives a bounce pass from B.*

of feint should be used to cause the opponent to lower her arms. The ball is then raised overhead with elbows slightly flexed and the ball held slightly behind the head, wrists radially flexed. (This often causes a defense player to move in closer to the ball handler and permits her to drive around the defender.) The pass is executed by a forceful extension of the arms, accompanied by radial abduction (turning backs of hands toward one another). The pass may be made from a forward-backward stride so that weight may be transferred to give more force to the pass. The ball should be aimed so that the receiver may catch it at shoulder level or slightly higher. Otherwise, its downward arc from an overhead position makes it extremely difficult to catch. This is a pass that should be used extensively by a player who is taller than her opponent, and should be used infrequently by one who is shorter than her opponent (Fig. 1.8).

Two-Hand Underhand Pass

The long two-hand underhand pass (6–12 ft.) is relatively slow because of its extended backswing and preparatory movement. It is effective particularly against a player who is guarding the passer closely, and is used primarily for guard to guard and guard to forward passes. The pass is one that is thrown from the hip (or from the side) and should be perfected from both sides.

Wrists cock slightly to permit thumbs to rest on top of the ball with fingers extended toward the floor at the start of the pass. Arms are extended comfortably to the rear (the extent depending upon the distance to throw and force necessary). Arms swing forward, the ball is released near waist level, and arms follow through in the direction of the pass. As arms swing back toward the hip on the backswing, a stride is started across the body with the opposite foot (right foot if throwing to the left). The stride is

a   b

Fig. 1.8 *Two-Hand Overhead Pass. The ball is raised overhead with arms flexed* (a). *Weight is transferred and arms are extended for release* (b).

DRILLS FOR OVERHEAD PASS

1. Partners stand about 10 ft. apart. Pass ball back and forth, emphasizing snappy passes and receptions at shoulder level or higher.

2. Each player stands about 6 ft. from the wall and passes against the wall. Emphasis is on proper release.

3. Partners position themselves as pivot player in a high post position and guard. The guard uses an overhead pass to the pivot, who turns to face the basket and gives an overhead pass to the cutting guard.

4. Same as drill 3 above, but add defense players.

5. Partners position themselves as forward and guard. The guard gives an overhead pass to the forward who returns a bounce pass to the guard as she cuts for the basket.

6. Same as drill 5 above, only add defenders.

7. Groups of three—one pivot player in a high post position and two guards (or one guard and one forward). One guard gives an overhead pass to the pivot who turns and gives an overhead pass to the other cutting guard (or forward).

8. Same as drill 7 above, only add defenders.

completed as the arms project the ball forward (Fig. 1.10). The short pass can be released quickly because its backswing is short and the crossover step can be eliminated.

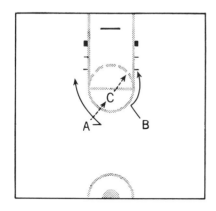

Fig. 1.9 *Player A gives an overhead pass to C, who pivots to face the basket and gives an overhead pass to B who cuts.*

a

b

c

Fig. 1.10 *Two-Hand Underhand Pass. Hands are well spread on the ball* (a). *The right leg is brought forward as the arms swing backward* (b). *Weight is transferred forward as arms swing forward in pendular fashion* (c).

DRILLS FOR TWO-HAND UNDERHAND PASS

1. Partners position themselves as guard and forward. The guard uses the crossover step and passes to the forward.

2. Same as drill 1 above, only add defense players.

3. Partners position themselves as forward and guard in their usual position on the right side of the court. The guard dribbles to her left, pivots back, and gives the two-hand underhand pass to the forward. Repeat from the other side. Add defenders.

4. Partners position themselves as two guards. The guard on the left dribbles toward the left corner, stops, reverses, and passes to the other guard. Repeat from the other side. Add defense players.

One-Hand Underhand Pass

This pass is used for short distances and, once started, is difficult to stop. The execution is the same as for the two-hand underhand pass with the exception of the grip. The player simply rolls the ball over so that her throwing hand is underneath the ball and the other hand on top. The top hand helps initiate the backswing by pushing against the ball, thus forcing it backward and against the passing hand. The ball is cupped in the throwing hand as the backswing is completed. With a straight arm the ball is brought forward and released similar to the description above. A player with small hands will have difficulty in controlling the ball for this pass. It may be executed directly from a dribble.

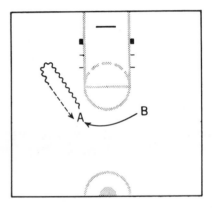

Fig. 1.11 *Player A dribbles toward the left corner and B moves over to replace her; A pivots and gives a two-hand underhand pass back to B.*

DRILL FOR ONE-HAND UNDERHAND PASS

Partners position themselves as forward and guard. The guard dribbles toward the forward and gives the forward an underhand pass directly from the dribble without catching it. Repeat from the other side. Add defense players.

Overarm or Baseball Pass

This pass is difficult to control and is unnecessary for beginners to learn. It is used when both speed and distance are desirable, on a fast break attempt, or on any half- or full court throw. Its execution is accomplished in the same manner as any overarm throw. A forward-backward stride is taken, hips and trunk rotate, and the throwing arm is abducted and laterally rotated during the backswing, fingers spread behind the ball. As the arm is brought forward, it abducts and medially rotates while the elbow extends and wrist and fingers flex to give final force to the ball. During the release the weight is transferred to the forward foot. Because the preparatory movements are relatively slow due to the long backswing and because the ball is vulnerable behind the body on the backswing, this pass can be used only when the player is wide open.

Controlling the pass is difficult, particularly for girls because of their relatively small hands. Frequently during the release the ball is rotated slightly so that the fingers are to the side of the ball, thus applying force off-center and resulting in sidespin as the ball is released. Over a long distance this sidespin is magnified and the ball may curve completely out of range of the receiver. On this pass some backspin is desirable to prevent the ball from drifting, and this is placed on the ball automatically with correct execution.

Handoff Pass

This is a pass that may be used any time a player cuts closely by a teammate with the ball. It is commonly used by the post player on scissoring maneuvers and by other players on inside and outside screen plays. As its title implies, the ball is simply handed to a teammate, although most coaches recommend that there be a slight flexion of the fingers at release so that the ball is slightly elevated from the hand. The release should be so timed that the receiver can catch the ball at waist level (Fig. 1.14).

Flip Pass

This is a backward pass most commonly executed over the shoulder. The backward flip also can be done underhand from hip level, bounced, or behind the back in a modified hook. It may be used by a pivot player after faking an opponent to a lower level or may be passed to a trailer on a fast break or a back screen.

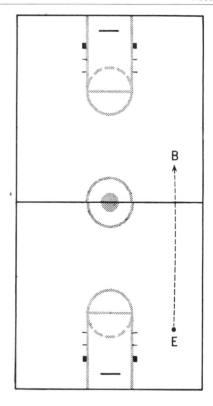

Fig. 1.12 *Player E throws an overarm pass to player B.*

DRILLS FOR OVERARM PASS

1. Partners stand about 25 ft. apart. Using the overarm pass, throw back and forth, emphasizing as rapid release as possible.

2. Partners position themselves as guard and forward in the back court. The guard cuts downcourt, looking over her shoulder for the overarm pass. Emphasize accuracy of the pass and correct release so that excessive spin is not produced.

3. Partners position themselves as guard and forward as shown in Fig. 1.12. (This situation occurs when defense players casually return to their defensive back court without paying attention to the ball's position. A long overarm pass may find a guard open.) Both guard and forward are stationary. The forward gives an overarm pass to the guard.

4. Partners position themselves as guard and forward. The forward starts under the basket as though she had rebounded, dribbles toward the sideline, and gives a pass downcourt to the guard as she cuts. Repeat, with the forward tossing the ball against the backboard and rebounding before moving toward the sideline.

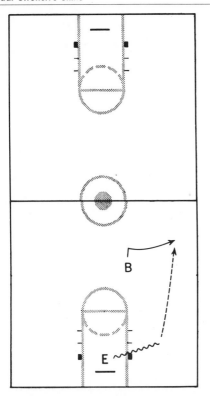

◀ **Fig. 1.13** *Player E starts under the basket, dribbles toward the side, and gives an overarm pass to B.*

Fig. 1.14 *Handoff. Although the receiver is too far from the passer, the pass is given with slight flexion of the fingers to elevate the ball to waist level for the receiver.* ▼

DRILLS FOR HANDOFF PASS

1. Partners. Player C stands with her back to the basket at the free throw line and player B has a ball and stands about 12–15 ft. from her and facing her. Player B passes the ball to C, fakes outside, and cuts close by C who hands off to B. B drives in for a layup. Work from both sides. Exchange places. Later, add a defense player against C.

2. Groups of three. One ball per group. Players C and B take the same positions as in drill 1 above, and player A takes a position about 10 ft. to the side of B. Player B starts with the ball, which is passed to C. Player B cuts first by C, followed closely by A around the other side of C. Player C may hand off to either player. Let A and B alternate starting the play. Rotate positions. Later, add defense players.

3. Repeat drill 2 above, except replace A with a forward to the side of the basket. Execute with either player starting the pass and practice from both sides of the basket.

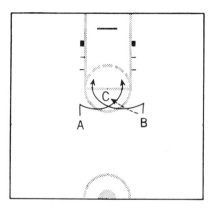

Fig. 1.15 *Player B passes to C and cuts close to C. Player A follows and cuts to the other side of C. C may hand off to either A or B.*

Fig. 1.16 *Player E passes in to player C and cuts around her. Player B cuts to the other side of C. C hands off to either player.*

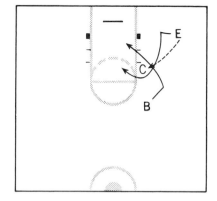

For the shoulder level pass the ball is rotated so that the passing hand is in front of the ball. The lower arm flexes followed by finger flexion to give the final impetus. It is a short pass and is received just behind the passer (Fig. 1.17). For the underhand pass the arm is extended at the side, the ball is cupped in the passing hand, the arm is extended backward, and finger flexion gives the final force. Rather than the underhand pass, the ball may be bounced. The passing hand is on the front side (height depending on angle desired for bounce — higher for a short pass, lower for a longer pass). The arm extends downward and fingers flex at release to cause the bounce.

The ball is flipped behind the back in a modified hook when a player is guarded closely on one side and a teammate is free on the other side. It is also useful for the middle man on a fast break. In the latter instance it is executed following a dribble. The ball is brought up close to shoulder level with two hands, at which time one hand is removed and the other is in front but to the side of the ball. For this pass the ball is out to the side of the body rather than in front during the preparation. The lower arm is then flexed, followed by finger flexion to give the impetus to the ball over the shoulder and behind the head (Fig. 1.18).

Hook Pass

A hook pass is used only when a player is closely guarded and when a pass in front of the body is impossible. The pass is made to a teammate who is either beside or behind the passer. To execute a pass to the left, the player steps with her left foot, rotates her trunk so that her shoulders are aligned with the direction of the pass, and looks over her left shoulder. Her throwing hand is under the ball and, with arm extended laterally, the ball is pulled up overhead and released with a final flick of the fingers. The arm follows through overhead (Fig. 1.19). Girls may find it necessary to allow the ball to rest against the forearm at the start of the throw. As the pass is started, most players also find it helpful to jump off the forward foot (left foot for a right-handed player) and return to the floor in the direction the player was originally facing.

DRILLS FOR FLIP PASS

1. Partners. One ball per pair. Use the same series of drills as explained under handoff (page 15), except fake a handoff and use a flip shoulder pass.

2. Partners. Any position on the floor about 10 ft. apart, even with one another and both facing the basket; one ball per pair. Player A passes the ball to B and runs behind her (back screen) to receive a shoulder flip pass. Player A then may shoot or drive for the basket. Alternate passers and start from different positions on the floor. Later, add defense players.

3. Partners. One ball per group. Player A dribbles (3 or 4 times) and then uses a shoulder flip pass back to B who is trailing. Exchange places. Also try the underhand and bounce pass.

4. Same as drill 3 above, only add a defense player who moves out to force player A to pass off.

5. Partners. Player B stands in the middle of the court with the ball; A is on her left. B starts dribbling with A cutting downcourt in the left lane. At the free throw line, B gives a back flip pass to A who drives in for the layup. Exchange places; place B to the right of A.

6. Groups of three. One ball per group. Player A is flanked by players B and C. A dribbles downcourt as B and C cut in their lanes. A has a choice of passing to B or C.

7. Same as drill 6 above, only add two defense players who are stationed between the free throw line and the basket. Let the defense players defend in any manner they wish and force A to find the open player. Exchange positions.

a

b

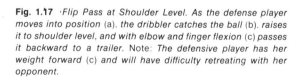

Fig. 1.17 ·*Flip Pass at Shoulder Level. As the defense player moves into position* (a), *the dribbler catches the ball* (b), *raises it to shoulder level, and with elbow and finger flexion* (c) *passes it backward to a trailer. Note: The defensive player has her weight forward* (c) *and will have difficulty retreating with her opponent.*

c

a

b

c

d

Fig. 1.18 *Flip Pass—Behind the Back. The opponent moves into good defensive position, preventing a chest or bounce pass to the dribbler's left (a). Fingers are well spread on the ball, and flexion of the lower arm has started (b). Fingers are flexed at release and during the follow-through (c). Notice the perfectly-placed pass to the teammate running at full speed and the receiver's widespread fingers.*

a   b

Fig. 1.19 *Hook Pass. The defensive player is well positioned to force the hook pass* (a). *Note the cupped position of the ball as the fully extended arm is raised overhead* (b).

DRILLS FOR HOOK PASS

1. Partners face each other about 12 ft. apart; each pair has a ball. The player with the ball pivots away from her partner and hooks to her. Player B pivots away and returns a hook pass to her partner. Continue. Later, add a dribble and pass.

2. Circle of five or six players with one ball per circle. Players form a wide circle and are well spaced. All players start trotting counterclockwise around the circle. The player with the ball dribbles and executes a hook pass to the player behind her. That player dribbles and hooks to the player behind her. Continue. Watch for traveling. Later, eliminate the dribble.

Lob Pass

A lob pass is a modified chest pass used to lead a player on a cut or to pass the ball to a teammate whose opponent is playing in front of her. Typical is the lob pass given to the pivot player when her opponent is guarding her from the front. When the opposing team is using a pressing defense and face guarding, the lob pass is often used in the backcourt by the player trying to in-bound the ball from the end line. Its execution is identical to the chest pass except that it is released higher and more softly. It can be a dangerous pass to use in the backcourt, as the opponents may divert a player to cover the area into which the pass would go. Therefore, it should be used with great caution.

DRILLS FOR LOB PASS

1. Partners. Player A plays in a medium pivot position outside the lane and player B plays about 10 ft. from A. Player A pivots and extends one arm into the air. Player B gives A a lob pass and A shoots. Later, player A should try to shoot before returning to the floor following the reception. Exchange places, if desirable. Practice from both sides of the court.

2. Same as drill 1 above, only add two defense players; the player guards the pivot fronting her.

3. Groups of four players—two attack and two defense. The attack player has the ball out of bounds at the end line and is guarded by an opponent. The other attack player starts close to the end line. She is guarded closely by a defense player who is face guarding and between her opponent and the ball. The attack player fakes a cut toward the end line and then cuts back with arm raised. A lob pass is made over the defense player's head. Rotate positions. Practice from both sides.

Behind the Back Pass

When a player is closely guarded, she might use this pass, but only as a last resort. Accuracy is difficult to attain because of its sidearm nature. The ball is cupped in the throwing hand and the arm is extended and swung in a circular path to the side of the body and then behind the back. Final force is given by finger flexion. This pass may be modified by a player who bounce passes behind her back.

Tip Pass

This pass is executed much like a volley in the game of volleyball. As the ball is received, it is not caught but flicked or volleyed to the intended receiver. Although not executed in the same manner, a slap pass from a dribble without an interceding catch might also be placed in this category. Opportunities for using these passes do not occur very often during the course of a season.

DRIBBLING

Unquestionably dribbling is a highly important skill for every player to learn, although sometimes it appears that teacher/coaches should spend more time on *when* to dribble rather than *how* to dribble. Nevertheless, players at an advanced level must be able to control the ball while dribbling with a variety of moves.

Dribbling is used by a player

- to move away from a congested area when no teammate is free for a pass
- to initiate and continue a fast break situation

- to advance the ball from the backcourt to the front court
- to advance the ball against a pressing defense
- to move the ball closer to a teammate for a shorter pass
- to drive for a goal

Players must be reminded constantly that passing promotes a faster game than does constant dribbling. Dribbling serves a very real purpose, but beginners must be taught early that the only time they should dribble is when it meets one of the criteria stated above. If this impression is strong enough, a player will not develop the habit of taking one bounce, or of dribbling every time she receives the ball. Once developed, this bad habit is difficult to eliminate. Players who cultivate this custom decrease their effectiveness and actually aid the defense. Often a player automatically bounces and catches the bounce as soon as an opponent moves in to guard her closely. This eliminates the future possibility of driving and reduces the choices of offensive action from three to two. The defender then only needs to be concerned with defending against a pass or shot.

In executing any type of dribble, the hand is cupped and fingers are spread. The ball is pushed against the floor by flexion of the fingers. Little force is necessary. As the ball rebounds from the floor, fingers meet it, the hand rides up slightly with the ball in contact before the next push, and bounce is started.

When starting any dribbling maneuver, the ball should be held at waist level or lower, and the push should be initiated from there. If the ball is started any higher, as beginners often do, there is a tendency to "carry" the ball before releasing it. When players are first learning the technique of dribbling, teacher/

MORE PASSING DRILLS

The following drills are included to help players needing improvement in attributes necessary for good passing. Drills 1–3 are devised for improving finger and wrist strength. Drills 5–8 will help players to release the ball more quickly and will improve their peripheral vision.

1. One ball per player. Each player stands about 8 ft. from a smooth surfaced wall. Using a chest pass, players throw the ball as hard against the wall as possible. Later, give them a 30-sec. time period and have them count the number of passes during that period. Keep a daily record to show improvement. Increase distance from the wall.

2. Individually and informally suggest to players with weak wrists and fingers that they obtain an old tennis ball and squeeze it at their convenience.

3. Same as drill 1 above, but use a weighted basketball. Take an old basketball and fill it with rags, newspaper, or sand.

4. Partners stand about 10–12 ft. apart and face each other; one ball per couple. Players pass the ball back and forth as though it were a hot potato—catch and pass, catch and pass, etc. Later, each player should vary the level at which the receiver must catch the ball and return the ball by using a pass suitable for that level—i.e., the ball must be released at the same height at which it is caught.

5. Circle of six players with a leader in the center. The leader passes the ball to each player who immediately returns it back to her.

6. Same as drill 5 above, except a second ball is added. The leader, A, and a player in the outside circle, B, have a ball. A and B pass at the same time—A to C and B to A. The passing should continue twice around the circle; then someone replaces A. Players in the circle always return the pass to A, and A always passes to the next player in the circle. The purpose of this drill is to improve reaction time, to increase peripheral vision, and to improve accuracy in passing. Therefore, all players should return the ball to A as soon as they have caught it. Keep A moving quickly.

7. Same description as drill 6 above, except players are in a semicircle and A passes to any player rather than always to the next player in the semicircle.

8. Groups of three in a triangle. Two players with a ball pass alternately to the player without the ball. Pass quickly. Increase the pace. Change positions.

coaches must carefully watch the pivot foot to see that it is not dragged along the floor, or that a step is not taken with the pivot foot before the ball is released. Starting the ball low on the dribble should eliminate both of these problems.

While dribbling, the player should keep her head up so that she can pass to a teammate as soon as she is free. Although eyes are focused ahead, some visual contact with the ball is afforded. The trunk is flexed but the back is relatively straight. The right hand should be used when dribbling to the right and the left hand when dribbling to the left while a player is being guarded. Failure to do so leaves the ball open for a defensive steal. If a player is wide open there is

no reason why she cannot use her preferred hand, however. Considerable attention must be devoted to dribbling with the correct hand.

The distance that a player wishes to cover will determine where the fingers will contact the ball and, therefore, the angle of the bounce. When a player is open, she can angle the ball further forward and cover greater distance with fewer dribbles. To do this the fingers contact behind the ball. If a more controlled dribble is necessary, contact will be made closer to the top of the ball. If a change in direction is desirable, contact on the left side will push the ball to the right side and vice versa; contact on the front side of the ball will pull the ball back toward the dribbler.

Speed or High Dribble

This dribble is used only when a player is wide open. It is the common means for advancing the ball on a fast break until an opponent is approached. The player is only slightly crouched and pushes the ball further forward so that fewer bounces are necessary to reach the desired objective at maximum speed. Each dribble is made approximately from hip level. The ball is dribbled in front of the body. Shoulders can remain square and the nondribbling hand should remain at the side since there is no need to protect the ball.

Control or Low Dribble

This dribble is used when a player is being closely guarded, when in a congested area, or while waiting for teammates to regain offensive balance after an unsuccessful scoring attempt. Because of the possibility of an opponent stealing the ball, it must be dribbled lower with frequent contacts for control and change of direction. The ball is contacted at knee level, which forces the trunk to flex; knees are well flexed so that the body is low. The nondribbling (free) arm is flexed with the shoulder forward to help protect the ball.

Change of Direction

When a player is advancing the ball and being guarded loosely, it is wise for her to change the direction of her dribble frequently to cause her opponent to adjust and possibly force her off balance. The directional change is also wise to prevent a defense player, slow in recovering, from approaching from the rear and tapping the ball away. Such a tactic is much easier when a dribbler is moving in a straight path. As the dribbler only wants to zigzag downcourt, a sharp lateral movement is not necessary. Forward progress is still desired so that the ball is contacted high behind the ball but only slightly off center. The rebound is then received by the other hand, which continues to dribble until another change is desired.

Crossover

A sharp directional change is accomplished by this technique. It is used when a player is being guarded closely and wishes to evade her opponent or place her at a disadvantage. It is also effective when the dribbler is being overplayed. If dribbling to the right, the change of direction is started when the right foot is forward. The dribbler reaches down to contact the ball sooner than usual — to get the ball on a short hop, so to speak. The ball is contacted on the right side so that very little forward momentum is given. As the ball is pushed across the body, the right foot pushes off and

a step is taken with the left foot as the left hand resumes the dribble. The right shoulder is lowered and brought forward to protect the ball. It is important that the lateral movement of the ball be accomplished with one bounce only and that the ball be protected immediately after it crosses the body (Fig. 1.20).

Change of Pace

This technique is designed to make the opponent believe the dribbler is slowing or will stop, thus slowing her reaction to backward pursuit. The dribbler decreases her forward speed by raising her trunk to a more erect position and contacting the ball closer to the top. When it appears as though the defender is lulled into a sense of security, a hard push-off is made by the right foot (when dribbling with the right hand), the ball is contacted further to the rear, and the left foot moves forward to aid in protecting the ball. It should be noted that in this technique the player continues to dribble with the same hand and in the same direction as before the hesitation (Fig. 1.21). Because of this, this technique cannot be used when an opponent is overplaying the dribbler. This technique also requires a reasonable amount of space for the change of pace to be effective. Several changes in speed may be necessary to elude an opponent. Therefore, it is used most often when advancing the ball into the front court, or just after the dribbler has crossed the division line.

Behind the Back

Advanced players may find this technique a valuable tool to add to their dribbling repertoire. Although a player should never dribble behind her back when the crossover dribble can be used, it is useful when a dribbler is closely guarded and being overplayed. It can also be used occasionally for the psychological advantage that is gained, since few players are adept at dribbling in this manner.

To start the behind-the-back dribble the player moves slightly ahead of the ball. If the ball is being dribbled with the right hand, weight should be on the right foot as the right hand is placed on the outside of the ball. A gentle push is given so that the ball will bounce behind the back and rebound slightly forward as the left leg moves forward and out of the way. The left hand then controls the ball and the dribble is continued. Since the ball is bounced almost laterally behind the back, forward movement is delayed temporarily (Fig. 1.22).

A modification of this technique was utilized by Rita Horky, an All-American player for many years. Before starting the bounce behind her back, Rita moved so that she had overrun the ball and the ball

a

b

c

d

Fig. 1.20 *Crossover Dribble. The dribbler approaches the defender at an angle (a). As her right foot is forward, the dribbler contacts the ball on its right side and bounces it across her body (b and c). The ball is then dribbled with the left hand forward (d).*

23

a   b

Fig. 1.21 *Change-of-Pace Dribble. The dribbler is moving at full speed* (a). *She is slowed down* (b) *and pulls her trunk erect to give the appearance of stopping, and has caused the defender to raise her arms* (c). *She flexes her trunk to proceed forward* (d) *and has beaten her opponent* (e and f).

c

d

e

f

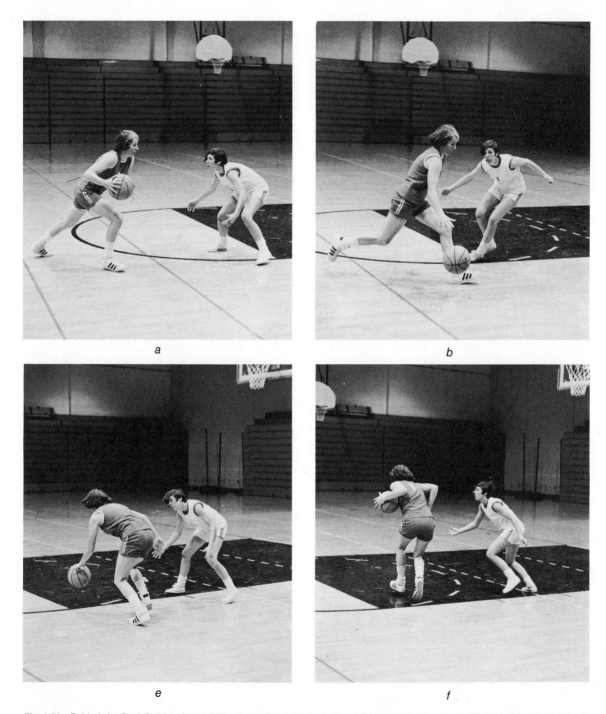

a

b

e

f

Fig. 1.22 *Behind-the-Back Dribble. The dribbler draws the defender to the right (a and b). She stops with the ball behind her back and her fingers placed on the right side of the ball (c). She pushes off from her right foot and steps left as the ball bounces to the left*

c

d

g

h

(d). *The ball is recovered with the left hand as a step is taken forward with the right foot* (e). *The player prepares and executes a jump shot* (f–h).

was directly behind her. Then she was able to place her hand behind the ball and push it forward so that full speed could be maintained.

Reverse Dribble

The reverse dribble is another means of changing direction when being overplayed and when the cross-over dribble is too dangerous to attempt. Because of its nature, this technique is the slowest means of changing direction and should be used only when the crossover is not feasible and when the behind-the-back dribble has not been perfected. The advantage of this dribble is that a player may maintain visual contact with the ball throughout the maneuver. Its disadvantages are that the player must turn her back to the basket and lose visual contact with the basket and teammates ahead, and be susceptible to a double team effort from her blind side.

During the execution of this evasive technique, a player reverses her direction and therefore must overcome her forward momentum prior to the execution of the reverse motion. To do this, she slows her forward speed slightly, and if dribbling with the right hand, stops by bending her right knee and bringing her weight back over her right foot. This is done with the left leg across the body to protect the ball which is slightly behind the player and opposite her right hip. As the player comes to a stop, she pushes off from her left foot, looks over her right shoulder, takes a short step with her right foot to her right (while facing the opposite direction from which she is going), bounces the ball with her left hand across her body, pivots on her right foot to face her intended direction, and steps left and continues to dribble with her left hand (Fig. 1.23).

It should be noted that only one bounce is required while the body turns. The subsequent bounce should be forward. Too often beginners do not turn quickly enough and require several bounces before they can proceed in a forward direction. The turn can be made rapidly, provided the dribbler swings in a 180-degree turn and places her foot opposite that of the defender. By the very nature of the reverse movement of the dribbler, the action is telegraphed to the opponent. If more than one bounce is required before the dribbler is turned, the opponent has time to adjust and can assume an overplaying position in the other direction.

Backward Dribble

Although this dribble is not used in the normal course of the game, it is a means of recovering a ball that is too far in advance of a player when an opponent approaches. It can also be used when a player slips

a

d

Fig. 1.23 *Reverse Dribble. The player is driving for the basket* (a). *She stops with her left foot forward* (b), *pushes hard off it as she contacts the ball with her left hand* (c), *continues around* (d), *and has her opponent beaten* (e *and* f).

or otherwise loses her balance. Since the attempt is being made to pull the ball back toward the player, fingers are placed on the far side of the ball. The ball should bounce toward the player so that a more controlled dribble can be continued, or the ball may be caught followed by an immediate pass.

DRILLS

1. Columns at one end of the court. The first person in each column speed dribbles downcourt with the right hand and back with the left hand. Give the ball to the next person and go to the end of the same column. Repeat.

2. Same as drill 1 above, except speed dribble halfway down, control dribble the rest of the way. Repeat and return to place.

3. Same as drill 1 above, except players change hands and direction on signal. Therefore, dribbling will be in a zigzag manner.

4. All players hold a ball of some type. All dribble simultaneously and in any direction, avoiding collisions. Make sure all change hands and direction during the dribbling activity. Avoid letting players move in a circle. They have fun maneuvering in and out and, to one's amazement, avoid collisions. This is a control dribble and the ball must be kept low for changing direction.

5. Columns of six or seven players are spaced about 6 ft. apart. The last player in the column has the ball and dribbles to the left of the first player, to the right of the second, and so on, until she has gone down and returned to her starting position. She gives the ball to the next player, who continues. Repeat until all have participated. When a dribbler goes around a player to the left, she dribbles with her left hand; when she goes around the player to the right, she dribbles with her right hand.

6. One column is in the middle behind the end line with chairs spaced as shown in Fig. 1.24. The first player dribbles as shown, always going to the inside of the chair, around it to the outside, and continuing. Dribblers stay at the opposite end in a column. The next dribbler may start as soon as the preceding one is around the first chair. Emphasize use of correct dribbling hand.

7. Each player has a ball. Dribble in place, moving the ball to the left, right, across in front and in back, in any sequence.

8. Ike-Mike Drill. Separate players into groups of eight or ten players with a leader. The leader facing the group dribbles in any direction but changes direction frequently, moving left, right, forward, and back. The players in the group mimic her and move in the same direction of progress—that is, if the leader moves forward, the group moves backward. Change leaders.

9. Same as drill 8 above, only play tag. The leader tries to touch anyone while continuing to control her dribble. When a player is touched, places are exchanged. Caution the players that they must follow only the directional changes of the leader to escape a tag.

10. Paris. The dribbler utilizes a zigzag dribble to the opposite end. Her opponent starts two steps behind the dribbler. Without fouling, the opponent tries from the rear to slap the ball away from the dribbler. Emphasize an upward, underhand motion to send the ball forward. (In a game a teammate would be ready to recover the ball for the defender.) Remind the dribblers that they are trying to advance to the opposite end as fast as possible; therefore, the zigs and zags should be as short as possible

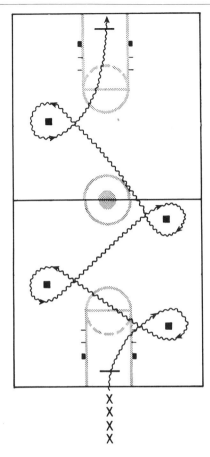

Fig. 1.24 *Players dribble to the inside of the chair, around it to the outside, and on to the next chair.*

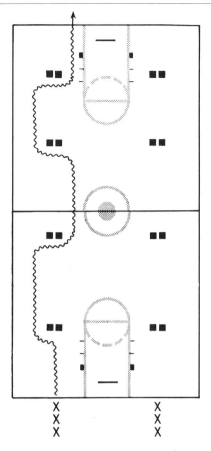

Fig. 1.25 *Players practice the crossover dribble as the chairs are approached.*

so that their forward direction is little delayed. Be certain to give all players an opportunity to dribble under stress and to be a chaser.

11. Columns. Place eight chairs in front of each column as shown in Fig. 1.25. The first player starts dribbling with her right hand and approaches the chair on the right in the first group of chairs. As she reaches the chair, she does a crossover dribble and continues dribbling with her left hand past the chairs. At the next group of chairs she approaches the chair on the left and uses the left-to-right crossover. She continues to the other end. Insist that players dribble up to the chairs before starting the crossover; otherwise the desirable lateral movement of the ball will not be acquired.

12. Columns at one end of the court. The first player becomes the dribbler and the second player becomes the opponent who takes her position about 6–8 ft. in front of the dribbler. The purpose of this drill is for the dribbler to use the crossover dribble frequently while progressing downcourt and for the defender to make a stab at the ball only if she is certain she can gain possession of it.

13. Shuttle formation with no more than two groups at each end of the court, and two players spaced as shown in Fig. 1.26. The player with the ball dribbles toward the opposite end. As the dribbler approaches, player No. 1 moves laterally to try to defend. The dribbler uses a crossover dribble to continue in the direction *from* which the defender came. As No. 2 is approached, another crossover is executed and the dribbler continues to the end of the court. Continue.

14. Same as drill 13 above, only four defenders are on the court as shown in Fig. 1.27. As the dribbler approaches each set of defenders, one of them (designated ahead of time) approaches the dribbler. In this drill the dribbler cannot predetermine to which direction she will cross over; it depends on the direction from which the defender comes, which is more gamelike.

15. Shuttle formation with groups at each end of the court. The first dribbler progresses downcourt using a change of pace maneuver. Use the right hand going downcourt and the left hand when returning. Later, alternate hands during each trip and add a defender.

16. Same as drill 15 above, only try the behind the back or reverse dribble.

17. Shuttle formation with no more than two groups at each end of the court. The first player in each column is the dribbler; the second, the defender. The dribbler tries to progress to the opposite end by using any dribbling maneuver. During each trip, try several maneuvers. Repeat.

18. Pairs at each restraining circle. One player dribbles while her opponent tries to obtain possession of the ball. Both players must stay within the boundaries of the circle. Exchange places. Use all types of dribbles.

SHOOTING

Usually there is little difficulty in motivating students to learn to shoot. Most students want to learn and perfect this skill. After ball handling (passing, catching, and dribbling), shooting probably ranks next in importance. All players must develop some degree of proficiency in shooting. If a player is recognized as one who takes few shots and is relatively inaccurate in those that she does take, an opponent does not have to be very concerned about this player's scoring ability. Instead, she can focus her attention on assisting teammates who have more difficult opponents to guard. By being able to sag off her own opponent, a defender can help immensely in developing a better team defense. A good player must develop a jump shot, set shot, and ability to drive. With these three shots she is a threat from almost any position on the floor and will demand a great deal of attention from the opponents.

In developing shooting technique, attention should be devoted to correct shooting principles. Accuracy is dependent upon balance, concentration, confidence, and correct release. Balance can be achieved by keeping the center of gravity over the base. The head should be turned toward the basket, and shoulders, hips, and feet should be squared to the basket. This brings the body in line with the target.

Shooters should concentrate on the target while taking aim, during the shot and after the ball has been released. Shooters should not watch the arc of the flight, for they tend to raise their head slightly early causing the shoulders and trunk to be elevated which, in turn, may cause inaccuracy.

Confidence develops after players become aware that they are successful within a certain range of the basket. This confidence increases with additional game experience against various types of defenses. To be a successful shooter a player must believe that every attempt she makes will result in a score. Individual defense or team defense against an opposing team may be geared to break down the confidence of good scorers. After being intimidated several times, a shooter's confidence is jeopardized and she tends to begin to pass off to other players without taking her normal number of shots. The psychological advantage of a Bill Russell or a Lew Alcindor blocking shots cannot be underestimated. Even in beginning play a good defense player can intimidate an offensive player to the extent that she rarely takes a shot; or even to the

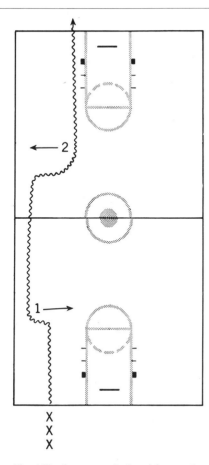

Fig. 1.26 *As opponents 1 and 2 move to defend, the dribbler uses a crossover dribble toward the direction from which the defender comes.*

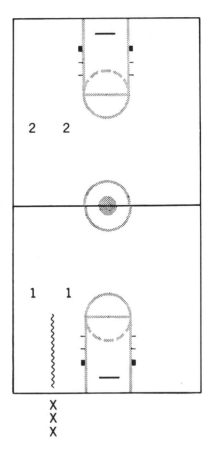

Fig. 1.27 *As a defender approaches, the dribbler uses a crossover dribble toward the direction from which she came.*

point where she may receive passes infrequently. Shooters can gain confidence by practicing against different defense players and acquiring moves to place the opponent at a disadvantage.

When attempting a shot the player should be relaxed. The ball should be held loosely on the fingertips without a great deal of pressure from the thumbs. The body should be square to the target as previously described. On one-hand shots the wrists and fingers flex as the ball is released. On two-hand shots the fingers push up and out at release so that during the follow-through the backs of the hands face one another. The ball should be released so that it rolls upward off the distal portion of the fingertips of the middle three fingers of the shooting hand(s). This action produces the backspin.

During flight some spin on the ball is desirable so that it does not "float." The latter is caused by air resistance building up on the rather large circumference of the ball. A moderate degree of any type of spin will eliminate this problem. Backspin seems to be the most desirable type of spin since it occurs naturally with proper release and produces desirable downward action when the ball hits the backboard.

On the follow-through for all shots, arms should be extended up toward the basket and hands should end in a relaxed flexed position. Eyes should continue to focus on the target. Release of the ball off the fingertips is an extremely important factor in developing accuracy. At the instant of release, just the ends of the fingers are in contact with the ball. Often beginners and poor shooters release the ball while it is in con-

33

tact with the greater portion of all of the fingers. This produces what is commonly called a heavy touch, and the ball hits hard against the backboard when it is used. Fingertip control provides the light touch which is more desirable.

After practicing for any length of time, players become aware of their shooting range and the types of shots with which they are most proficient. They also know the places on the court from which they are most successful. They should continue to maintain their proficiency from these areas but also work to develop other shots and from a greater range. However, during a game, players should only attempt shots in which they have great confidence and only if they have balance and time to take an unhurried shot.

Another important factor for all players to remember is the desirability of taking high percentage shots. The closer a player is to the basket, the greater chance she has of making the shot. Therefore, for beginning players it is highly desirable that most scoring efforts be limited to layup shots or other shots within 6–8 ft. of the basket. More highly skilled players will be forced to take longer shots because of the better defense against which they will be playing. Nevertheless most of their shots should be taken within a 15- to 20-ft. radius of the basket. Beyond the 20-ft. radius the percentage of successful shots decreases rapidly. This point should be made very clear to all players so that they can maintain their poise and patience until they can move the ball into good shooting territory. Team offenses should be dedicated to maneuvering the ball for as many layups and shots within a 10-ft. radius of the basket as possible.

When practicing shooting, drills should be presented and players should be encouraged to practice the aforementioned types of shots that are so important for each player to develop—mainly, the set shot, jump shot, and driving layup shot. Practice should be devoted to drills utilizing the various kinds of shots from appropriate places on the court. Increased maneuverability in driving shots, greater accuracy in executing all types of shots, and increased range for these attempts are of great consequence.

Some players develop a favorite spot on the court from which they like to shoot. Once the defense is aware of this, they can overplay the opponent in this area and prevent her from shooting, or at least impose considerable harassment. If the shooter lacks confidence from other areas on the court, the defense can render her practically useless as a scoring threat.

Although there is a need for players to learn to shoot with confidence from various places on the court, it is important for players to practice from those places where they will most likely take their shots. It is from these spots that they must learn to receive a pass, pivot (if necessary), shoot immediately, or drive for the goal. Much practice time should be devoted to perfecting these moves. *All* players therefore need not practice shooting from the same spots unless the offensive pattern requires rotation of players to all positions. If this is not the case, it is more beneficial for each player to practice the type of shots she is likely to use in the game plan.

It is also important for players to learn to release the ball as rapidly as possible. The principle in softball where the catch becomes part of the throw should be followed in basketball. When a player is open and in scoring range the shot should be taken immediately. Often in practice players receive a pass from a rebounder, bounce the ball a few times, and then take a shot. This is not very gamelike. It would be much better practice to receive the pass and take the shot immediately or practice whatever feinting techniques are desirable before the attempted shot. Whatever the situation, players must learn to release the shot quickly when the opportunity arises. In highly competitive play, the opening rarely exists for more than a split second. This is not to say that a player should rush a shot. Far from this. The faster a player can release the ball though, the fewer times she will be rushed; consequently, the more times she will be able to shoot in the game.

Another point should be made very clear and emphasized repeatedly. Even though a player is in good shooting position and well within her range, it is far better to pass off to a teammate who is open and closer to the basket for a shorter shot. A layup is more likely to score than even a 10-footer! It is important to instill players with the concept that an assist for a field goal is as important as the scoring of the field goal itself. Development of this belief was one of the reasons for the Boston Celtic dynasty for so many years. This was particularly evident in the playoffs of 1969 when they were opposed by the Los Angeles Lakers. At the conclusion of the playoffs won by the Celtics, one of the Lakers admitted that they had far better personnel but that the Celtics were a far better team! Teamwork and unselfishness does a great deal to overcome individual weaknesses.

Arc of Flight

As is the case of any projectile a shot follows the path of a parabola; but since the ball does not drop to the same height from which it was released, the height of its arc will occur closer to the basket than to the shooter. This trajectory of the ball's flight is dependent upon its velocity and angle of release. Since excessive distance is not involved in shooting, velocity is not the greatest concern. The angle of release becomes the primary matter of interest.

Since the basket is supported 10 ft. above the floor, the ball must descend from above through the net. One can easily visualize that if the ball could drop vertically at a 90-degree angle with the floor, it has the greatest chance of passing through the basket. As that angle is reduced from 90 degrees, the opening to the basket reduces sharply. As the angle diminishes, there is a greater chance of the ball hitting the front or back rim and rebounding away from the basket. Therefore, the higher the arc, the greater the chance of the ball dropping through the basket. The lower the arc (flatter the trajectory), the less chance of the ball entering the target—or, said in another way, the greater accuracy that is needed. However, the higher the arc the greater the ball's velocity. Therefore, the greater the rebound when the ball strikes the backboard or rim of the basket. A high arc also requires greater strength than a low arc because the ball must travel further. All factors considered, it appears as though it is best to encourage shooters to release the ball at a 45-degree angle. However, if this desirable release cannot be achieved it is better to err in shooting at a greater angle rather than a smaller angle because of the diminished diameter of the basket at right angle to the flight.

Use of the Backboard

There seems to be a trend away from using the backboard to bank shots into the basket, except when shooting layups or other shots to the side and close to the basket. This is due to the fact that as the arc and force of the shot changes and as the angle of the player to the basket changes, her point of aim on the backboard must also change; but, if the point of aim is the basket, the target remains constant regardless of other factors. Also, backboards are manufactured from different materials (wood, metal, glass) and each has a different resiliency which necessitates slight adjustments in shooting. This is not necessary when players shoot for the basket only.

Since players do not shoot with the same arc and force, it is erroneous to identify a point of aim for all shooters. For any specified shot there is probably no one spot that all shooters could use with ease and obtain similar success. The layup shot probably comes closest, but there still would be some variation unless the spot is made large enough.

If the backboard is used, the point of aim moves further from the basket or closer to the edge of the backboard as a player moves closer to the sideline. Her point of aim moves closer to the basket as she moves closer to the center of the floor. The height of the shot against the backboard depends on the arc and force of the shot and the distance from the basket that the ball strikes the backboard. The greater the arc, the

higher the ball should strike the backboard; the flatter the arc, the lower it must hit. It can be seen in Fig. 1.28 that the ball striking higher on the backboard

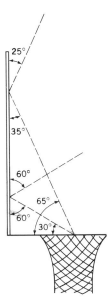

Fig. 1.28 *The ball approaches the basket at these angles when rebounded from different spots (gravity and spin neglected).*[1]

approaches the basket at a greater angle than the one hitting lower on the backboard. The ball that approaches the backboard at a 25-degree angle approaches the basket at a 65-degree angle whereas the ball that approaches the backboard at a 60-degree angle approaches the basket at a 30-degree angle. This means that the ball striking higher on the backboard has a better chance of entering the basket because it approaches the basket more nearly at a right angle and, therefore, requires less accuracy to score.

A ball shot with much force must hit lower on the backboard than a ball shot with a lighter touch; otherwise the force causes the ball to rebound away from the basket before it has time to drop through. A ball shot closer to the sideline must hit higher on the backboard than a ball shot closer to the basket with the same arc because the ball must hit out further from the basket (Fig. 1.29). Since it has a longer distance to rebound, it will take more time to reach the basket, and gravity has a longer time to act on it. Side shots must also be shot with somewhat greater force, because the ball has further to carry after it strikes the

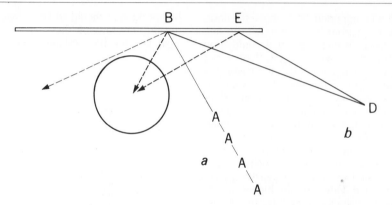

Fig. 1.29 (a) *Use of the same spot on the backboard when shots are taken from the same angle (A–B) but at varying distances from the basket; (b) a shot taken from closer to the sideline must strike the backboard further from the basket (D–E) in order to be successful. If a shot is taken from D and hits the backboard at B, it will miss the basket entirely.*[2]

backboard. A player who shoots at the same angle from the basket but at varying distances can use the same point of aim against the backboard, provided that arc and force are relatively the same. This is shown in Fig. 1.29. Some variation is possible because the ball need not enter the center of the basket.

Backspin on the ball will decrease the angle of the rebound and so increase the angle of approach to the basket. This occurs because a ball with backspin pushes upward against the backboard on contact and consequently is pushed downward. Since it will drop closer to the backboard and fall more quickly (because of the downward push rendered by the backboard and the force of gravity), backspin helps to compensate for the effects of a ball hitting too hard against the backboard.

TYPES OF SHOTS

Layup Shot

The layup is probably the most important of all shots. It is a shot that skilled players can ill afford to miss and one with which beginning players can achieve reasonable success. It is the shot used when a player is close to the basket and is used to culminate a fast break. Because it is taken close to the basket, a layup shot must descend into the basket quickly. Therefore, it must be shot softly against the backboard or it will rebound past the basket.

In executing the shot from the right side of the basket the player catches the ball as she steps on her right foot. She then steps left and jumps high into the air while carrying the ball high overhead. The ball is laid gently against the backboard as the player follows through toward the point of aim which is slightly higher and to the right of the basket. A soft shot will result if the player carries the ball high above her head before the release and lets the ball roll off her fingertips (Fig. 1.30). Very little spin is desired. The follow-through is completed as the player lands with ankles and knees flexed and is ready to rebound or go on defense.

Beginners have difficulty with the shot

- when they approach from a poor angle (either too acute or too wide)
- when they start to release the ball at chest, shoulder, or head level
- when they attempt to use two hands (tried more often on the side of the nonpreferred hand)
- when the shooting hand is under the ball so that after the ball hits the backboard it is still traveling in an upward flight.

Elimination of any of these problems should bring better results. Greatest emphasis should probably be placed on raising the ball high overhead. This tends to allow the ball to roll off the fingertips and reduces the force.

When shooting from the left side the ball should be caught with the step on the left foot and the shot should be taken with the jump from the right foot. The ball should be shot from the left hand. Beginners or less skilled players may be permitted to shoot with the preferred hand at all times. Takeoff should be from

a

b

Fig. 1.30 *Layup Shot. From a drive the player catches the ball with her weight on her right foot* (a), *steps left as she raises the ball* (b), *and jumps for the release to lay the ball against the backboard* (c)

c

a   b

the appropriate foot (left foot for right-handed shooters). When the approach is down the middle the ball can be shot with either hand (the one away from the defender) and the takeoff should be made from the appropriate foot. The point of aim is just over the front rim of the basket, not the backboard. The approach down the center should be used only when there is no alternative. Anytime it is possible, the player should veer to one side or the other and shoot with the preferred hand. After the shot, the player should be ready to rebound if the shot is missed or to hurry back on defense if the attempt is successful.

Set Shot

The set shot is generally limited to shooting from those areas that are considered long shots. This distance will vary depending upon the skill of the players. For experienced teams, however, the set shot should probably be used in the range of 20–25 ft. from the basket. For beginning players a "long shot" may be a distance of only 10–15 ft. Regardless of the players' potential, they should only attempt shots for which they do not have to strain. Therefore, the type of shot and range must depend on the ability of the individual player. In advanced play teams will have difficulty in penetrating the defense for close shots if they do not have a potential outside shooter. Without an outside scoring threat the defense can sag and wait for the offense to try to penetrate.

There are two types of set shots—namely, the two-hand set (chest shot) and the one-hand set (push shot). The one-hand set can be released somewhat quicker

than the two-hand shot, but some girls with limited strength may have better success with the two-hand shot.

One-Hand Set

This shot can be attempted as soon as a player receives a pass if she is free or following a dribble. If a dribble precedes it, the player should stop quickly with the left foot forward and draw it back behind the right foot to give better balance for the shot. If the player stops with her left foot forward, her weight should be shifted back over her base before she attempts her shot. The right foot should be just slightly ahead of the left foot and pointing toward the target, although some coaches prefer feet to be parallel. The reason for the weight shift back over the base is to allow the player to extend her body or jump upward rather than forward, possibly committing a foul.

Knees should be flexed and the ball should be brought to eye level or slightly higher. The ball is raised close to the body so that the metacarpal knuckles brush past the nose when elevated to this height. The ball should be held at the midline of the body. Fingers on the shooting hand are well spread and behind but slightly under the ball. Fingers on the left hand are spread, under and slightly in front of the ball. This hand supports the ball as long as possible. The upper arm is parallel to the floor prior to the shot. The ball is released as legs and elbow extend, and fingers flex to give final impetus to the shot. A jump may accompany the shot, in which case the ball is released before the player reaches the peak of her jump. Follow-through is in the direction of the target (Fig. 1.31).

Fig. 1.31 *One-Hand Set* (a–c). *The player eyes the basket and moves toward a forward-backward stride* (a). *Her knees are flexed and the ball is raised overhead* (b). *Legs are extended and she follows through* (c).

Moving One-Hand Set (d–h). *The player fakes to her left* (d and e). *Note the good position of the ball. She pushes off from her right foot* (f), *steps across with her left foot* (g), *and releases the shot* (h).

Two-Hand Set

This shot is usually executed without using the dribble. Knees should be flexed and the ball is held with the fingers well spread and thumbs behind the ball and pointing toward each other, in a position similar to that used for the chest pass. Feet are about shoulder width apart, the right foot slightly ahead of the left foot and toes pointing toward the target. Elbows are close to the sides of the body and the ball is raised with elbows close to the chest; backs of hands pass very close to the face. Force for the shot comes from the extension of knees, elbows, and flexion of the fingers at release. Fingers push outward on the sides of the ball so that backs of the hands face one another just after release. A player may rise onto her toes at release or she may jump; but, if she jumps she should jump straight up—not forward—and land on the same spot from which she took off (Fig. 1.32).

Beginners have difficulty developing this shot because they tend to point their elbows out rather than toward the floor prior to their extension. They also tend to start the release when the ball is too low. Both problems can be alleviated if the player draws her arms upward close to her body and delays the release until the ball is overhead. Beginners often jump for-

a

b

c

Fig. 1.32 *Two-Hand Set. Preparation* (a); *knee flexion and raising the ball close to the chest* (b); *weight has been transferred and good follow-through results* (c).

ward rather than up because they are straining to get distance. This problem can be reduced if they move closer to the basket. They can also acquire more force with less effort if the shot is started with the ball close to the body to provide more distance over which the force can be applied.

To help students acquire the kinesthetic sense of the proper release for both the *one-hand* and *two-hand* sets, players may be spaced informally around the gymnasium, each with a ball. Each player raises the ball overhead properly and attempts to gain the feeling of the ball rolling off her fingertips as she releases it straight up into the air so that she may catch it without moving. Little force is necessary at the start and then the ball may be "shot" higher with more force, still allowing the player to catch her "shot" without moving. This is an excellent technique for beginning players to use if they tend to release the ball too low or from the palm of the hand or the greater portion of all of the fingers at the same time.

Jump Shot

The jump shot has revolutionized the game of basketball. Every good player should have this shot in her repertoire. It is a shot that can be used from all ranges — short, medium, or long (although limited generally for women to the short and medium ranges). Because this shot is released at the peak of the jump, all the force must be exerted from the shooting arm and hand; thus, greater strength is necessary for shooting this shot in contrast to others from comparable distances.

In order to block this shot a defense player of the same height must jump as soon as the shooter. Any type of feint should delay the defender's jump and, therefore, prevent her from blocking the shot. The shooter should have difficulty in getting the shot off only against a much taller opponent. The jump shot may be executed by a player facing in any direction, although the release is always made when the player has turned to face the basket. The player may start with her back to the basket, in which case she generally does a fall away jump shot. She may be facing the end line on either side of the court or facing the sideline prior to her shot. In either case, as she makes her jump into the air she also turns to face the basket before the release.

The shot may be made while a player is stationary, following a dribble or following the reception of a pass on a cut (Fig. 1.33). In the first instance the shot must be preceded by some kind of a fake to give the shooter a split-second advantage if she is guarded rather closely. If not, a fake is undesirable. In either of the other two instances, if the player gains a slight advantage over her defender, the shot can be made immediately; otherwise it, too, should be preceded by

a feint of some sort. When a player is on the move, either dribbling or receiving a pass while cutting, the shot (if made immediately) may be made from a greater distance from the basket because of the added momentum that the body has gained. When shooting from a stationary position, this means that greater success will be achieved when the player is closer to the basket. If a player drives, stops, and fakes and then goes up for her shot, she has lost some of her forward momentum and her shooting range will diminish. Players should be made aware of these factors and encouraged to shoot from varying ranges accordingly.

Girls generally need the force from a 2-ft. takeoff regardless of what movement has preceded the start of the shot. Stronger players may be able to use the 1-ft. takeoff if they are on the move. If this is the case, the takeoff should be from the foot opposite the shooting hand. If the 2-ft. takeoff is used, it may be from either a side stride or forward-backward stride — the latter most commonly used when a player is on the move, since it provides better balance stopping the forward movement. As the shot is started, ankles, knees, and hips flex to provide a powerful extension directly upward. Arms raise so that upper arms are parallel to the floor and the shooting elbow points toward the basket. As the player jumps in the air, hands turn the ball so that the shooting hand is behind and under the ball and the other hand steadies the ball until the shot is released. This occurs at the peak of the jump. The player literally tries to "hang" in the air before releasing the ball. Shooting on the way up (a common mistake) or on the way down defeats the purpose of the jump shot. Timing the release is critical. The position of the ball overhead varies with individual players. Some prefer to have it directly above the head while others prefer it slightly to the side of the head. Taller players tend to raise it directly overhead. The ball is released by extension of the arm and hand and finger flexion. Follow-through is high and toward the basket.

The greatest problem for beginners seems to be in acquiring the feeling of releasing the ball at the apex of the jump. Some preliminary techniques may help them acquire this kinesthetic sense. Players (each with a ball) can be positioned informally around the gym, or they may imagine they are holding a ball. On signal, they jump into the air, raise their arms overhead so that upper arms are parallel to the floor (particularly the shooting arm) and the elbow of the shooting arm points toward the basket. They return to the floor with the ball still in their hands. Repeat a few times. After making any general corrections, let them continue jumping at their own speed. Next, let them find a partner and stand about 6 ft. apart. Each twosome should have a ball. Let them practice jump passing to each other, emphasizing a high arc as for a shot. Once

a   b   c

they seem to acquire the correct technique, let them try the shot at a basket. Encourage them to stay close to the basket—up to 6 ft. from it. As they become proficient at this distance, they may move further from the basket.

Hook Shot

The hook shot is used most extensively by pivot players, although forwards may also find it useful. Its use is generally limited to short ranges when a player is closely guarded. The shot may be executed either while a player is stationary or following a dribble. This shot is made with the back to the basket while stepping away from the basket so that the shooter is in poor rebounding position.

For a right-hand hook shot the player steps to her right with her left foot and, at the same time, rotates her trunk slightly left and looks over her left shoulder for her point of aim. The ball is held in the right hand, supported by the forearm. The shooting arm extends in a horizontal plane and the arm is brought up overhead while remaining in an extended position. The ball is released by hand and finger flexion when the ball is almost directly overhead. The arm follows through overhead and toward the basket, and the body turns to face the basket on landing (Fig. 1.35). Beginners tend to flex the arm while raising it overhead and/or bring the arm in front of the face for the release

rather than overhead. These points must be emphasized.

This shot is impossible to defend by an opponent between the shooter and the basket, which is why it is so effective when close to the basket. However, the shooter does need several feet of space to the side of her shooting arm because her arm is extended throughout the shot and it takes a relatively long time to raise the arm overhead in this position. A teammate's defender may try to block the shot from the rear or side.

The shot can be used following a rebound if there is sufficient space. It is also effective following a drive. In this instance, the player has some momentum from moving, so the shot must be made with greater fingertip control. Pivot players, in particular, should learn to execute this shot well, going in either direction and using either hand.

Layback Shot

When a player is guarded closely near the basket on her nonpreferred shooting hand side (left side for right-handed shooter), the layback shot may be used in preference to a hook. The player may have recovered a loose ball or a rebound on that side of the basket, or she may have been dribbling in on the right side of the basket, forced under the basket and around to the left side. In any case the shot is started when the player has her back to the basket (pivoting

Fig. 1.33 *Jump Shot. Following a drive, the player eyes the basket as she prepares for her jump (a), shot (b), and follow-through (c). Another player pushes hard off her right foot (d), drives around her opponent (e), lands with a two-foot stop with both knees well flexed (f), and extends for the shot (g).*

Fig. 1.34 *Jump Shot. The player slows down her drive (a and b). She stops her drive with her right foot forward and fakes a shot (c), steps across with her right foot (d), extends and raises the ball overhead (e), and follows through (f).*

c

d

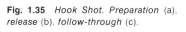

a

b

c

Fig. 1.35 *Hook Shot. Preparation* (a), *release* (b), *follow-through* (c).

if necessary to get into this position). She looks back toward the basket, takes a step with the foot opposite her shooting hand, raises her shooting hand, and releases the ball as high as possible (Fig. 1.36).

Tip-In

The tip-in is an excellent tactic used successfully in men's basketball. It does not retain quite the same degree of importance in women's play simply because few women possess the height advantage of men. Without it the ball drops to a lower position before it can be tapped, necessitating greater strength to return the ball higher than the basket. Since women have less wrist strength than men, this shot is considerably more difficult for them. Nevertheless, tall players with sufficient skill, timing, and strength should be encouraged to learn the tip-in and use it to their advantage. Other players would benefit more from practicing other shots.

To execute the shot the player must have previously acquired good rebounding position in front of her defensive player and within a few feet of the basket.

Her hips, knees, and ankles are flexed; hands are up, elbows about shoulder high. (Although more height can be gained by starting with the arms in a lower position, in the congested rebounding area a player may not have enough space to raise her arms when desired.) As a missed shot rebounds off the backboard the player must judge the angle at which it is descending and time her jump so that she can tap the ball at the peak of her jump. In essence, as she contacts the ball she controls it with her fingertips instantaneously and then pushes it upward just as she would in executing a layup shot. She lands with ankles, knees, and hips flexed ready to make another attempt if the shot is missed (Fig. 1.37).

Offensive Rebound Shot

When the offensive player has rebound position on the defender but is too far from the basket to attempt a tip-in, she should catch the rebound and then go back up for her shot. It is advisable for her to move toward the basket in this maneuver. In other words, some type of layup is preferable to a jump or hook

a   b   c

Fig. 1.36 *Layback Shot. Note that the eyes are on the point of aim throughout the shot.*

a　　　　*b*

c　　　　*d*

Fig. 1.37 *Tip-In Shot. Fingers control the ball as it is pushed upward.*

shot. It takes her closer to the basket for the shot and also may cause the defender to foul her.

Once the player has rebounded the ball, she gives a quick fake with her head, eyes, shoulders, and ball, thus causing the defensive player to jump in the air. The shooter then takes a step toward the basket holding the ball firmly and protecting it from the defender. She carries the ball high overhead before releasing it. The follow-through is similar to any other one-hand shot.

47

Free Throw

The importance of free throw shooting should not be underestimated. It is one of the most vital scoring opportunities in any game. Looking over statistics from previous years it can be seen that in roughly 20–30 percent of all games the winning team makes more free throws than the losing team. This may mean the difference in winning several games during the season. It may also mean the difference between a winning season and a losing season.

Free throw practice should be incorporated into every practice session. For best results, practice should be held at various times in the daily schedule during the season. Shooting early in the practice session when players are fresh is common early in the season as shooting form is perfected or while beginners are learning. After the shot is learned, practice should be made when players are somewhat fatigued under more gamelike conditions. At this stage players should take no more than two shots at a time to simulate game conditions. Shooting ten in a row is of little value beyond the early learning stage.

Players should be encouraged to use the same type of shot for free throws that they use successfully on other 15-ft. shots. For some, it will be a two-hand set; for others a one-hand set; and, possibly for a few, it will be a jump shot. For those players who have little success with any of those shots from this range, the two-hand underhand shot should be attempted. For this style the player assumes a comfortable side stride position and holds the ball with fingers spread and along the side. Arms extend in front of the player at about shoulder height. The player flexes her ankles and knees to lower the ball, but keeps her back straight. Arms swing upward and the ball is released at about waist or chest level. The player follows through high, with the weight going onto the balls of the feet. If a player has tight Achilles tendons, her ability to flex at the ankle without rising onto the balls of the feet is limited. If her balance is precarious in this position and her accuracy thus affected, it would be wise for this player to try to perfect another type of free throw.

Regardless of the style of the shot, a player should establish a certain routine that is followed automatically under game conditions. Of course, these must be learned in practice sessions so that their use becomes automatic.

1. Once in the free throw area the player should check the positioning of her teammates and that of the opponents.
2. She should then approach the free throw line, accept the ball from the official, and place her feet behind the line. (When players are learning, particular attention should be given to their foot position to assure that they do not touch or go over the line during the shot or on the follow-through.)

3. The player should bounce the ball a few times to get the feel of the ball and also to relax shoulders, arms, and fingers.
4. The shooter should then place her hands on the ball in the position she desires and sight her target.
5. She should take a deep breath for further relaxation and then shoot.

The free throw is deserving of extensive practice. Approximately 25 percent of all points made in a game are scored by this means. Is ample time spent on this technique in practice sessions? In practice all players should be able to shoot between 70 and 80 percent of their attempts. This may be somewhat reduced under game conditions.

Drills

When players are learning a particular shot, they should practice without opposition and from a relatively close range—that is, jump shots within a 6–8-ft. range, hook shots under the basket, etc. Once they learn the technique of the shot and become somewhat proficient in its use, more gamelike conditions should be added in a progressive sequence.

Depending upon the type of shot, the next progression would permit the shooter to dribble or receive a pass prior to the shot. Since the player has control of the ball, the addition of the dribble is easiest. This can be done while learning the layup, jump, and hook shots. Following the dribble sequence, the player should then receive a pass and execute the shot directly; later, a dribble can follow the reception of the pass if court position permits. It is better not to precede set shots with a dribble. The player should shoot immediately after receiving a pass.

An opponent should then be added. At first the defender should remain stationary, putting a hand up to block the shot and offering only token resistance. Next, the defender should be permitted to move just one foot and finally she is free to try to oppose the shooter under gamelike conditions. The shooter then should add a feint to the sequence to gain an advantage over the defender.

Throughout this progression the instructor can assure that the shooter is able to get her shot off by designating where the defender may take her position. For example, if set shots are being attempted, the defense player should be instructed to guard loosely. If driving shots are being practiced, the defender should move in closer to the shooter. As the shooter gains confidence and improves in marksmanship, the defense player should be permitted to defend in any manner she wishes so that the shooter can learn to adjust to the defender's position—that is, to drive if she is close and to set if she is loose.

LAYUP DRILLS

1. Five or six players at each basket with two or three balls. Two or three players shoot while positioned to the side or in front of the basket. Each player shoots four or five shots and gives the ball to another player.

2. Two columns, one on each side of the basket at a 45-degree angle (Fig. 1.38). The first player in each column stands at the edge of the free throw line. More advanced players should start from the top of the restraining circle. For beginners, lines can be placed on the floor at a 45-degree angle to the basket so that they can approach the basket from a good angle. (Beginners have a tendency to increase this angle—move closer to the sideline—which makes the shot more difficult.) The right line is the shooting line and the left is the rebounding line. The first player in the shooting line dribbles in, takes her layup, continues running under the basket while watching to see if her shot is successful, and then goes to the outside and end of the line on the left. The first player from the line on the left runs in, obtains the rebound, pivots to face the next shooter, passes to her, and runs to the inside and end of the right-hand line. Continue. Shoot also from the left and down the center. With beginners, several items must be stressed. They tend to rebound their own shot and get in the way of the proper rebounder. If this is a problem, they may be instructed to continue under the basket and touch the wall before continuing to the end of the line on the left. Rebounders must be encouraged to jump for the rebound and not permit any ball to hit the floor. If the shot should bounce off the rim away from the rebounder, she should hustle to retrieve it, pivot from that position to face the shooter, and pass to her. The rebounder should not retrieve the ball and walk back under the basket before passing it to the shooter.

3. Same as drill 2 above, only the shooters do not dribble in for the layup. As the rebounder gets the ball in her hands, the shooter cuts in to receive a pass from the rebounder and then shoots without benefit of a dribble. Emphasis must be placed on the two-step takeoff for the shot. Rebounders must be instructed *not* to pass until the shooter is cutting. Shooters must not start their cut until the rebounder has retrieved the ball.

4. Give and go. Players are lined up at each basket (Fig. 1.39). Player A passes to B and cuts for the basket; B passes to A for a layup. Player A "gives" a pass and "goes" for the basket. Practice from both sides.

5. Players line up (Fig. 1.40). A passes to C and cuts close to and around her; B cuts after A and goes to the other side of C; C hands off to either player for a layup. While players A and B recover the rebound, the next player in the line on the left passes in to C with a second ball. Continue. Start the ball with the line on the right. Move the two lines to another angle. Occasionally, let player C fake to A or B and then go up with a hook or jump shot herself.

6. Columns (Fig. 1.41). It can be seen that player A has a two-step advantage on player 1. Player A drives for goal while 1 tries to defend. Players A and 1 rebound while the next players in line start with another ball.

7. Columns at each side of the basket starting near the free throw line. First player in each line with a ball. The shooter drives toward the baseline, stops with her outside foot forward (right foot on the right side), pivots toward the basket, and shoots (Fig. 1.34). She recovers her own rebound, passes it back to the line from which she shot, and goes to the end of the other line.

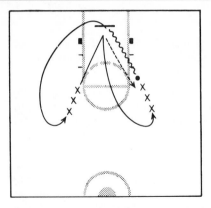

Fig. 1.38 *Two lines for layup drill: shooting from the right and rebounding from the left.*

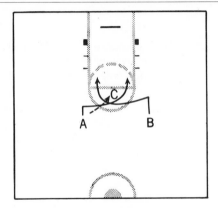

Fig. 1.40 *Practice of a Scissor Maneuver. Two guards practice cutting techniques and the pivot hands off to either one.*

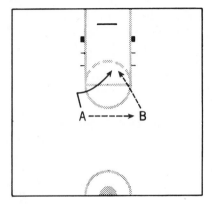

Fig. 1.39 *Give-and-Go Play. A passes to B and receives a return pass as she cuts for goal.*

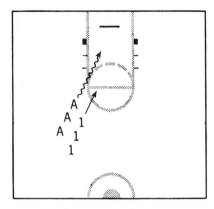

Fig. 1.41 *Player 1 attempts to overcome a two-step advantage as A drives for goal.*

Set Shot

1. Five or six players stand at each basket with two or three balls. Two or three players shoot from a range within their ability, rebound, and pass to another player. After the player rebounds she takes a layup, if desired. If preferred, one or two players may rebound all shots and pass out to the shooters who take only the set shot. Places are exchanged. Another variation allows players to shoot and rebound for a few minutes while the others await their turn. Exchange places.

2. Competitive shooting. A column is formed at each basket behind a designated spot. Two or more balls at each basket. Each player in turn shoots from the spot, recovers her rebound, and passes to the next shooter. Each shot that is made is counted, and the group that reaches 25 (50, 75, 100, 200, 300) first wins.

3. "21". Four or five players at each basket (one ball). Each player in turn takes a long shot from behind a designated spot and follows her shot with a layup. If made, the long shot counts 2 points; the layup counts 1 point. If both shots are made, the player has another turn. The first player to reach 21 points wins.

4. "Ghost." Four or five players stand at each basket (one ball). The first player shoots any type of shot from any place on the court. If the shot is made, the next player must attempt and make the same shot; if she does not, she becomes a "G." For every miss, another letter is added until GHOST is spelled, and that player is eliminated from competition. The last player to remain is the winner.

5. Eight players stand at each basket (two balls). Each player has a partner. One player with a ball stands near the baseline and passes out to her partner who shoots. The passer moves out to try to block the shot. Exchange places. Repeat. Alternate with other couples. Shoot from different places on the court.

6. Pairs stand informally at each basket. The shooter has the ball and is guarded closely. The shooter fakes a drive for the basket, forcing her opponent to drop back. She then takes a long shot. Exchange places. Attempt from different places on the court.

Jump Shot

Any of the drills described for set shots may be used to practice jump shots from a stationary position. For the drills described below a layup shot can be substituted for the jump shot if the player is close to the basket.

1. Five or six players at each basket (two or three balls). Player with the ball drives, stops, and executes a jump shot. She rebounds her own shot and passes to another player. As she gains confidence in this shot, she should try adding a feint prior to her shot.

2. Two columns at each basket (Fig. 1.42). The first player drives and executes a jump shot. Both players rebound and pass to the next player.

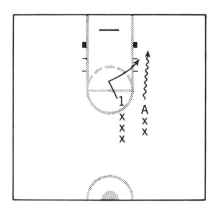

Fig. 1.42 *Player A drives for a shot as 1 tries to prevent it. Both rebound.*

3. Pairs stand informally at each basket. The shooter is guarded closely. She fakes in one direction, drives to another, and does a jump shot. If the guard is able to remain with her, the shooter fakes before shooting her jump shot. Exchange places.

4. Pairs stand informally at each basket. The shooter is guarded closely. She fakes a shot and drives around her opponent for a jump shot. Rebound and exchange places.

5. Pairs stand informally at each basket. The shooter is guarded closely. She uses a rocker step to fake the guard out of position (fake a drive, fake a shot, and drive) and does her jump shot. Exchange places.

6. Pivot player in a medium or low post position and her opponent. The pivot player fakes to the inside (toward the lane), steps toward the outside, and shoots (Fig. 1.43).

7. Pairs stand informally at each basket. The shooter starts on the left side of the basket, drives across the lane, stops, fakes a shot drawing her opponent in the air, steps to the left with her right foot, and executes a jump shot.

Hook Shot

1. One player with the ball near the baseline at each basket; others waiting their turn. From a position under the basket, step to the side and shoot the hook. Try several times and pass to another player.

2. Same as drill 1 above, except start to the left of the basket, dribble across and shoot a hook. Later, move further from the basket.

3. Any layup drill. Use the hook shot instead of the layup.

4. Pivot player practice. Have the pivot player position herself anywhere along the key. A teammate passes into her and she drives and hooks or turns and hooks. Add an opponent against her.

Tip-in Shot

1. Two or three players at each basket with a ball; other players waiting their turn. One player tosses the ball against the backboard so that it will rebound without hitting the rim; the other player attempts a tip-in. Repeat and exchange places. Attempt from both sides of the basket.

2. Same as drill 1 above, except use a device that covers the basket so that the ball will not drop through. This will allow for continuous practice.

Rebound Shot

Pairs stand informally at each basket (one ball). One player with the ball goes under the basket and tosses the ball against the backboard so that the ball rebounds out 5–6 ft. from the basket. She then becomes the defense player. Because it is too far for a tip-in, the other player rebounds, fakes a shot, and then does a rebound shot. Exchange places and alternate with the others in the group. Attempt from both sides.

Free Throw Shooting

Rarely should more than two players be involved with free throw shooting at any one basket. One player can shoot, the other one can rebound; any additional

Fig. 1.43 *Pivot Fake. The pivot player fakes a drive into the lane* (a), *reverses direction* (b and c), *and prepares for a jump shot* (d and e)

players are unnecessary and could better use the time by practicing other techniques until a basket is free at which time they can practice their free throw shooting.

1. Pairs. One player shoots two free throws and the other player rebounds. Rotate.
2. Pairs at each basket. Competitive shooting; each player shoots two and rotates; first team to make 25 (50, 100) shots wins.
3. Pairs. Shoot two and rotate; shoot a total of 50 free throws; record number made.
4. Pairs. Each player shoots one free throw at a basket and rotates clockwise to next basket; first player to make 25 (50, 100) free throws wins. (Leave the ball at the basket.)
5. For any of the above drills, at the proper stage in the learning process, the player may be instructed to run a lap for every missed free throw.
6. At the end of a practice session, each player must shoot three (four, five) consecutive free throws before leaving. Place a time limit.
7. At the end of practice each team must shoot five (10, 15, 20) consecutive free throws before leaving. Alternate players. Place a time limit.

FOOTWORK

Without question, footwork must be considered one of the most important elements of the game. Footwork is basic to body control and balance and without it very few other fundamentals may be learned effectively. Good footwork refers to the ability to start and stop quickly, change direction, pivot, and employ various feinting techniques requiring footwork for their success.

Speed is another important factor. Players with exceptional speed can be a great asset to a team. Numerous instances can be documented in which a faster team literally "ran circles" around a slower team with otherwise superior personnel. If a team possesses speedy individuals, its assets should be used to the best advantage in both the offensive and defensive aspects of the game.

Starts

Many players automatically start a move in the correct manner. For those few who do not, the following directions may be of help. The player should lower her shoulder and lean with her head and shoulder in the direction she wishes to go. At the same time, she plants her opposite foot hard against the floor, pushes off, and takes short quick steps until momentum is gained. The arms are used for balance, and their pumping motion may assist in acquiring speed (Fig. 1.44).

Stops

Players must move at a pace whereby they can stop efficiently without loss of balance. Beginning players

a

b

Fig. 1.44 *Start. The player fakes to her left* (a) *and pushes hard off her right foot* (b).

with poor body control may be forced to move at a pace considerably less than full speed in order to stop and change direction to avoid fouls and/or violations.

Basically, there are two ways in which a player can come to a stop—the two-step stop and jump stop. Beginners should concentrate on the two-step stop which is made in a forward-backward stride in the direction of movement. Because of this, balance is easier to maintain than with the two-foot jump stop. Advanced players should be adept at either one.

Whichever stop is used, it is important that hips are low, knees are flexed, back is straight, and trunk is leaning slightly forward with the head over the midline of the body. Arms should be flexed. If the stop follows a reception of a pass, elbows are brought close to the body to protect the ball.

Two-Step Stop

The player lands in a two-step stop with one foot landing first, followed by the other foot in a forward-backward stride with the feet 2–3 ft. apart (Fig. 1.45). The rear foot must become the pivot foot. This stop is more suitable when the defense is not harassing the offense and when a player is in scoring territory. With a quick pivot after receiving the ball, the player may drive for the basket or shoot immediately (Fig. 1.45). Most coaches recommend that players on the right side of the court use the right foot as their pivot foot and that players on the left side of the court use the left foot as their pivot foot. Other coaches recommend that a right-handed player use the left foot as a pivot foot and that a left-handed player use the right foot as the pivot foot regardless of which side of the court the individual is playing on.

Jump Stop

The entire surfaces of both feet contact the floor simultaneously in a side stride about shoulder width apart or slightly wider. Balance is hazardous with a much narrower stride. This stop is often used when a defense player is pressuring a dribbler and forcing her to the sideline. By using this stop, a pivot can be executed quickly away from the opponent, followed immediately by a pass to a teammate (Fig. 1.46). It is also used frequently prior to a jump shot.

Change of Direction

While a player is running in a given direction, it is sometimes desirable to change that direction. This is frequently done to fake an opponent out of position. It is also used after a defensive player reacts to a particular move and the offensive player reacts to the new defensive position of her opponent with a change of direction. It is effective for an offensive player to change direction frequently and to move in a zigzag pattern when closely guarded. This type of maneuver is much more difficult to defend against in contrast to a move in one direction only or any type of curved or rounded pattern.

a

b

Fig. 1.45 *Two-Step Stop. The player catches the ball on her right foot* (a). *The second step is taken on the left foot as the right knee flexes to allow the center of gravity to fall over her feet* (b).

a   b

c   d

Fig. 1.46 *Two-Step Jump Stop. The dribbler moves toward the sideline* (a). *She comes to a jump stop* (b and c), *and pivots and prepares to pass* (d).

DRILLS
(effective for starts and stops unless otherwise stated)

1. Informally, all players face the same direction. All run forward; on signal, all stop. Continue. Designate which stop should be used.

2. Each player with a ball dribbles anywhere on the court and comes to a two-step stop on signal.

3. Each player with a ball dribbles diagonally toward the sideline and uses a jump stop.

4. Two columns on each side of every basket with a ball, one column in the guard position, and one in a low post position. A player in the guard position passes into a pivot player moving from a low to a high post position. The pivot player uses a two-foot jump stop. The pivot player passes to the next player in the guard position. Continue. Exchange places, if desired.

5. Same as drill 4 above, except move the column from the low post position to the forward position. The forward cuts up to receive a pass in a stride position. Continue.

DRILLS

1. Columns at one end of the court. On signal, the first person in each column starts to her left, takes three steps in that direction, three steps in the other direction, and continues downcourt. Each successive player starts when there is sufficient space for her speed.

2. Columns. Designate spots on the floor. Each person in turn runs to that spot, changes direction, and runs to the next spot, etc. Emphasize quick changes on the spot.

3. Players in their normal playing positions are spaced at each basket. Forwards take a few steps toward the basket and then cut out for an imaginary pass from a guard; post players cut toward the sideline and then up toward a player with an imaginary ball; guards cut toward the sideline or toward the basket and back for an imaginary pass from the other guard. Later, add a passer for each group.

4. Two columns—one offensive and one defensive at each basket. An offense player starts in a guard position with an opponent defending against her. An extra player in a forward position has the ball. The guard uses zigzag cuts to free herself of her opponent for a pass from the forward and a layup. Rotate positions and start from different places on the floor.

5. Pairs. The attack player tries to evade the defense player by stops, starts, and changes of direction.

To change direction when running, the movement should be quick and abrupt. When a player wishes to cut to the right, she plants her left foot, pushes off sharply from it, lowers her right shoulder, faces to the right, and starts in that direction with her right foot. The action is similar to a start. A crossover step is not recommended because the directional change cannot be as sharp or quick. The change of direction to the left is made in the opposite manner.

Pivots or Turns

There seems to be little agreement on the difference between a pivot and a turn. For the purposes of this book, the terms will be used interchangeably.

Simple Turn

A simple turn is made by pivoting on the balls of both feet. Feet may be in any position, but the turn is made without lifting either foot. Beginning players need to practice this technique to avoid throwing poor passes, because their legs become tangled. When passing, beginning players should face the direction of the pass; this can be accomplished by using the simple turn. If a foot fake or a two-step stop has been executed, a pivot is made on the ball of the pivot foot

while the other foot steps toward the direction of the pass.

Reverse Turn

One of the most commonly used turns is the reverse turn in which a player is moving forward (or backward) and desires to change direction immediately to go in the opposite direction. This might occur when the offensive team loses the ball due to an interception or rebound, or when a defense player slides toward the basket to prevent the give and go. Offensively, it is used to move in one direction and cut back for the ball and to cut toward the ball and then reverse toward the basket.

The technique is similar to that for changing direction. The player stops in a forward-backward stride position. Body weight is thrown back over the rear foot as the pivot is made on that foot. The forward foot during the stop takes the first step in the opposite direction as the shoulder on that side is lowered and the push-off is given by the other foot. This reverse turn is often done as a half- or three-quarter turn. It becomes a half-turn when the player simply wants to reverse direction. The three-quarter turn is used when a player cuts in one direction with an opponent on her side, reverses in a three-quarter turn, and cuts behind the opponent.

Inside Turn

This turn is used following a jump stop when a player is forced toward the sideline and must quickly turn in toward the court to sight her teammates and pass. The player pivots on her inside foot (the one closer to midcourt) and swings the other leg backward in a half-turn until she is facing the opposite direction from which she started. The resultant stride position should be sufficiently wide so that balance is not lost. During the turn the ball is protected by keeping elbows bent and close to the body (Fig. 1.47). The ball should be passed immediately. The turn is used by a pivot player to face the basket.

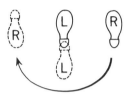

Fig. 1.47 *Inside Turn. The pivot is made on the inside foot, as the outside foot swings around so that the player has her back to the basket she is attacking. In this case the player is near the right sideline, so her left foot is the inside foot. If she were near the left sideline, her right foot would be her pivot foot and she would swing her left foot around.*

Outside Turn

Following a jump stop, this turn is executed identically to the inside turn except the outside foot (the one closer to the sideline) becomes the pivot foot. This turn should never be used close to the sideline where the player could be hemmed in by an opponent (Fig. 1.48). This turn is also used by pivot players starting with their back to the basket to turn to face the basket.

Drills

(Use the same drills described for stops; follow by one of the turns described.)

FEINTING

Feinting is a technique used to deceive an opponent. It is a move made usually opposite to the intended direction. Although generally considered an offensive

technique, it can be used with equal success by defensive players.

Offensively, feints or fakes are used either when a player has the ball or when she is trying to free herself to receive a pass. One often sees players practicing fakes with the ball, but often they give little attention to fakes without the ball. Perhaps more time could be spent wisely on these maneuvers. It is often because players are unable to get free that one sees a passer under stress throw the ball where she hopes her teammate will be. This is evident not only in beginning play, but also by some advanced players when they encounter a pressing defense. Fakes normally are done with the head, eyes, shoulder, body, arms, and feet. Ball fakes can be used, but elbows should be kept in contact with the body so that the ball stays within the lines of the body. Extending the ball beyond the lines of the body is an invitation for an opponent to slap at the ball and tends to send the center of gravity beyond the base. It is important to keep the center of gravity over the base when executing any of the fakes. If the center of gravity is forced outside the base or near the edge of the base, time is required to move the center of gravity back over the base, thus limiting the quickness with which an alternate move may be made. While time is being consumed during this action, the defense player is also given time to recover to make a new move. On all feints, it is also important that the head turns in the direction of the feint and that eyes focus in that direction.

Feints Without the Ball

Fakes of this nature are made to free a player or to take an opponent away from the play. When a fast

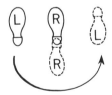

Fig. 1.48 *Outside Turn. The outside foot (nearest the sideline) is the pivot foot, and the other foot swings around so that the player ends up with her back to the basket. The right foot is the pivot foot to the right side of the midline of the court. The left foot is the pivot foot to the left side as the right foot swings around.*

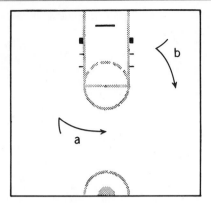

Fig. 1.49 *Examples of V cuts:* (a) *by a guard,* (b) *by a forward.*

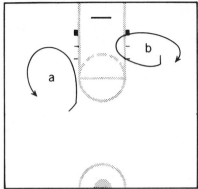

Fig. 1.50 *Examples of a buttonhook cut:* (a) *by a guard,* (b) *by a forward.*

directional change is required, the player takes a step with one foot, pushes hard off it, and takes a step in the opposite direction with the other foot (refer to Fig. 1.44). (When the initial step is taken, the opposite knee flexes to keep the center of gravity over the base.) This technique is used when working a give and go, splitting the pivot, or simply getting open for a pass. A simple head and shoulder fake may accomplish the same purpose.

A player may also cut in one direction followed by a quick change of direction. This is a slow means, since several steps are taken before the change in direction is made. This method is used more often when an opponent is being lured out of the play or when she is not involved with the ball immediately before she is to receive a pass. This type of cut is most commonly made in a V (Fig. 1.49) or a buttonhook pattern (Fig. 1.50).

If a defense player is guarding closely, a player may cut toward the ball, do a reverse turn, and cut behind the defense player for the basket simulating a backdoor play (Fig. 1.51).

A change of pace is another means of deceiving an opponent. It is usually accomplished by a player running at normal speed, slowing down, and then speeding up. It is accomplished by placing one foot in advance of the center of gravity and extending (straightening) the trunk which causes a decreased speed. To speed up, the trunk flexes, causing the center of gravity to fall outside the base; the front foot pushes off as the leg extends.

Another technique that can be used on occasion by advanced players is one in which the opponent is lulled into a belief that her opponent will not become involved in the action. This is accomplished by standing in a relaxed manner, arms at sides, weight on one foot, and generally giving the appearance of watching the play. As soon as the opponent has been duped, the player cuts hard for a pass. If an opponent does not watch the ball, a player may stand innocently with her arms at her sides and, at the last instant, reach up for a pass. Similarly, a player can fake a reception to draw her opponent closer before cutting on her.

Feints with the Ball

Feints with the ball are designed to open passing lanes, to free oneself for a shot, or to drive toward the basket. Feinting with the ball is much easier than without it because the defense player must try to defend against a pass, shot, or a drive. To defend against a shot, the opponent must draw close; to defend against the drive, she must play looser. Because of the dilemma this places the defense player in, it is imperative that offensive players use the dribble wisely. Simply bouncing the ball in place or taking an automatic bounce whenever the ball is received plays right into the defensive player's hands because one of the options has been used and the defender need be concerned only with the shot or pass. Regardless of the type of feint used, the ball always stays close to the body and the center of gravity over the base. Otherwise no advantage is gained by the ball handler following her feint.

Feints to Open Passing Lanes

Use of the head, eyes, shoulders, arms, and feet can be used for this purpose. Ball fakes can also be used if the ball stays near the midline of the body. Regardless of the type of fake used, it should involve the use of the head and eyes. Following a fake in one direc-

Fig. 1.51 *Reverse Turn. The player cuts toward the ball* (a). *She raises her trunk and prepares to reverse as her inside foot (left) strikes the floor* (b). *She pushes off from her left foot* (c). *Her step with the right foot takes her beyond her opponent* (d), *and she is free for a pass* (e).

tion, the player should pass in another. A player may fake left and pass right, or she may fake a pass at one level and pass at another. For example, a player may fake a shot or an overhead pass and follow it with a bounce pass. Whichever technique is used, the ball must be passed immediately after the fake so that the opponent does not have time to readjust her position. Following a fake there is not time for a long back-swing, so players must develop arm and hand strength to produce the required force for a pass primarily with wrist action. During the fake and subsequent action, beginners tend to throw their body too close

---

DRILLS

1. Fake left, cut right; fake right, cut left; fake forward, cut left; fake forward, cut right; fake forward, cut back. Repeat.

2. Place the players at each basket in their normal playing positions. Let each player try the fakes she will most likely use from her position: *guards* — fake left or right and cut in the opposite direction, or fake left or right and cut toward the basket; *forwards* — fake toward the basket and cut toward a guard; fake toward the guard and cut toward the basket; *center* — fake left or right and cut opposite; fake left or right and cut toward a guard; fake toward a guard and cut to the opposite side of the key.

3. Same as drill 2 above, but add an opponent against each player. In turn, let each player try to get free from her opponent.

4. Two players (two guards, a guard and a forward on the same side of the court, or a forward and center) in their normal playing positions and their opponents. Start the ball with either attack player. Her teammate uses some feint to free herself for a pass. Repeat.

5. Players execute a change of pace. Add an opponent. Alternate.

6. Place players and their opponents on the court in their normal playing positions. Any offensive player may start with the ball (preferably a guard) and the other players try to get free only by using a change of pace or by lulling their opponent to sleep. Each player should watch closely to see if her opponent turns her head. If she does, a sharp cut should be made toward the ball or the basket depending upon the situation.

7. Same as drill 6 above, except offensive players should vary their fakes.

8. Same as drill 6 above, but request the defense to play tight or press their opponent. Offensive players should try the backdoor play when the opportunity presents itself.

---

to the edge of the base or take too long a backswing for the throw. These problems must be overcome.

Feints for a Shot or a Drive

Generally, the purpose of these feints is twofold: to fake a shot and draw an opponent close so that a player can drive around her; or to fake a drive, forcing the opponent to give ground, and then shoot. Players may also fake in one direction and move in the opposite. Players should recognize that a defense player is more vulnerable when a drive is made in the direction of her front foot. If an opponent is playing with her left foot forward, she will have more difficulty defending against a drive in this direction. Greater advantage should be made of this fact, particularly against teams that do not sag or float to help teammates. Whenever a ball handler is contemplating a drive or shot, she should focus her attention on her defender's feet. In this way she can observe the weight shift of the defensive player and/or a foot being lifted from the floor. This indicates to the ball handler when and in what direction she is free to move.

There are several fakes that may be used to achieve the purposes stated above. All feints can be done in either direction, but a description is given to one side only.

Jab Step

The player with the ball takes a side stride position. She takes a quick, short step in any direction and returns to the starting position. Several steps taken in this manner should drive an opponent off balance (Fig. 1.52). A sequence such as forward, return, left, return, followed by a drive to the right may be successful.

Crossover

The player fakes a drive to the left with the left foot while keeping the right knee flexed to keep her center of gravity over her base. The left foot crosses over to the right side, placing the left shoulder between the opponent and the ball. The drive is started to the right as the ball is dribbled with the right hand. In order to

Fig. 1.52 *Jab Step. The player jabs to the left with her left foot* (a), *jabs to the right with the left foot* (b and c), *brings the left foot back* (d), *pushes hard off the right foot* (e), *and drives by her opponent* (f).

profit from a successful feint, the crossover step should be outside the opponent's foot on that side so that the head and shoulders are immediately ahead of the defensive player (Fig. 1.53).

Double Fake

A player fakes in one direction, fakes in the opposite direction, and drives in the direction of the first fake.

61

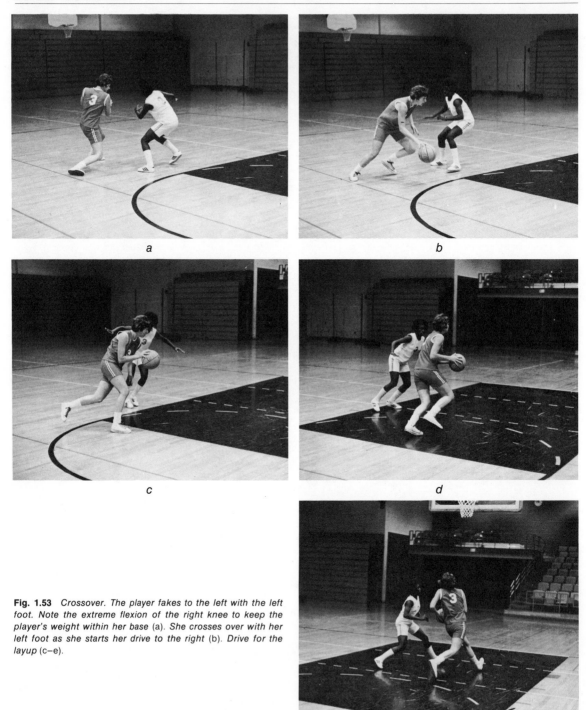

Fig. 1.53 *Crossover. The player fakes to the left with the left foot. Note the extreme flexion of the right knee to keep the player's weight within her base (a). She crosses over with her left foot as she starts her drive to the right (b). Drive for the layup (c–e).*

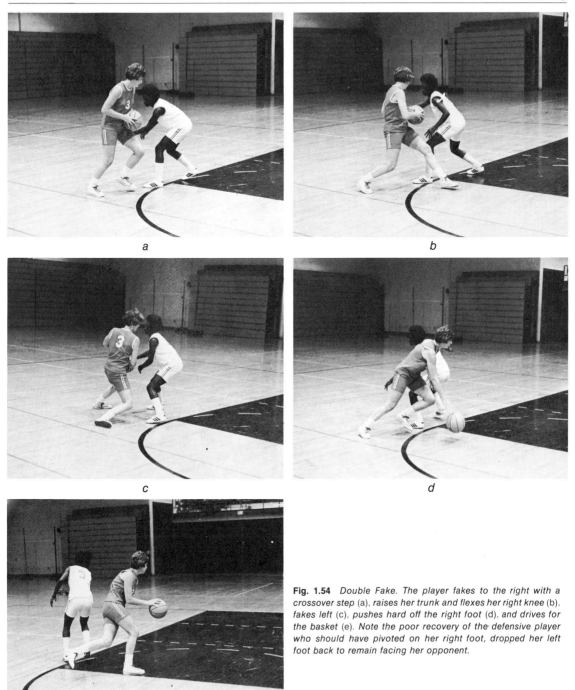

a

b

c

d

e

Fig. 1.54 *Double Fake. The player fakes to the right with a crossover step (a), raises her trunk and flexes her right knee (b), fakes left (c), pushes hard off the right foot (d), and drives for the basket (e). Note the poor recovery of the defensive player who should have pivoted on her right foot, dropped her left foot back to remain facing her opponent.*

Usually the drive is taken to the side where the cross-over step can be utilized to protect the ball with the body. Therefore, the first fake is made with a crossover step. The player crosses over with the left foot while keeping the right knee flexed, and then pushes hard off the left foot to push the body back to the left. The stride is long enough to show the intent of driving in that direction and then a hard push is given once more as the left leg crosses over and the drive is made to the right as described previously (Fig. 1.54).

Fake and Drive in the Same Direction

By using a hesitation rather than a double fake, a player can drive in the direction of her original fake. The player uses a crossover step with the left foot and then extends her trunk by pulling her head and shoulders up and back. The trunk is flexed immediately afterward, placing gravity outside the base again; the right leg extends, giving the initial push-off. A forceful extension of the left leg is also necessary to gather momentum (Fig. 1.55).

Rocker Step

In this move the player fakes a drive, pulls back to fake a shot, and then drives in the direction of the original fake. For example, the player fakes left with her left foot, keeping her right leg flexed and hips low and over the base. Then she draws her left foot back behind the right, keeping the trunk flexed and gravity near the front edge of the base. At the same time a shot is faked to draw the opponent close, at which time the right leg extends as a step is taken to the left and the drive is started. The ball is dribbled with the left hand (Fig. 1.56).

Fake a Shot and Drive (up and under)

The player fakes a shot by using her head, eyes, arms, and hands in the same manner that she normally does for a shot from that position on the floor. As the defense player moves in to defend against the shot, the offensive player may drive in either direction but preferably toward the defender's forward foot and arm. This is because the defender's weight must be returned over her base before her forward foot can be moved backward.

No Feint

Sometimes an opponent can be caught off balance if a player starts a drive as soon as she catches the ball without any preliminary feint. Since the defense player is usually playing ball side of her opponent, the drive is made to the other side. If a player receives the ball from the right, she immediately steps left with her left foot and starts her drive in that direction.

CUTTING

To participate in any offensive action, a player must be able to cut. Cutting means running to get free to receive a pass or running away from the possible pass area to clear it for a teammate. Usually a cut is preceded by some type of fake to cause the defensive player to start in the wrong direction and enable the offensive player to get at least a half a step advantage on her opponent. This means that in order to cut a player must be adept at starting, stopping, faking, and changing direction quickly. One of the greatest faults of beginning players is the inability to cut. Rather than

---

DRILLS

1. Groups of three—two offensive and one defensive player guarding the player with the ball. The offensive players must remain stationary and attempt to pass the ball back and forth. The defensive player guards the player with the ball and a pass may not be attempted until she is in position to guard. All types of fakes should be attempted, and various passes at different levels should be used. Rotate players and repeat.

2. Each player has a ball. All try two or three of the fakes described. (*Note:* For all of the following, initially instruct the defender to "take" the fake (if it is well executed); later, instruct them not to "take" the fake, forcing the fakes to continue with original movement; then, let the defender use either alternative.)

3. Pairs position themselves as one offensive and one defensive player in their normal playing position. The offensive player tries any of the fakes she knows against her opponent. Exchange places. Emphasize improving all fakes and possibilities.

Fig. 1.55 *Fake and Drive in the Same Direction. The player fakes to the right* (a *and* b). *She straightens her trunk and pulls back* (c). *The trunk inclines forward, and the push comes from the right foot as she has brought the defender toward her* (d). *Drive for the basket* (e) *and* (f).

Fig. 1.56 *Rocker Step. The player fakes to her right* (a) *and brings her left foot back and fakes a shot which brings the defender close to her* (b). *She pushes off hard from the right foot* (c) *and drives for the layup* (d–f). *Note the height of the ball before release.*

running, beginning players often attempt to get free by sliding three or four steps in one direction and then an equal number of steps in the opposite direction. In essence, they are sliding back and forth in one place and this type of tactic is very easy to defend against. Beginners must learn that on offense all movement patterns are made by running, not sliding.

Most cuts should be made sharply and angularly. A cut performed in this manner is much more difficult to defend against than is a cut in an arc or circle (Fig. 1.57a). When an offensive player chooses to move in an arc, the defensive player can follow a straight path and beat her opponent to her desired position (Fig. 1.57b).

Not only is it important to know how to cut but also when and where to cut. Where the cut is made depends on the position of the offensive player's opponent and the team offensive system being played. Basically, only one cutter should be moving at a time. If two players have cut simultaneously, only the player in the better position for receiving a pass should continue her cut into the receiving area. The other player should move away from the primary receiver so that the passing lane remains open.

The timing of the cut is equally important. The cutter must reach the desired receiving area when that area is cleared of other players. Secondary receivers must be ready to make their cuts if the passer finds

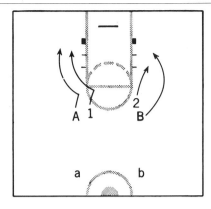

Fig. 1.57 *Player A makes an angular cut and B makes a cut in an arc. A defense player can guard against this cut to an easier degree.*

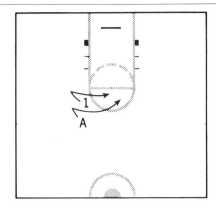

Fig. 1.58 *Front cut made by player A and the accompanying move made by 1.*

that the primary cutter is not free. Generally, one cut follows another in a sequential pattern. No two people are cutting into the same area at the same time, but someone is cutting all of the time. On offense there should be extensive movement. A team that stands around will not have much success. But it must be recognized early that everyone cannot be moving into the same area. This is what makes offensive play so difficult to coordinate. Each player must adjust her moves according to what her teammates are doing. One player should cut into the passing lane, followed by another and another. If the initial cutter does not receive a pass she must clear the area for a second cutter. In this way a passing lane should remain open at all times.

There are three types of cuts that can be used, each with their own modifications. All of these cuts are effective both when advancing the ball from the back court to the front court and for offensive maneuvers in the front court for scoring possibilities.

Front Cut

The front cut is preceded by a fake in the opposite direction followed by a quick change of direction. The player should move in front of and ball side of the opponent. This move is effective when the defense player is not overplaying her opponent to the ball side. If the player is successful in making her front cut, she should be free for a pass (Fig. 1.58).

Reverse Cut

When the defense player is overplaying and pressing her opponent, the offensive player finds the reverse cut (also called the back or backdoor cut) more

suitable. Because of the defense player's position, she is unable to cut in front of her to open a passing lane; the open lane is behind the defense player. The offensive player fakes toward the ball and, with a quick change of direction, cuts behind the defensive player. If executed quickly, the cutter should be free for a pass (Fig. 1.59). A more subtle use of this maneuver can be executed by a player on the weak side, usually a forward. With good acting the offensive player can give the appearance of being uninvolved in the play pattern being executed. By standing nonchalantly the player may cause her opponent to relax slightly. As that occurs, the offensive player can cut behind the defensive player to receive a pass. In this instance the preliminary fake prior to the cut

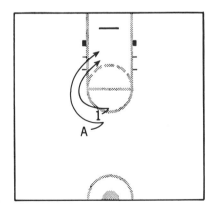

Fig. 1.59 *Reverse cut made by player A when 1 presses.*

is unnecessary and only alerts the defender to the move.

V Cut

A third method of cutting is known as a V cut. It differs from the front and reverse cuts only in that the intended cut is preceded by several steps in a different direction rather than the simple fake. Because of this, it takes longer to execute and therefore must be started sooner than the front or reverse cut in order to reach the passing area at the proper time. Use of this cut may be necessary if the opponent is exceptionally good defensively, or it may be used in order to clear the space into which the cutter wishes to move. By cutting in another direction and taking the defensive player with her, the offensive player can cut back into the space just vacated. This type of cut is also used to drive an opponent into a screen (Fig. 1.60).

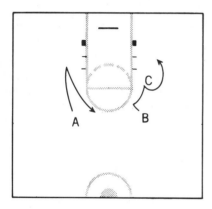

Fig. 1.60 *V cut made by player A to free a space to receive a pass; player B makes a V cut as she uses player C as a screen.*

OFFENSIVE REBOUNDING

Rebounding is probably one of the most overlooked aspects of all offensive tactics. For some reason, teachers and coaches seem to attach little importance to offensive rebounding. At least from the time spent in practicing offensive rebounding it appears that the importance of this technique is underestimated. When one considers that few women's teams can boast a shooting percentage higher than 35–45 percent, one can better understand the importance of good rebounding techniques. If one does not develop offensive rebounders, a team is permitting its opponents to obtain the rebound on approximately three out of

five shots. This seems rather futile when generally the team that gains the greatest number of rebounds wins.

It is generally conceded that offensive rebounding is the responsibility primarily of the pivot player and two forwards. Often they are in a position closer to the basket than are the guards and therefore are in better rebounding position. It is also important to recognize that on any attempted field goal a team must maintain defensive court balance so that the opponents cannot gain a fast break opportunity. This means generally that a team deploys two players—one at the free throw line and the other back near the top of the circle, for this purpose. If a guard has been used in a cutting maneuver, a forward must move back to the free throw line to maintain this proper defensive alignment.

Whichever players happen to be involved in rebounding assignments, they must be aggressive in order to gain good position for rebounding. There is no question but that the defensive team has a distinct advantage in any rebounding situation. If they have been in proper position, they are closer to the basket than any of the offensive players and therefore should be in a position to block off the offensive rebounders. This means then that the offensive players must anticipate the shooting attempts of their teammates and must use whatever fakes and maneuvers are necessary to get into rebounding position. In one sense they have the advantage of knowing when a teammate is likely to shoot. Beginning players, especially, must be reminded immediately to rebound any shot rather than to stand and admire the beauty of its flight. Of course, if they are in a guard position or have defensive responsibilities, this suggestion does not apply.

In man-to-man defense each player is assigned an opponent to guard and should be between that player and the basket at the time of the shot. It is then relatively easy for the defensive players to step in front of the offensive player and block her out from the ensuing play. Against a zone defense or a sagging man-to-man defense, the defensive players do not have as good rebounding position against their opponents—i.e., they are not in a position to block out an opponent immediately. Zone defense players are particularly vulnerable since they are generally assigned an area to rebound rather than to block out a specific player. This means that the offensive players should be able to maneuver into good rebounding position more easily against this type of defense.

Regardless of the defense employed, offense players should make an effort to acquire good rebounding position. This may be done by faking toward the inside and moving to the outside or vice versa. The fastest route to the rebound is by means of cutting

---

REBOUND DRILLS

1. Groups of three. One player tosses the ball against the backboard. Another player times the jump, catches it, pulls it into her chest, pivots, and passes to a teammate near the sideline.

2. Pairs. One offensive player with the ball and one defensive player playing 4–5 ft. away from the offensive player. The offensive player takes a set shot and attempts to outmaneuver the defense player who tries to block her out.

3. Pairs—offensive player with the ball and a defensive player guarding her. The offensive player works one on one against the opponent and shoots when the opportunity arises. She immediately attempts to follow in her shot for a rebound; meanwhile, the defense player attempts to block her out.

4. Four players—two offensive and two defensive players. They play two on two and shoot when the opportunity arises. Both defensive players try to block out their opponents while the offensive players try to get in position for the rebound.

5. Same as drill 4 above, only with three offensive players and three defensive players.

6. Play five against five, emphasizing defensive balance. Two players stay back at the top of the key and the others work for offensive rebounds.

---

inside, but generally the defender protects this side better than an outside cut. The fakes should be varied. It may be possible to fake in one direction and cut in the opposite direction two or three times. A subsequent fake in the same direction, followed by a cut to that direction may deceive an opponent. It is also possible to attempt no fake and simply stand initially directly behind the defender. This often causes her to turn her head to see in what direction the offensive player intends to maneuver. As soon as the offensive player sees the defender's head turn, she should cut to the opposite side.

Often by maneuvering for rebounding position, offensive players can force one or more of the defense players close to the backboard so that the rebound will ricochet over the defender's head and allow the offensive rebounder to obtain the ball or at least tie it up. When maneuvering into position, the offensive player must utilize fakes and anticipate the direction of the rebound. As she makes her moves she must avoid being forced so far under the basket that the rebound will ricochet beyond her outstretched arms.

When an offensive player is in a position to obtain the rebound, she should take a wide stance to give her a firm base in case any contact occurs under the basket. Her knees and ankles should be flexed, her elbows should be at shoulder level, and her forearms

and hands should be extended. This places her in a good jumping position and also makes her wide so that she cannot be easily nudged out of position. Of course, the timing of the jump is important and this timing can be learned only through considerable practice.

When a player goes up for a rebound, she has three options: She may attempt a tip-in, tip the ball back to one of her guards, or catch the ball and follow it with a shot or a pass to a teammate. If a player is not in position to catch a rebound, her next alternative should be that of tipping the ball back to a guard who may then set up the offensive play action from that point. If the player has gained good position and the ball is well within the grasp she should try to catch it and, if free, go back up for a shot. If she is not free, the ball should be brought down with one hand on top of the ball and brought in near her chest so that it may be protected. An outward pass should be made as quickly as possible, and the offense is resumed.

REFERENCES

1. Adapted with permission from Broer, Marion. *Efficiency of Human Motion*, Philadelphia, Pa.: W. B. Saunders Co., 1966, p. 302.

2. *Ibid*, pp. 304, 305.

2

Two-, Three-, and Four-Player Offensive Tactics

There are several tactics that an offensive player can use in combination with one or more teammates that may prove successful against varying types of defenses. The maneuvers that will be described are basic to all offensive tactics. Some are more useful against man-to-man defense whereas others are equally effective against both man-to-man and zone defenses. The pass and cut and running screens are effective against both types of defenses; scissoring and screens encouraging a switch of defensive player assignments are effective only against man-to-man style defenses.

PASS AND CUT

Once beginners learn to cut they are then ready to execute the most elementary of all offensive plays—the pass and cut maneuver (often called the give and go) in which a player passes to a teammate and then cuts for the basket. It is a play in which the original passer re-acquires the ball in a position closer to the basket, either to shoot immediately or to drive closer to the goal. Either the front or reverse cutting techniques may be used, depending upon the position of the defense players. This play is executed most often with the guard starting the play by passing to a forward. If the defense guards this maneuver well, the cutter must continue her cut to a position near the end line and then clear the area. In so doing she may clear to the opposite side of the court or stay on the same side of the court and set a running screen for the forward

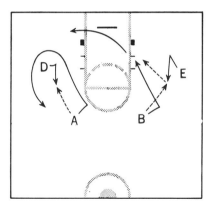

Fig. 2.1 *Players B and E execute a pass and cut play. If E cannot pass in to B, B may clear to the opposite side; player A started a pass and cut with D but was not free, so she set a running screen for D and then buttonhooked back to her position.*

with the ball (Fig. 2.1). It may also be successful when executed by the two guards if the pivot player has cleared the lane.

SCREENING

The purpose of screening is threefold:

1. to provide a teammate with the ball the oppor-

tunity to shoot or drive for goal

2. to free a teammate without the ball for a pass
3. to go behind a teammate to receive a hand-off with the option of shooting or driving for goal

In advanced play, screening is also used to force the defensive players to switch opponents, causing a mismatch in height and/or ability on the exchange of defensive assignments. By forcing a short defensive player to switch to a taller opponent, it should provide the offensive team with a good scoring opportunity.

There are three ways of setting a screen. The player sets the screen

1. closer to the basket than her teammate's opponent (outside or rear screen—Fig. 2.2)

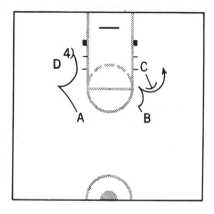

Fig. 2.2 *Player A sets an outside screen for player D. Player C moves up to set a rear screen for player B.*

2. between her teammate and her teammate's opponent (inside or back screen—Fig. 2.3)
3. to either side of her teammate's opponent (lateral screen—Fig. 2.4).

The position of the teammate's opponent is the deciding factor in determining where the screen is set. When an opponent is guarding loosely or sagging, the inside or back screen is generally used. When the opponent is guarding closely the outside, rear, or lateral screens are generally used. The reason for this will be understood as the description of each screen is read.

The player may set the desired screen in either of two ways. She may cut over to set the screen on the defensive player or she may dribble into position for the screen. Both techniques may be employed to set either a moving or stationary screen although the dribbling technique usually involves a moving screen. Screen plays may involve two, three, or four players. Beginners should learn how to screen first with two players; and, once the moves and timing are acquired for that technique, then three-player screens may be attempted, followed by four-player screens—commonly called double screens.

Whenever possible, players should set screens facing the basket. Following the cut off the screen, the screener can sight the basket as well as many of the other offensive players. Positioning herself in this manner avoids delay caused by pivoting in order to face the basket.

Whenever a screen is set, the player for whom the screen is set is responsible for using it. She must cut off the screen to relieve congestion in that area and also to relieve the defensive pressure on the ball. On a lateral screen the cutter usually moves toward

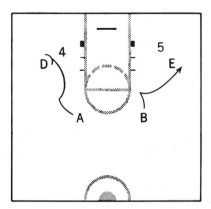

Fig. 2.3 *Player A sets an inside screen for player D, and player B cuts behind player E to effect a back screen.*

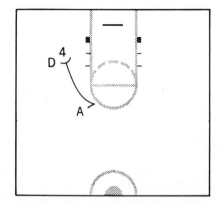

Fig. 2.4 *Player A sets a lateral screen for player D.*

a　　　　　　　　　　　　　　　b

Fig. 2.5 *Inside Screen. Dark No. 5 moves over to set a screen against defender No. 3, who is guarding loosely* (a and b). *As No. 3 moves toward the ball handler, No. 4 drives in the opposite direction* (c). *No. 5 (dark uniform) has pivoted on her left foot to block out her opponent* (d). *The pass is made for the layup* (e).

the side of the screen. On all other screens the cutter may go in either direction.

In many instances the offensive team can gain a real advantage if the opponents are forced to switch defensive assignments on screens. This advantage is gained by forcing a shorter opponent to guard a tall offensive player. This maneuver can be effected either by the short or tall player initiating the screen for her teammate. Should the short player screen for her teammate, the taller player will be guarded by a shorter guard on her cut for the basket if the switch is necessary. The height advantage should give the tall player the opportunity to drive and score reasonably easy. If a tall player screens for a shorter teammate, the tall player will be guarded by the short defensive player on the switch as she rolls following the screen. This should also result in a relatively easy shot. Players should look for mismatches in height at any time, although they are most likely to occur on guard to forward moves, guard to pivot moves, and forward and pivot moves.

Inside Screen

An inside screen is executed by a player moving between a teammate and her opponent who is guarding loosely, and is most commonly used by two guards or by a guard and a forward. The screen may be estab-

lished by a player cutting between her teammate and her opponent and stopping to form a stationary screen, or the screen may be set as a player cuts between a teammate and her opponent or dribbles between the two players, thus forming a moving screen. In all cases the screener should face the basket.

Guard to Guard

If the inside screen is set by a guard who passes to a teammate and cuts in front of her and stops, the player with the ball has several options. If she is within her shooting range, she may shoot from behind the screen. If either defense player moves around the screen to guard her more closely, she can drive in the opposite direction. If neither defense player moves in to guard her, she may drive for the basket.

It is easily understandable that the alternative chosen by the player with the ball depends upon the defensive moves of the opponents. This is also true of the subsequent action of the screener. If either defense player moves to guard the player with the ball, the screener blocks out the other defender so that she (the screener) should be free for an ensuing pass. Having set the screen while facing the basket, the screener will have both defenders in front of her and probably side by side. If the defender on her right moves in to guard the player with the ball, the screener quickly

c

d

e

Fig. 2.5 *continued.*

74

steps forward with her left foot to place the defender on her left behind her. She is then free for a quick pass. If the defender on the screener's left moves in to guard the player with the ball, the screener then steps forward with her right foot to block out the defender on her right. The blocking out and roll toward the basket is started as soon as the switch in defensive assignments is made, and the pass to the rolling player must be made immediately. A bounce pass is usually most effective. If the pass is delayed the defensive team has time to reposition and possibly intercept the pass (Fig. 2.5).

The moving screen is more commonly seen in guard maneuvers. The guard with the ball dribbles between a teammate and her opponent (or cuts between them). The teammate then cuts in the direction from which the dribbler came, receives a hand-off, and drives for the basket. Her own opponent should be at a defensive disadvantage or, if the opponents switch, her teammate should have a half-step advantage on her new opponent (Fig. 2.6). (*Note:* The two defensive players came shoulder to shoulder before the switch was started.) If the defensive players had anticipated the screen and if the dribbler's opponent had started her switch too soon, this would have permitted the dribbler to cut between the two guards after her hand-off, thus affecting an outside screen enabling her to be free for a subsequent pass (Fig. 2.7).

Guard to Forward

The same options are available on the inside screen when the guard sets a screen for the forward. The forward must be cautious in her positioning if she wants to take advantage of this type of screen. She must be between 12 and 15 ft. from the end line. If she is too close to the end line when the screen is set, the screen is ineffective because the drive may be made in only one direction.

Three-Player Inside Screen

This play may be executed by a pivot, guard, and forward. As the pivot player receives the pass the guard can cut down and set the inside screen for the forward. The same options are available for the forward, and the pivot player looks for either the forward or the guard—whichever player appears to be more free. The pivot player should be particularly aware of any mismatches in defensive assignments that may develop (Fig. 2.8).

Back Screens

Whenever a back screen is set, the same situations

Fig. 2.6 *Inside Screen. Dark No. 5 has dribbled over and handed the ball to No. 4* (a). *As both defenders are concerned with the drive* (b), *No. 4 passes* (c) *to her free teammate* (d).

develop as occurred when the inside screen was set. This is true because on a back screen the two offensive and two defensive players have the same relative position as they had during the inside screen — i.e., the two defense players are closer to the basket than either of the offensive players. A back screen may occur when a player cuts behind a teammate in possession of the ball, or when a player with the ball dribbles behind a teammate. In both cases the options are the same as occurred with the inside screen.

Guard to Guard

This technique is used less frequently with the guards because the player with the ball is often beyond her shooting range. Nevertheless, the back screen be-tween the two guards may be effective since the other options are still usable.

Guard to Forward

The guard may intentionally dribble behind the forward and utilize any of the options described. The screen may also develop when the guard starts to set an inside screen for the forward but the forward's opponent moves close to prevent the inside screen from being set. The guard is forced to change her tactic and dribbles behind the forward (Fig. 2.9). The same situation may occur when the guard passes to the forward and tries to set an inside screen. If the inside screen cannot be set, she may cut behind the forward for a hand-off. In either situation a back screen has occurred and the guard has the various options to use.

Fig. 2.7 *Inside Screen. Dark No. 5 dribbles toward her teammate* (a and b). *She has handed the ball to No. 4 and sees that the two defenders have not moved shoulder to shoulder* (c). *No. 5 cuts between the defenders* (d), *receives the pass* (e), *and shoots* (f).

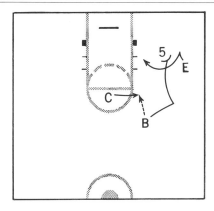

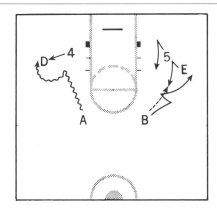

Fig. 2.8 *Three-Player Inside Screen. Player B passes to C and cuts down to set an inside screen for E. Player C passes to either E on her cut or to B on her roll.*

Fig. 2.9 *Player A dribbles toward D to set an inside screen, but No. 4 moves to guard closely so A dribbles behind D to effect a back screen. Player B passes to E and tries to set an inside screen but goes behind E as No. 5 moves in to guard closely.*

a

b

c

d

e

Fig. 2.10 *Outside Screen. Light No. 5 passes to her teammate* (a) *and moves over to set a screen behind dark No. 4. No. 3 fakes and drives, causing dark No. 4 to move into the screen while her teammate fakes* (b and c). *No. 3 drives, forcing her opponent into the screen* (d) *and is free for the layup* (e).

Outside Screens

The outside screen is set basket side of a teammate's opponent and is used when the defensive player is guarding a teammate rather closely. It may be used in preference to a lateral screen since the outside screen is more easily disguised and the opponent is not as aware that a screen has been set. When setting an outside screen, the screener must be certain that she is on a direct line between the player screened and the basket and, when possible, she should face the basket. The screen is extremely effective either when set for a player with the ball or when set for a player away from the ball who may then cut off the screen for a pass and an attempted shot. The screen can be used effectively by two guards, guard and forward, or pivot player and forward. When using the screen it may be necessary to fake or cut a few steps below (beyond) the screen and then cut back in order to force the opponent into the screen.

Once an outside screen is set, the player for whom the screen is set must always cut off the screen and continue away from it. This relieves congestion in the area and enables the screener to step in front of the closer opponent and roll toward the basket for a pass. As was the case for the inside screen, the outside screen may be executed either moving or stationary, and may be initiated by a player dribbling or cutting into position for the screen.

Guard to Guard

One guard may pass the ball to her teammate and cut over behind her teammate's opponent. The player with the ball usually fakes toward the direction from which the screen is coming and then drives around the screen in the opposite direction. If the defense players switch off, the screener should step in front of her new opponent and roll for the basket. She should receive a pass immediately. The same maneuver may materialize if the guard dribbles over toward her teammate, hands off to her, and then continues to cut behind her teammate's opponent.

A slight variation of this maneuver is demonstrated by a guard who dribbles over behind her teammate's opponent and stops to set a stationary screen at that point. The screened player then utilizes fakes to force her opponent into the screen and cuts in the opposite direction to receive a hand-off from the ball handler.

Guard to Forward and Pivot to Forward

The same options are available for these two players as identified for the two guards. Again the forward must be at least 12 ft. from the end line so that she is able to maneuver in either direction as a guard (Fig. 2.10) or pivot player screens for her.

Three-Player Screen

The purpose of the three-player screen is to set the screen for a player away from the ball to enable her to cut to receive a pass for a possible field goal attempt. One example of this play occurs when a guard passes into a pivot and cuts down to set a screen for a forward. The forward maneuvers her opponent into the

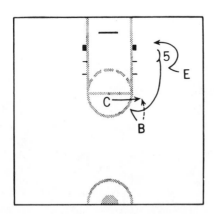

Fig. 2.11 *Three-Player Outside Screen. Player B passes to C and cuts down to set an outside screen for E. Player E fakes toward the screen and cuts opposite, forcing No. 5 into the screen.*

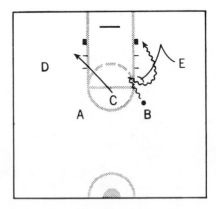

Fig. 2.12 *Rear Screen. Player C cuts to the weak side. Player E cuts to set a rear screen for player B, who dribbles her opponent into it and drives around the screen for a shot.*

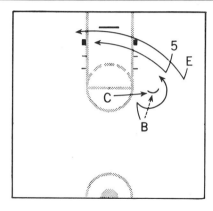

Fig. 2.13 *Player C cuts to set a rear screen for player B. E clears to the opposite side. B passes to C, who pivots to face the basket. B forces her opponent into the screen and receives a hand-off from C.*

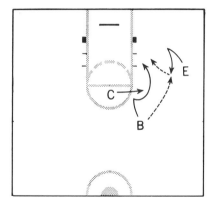

Fig. 2.14 *Three-Player Rear Screen. Player C cuts to set a rear screen. Player E does not clear, and B passes to her. B cuts off the screen to receive a pass from E. If B is not free, E can pass to C as she cuts for the basket.*

screen, cuts around it, and receives a pass from the pivot player (Fig. 2.11). This tactic is also effective for an out-of-bounds play.

Rear Screen

The principles and options for the rear screen are the same as those described for the outside screen, except the rear screen is always set at a distance from the player with the ball, or at a distance from the player for whom the screen is intended. It is most commonly set by a forward or a pivot player who is closer to the basket than the player for whom the screen is set. The rear screen can be a highly effective tool when set for a player who works one-on-one effectively. A rear screen is always set in a stationary manner in an uncongested area on the court.

Forward for Guard

A guard has possession of the ball and a forward cuts out from her corner position to an uncongested area 15–18 ft. from the basket, generally at an extension of the free throw line. She sets her screen and the guard dribbles her opponent into the screen thus allowing the guard to continue her drive around the screen for an attempted shot (Fig. 2.12). If the defense players switch, the screener steps in front of her new opponent, cuts for the basket, and should receive a pass. The pivot player clears to the other side. A variation of this play is executed when the forward cuts up toward the guard and the guard passes to her. The forward immediately pivots to face the basket and the

guard maneuvers her opponent into the screen and cuts in the opposite direction around the forward for a hand-off. If the guards switch defensive assignments, the forward is free to shoot a jump shot or drive for the basket.

Pivot for Guard

The same options as described for forward and guard maneuvers are useful for these two players. The pivot player may cut diagonally up toward the guard or laterally to an extension of the free throw line to set the rear screen. The near side forward clears to the far side of the court (Fig. 2.13).

Three-Player Screen

A pivot player sets a rear screen at the extension of the free throw line. A guard passes the ball to a forward and cuts off the screen for a return pass from the forward. The pivot player then cuts for the basket and the forward passes to whichever player is freer (Fig. 2.14).

Lateral Screens

A lateral screen is executed by a player either for a player with the ball or away from the ball to free a player to receive a pass. The lateral screen is effective only if the defensive player is guarding closely. If the defender is guarding loosely, an inside screen should be set in preference to the lateral screen. In setting the lateral screen, a player sets her body perpendicular to her opponent and as close as possible while avoiding the possibility of fouling her. One of the disad-

Fig. 2.15 *Lateral Screen. Light No. 5 moves over to set the screen on dark No. 4 as No. 3 fakes in the other direction (a and b). No. 3 drives toward the screen (c). No. 5 pivots on her left foot to start her roll (d). Both players are free because of poor defensive moves (e).*

vantages of the lateral screen is the screener's position in relation to the basket. With her body perpendicular and facing her opponent, she must pivot before she can face the basket. After setting the screen, the player holds it until her teammate starts her drive. Then the screener rolls for the basket. If the screen is set with the left foot closer to the basket than the right foot, the screener moves her left foot slightly to the left to assure that the defender being screened is forced to remain behind the screener. After taking the slight move to her left, she pivots on her left foot and cuts for the basket with her right foot. If the screen is set on the other side of the court when the player has her right foot closer to the basket, the screener moves her right foot slightly to her right, pivots off her right foot, and starts for the basket with her left foot. With beginning players it is not necessary for the screener to move her rear foot slightly to the side to keep the

opponent behind her.

There is an alternate method of setting a lateral screen that is used less frequently. Rather than facing the defense player, the screener sets the screen with her back to her. This has the advantage of eliminating the pivot prior to the roll for the basket but is disadvantageous to the screener if the player screened for cuts or drives away from the side on which the screen is set. This position does not allow the screener to detect this move during the initial stage. If a player chooses to set the screen in this manner, her approach is slightly different than previously described. If the screen is to be set to the screener's right, she cuts over and stops with her left foot opposite the front foot of the defender to be screened. She does a reverse pivot so that her right foot is behind the defender's rear foot. She now is in the same relative position as she would be had she set the screen in the

Fig. 2.16 *Lateral Screen. Light No. 5 sets the screen on dark No. 4 as light No. 3 fakes (a and* b). *Dark No. 5 switches opponents and moves to guard light No. 3 (c). Light No. 5 pivots and rolls as No. 3 passes (d). No. 5 is free for a drive (e).*

more standard way except she has her back to the defense player. As she starts her roll, she takes a slight step with her right foot to keep the defender behind her and cuts toward the basket with her left foot.

For a lateral screen to be successful it is important that the player, for whom the screen is set, looks away from the direction from which the screen is coming and fakes in another direction. For example, if the screen is coming from the player's left, she can look toward the basket or to her right, fake to her right, and then cut left around the screen. Otherwise the defender is alerted for the screen and can take measures to reduce its effectiveness.

It is the responsibility of the player for whom the screen is set to avoid causing a foul. She must wait for the screener to come to a stationary position before the cut or drive is made. If she starts her cut or drive around the screen too soon, her teammate is likely to

be called for blocking if contact results between her and an opponent.

There are a number of possibilities for using lateral screens. They may be used by a guard setting the screen for another guard, a guard screening for a forward, a pivot player screening for a forward, or a forward screening for another forward. Use of the lateral screen is made to a lesser extent by a forward screening for a guard or a pivot screening for a guard. In both of these instances, the rear screen is more effective. A lateral screen is a very effective means for freeing a forward who is close to the baseline. Because of her inability to cut toward the end line side, it is the only effective screen when she is in this position.

Guard to Guard

A guard passes to her teammate and cuts over to set a

Fig. 2.17 *Lateral Screen. Dark No. 2 passes to her teammate and moves to set a screen (a and b). Light No. 1 anticipates the screen and moves toward the direction of the anticipated drive (c). Dark No. 1 drives away from the screen (d) and is free for the layup before the defense can recover (e–g).*

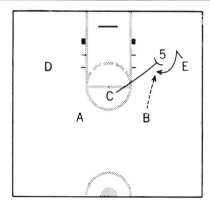

Fig. 2.18 *Three-Player Lateral Screen. Player C sets a screen for E. E fakes away from the screen and cuts back for a pass from B. If E is not free, B can pass to C on her roll.*

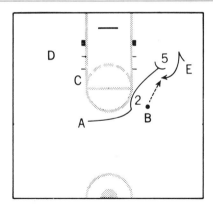

Fig. 2.19 *Three-Player Lateral Screen. Player A cuts behind No. 2 and continues to set a screen for E. Player E fakes and cuts around the screen for a pass from B. Player B also has the option of passing to A.*

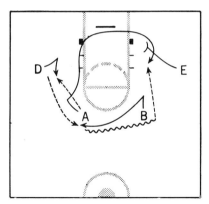

Fig. 2.20 *Lateral Screen Set in Open Space. Player A passes to D and cuts for the basket. Player B fills the space, and D passes back to B. E moves toward the lane and sets a diagonal screen for A to cut around. B dribbles to her right and passes to A or E on her subsequent roll.*

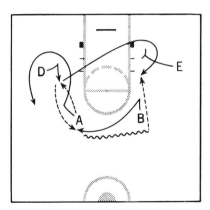

Fig. 2.21 *Variation of Fig. 2.20. Player A passes to D and cuts for the goal. When A does not get a return pass, she buttonhooks back as D passes to B. Player B dribbles to her right and passes to D as she cuts around E's screen, or she may pass to E if she is free on her roll.*

lateral screen on her teammate's opponent. The player with the ball generally cuts toward the side of the screen, thus forcing her opponent into the screen. If the defensive players do not switch, the ball handler is free to drive toward the basket (Fig. 2.15). If the defense players switch, the screener pivots and rolls toward the basket and should be free for a pass (Fig. 2.16).

If a defense player anticipates a screen and moves toward the screening side before the screen is set, the player with the ball should cut away from the screen and should be free on her drive toward the basket (Fig. 2.17).

Other Players

As mentioned previously, other players may team up to work a lateral screen and the options for its use are the same for them as described for the two guards.

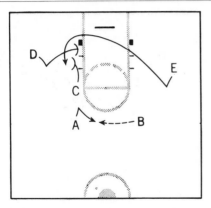

Fig. 2.22 *Double Screen Along the Lane. As player B passes to A, C and D both cut to set the double screen. E cuts around the double screen. Player A passes to E or to C or D, depending upon the action of the defense.*

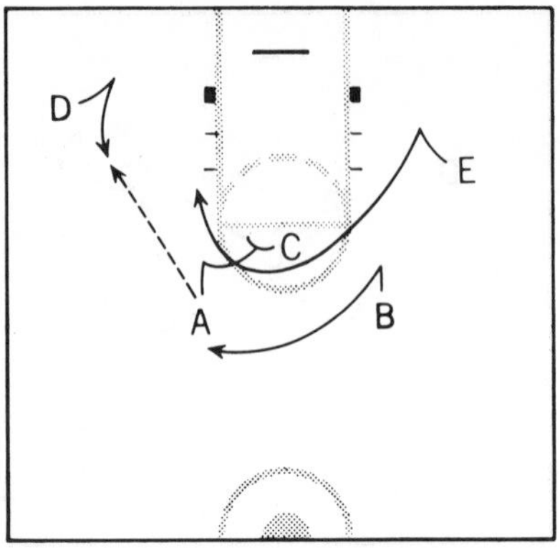

Fig. 2.23 *Double Screen at the Free Throw Line. Player A passes to D and screens beside C. Player E cuts around the screen for a pass from D.*

Three-Player Lateral Screens

Several combinations of this maneuver are practical and most of them occur when a guard has the ball. A pivot player may set a screen for a forward who receives the pass from the guard (Fig. 2.18). When the weak side guard has the ball, the strong side guard may make a diagonal cut and screen for the weak side forward who receives the pass (Fig. 2.19). A guard or pivot player may have the ball as a forward screens for the other forward. The pivot player may have the ball as a guard screens for a forward. A lateral screen may also be set in an open space (Figs. 2.20 and 2.21). Regardless of whether the screen is for two or three players, the options for the lateral screen remain the same.

Double Screens

A double screen always requires four players and because of the number of players involved, the timing of this screen is more difficult than any of the others. Two players are always used to form the screen as a third player cuts behind the screen to receive a pass from the fourth player. Basically, the purpose of the double screen is to permit a player to be relatively free for an immediate shot. If this does not materialize, the player can drive beyond the screen for a short jump shot or continue to drive for the basket. If the defense players switch, then the appropriate screener should roll to receive a pass.

Double screens are usually formed when a guard

has possession of the ball and a pivot and forward or pivot and guard set the screen. Following the double screen, players must hasten to regain court balance in case the ball is intercepted or the opponents recover a rebound.

Because of the nature of double screens, they are used less often than other screens. Their use is limited in terms of frequency and position on the court where they can be set. The double screen is always set along one of the lane lines or at the free throw line.

One example of a double screen utilizes a pivot player moving to a low post position and a forward on that side cutting to the lane line beside the pivot for the double screen. The strong side guard (one on that side of the court) has the ball and the forward on the weak side cuts through the key under the basket and behind the double screen to receive the pass. She either shoots from behind the screen or drives around it (Fig. 2.22). Another double screen is possible when the guard on the strong side passes to the weak side guard and immediately cuts along the key beside the pivot in the low or medium post position. The strong side forward then cuts around the screen to receive a pass from the guard.

A third example of a double screen occurs when a forward has the ball. A guard and pivot form a double screen at the free throw line and the weak side forward cuts up and around the double screen for a pass (Fig. 2.23). The same situation can develop with the pivot and forward forming the screen at the free throw line and the weak side guard cuts around it for the pass.

Fig. 2.24 *Scissor. Dark No. 2 fakes* (a). *After passing into the pivot, she becomes the first cutter* (b and c). *No. 3 fakes the hand-off to No. 2* (d). *In this instance, No. 2 was free for the hand-off due to the poor position of her opponent (light No. 2, who did not anticipate the cut). Having faked previously, No. 1 becomes the second cutter* (e and f). *By cutting tight off the pivot, her opponent does not have space to follow, and No. 1 is given a hand-off* (g). *She drives for the layup* (h–k). *After the hand-off, dark No. 3 should have cut in for a possible rebound.*

h

i

j

k

Fig. 2.24 *continued.*

Drills

The success of any of the screen plays is entirely dependent upon the timing of the cuts and the correct execution of the screen itself. It is also necessary for the offensive players to observe the deployment of the defense players so that they can counteract the defensive move and make the screen play effective. This means that considerable practice time must be devoted to the two- and three-player screens by the players involved so that they may develop the game sense necessary for proficient execution. While two guards are practicing various screens, the pivot and one forward may also work on their screen moves. At another time the guard and forward on each side of the court can work on their moves while the pivot player may be working on her individual moves at another basket.

At the initial stage of learning, the position of defense players in relation to ball handlers must be stipulated so that the two offense players may practice a designated screen. For example, if two players are preparing to practice an inside screen, the defensive player must be instructed to sag so that there is space in which the inside screen may be set. Later the defenders should be instructed to press or play closely so that the offense may use a lateral, outside, or back screen as instructed.

Initially, the defense player should be instructed to play strict man-to-man rather than switching defense so that the offense can learn how to react to this situation. Later, the defense should be instructed to switch each time the screen is practiced so that the offensive players can practice the roll and subsequent pass. Somewhat later the defensive players can be encouraged to use their own discretion and play either strict man-to-man or switching defense so that the offensive players learn to recognize which tactic is being used and learn to combat it.

After the offensive players have gained some wis-

Fig. 2.25 *Scissor. The pass is made to the pivot, and the two guards time their cuts (a–c). The pivot's defender, light No. 3, begins to hedge toward the side of the second cutter (d and e). The pivot sees the position of her opponent (f) and turns to shoot a jump shot (g–i). Again, light No. 2 has poor defensive position and her opponent was free throughout the maneuver.*

h

i

Fig. 2.25 *continued.*

dom and skill in the use of these screens, the defensive players can be encouraged to attempt to counteract the desired screen that the offense wishes to employ. For example, if a defensive player is sagging and can see that an inside screen is desired by the offensive players, she can move up to a position closer to the offensive player so that the offense must then set a different type of screen in order to be effective. In this particular situation as the defensive player moves close to the offensive player, the screener can

then change from an inside screen to a lateral screen, back screen, or outside screen.

There is no question but that considerable time must be devoted to two- and three-player maneuvers in practice sessions. Offensive players must be able to react to whatever defensive tactics are employed and be able to change their tactics to counteract those of the defense. Understanding and acquisition of these skills takes time and considerable team work between the players involved. All of these screens

a

b

c

Fig. 2.26 *Scissor. The ball is passed to the pivot (a). Both guards move back in front of the pivot in position to switch opponents as they cross (b). The ball cannot be handed to the first cutter (c). The second cutter observes the defensive plan and changes direction (d). She cuts in the same direction as the first cutter (e) and receives the hand-off (f). She drives and is free to shoot as dark No. 2 screens out her new opponent (g–i).*

d

e

f

g

h

i

are the heart of offensive patterns that may be selected for team use. They must be learned and practiced to the extent that players can react instantly to any defensive tactic employed by the opponents in a game situation.

SCISSORING

Scissoring is a maneuver involving the pivot player and two other players (two guards or a guard and forward) who cross and cut on either side of the pivot. The purpose is to free one of the cutters for a pass or an attempted shot for the basket.

Pivot and Two Guards

The scissor maneuver is executed most frequently by these three players. The play is initiated by one of the guards who passes the ball into the pivot who has moved to the high post position with her back to the basket. The player who passes in to the pivot *always* makes the first cut. She fakes down her side of the court and then cuts around and as close as possible to the pivot player. The other guard delays her cut momentarily and then fakes down her side of the court and cuts "off the back" (very close behind) of the first cutter to the other side of the pivot. The pivot player may pass to either player, whichever one appears to be more free. Generally, the second cutter will be the freer player since her opponent should be forced into the screen provided by the first cutter. It is important that the cutters move as close as possible to the pivot player so that their opponents cannot maneuver between them and the pivot player. (Beginners tend to cut in a wide arc and this must be corrected immediately.)

Variations

Whenever the scissor maneuver is executed, the offensive players should be aware of how the defense attempts to defeat the effectiveness of the scissor play. If the defense play is strictly man-to-man and each defense player follows her opponent in the scissor maneuver, the second cutter should always be free to receive the pass (Fig. 2.24). However, the defense players often try other tactics to prevent the success of the scissor maneuver. In one such tactic the pivot player's opponent anticipates the pass to the second cutter and moves slightly in that direction (hedging). Since the pivot player has her back to the basket, she must use her peripheral vision to observe the defensive position of her opponent. As she sees her hedge, the pivot player should fake a hand-off to the second cutter and then pivot and take a jump shot immediately; or, if the lane is open she should drive for a layup or a short jump shot (Fig. 2.25).

Occasionally, the defense tries to counteract the scissor play by having both of the guards' opponents drop back in front of the pivot so that they may switch opponents when the opponents cross. If this occurs, the first cutter makes her normal cut and the second cutter starts her usual cut; instead of continuing around the pivot player, however, she reverses her cut and cuts down the same side of the pivot player as the first player. The pivot player hands off to the second cutter who should be free for a jump shot or a drive for a layup (Fig. 2.26).

If the defense fears the effectiveness of the scissor play, one defender may drop back to help protect against the ball being passed into the pivot. This means that the guard without the ball is left open. As the ball is passed into the pivot, the guard may quickly cut down her side of the court in executing a reverse cut (backdoor play). In this instance, she does not time her cut after the passer starts, but moves immediately as the pass goes successfully into the pivot. The pivot player passes quickly to her for the layup or short jump shot (Fig. 2.27). In order for this play to be effective, the forward in the corner must clear that side of the court or her opponent will float and be in a position to prevent the layup or at least reduce its effectiveness.

The other way in which the defense attempts to counteract the scissor is by sending the second cutter's opponent behind the post player so that she is not screened by the move of the first cutter. By moving behind the pivot, she is in position to recover good guarding position as the second cutter moves past the pivot. When the first cutter observes this action she should stop behind the pivot player to form a double screen. The second cutter delays her cut and stops behind the double screen to receive a hand-off. She then may execute a set shot or utilize any of the other options that are useful from a double screen position (Fig. 2.28).

Pivot, Forward, and Guard

The same scissor maneuver and all of its variations may be used by a pivot player and a forward and guard. Usually, the ball starts with the forward who passes to the pivot in a medium post position along the lane line. Again the pivot player receives the pass with her back to the basket. Following the pass in, the forward fakes a cut in one direction and moves around the opposite side of the pivot. The guard cuts off the back of the forward and the post player may pass to either player. Once again, the second player around the pivot should be the freer player. According to the actions of the defense players, any of the options described previously can be used to counteract their moves (Fig. 2.29).

Fig. 2.27 *Scissor. The ball is passed to the pivot even though defensive guard (light No. 1) has retreated to hinder this move* (a). *Dark No. 1 observes the position of her opponent and cuts directly for the basket* (b). *The pivot passes to No. 1, who is free to shoot* (c–f). *Notice that the player who passed to the pivot altered her usual move and cut down the other side of the pivot.*

a

b

c

d

e

f

Fig. 2.28 *Scissor. The ball is passed to the pivot and the cutters start their usual moves* (a–d). *Light No. 1 cuts behind the pivot to meet her opponent on the other side* (e). *Dark No. 1 observes this action and changes direction* (f). *Dark No. 2 moves to set a double screen with the pivot* (g and h). *No. 1 is free for a shot* (i and j).

g   h

i   j

Drills for Scissor Plays

Scissor plays deserve considerable practice if they are to become effective offensive tactics in a game situation. The two guards and pivot player should work on the moves before defensive players are added. Emphasis should be placed on the timing of the guard cuts and the cuts close to the pivot player. The pivot should be encouraged to pass to the second cutter most of the time. When these moves are learned, opponents can be added with instructions to play only man-to-man. Now it will become apparent that the second cutter is free more often.

Some time later the pivot player's opponent can hedge and force the offensive players to respond correctly to that defensive tactic. Later the defense can back up in front of the pivot and the offense can counteract by using the backdoor play or by sending both cutters down the same side of the pivot. In time the defense players may use their own discretion in the type of defense to use against the pivot cuts. In this situation the offense must react to the type of defense and move accordingly. The same procedure should be followed for pivot, forward, and guard scissor maneuvers.

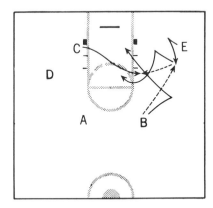

Fig. 2.29 *Forward, Pivot, and Guard Scissor Play. Player B passes to E as C cuts to medium post position. E passes to C. E cuts off the screen followed by B. C passes to the free player or executes a jump shot.*

93

3

Team Offense

When building any type of offense the teacher/coach must consider her players' abilities and potential development. The devised offense may be either simple or very complicated. It may range from the use of give-and-go tactics only to a pattern offense that utilizes cuts of all kinds and various screening maneuvers. Regardless of the offense selected there are certain aspects which should be emphasized and basic principles which are applicable to any offensive system.

BASIC OFFENSIVE PRINCIPLES

Ball Handling

1. Ball possession must be considered extremely important. A team cannot score unless it has possession of the ball, and opponents cannot score when they do not have the ball. The importance of gaining the ball and keeping it once it is gained until a score is made must be impressed continually upon the players. They must recognize the importance of good ball handling skills and how poor ball handling jeopardizes the entire offensive structure of the team.
2. All passes must be accurate and crisp. Lob passes should be made with caution, as they allow the defense time to realign and lead to interceptions. Short passes tend to be more accurate than long ones. Passes should be made to where a player is moving, not where the passer wishes she were. A pass interception, a pass that goes out of bounds, or a pass that is fumbled by the receiver is almost

always the fault of the passer rather than the receiver.
3. Pass receivers must move to meet the ball. A pass should rarely be made to a player who is standing still. If the defense is passive (sagging or playing loosely), cutting to meet the ball may not be as necessary; but, offensive players should not be deceived by the defender's apparent position. It may only be a ruse so that an interception may be attempted. When the defense is playing aggressively (closely), offensive players must cut to meet a pass and the pass should be made toward the shoulder away from the opponent.
4. Pass receivers should be facing the basket when they receive a pass (with the exception of the pivot player). Receiving a pass with her back to the basket is a great weakness of many beginning players —particularly forwards. This action limits offensive play considerably. The player with the ball is unable to see any teammate cutting free for the basket behind her and she is not in a position to shoot. This means that the defense players have an opportunity to regain a good defensive position while the ball handler contemplates her next move. When the defense is sagging a player should have no difficulty in receiving a pass while facing the basket. The cut to meet the ball should be made on a diagonal so that as the player stops she can be facing the basket. The same action should be followed by a player who is closely guarded. She must cut on a diagonal to receive a pass which should be aimed at her ''off'' shoulder (shoulder away from her opponent). The foot position on her stop may allow her to face the basket as she re-

ceives the pass. If not, she should land facing the passer so that a short pivot permits her to face the basket (Fig. 3.1). If a potential receiver discovers that her defender is pressing often, she should attempt a backdoor cut to discourage her from playing too close.

5. Players should dribble only when they are unable to pass to a player in a better position. Highly skilled dribblers should be encouraged to demonstrate their abilities only when necessary and to think of passing before dribbling. An "alive" player (one who has not dribbled) is a more dangerous threat to the defense than one who has already dribbled and caught the ball. Regardless of skill, all players must be discouraged from dribbling unless there is some purpose for it. A reception of a pass followed by an immediate bounce is a sign of an ineffective player and this habit must be corrected quickly. A player should not stop dribbling until she is ready to pass or shoot. This keeps her alive and discourages double-teaming efforts by the opponents. When challenged by a defense player, beginning players often stop dribbling, whereupon one or more defense players guard her closely, frequently causing a violation or a bad pass. Players must acquire an early understanding of the values and disadvantages of the dribble, including when and how to use it effectively.

Positioning and Cutting

1. Whatever offensive system is utilized, it must contain both ball and player movement. An offense where players basically stay in the same position is far easier to defend than one in which the defense must be aware of the changing position of players and ball. This is true for both an offense against a man-to-man and zone defense. Players must pass and cut to force the defense to readjust constantly. They must keep the defense busy physically and mentally. Guards can move laterally or cut to the corners; forwards and the pivot can use baseline cuts. All players may cut through the lane; a team should not rely wholly on passing into that area, however, for it is easily congested by the defense.

2. At the start of any offensive thrust players should remain apart 12 ft. or more. They must make every effort to discourage double-teaming tactics and to keep the defense spread so that one defender cannot guard two offensive players. Beginning players tend to edge toward the ball and/or the lane, thus bringing the defense players in tighter and closing the passing lanes. Of course, once an offensive thrust is started it is impossible and undesirable to keep this distance as players use cuts and screens to free themselves.

a *b*

Fig. 3.1 *Receiving a Pass. The player receives a pass* (a). *She pivots immediately to face the basket* (b).

3. Cuts on offense must be well timed. This is one of the most difficult aspects for players to learn. This is also what makes teaching offense more difficult than teaching defense. How often one sees two or three beginning players cutting for a pass and all arriving in the same spot at practically the same time! This must be avoided! One player may cut to a space and when she clears it another player may cut through the space—but not both at the same time! As one player leaves a spot, another player may fill it.

4. Players should be assigned positions on every offensive movement so that every player knows where she should be at all times. This is true whether a team is using a free lance system or not. Teams that choose this type of offense generally are made up of players who have played with one another for a period of time and who intuitively know the moves of their teammates. Players must possess the "game sense" to know what spaces should be filled. In any other attack system the movements of the individual players are devised so that players remain spread and cover the trailer position. This prevents crowding in a particular location, opens cutting lanes, and helps players to acquire the timing for an offensive thrust.

5. Under most circumstances a player cutting for the ball should receive a pass from a player whom she is facing. This is the easiest way for a receiver to catch a pass and it is also the easiest way for a player to give an accurate pass. This means that generally when a pivot cuts to the high post position she should receive a pass from a player in the guard position. As a guard cuts for the basket she should receive a pass from a player in the corner or low or medium pivot position. As a player in the corner position makes a cut through the lane under the basket or makes a cut up and through the lower half of the restraining circle, she should receive a pass from a player in the opposite corner or in the low or medium post position on the side toward which she is cutting. Although passing in this manner is desirable and most maneuvers should be designed with this principle in mind, it is not always possible or desirable to follow. For example, use of a roll following a screen, scissor maneuvers, and reverse cuts all necessitate a pass being received as a player is cutting away from the ball. This type of pass is most difficult to give accurately and should be used only when necessary.

6. The ball should be passed back out when continued penetration is not feasible. Ideally, the attack wishes to pass the ball toward the basket until a score can result. This may not always be possible. A defense may adjust to the ball and player movement so well that continued advancement of the ball toward the basket would result in a charging foul or pass interception. In this case the ball should be passed back, forcing the defense to realign and making it possible to start an offensive thrust again.

The action may be started again on the same side, or the ball may be passed from the strong side around the perimeter of the defense to penetrate it from the weak side.

7. Players should clear the area when a player is driving. Teammates should cut away from the dribbler to draw their opponent with them and prevent the defense from collapsing around the dribbler. This is particularly important against a zone defense. If a player can penetrate the perimeter of the zone, she will draw another defender; this should leave a teammate open for a pass so long as she has pulled away far enough so that the same defender cannot guard both players. Against a man-to-man defense it is possible to free one player to operate one-on-one if the ball is passed to the weak side, providing the other player clears the area (Fig. 3.2).

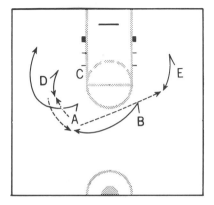

Fig. 3.2 *Pass to the Weak Side to Allow a Forward to Work One on One. Player A passes to D and cuts to the corner. D passes back to B, who passes to E. Player E can work one-on-one against her opponent.*

Shooting and Cutting

1. A team must have players who can shoot accurately from the inside and outside. Long shots do not produce a high scoring percentage, and a team that must rely on these for scoring only will not win many games. Likewise the team that can shoot only from within 10–15 ft. of the basket will have difficulty in scoring, as the defense will collapse to this area and permit and encourage longer shots.

2. Whenever a tall player shoots, she should use her height to advantage and execute overhead layups, jump shots, and set shots. When a short player moves through the lane she probably will have the greatest success by faking an overhead layup and using an underhand shot or by stopping short of the layup and taking a jump shot 6–8 ft. in front of the basket.

3. Although a team may possess good outside shooters, it should continually attempt to free players within the 8- to 10-ft. range. Shots taken from this area will produce a high percentage for success. If shots cannot be attained from this area, the next highest percentage area falls between 10 and 15 ft. The least desirable shooting distance would be from 15–21 ft. Few shots should be taken from beyond this area (Fig. 3.3).

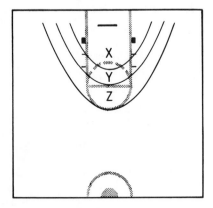

Fig. 3.3 *Shooting Distances. Area X contains the area within 10 ft. of the basket. Most shots should be taken from within this area. Area Y includes the area between 10 and 15 ft. of the basket. Area Z includes the area 15–21 ft. from the basket. Few shots should be attempted from beyond this area.*

4. Patience must be the byword of an attacking team. They must not hurry their scoring thrust but cut and pass to obtain the high percentage shot. Offensive maneuvers must be designed with this in mind and will provide many opportunities for players to be free within a short distance of the basket.

5. The offense should be devised to give every player an opportunity for scoring. This helps team morale. A team that has only two or three good shooters must provide those players with most of the scoring opportunities, however. A team should not reduce its scoring effectiveness to satisfy the desires of inaccurate shooters.

6. Players should not shoot if another player is free and in a better position to do so. Unselfishness is a characteristic that players must be taught if they do not already possess it. A player who is free under the basket is more likely to score than another player 10 ft. from the basket.

7. Whenever a shot is attempted, four conditions must be met:

a. the shooter must be in a better position than any other player to shoot
b. she must not be hurried or off-balance as she attempts her shot
c. she must be within her shooting range
d. rebounders must be in position unless the shooter is attempting a layup or a shot within 5 ft. of the basket

A team usually has worked hard to obtain the ball and to get it in position for a shot. It is senseless to take a shot that has little possibility of scoring, and it is even more questionable to take it without rebounders in position.

8. Unless directed otherwise, any player who shoots should follow her shot for the rebound. She is in the best position to know where the ball is likely to rebound if it is unsuccessful, and she can gain a quick start in that direction.

General

1. Screens should be considered a vital part of any offensive system. Contrary to the beliefs of some coaches, screens are effective against both man-to-man and a zone defense. Many zone offenses utilize running screens to free players and they have been found an effective measure. Against a zone, screens are also set at a spot to prevent a zone defender from moving to her new position as the ball changes position. The value of screens against a man-to-man defense is unchallenged. Their use should be perfected to garner advantages against both types of defense. To make the screen effective, a player must fake away from the screen prior to using it and must not alert an opponent that a screen is being set.

2. Maneuvers that are designed to use a screen and roll should be started approximately 15 ft. from the basket. If started closer than this, there is not sufficient space for the screener to roll toward the basket and receive a pass. Often the area within 8–10 ft. of the basket is quite congested.

3. Any designed offense should exploit the strengths of the offensive players. Maneuvers should be designed to free the best shooters. Advantage should be taken of good ball handlers, and an effort should be made to hide weak ball handlers and shooters. These players should deploy their defenders by fakes and cuts to keep their opponents occupied. The best rebounders should be placed in a position favorable for this task. All players should be involved in every scoring effort in one way or another. Those who are not given many scoring opportunities must be congratulated for their particular contribution to any score. All players must gain a sense of importance in the offensive system.

4. An offense should not only exploit the strengths of its own players but also the weaknesses of the opponents. If the opposing team has one or more

weak defensive players the scoring thrusts should be made in their direction. Soon better skilled teammates will try to help them, thus weakening their own defensive responsibility. If the opponents are slower, the ball should be advanced quickly downcourt. Players can use various cuts to get free and drives to gain a step advantage. If the opponents lack height or jumping ability, taller players may be assigned those positions which bring them close to the basket and passes should be directed to them.

5. A team must provide defensive protection while it is on offense. There must be at least one or two players 20–25 ft. from the basket at all times. As a guard cuts toward the basket, she is replaced by another player and that player is replaced by another. Fig. 3.4 shows how this may be done during a very simple and common maneuver. It is evident from this diagram that this deployment does not involve the same players at all times, although the guards are likely to be in this position more often than the others. Essentially, the purpose of this tactic is twofold:
   a. it provides the offense with a trailer who can receive a pass when forward penetration with the ball is not feasible
   b. it serves as a safety valve in case the ball is intercepted. All offensive maneuvers must use this very important principle.
6. Above all, players must understand the importance of team cooperation and recognize the contribution that each player makes in the total offensive effort.

OTHER CONSIDERATIONS

Getting the Ball from the Back Court to the Front Court

A team may acquire the ball in its defensive end by intercepting it, obtaining a rebound, or by getting the ball out of bounds following a violation or score. There are two ways to advance the ball—either by means of a fast break or a controlled style of play. If the team uses a fast break, the passes are made quickly to gain a player advantage. On an out-of-bounds play a forward (or pivot) puts the ball in play, as she is the closest player to the end line. The ball is in-bounded as rapidly as possible so that the fast break can be initiated.

If a team chooses to use a controlled type of offense, the ball is given to the best ball handler while the rest of the players move to the front court and get into position. The player with the ball dribbles into the front court and sets up the attack. If the ball is put in play from out of bounds the best passer is given this assignment. The ball is in-bounded to a guard while forwards and pivot player move to the front

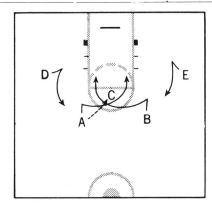

Fig. 3.4 *Players Filling the Spaces to Retain Defensive Balance. On a scissor maneuver by the guards, the two forwards clear the area and come back to provide defensive balance. Fig. 3.2 shows player B providing balance.*

court. The best ball handler is given the responsibility of dribbling the ball downcourt to set up the offensive maneuver.

Following a score the team putting the ball in play from out of bounds may need more help if the opponents press them. In this case the forwards may remain in the back court to assist in beating the press. The pivot moves to the front court as usual. The manner in which a team copes with a press is discussed later in this chapter.

The 30-Sec. Clock

The purpose of the clock is to force the ball to exchange hands reasonably often and, as a result, to prevent any type of stall offense to develop for more than 30 sec. Although the purpose of the clock is to speed up play, there are very few occasions when a team is unable to establish its offense in the manner in which it would like and obtain a high percentage shot. Thirty seconds is a long time, when one considers that it takes only 4 or 5 sec. (or less) to advance the ball into the front court.

Coaches should impress upon their players that there is no need to hurry an attack and that they should be patient in maneuvering for an open shot. Although a pressing defense may delay the crossing into the front court, there still should be ample time to develop the offense in the usual manner. Many teams have been clocked on the time it takes them to obtain a shot, and most are amazed with the alacrity with which they shoot. It is not unusual for a team to shoot within 15 sec. of the time they obtain the ball. If for some reason a team is slow in obtaining a good shot, it may be wise for substitutes or a manager to inform the players when there are only 5 or 8 sec. left, if the 30-sec. clock is not visible to the players.

Determining the Type of Defense Being Used

At the beginning of each quarter the attack should learn specifically what type of defense is being played against them — man-to-man, switching man-to-man, the type of zone, or a combination defense. Each is attacked somewhat differently, so a team should run a simple maneuver to ascertain the moves of the defenders the first time it has possession of the ball. If a defense player follows each cutter, they are using some type of man-to-man defense. If they do not follow each player they are either playing a zone or a combination defense. The nature of either of these must be determined.

This initial maneuver should contain vertical and diagonal cuts by guards and baseline cuts by forwards. The best shooter should be involved in one of the cuts. Any play in an offense system that uses these cuts may become the first scoring thrust. Figs. 3.5 and 3.6 show a simple example of a play that would determine the defensive alignment.

There are other times when the defense may change alignment, but the start of each period is a logical one and the attack should be prepared to identify it immediately. Following a time out or other suspension of play are other times when the attack must be particularly alert for a change. Of course, some teams can make the transition from one defense to another without benefit of a time out. Any time an attack player observes a different alignment she should notify her teammates if the coach has not already done so.

Use of Signals

The practice of using signals of some description to designate a play or a pattern is familiar to all. Signals may be verbal or visual. Names of schools, colors, animals, athletes, and numbers are common verbal signals. The main criticism against the verbal signal is that it may not be heard above the crowd noise. The visual signal is preferred. One finger, two fingers, or a closed fist may be raised above the head to designate the play. This technique may be difficult to achieve against a pressing defense.

A means of accomplishing the same purpose and one that does not call attention to the defense is a more subtle visual signal. This involves movement of the ball. If the ball handler passes to her other guard it will signal a maneuver different from one indicated if the ball had been passed to the forward. The position of a key player may identify a series also. For example, a post player may position herself in the low, medium, or high post positions and her exact position may designate a play in any of them. The technique used most commonly is the movement of the player with the ball after she passes. If the guard cuts diagonally through the key, she establishes the beginning of a maneuver that differs from one indicated if she had gone behind the player to whom she passed.

TYPES OF OFFENSE

There are three types of offense: fast break, man-to-man offense, and zone offense. The fast break involves running and more running in an effort to outnumber the opponents in the offensive end of the court. Because players are moving at near top speed, bad

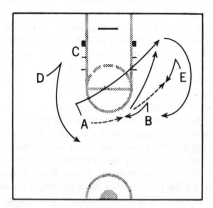

Fig. 3.5 *Player A passes to B and cuts for the corner; D replaces A; B passes to E and cuts down the side of the lane.*

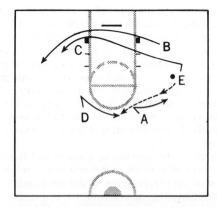

Fig. 3.6 *Player E passes back to A as B clears the area; A passes to D as E cuts under the basket; D can pass to B, E, or C as she makes a move.*

passes and traveling errors may be made. Man-to-man offense is used against a team that employs man-to-man defense. It is based on cutting, scissoring, and screen tactics. A zone offense is used against a team using some type of zone defense and is based on cutting, screens, and overload principles.

Various offensive alignments (positioning of players) may be used to attack either a man-to-man or zone defense. Regardless of the choice of offensive alignment, a team may choose to use a control style of play or a free lance system.

Control Style

The term *control* does not necessarily imply a slow-down style of play. Instead, it implies that a team advances the ball downcourt without undue haste and sets up their attack at the offensive end. A coach who believes completely in this style of play does not permit her team to fast break even if the opportunity arises. Once the team is positioned in the front court they run a predetermined pattern or play. After the action has started, all players follow the prescribed movements for that particular pattern or play. Individual initiative in moving in a different fashion is not permitted.

Use of this style of play assures proper court balance, rebounding assignments, and clear paths for cutting. One of its greatest advantages is that players know exactly where they should be at all times. It eliminates the possibility of two or more players cutting to the same position at the same time. For this reason it may be extremely useful for inexperienced players. Its greatest disadvantage is that it does not permit anyone but the ball handler and primary pass receiver to take advantage of an opponent's momentary defensive error.

Free Lance Style

The free lance style of play allows players to improvise whenever such action is warranted. If the opportunity arises, a team may fast break downcourt to take advantage of some defensive lapse. Otherwise the team moves into the front court and establishes its offensive alignment. From that position it usually runs a play or pattern that has been predetermined. However, instead of players dogmatically following their prescribed paths, individuals may move "on their own" to exploit a defensive weakness or error.

A team may also use a "pure" free lance system in which no pattern or play is prescribed and players cut as the openings arise. They rely on their game sense to take advantage of their opponents. In order to effectively use the free lance style in this manner, players must practice together for a considerable length of time in order to assure rebounding strength and court balance. Often substitutes have difficulty in fitting into the offense if their practice time with the other players is limited.

FAST BREAK

The purpose of the fast break is to provide the attack with a player advantage. It usually results in a two-on-one or three-on-two situation. The fast break is the quickest means of advancing the ball downcourt and may be started any time the defense acquires the ball in its back court. This may occur following an interception, rebound, violation, missed free throw, or any type of score. It must be started quickly so that the defense can be outnumbered.

This style of play produces many advantages. First, and quite obviously, it produces many scoring opportunities. Many easy layups should result with the opponents at a player disadvantage. If a team uses the fast break extensively, it forces the opponents to begin thinking about defense before they lose possession of the ball. Often after they shoot they begin to fall back to prevent the fast break and fail to rebound properly. Although this may limit the number of fast break opportunities it affords, it almost assures the fast breaking team of acquiring a large number of rebounds. Because the fast break is a running style of play, the opponents may become fatigued in the latter stages of the game and commit an unusual number of ball handling errors. The fast break also allows scoring to be distributed among a number of players, and those who are not high scorers enjoy this. It also allows players to free lance and to use their own initiative—particularly the middle player. She is the ball handler and can help distribute the scoring by various means.

The fast break can be used as the primary style of offense. In other words whenever a team obtains the ball, they think *fast break* and try to initiate it. Only when it is halted does the team consider a controlled style of play. Other teams use the fast break only when a specific situation arises in which they can easily gain the player advantage, whereas other teams prefer not to use the fast break and rely entirely on the controlled style of play.

The fast break does have some disadvantages. Players must be in excellent physical condition in order to use this style of play as the primary offense. If not, they will begin to commit ball handling errors and traveling violations, thereby negating the advantages that it may produce. The fast break is also frustrating to teach and learn during the beginning stages because players commit so many ball handling errors. They run at full speed, and the timing of passes and judgment of speed is far more difficult than under normal conditions. Players and the teacher/coach must be patient until the skills are developed for using the fast break effectively.

The fast break requires only one good ball handler. A team with two or more good ball handlers is particularly capable of using this style of play. The opposing team knows that the best way to prevent a fast break is to stop it before it gets started, so they will take some means to accomplish this. If a team has more than one player who can assume the responsibility of the middle player, they are less likely to stop the break by tightly defending one player.

This is an excellent offense to use when a team has small, quick players and must face much taller opponents. They are able to play them on a more equal basis by racing down the court for uncontested layups.

Development of the Fast Break

The most important factor for the success of the fast break is to start it quickly. If the play starts from an out-of-bounds situation, the ball must be in-bounded immediately. The player closest to the ball obtains it

and passes it in as rapidly as possible. If the fast break starts from a rebound, as is the case most of the time, the outlet pass must be made quickly. When the rebounder secures the ball she wishes to pass immediately toward the nearer sideline. (She rarely passes down the middle because of the imminent danger in this direction.) She may be able to turn and pass while she is still in the air, although this practice is not recommended for anyone except the highly skilled (Fig. 3.7). In order to pass quickly (even after she has returned to the floor) the rebounder must be assured that a player will be cutting to the sideline and in position to receive the outlet pass. In order to accomplish this purpose the fast breaking team must assign someone to be in that position. The two guards are generally designated to receive the outlet passes. This may be accomplished in two ways: Either player may be assigned to be in a certain spot or each player is assigned a designated side of the court. Depending upon the system selected, the rebounder either passes to a spot and to the guard who is there or looks down one side of the court for a specific player. In either case, the near side guard must free herself be-

a   b

Fig. 3.7 *Rebounding to Start a Fast Break. The player has gained good rebound positioning* (a). *She rebounds, turns in the air, and makes the outlet pass to a cutting teammate before landing from her jump* (b).

cause the defenders will attempt to prevent this initial pass. Either system may be used, or they may be used interchangeably.

When a team is using a zone defense it is usually easier for the guards to get into position quickly because they are assigned the outside positions in the zone defense. When playing man-to-man, their opponent may have cut under the basket, which takes them out of position for a subsequent outlet pass. In this case whichever player has replaced the guard in an outside position cuts for the outlet pass if the other guard is not in position to do so. If the rebounder is closely guarded, she may have to dribble toward the sideline before she can pass. She must hurry however, because any delay reduces the success of the fast break.

Once the rebound is secured and the outlet pass is made, players endeavor to fill the three lanes as fast as possible. One of the two guards moves to the middle position while the other guard and one forward (or pivot) fill the wing (outside) positions so that three players move down the court in line with one another. The ball should be passed or dribbled into the middle position as quickly as possible. The next player follows the front line downcourt by about 10 ft. She is the trailer to whom the middle player may pass if the opponents succeed in getting back three players. The fifth player, usually the rebounder (or in-bounder), follows the others downcourt in a safety position in case the ball is intercepted and the opponents start a fast break. Fig. 3.8 shows the relative positions of the fast breaking team as the top of the circle is approached.

There are several points of view on which player should be in the middle position. Some believe that the best ball handler is usually a guard who should always move into the center position. If the other guard receives the outlet pass, the best ball handler cuts to the middle to receive the subsequent pass. On the other hand, if the ball is rebounded on her side of the court the best ball handler must break to the sideline for the outlet pass. She then would dribble the ball into the middle position and continue downcourt. This method allows a team to always have the same player in the middle so that she can gain experience in analyzing the defense and deceiving them.

Others prefer to allow either guard to act as the middle player. One player receives the outlet pass and passes to the other guard who has cut to the middle position. Another method allows the weak side forward to dart to the middle position and she is flanked by both guards as they progress downcourt. This method is not used as frequently as the others because it may reduce rebounding strength, and the forward often is not an exceptionally good ball handler.

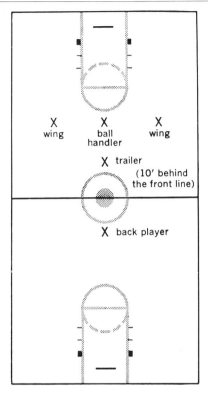

Fig. 3.8 *Position of Players as They Approach the Top of the Circle on a Fast Break.*

The desirability of utilizing one method in preference to another is a philosophical decision that must be made by the teacher/coach. If a team possesses one outstanding dribbler and ball handler, it may be desirable to have her in the middle all of the time. If it is difficult to determine who is the better ball handler, then a team might choose to use either one, depending upon the situation at the time.

During a fast break it is important that the ball be dribbled down the middle of the court. If the ball is advanced by one of the wings near the sideline, the opponents find it easier to defend since a pass can be made in one direction only; if the ball is brought down the middle, however, the pass can be made to either side—which complicates the task for the defense. There are some coaches who advocate passing while the ball is advanced. This action seems somewhat questionable since players are moving at top speed and the more players handling the ball, the greater chance there is for a ball handling error.

Fig. 3.9 shows the movement of players as they start downcourt to fill the closest lanes. This allows

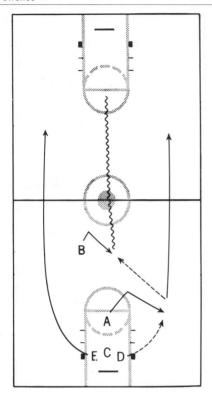

Fig. 3.9 *Filling the Lanes on the Fast Break. Player A cuts for the outlet pass and passes to B as she cuts to the middle. Player E hurries downcourt to fill the third lane. Player C becomes the trailer as rebounder D becomes the back player.*

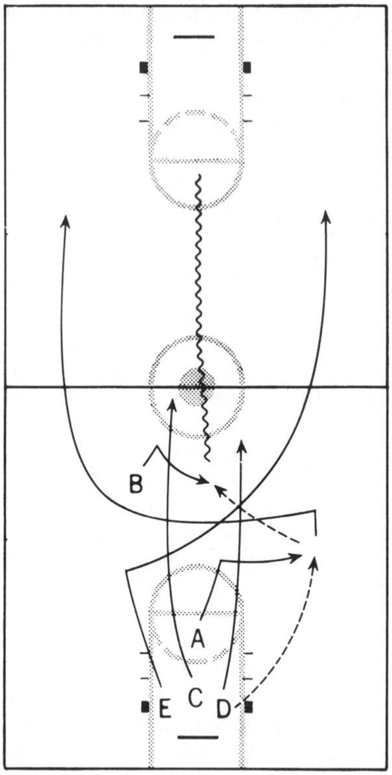

Fig. 3.10 *Crisscrossing to Fill the Lanes. Player D rebounds and passes to A who cuts for the outlet pass. A passes to B and A crosses to the left side of the court. Player E starts up the left side and then crosses to the right. Players C and D follow in the usual manner.*

the players to fill the lanes in the quickest way possible. Another method used is that of crisscrossing the wings as shown in Fig. 3.10. This method takes slightly longer than the other and forces the players to run further but may be used for variety.

As the middle player approaches the top of the circle, both wings should be even or slightly ahead of her. If they are not, the middle player must give the appearance of continuing toward the basket but must maneuver laterally to allow them time to catch up. As the dribbler reaches the top of the circle she should have complete control over the ball and her body, for it is here that her action determines the success or failure of the fast break. By dribbling slightly toward one direction, faking well before passing, or passing off the dribble (bounce passing without catching the ball after dribbling), she must maneuver the defenders so that they cannot interfere with the success of the

fast break. It is the middle player's responsibility to accurately analyze how the defense intends to cope with the situation and to make the proper move to assure that a layup is scored. Her pass to a wing player must be so timed that the player is ready to go up for her layup without benefit of a bounce.

In the fast break situation one defender usually moves out to inhibit the actions of the middle player as she approaches the free throw line. At this time the middle player uses some means of deception and bounce passes to one of her wings for the layup (Fig. 3.11). Following the pass the middle player stays near the free throw line. If a wing player is unable to shoot, she must pass back to the middle player in this position. An attempt to pass to the other wing will result in an interception as the defense recovers. As the middle player receives the pass, she should shoot if she is free. Chances are that if a third pass is necessary

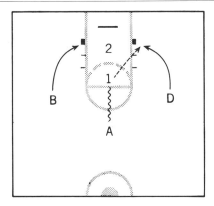

Fig. 3.11 *Fast Break, Three-on-Two. As player A approaches the free throw line, No. 1 moves to defend against her. Directly from her dribble, player A passes (with her right hand) to player D for the layup. Had she passed to player B, the pass should have been made from the left hand. After the pass, player A stays at the free throw line.*

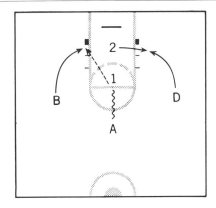

Fig. 3.12 *Fast Break, Three-on-Two. Player A stops at the free throw line and fakes a pass to D, which draws No. 2 toward D. Player A passes to B for the layup.*

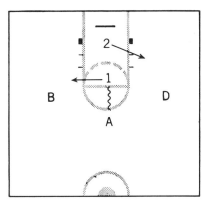

Fig. 3.13 *Fast Break, Three-on-Two. Player A stops at the free throw line and fakes a pass to D, which draws No. 2 toward D. No. 1 anticipates a pass to B and floats toward her. Witnessing the action of the defenders, player A shoots a jump shot.*

the other defenders will have recovered in time to intercept or prevent the layup. If the pass back to the middle player is necessary, the fast break has not been executed perfectly—either the middle player used poor judgment or the wing mishandled the pass.

The middle player must alter her actions so that the defense cannot anticipate accurately what the offense intends to do. More often than not she should pass to the forward on the wing rather than the guard, since the forward has a height advantage which may be useful. However, continual passes to the forward alert the defense and they should be prepared to deal with them.

Passes to the right should be made with the right hand and those to the left with the left hand so that the ball does not have to move in front of the passer's body where it can be deflected. A bounce pass is effective, and if possible the player should learn to execute the pass directly from her dribble. Beginners probably should catch the ball, fake, and pass; but, more experienced players should be able to pass from the bounce with equal success from both hands.

There are other options with which the middle player should become familiar. If the defender who moves out to guard her at the free throw line is slow, the middle player may fake and drive around her for the layup. If the second defender interferes with her drive, the middle player passes off to either wing for the layup. The middle player may also stop at the free throw line and fake to one wing to determine what the defense will do. If one opponent moves to

guard her and the other one edges toward one of the wing players, a bounce pass to the opposite wing should be successful (Fig. 3.12). If the front defender sags after the dribbler catches the ball to prevent a pass to a wing, the dribbler should shoot a jump shot from the free throw line (Fig. 3.13).

If the offense has been delayed slightly in advancing downcourt, there may be three defenders ready to combat the fast break. This should not deter the offense from attempting to maneuver against them. Playing three-against-three provides more openings than waiting until the remaining players for both teams arrive. A team that is fast breaking must learn to recognize when they no longer have a fast break situation, however. As soon as the defense has more players downcourt than does the offense, the fast break has not developed and the middle player should stop the fast break by dribbling to any free space. She waits for the rest of her teammates to move downcourt and sets up the secondary offense.

Should the three-on-three situation develop, players use simple screens to effect a scoring situation. The middle player may fake and drive around her own player if she is slow. If not, she can dribble toward one of her wings, set a lateral screen on the defender and hand off to her teammate who can drive for the layup (Fig. 3.14). If the opponents are zoning, the middle player may set an inside screen for her teammate to shoot. The middle player can also pass to one wing and screen opposite—i.e., she screens for the wing who did not receive the pass, allowing her to cut, receive the subsequent pass, and shoot her layup (Fig. 3.15). If the opponents are zoning, the middle player can pass to one wing, cut, and screen either the front or back guard for the other wing to cut around for a pass and shot. The first method suggested is probably more effective against a zone (Fig. 3.16).

If a three-on-three situation arises with a trailer approaching, the trailer should alert her teammates of her approach by calling ''With you'' or ''Coming.'' The wing players should remain wide while the dribbler drives toward one side. When the trailer is opposite the dribbler, an underhand pass with the closest hand is made. If the trailer needs more time to get' into position, the dribbler catches her dribble and pivots to give an underhand pass to the trailer. If the opponents are playing man-to-man against this situation, the trailer should be free for her layup. The wings should clear the under-basket area so that a defender cannot sag off to guard the trailer. If the defense is playing a zone, the trailer penetrates the zone as far as possible and passes to the free player (Fig. 3.17).

A three-on-two situation may develop near the division line in which one of the opponents attempts to delay the middle player. This leaves the defense extremely vulnerable, but a team may attempt this tactic against an inexperienced fast breaking team. The offense should take immediate advantage of the opponents' vulnerable position. The middle player should pass to one of her wings without delay so that they may proceed downcourt in a two-on-one situation. The two players should remain well spread, and the ball handler should drive for a layup. If she draws the lone defender she should pass to her teammate for the layup. The middle player may follow downcourt in a trailer position but should remain well to the rear of her teammates so that her opponent cannot guard her and one of her teammates.

Shooting the Layup

As a wing player receives a pass from the middle player, she should be moving at near top speed. Inexperienced players often miss the layup. They move faster than they normally do in practice and their momentum causes them to use too much force, allowing the ball to go beyond the basket. Sometimes they slow their speed or stop so that the above does not

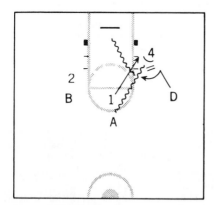

Fig. 3.14 *Fast Break, Three-on-Three Situation. Since the fast break has been nullified, player A dribbles over and screens for D, who cuts around the screen, receives a hand-off, and drives for goal.*

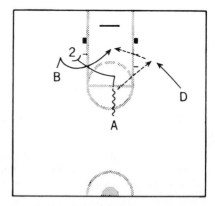

Fig. 3.15 *Fast Break, Three-on-Three. With the defense playing man-to-man, player A passes to D and cuts over to set a screen for B. Player B fakes and cuts around the screen for a pass from D.*

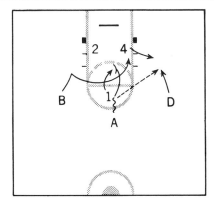

Fig. 3.16 *Fast Break, Three-on-Three, Triangle Zone. Player A passes to D, which draws No. 4. Player A then starts to cut down the lane but screens No. 1 so that B can cut around the screen for a pass from D. Player A could also continue down the lane and screen No. 2 for a more direct cut by B.*

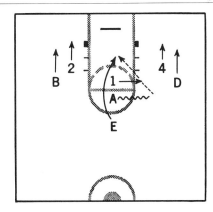

Fig. 3.17 *Fast Break with a Trailer. The three front players are guarded. The trailer signals she is coming. The middle player dribbles to the side and gives the trailer a pass when she is in position for a layup.*

happen, but this allows an opponent time to catch up. This usually results in a foul since the offense player stopped unexpectedly while the defender was still moving at full speed. Often the foul is made before the shot is attempted, which means the offense is awarded one free throw only. Had the player continued her forward movement rather than stopping she had a chance for two points. To prevent either of these situations from arising in a game, players should practice layups at full speed in fast breaking drills.

Need for a Rebounder

Any team that has great success with a fast break must have an outstanding rebounder. As has been stated previously the most important element for the development of a fast break is the quick outlet pass. For utmost speed in starting the fast break a pass receiver must be in position for the outlet pass as the rebounder catches the ball. This means that she cannot wait to see if her team obtains the rebound. She must cut considerably before that. In order to do this a team must have a player on whom they can rely to obtain almost every rebound, or they must be willing to gamble. If either of these conditions exist, the outlet receivers generally block out their opponent only for an instant and then cut for the pass. If a team does not have an exceptional rebounder or is not willing to take many chances on rebounds, the outlet receivers should continue to block out and delay their cut until they see that a teammate has acquired the rebound.

With an outstanding rebounder it may be possible for a player to sneak downcourt on occasion following

a shot. She does not block out her opponent at all and cuts downcourt as soon as a shot is taken. She may be open for a long pass and an easy layup. The long pass is extremely difficult for most girls to throw with accuracy, and teachers may wish to prohibit its use; but there is no need to do this if a player has success with it. Another problem with the long pass is that a player telegraphs her intention as she draws her arm back for the overhand throw. She requires a great deal of space so that an opponent cannot approach from behind and tap the ball from her hand or block the pass.

MAN-TO-MAN OFFENSE

Against a man-to-man defense, teams rely on cutting maneuvers, screens, of various kinds, and scissor maneuvers to free a player for a high percentage shot. Whenever a man-to-man defense is encountered, a team should quickly analyze whether the opponents play tight or loose, whether they sag and/or float, under what conditions (if any) they switch, which players possess defensive weaknesses, and which defenders are the primary rebounders. Whatever defensive weaknesses are discovered should be exploited.

OFFENSIVE ALIGNMENTS

When playing a control or free lance style of play it is possible to establish the offense with different alignments. The selected alignment is based on player

DRILLS FOR FAST BREAK

All drills should be practiced to the left and right sides.

1. Columns of four players 6 ft. in front of each basket, with another player tossing the ball against the backboard. The first person in each column moves forward observing correct rebounding technique and jumps for the rebound, lands on the floor, and immediately pivots toward the near sideline ready to pass. She should pivot toward the corner of the court and away from the middle or the under-basket area. She gives the ball back to the tosser, who repeats the drill with each succeeding player. As experienced players rebound, they can pivot in the air and land facing the near sideline.

2. Same as drill 1 above, only another player is positioned about 6 ft. in from the sideline and about 20 ft. from the basket. The same drill is repeated, only the rebounder passes to the outlet receiver.

3. Same as drill 2 above, only an opponent stands behind the rebounder and tries to harass the outlet pass. The rebounder may have to take a bounce in order to make an accurate pass.

4. One opponent shoots from the free throw line and a rebounder loosely guards her and two guards on the same team. The opponent shoots; the rebounder obtains the rebound, pivots, and passes to the guard who has cut to the near sideline. The other guard cuts to the middle and toward the division line for the subsequent pass. Emphasis should be on the guard receiving the outlet pass moving toward the front court as she receives the pass; it should also be on the second guard timing her cut so that she arrives near the division line at the time the pass does. There should be no waiting either to make the pass or to receive the pass.

5. Same as drill 4 above, but add another rebounder. The player who does not rebound and the guard receiving the outlet pass must move into the wing positions as the middle player dribbles downcourt to the free throw line. Emphasis should be placed on the timing of the cuts identified previously (drill 4 above) and the quick start to move up on a line with the middle player as fast as possible, but at least by the time the top of the circle is reached.

6. Two wings and a middle player starting at the division line in their own position. The middle player dribbles downcourt flanked by the wings and bounce passes to one of the wings from the free throw line. Repeat so the middle player gains experience in passing with either hand.

7. Same as drill 6 above, only place one defensive player at the free throw line to challenge the dribbler as she approaches.

8. Same as drill 6 above, with two defensive players in a front and back position at the defensive end. The middle player uses a variety of methods to obtain the layup, such as
   a. pass to the wing on her left
   b. pass to the wing on her right
   c. against a slow front player, change the pace of the dribble and drive by her
   d. stop at the free throw line
      1) pass to a wing if the front player moves to guard the middle player
      2) shoot if the front player sags to prevent a pass to a wing

For all of these drills involving defense players, the instructor should inform the defenders of the actions they should follow. At first they should be instructed to stay in the middle of the lane with the front player guarding the dribbler. Later the back player can be instructed to edge toward one wing or the other to see if the middle player can recognize the opening to the other side. The front player may also be instructed to sag as the dribbler approaches. Finally the defenders can move as they wish. In this way the middle player can recognize where the opening exists under a designated condition. Later when the defenders move as they wish she must make the correct decision to any number of variables.

9. Three defenders at the defensive end playing man-to-man against the three attackers as they approach the top of the circle. On consecutive plays the middle player practices the dribble screen to each side and later the screen opposite to each side.

10. Same as drill 9 above, only the defense plays zone and on consecutive plays the middle player dribble screens (inside) to each side and then screens either the front or back zone player.

11. Three defenders at the defensive end playing man-to-man. Three attack players start at the division line with a trailer 10 ft. behind. The middle player dribbles down the court flanked by the wings and followed by the trailer who indicates she is "coming." The middle player times her pass to the trailer so that she can go in for a layup. Later, start the trailer slightly further back and force the dribbler to pivot before the trailer is in position for the pass.

12. Same as drill 11 above, only the defenders play zone.

13. Two offensive players against one defensive player. One of the attack players has the ball at the division line and dribbles downcourt using proper techniques for scoring.

14. Five players in their back court in normal positions on defense. Another player tosses the ball against the backboard and the players react immediately for the start of the fast break. Emphasis should be on the wings hustling to position, the trailer about 10 ft. behind and the rebounder about 15 ft. behind the trailer.

15. Two teams at one end of the court. A player on the attacking team shoots and the opposing team immediately starts to fast break. The team that attempted the shot delays for a count of two and tries to recover. Again, emphasis is on the positioning of the attacking team. The rebounder should be trailing everyone down the court.

personnel and their qualifications for various positions. For example, a team with a tall, rather immobile player should choose an alignment that would permit her to maneuver under the basket. A team without tall players would benefit from playing from a posture other than a pivot.

The alignments are named by designating the number of players furthest from the basket (closer to the division line) first followed by those closer to the basket. For example, a three-two alignment would have three players on the outside and two players closer to the basket.

One-Three-One

The alignment shown in Fig. 3.18 is seldom seen but offers good possibilities for a double post to work in tandem (one high and the other low). An offense can be designed in which the pivots interchange; or, if one pivot is less agile, she may remain primarily in the low post while the other is assigned the high or medium post position. This is a good formation for a team with three small players and two tall players. The best ball handler of the three small players should be in the middle with the other two at the wing positions.

109

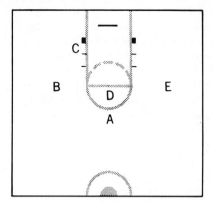

Fig. 3.18 One-Three-One Offensive Alignment.

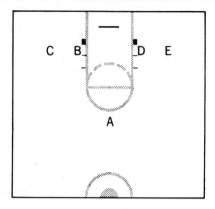

Fig. 3.20 One-Four Offensive Alignment (End Line).

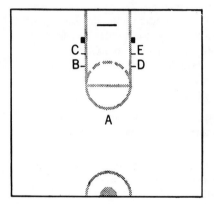

Fig. 3.19 One-Four Offensive Alignment (Stack).

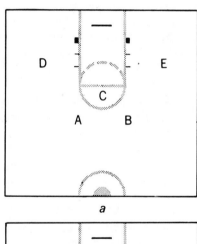

a

One-Four

This configuration popularized by Cousy is also called the stack offense. It is an excellent formation for a team with one good ball handler and four tall players. The position of the players is shown in Fig. 3.19. Rarely seen is another one-four alignment as shown in Fig. 3.20.

Two-Three

This formation is probably the most popular one in use today. It utilizes two players on the outside with three close to the basket and generally involves a post player at the high, medium, or low post position. This alignment provides good rebound strength and is effective for a team with two short players and three tall players. Fig. 3.21 shows possible placement of players for this formation.

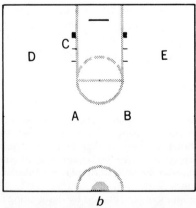

b

Fig. 3.21 Two-Three Offensive Alignment. *Possible placement of players: C is in the high post position* (a); *C is in the low post position and may move up to the medium post position* (b).

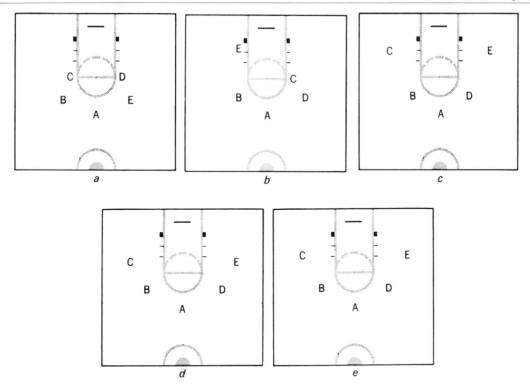

Fig. 3.22 *Three-Two Offensive Alignment. Possible placement of players: C and D are playing a double pivot in parallel position (a); C and E are playing a double pivot in a tandem position (b). All align without a pivot player to allow drives and cuts through the lane and to permit a flash pivot (any player moving into pivot position) (c–e).*

Three-Two

This alignment provides numerous possibilities for player positioning. It can be initiated from a double post with the players in a parallel (Fig. 3.22a) or a tandem position (Fig. 3.22b.) It may also be initiated without post players and all players on the outside (Fig. 3.22c–e). A team with three smaller players and two tall players may choose an alignment utilizing the double post. A team with all short players may select any of the formations where all the players are on the perimeter.

Four-One

Fig. 3.23 shows the basic formation. This alignment is often used against a zone defense because it involves overload principles. It is not used as often against man-

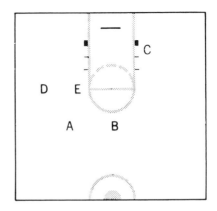

Fig. 3.23 *Four-One Alignment (Overload).*

to-man defense. It is not recommended as a primary offensive alignment because the possibilities for options are limited.

Basic Principles to Follow Against a Man-to-Man Defense

1. The basic technique to free a player is by means of a screen. The type or types of screens selected depend upon the offensive system devised, but any or all of them are effective against this type of defense. As the reader knows, the screen may be set toward or away from the ball, and the screen need not be set necessarily where a defender is positioned. A player should roll after she sets a screen. One of the offensive players involved in the screen should be free if the timing of the moves and cuts is perfected.

2. Lateral or rear screens may be set anywhere on the court for a teammate to use. If a player has a favorite place on the court from which to shoot, a teammate may set a screen at that site to free the player for a shot from that position. A screen of this nature may also be set to allow a cutter to cut off it or to allow a dribbler to drive around the screen. The purpose of both tactics is to free the attack player momentarily from her defender.

3. Prior to using a screen the player for whom the screen is set must always fake in the opposite direction. She must not alert her opponent to the setting of the screen.

4. The player being guarded by the weakest defensive opponent should be encouraged and given opportunities to work one-on-one against her. This is done by clearing one side of the court to provide the offensive player with space in which to maneuver against her opponent.

5. If the defenders use sagging and floating techniques, the offensive players being guarded by this method should maneuver to become free. By cutting away from the ball, they force their opponent to move away from the ball also, thus making their sagging and floating techniques less effective. Teammates can also set screens away from the ball to allow the offensive players being guarded in this manner to use them to free themselves for a pass.

6. There are two effective ways of dealing with a team that uses pressing measures. A team may use lateral screens near the ball or rear or lateral screens away from the ball to free the offensive players. When guarding closely, defenders are less able to avoid lateral screens. The attack players should also be skilled in backdoor maneuvers and use them effectively. A few successful layups scored by this means tend to make the defense a little more "honest" (guard more loosely).

7. If the defense overplays against lateral screens to make the screen less effective, the attack should cut away from the screen on numerous occasions.

This also tends to force the defense to guard in a more normal manner.

8. The offense should maneuver to acquire a disparity in heights and/or abilities against a team that utilizes a switching man-to-man defense. The offense should use numerous guard-forward, guard-pivot, and pivot-forward screens. This action should produce a height advantage for one of the attack players, and this tactic should be exploited.

9. The offensive team should employ lob passes over the defender's head against a team that fronts the pivot player in the medium or high pivot position. Whenever the weak side forward views the pivot being played in this manner, she should cut toward the strong side so that her opponent cannot float and intercept the pass to the pivot or be in a position to challenge the pivot once she receives the pass.

SINGLE PIVOT OFFENSE

A team that chooses to use a single post offense has one player who operates at an optimum level within 15 ft. of the basket. She generally is not sufficiently mobile to maneuver as effectively outside of the lane area. She is often the tallest player on the team who shoots effectively in this area. She should be the strongest rebounder on the team because, by virtue of her position in relation to the basket, she is in the best position to rebound and is involved in rebounding on every play.

When she plays in a high post position her main function is to feed cutters as they cut off her or as they utilize a screen from another player to free themselves for a pass. When playing in the medium post position, the pivot is in an excellent position to shoot or to pass to cutters. When cutting across the lane in this position she must have the ability to fake and front her opponent so that she is free in this high percentage shooting range. When in the low post area she must maneuver constantly to get free to receive a pass. She is too close to the basket in this position to allow players to cut off her so when she gets the ball she must shoot or return a pass back out if she is double-teamed and unable to obtain a good shot.

Regardless of the position she is playing she must use various tactics to free herself from her opponent. The pivot is always guarded closely unless her opponent has been forced into a screen. This means that she must acquire a number of different moves to get free and be able to move or drive either to her left or right. She must be able to protect the ball well in this congested area. She must rarely take more than one bounce and never more than two unless she is retreating away from the basket to establish another scoring thrust.

When a team is playing a single post offense team, members must work to pass the ball in to the pivot player. Because of her position in relation to the basket, she is always within a good shooting distance. In addition to the scoring possibilities this presents, it also forces the defense to make some adjustments. When a pivot player is successful in shooting, defense players guarding other opponents sag or float away from their opponent to assist their teammate in limiting the effectiveness of the pivot player. When this happens, other offense players are freed by the very action of the defense players. If a pivot receives the ball and defenders sag on her, she should immediately pass the ball to one of her free teammates. The faster the pivot is able to find a free teammate, the greater exploitation can be made of the defender's action. As the opponents learn that their sagging tactics permit outside shots, they should begin to delay their moves against the pivot; this in turn should open the passing or cutting lanes to the pivot once more. Providing a team has accurate outside shooting and an effective pivot player, extensive pressure is placed on the defensive team to limit the scoring of their opponents. Because of the effectiveness of this style of offense, it is one of the most widely used today.

Single Post in a High Pivot Position (two-three alignment)

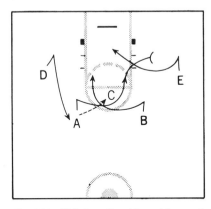

Fig. 3.24 *High Post (Two-Three Alignment). A passes to C and cuts off C. B cuts off A. D moves out for defensive balance as A continues her cut to screen E. C may pass to B or E. Player A may roll for a possible pass. If B does not receive a pass, she clears; likewise E and A. C may shoot or pass back to D. If B shoots, B, C, and E rebound. Player A goes to the medium rebound position and D to the deep position. If A shoots, A, E, and C rebound. B goes to the middle rebound position and D goes to the deep position.*

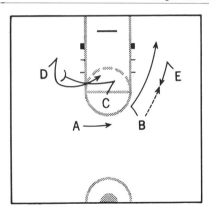

Fig. 3.25 *B passes to E and cuts to the corner. C fakes and screens for D, who fakes toward the baseline before cutting around the screen. E may pass to D, B, or back to A who slides over.*

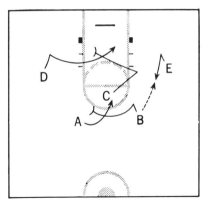

Fig. 3.26 *B passes to E. C fakes toward E and sets a screen in the lane. As C fakes toward E, D fakes toward the baseline and cuts into the lane around the screen. (The timing of the cut by D is extremely important so that C does not commit a lane violation.) B delays her fake toward the corner and moves over to screen A, who fakes and cuts around the screen as an alternate pass receiver.*

113

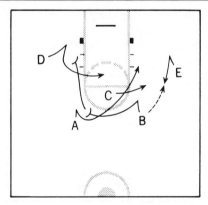

Fig. 3.27 *B passes to E, fakes toward the corner, and screens for A. A fakes and cuts around the screen. B continues and sets a screen outside the lane. D fakes toward the end line and cuts around the screen. E passes to A or D. After A cuts by, C cuts to the side of the lane.*

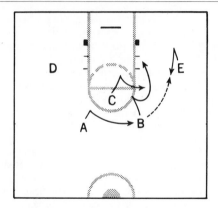

Fig. 3.29 *B passes to E. C cuts out opposite the free throw line to set a rear screen. B fakes inside and cuts around the screen for a pass from E.*

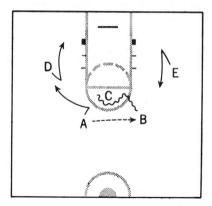

Fig. 3.28 *This option provides B with an opportunity to dribble using C as a screen to free herself for a shot from the 18-ft. range. A clears to the opposite side. B may also pass to E and run her defender in to C and receive a return pass for a shot.*

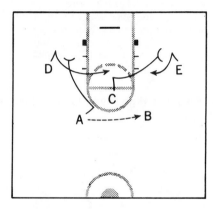

Fig. 3.30 *A passes to B. C fakes and cuts outside the lane to set a screen at the same time. E fakes toward the baseline and cuts around the screen. A delays, fakes, and cuts and screens for D who fakes toward the baseline and cuts around the screen. B passes to E or to D.*

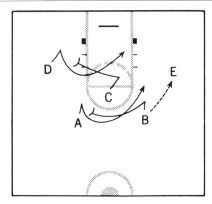

Fig. 3.31 *B passes to E, fakes toward the corner, and screens for A who fakes before cutting off the screen. C fakes toward the ball and screens outside the lane. D fakes before cutting around the screen. E passes to A or to D.*

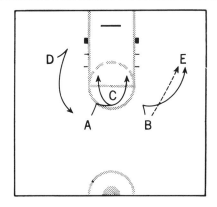

Fig. 3.33 *B basses to E, fakes toward the lane, and cuts behind E. A cuts either side of C. E passes to A or B.*

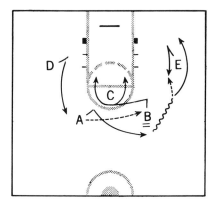

Fig. 3.32 *A passes to B, fakes, and cuts behind B for a handoff. A dribbles toward the corner and passes off to E and continues behind E. Meanwhile B cuts off either side of C. E passes to A, B, or C.*

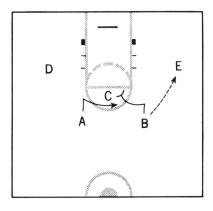

Fig. 3.34 *B passes to E, fakes toward the corner, and cuts to a position beside C to form a double screen. A fakes and cuts behind it to receive a pass from E. A has all the options for the double screen.*

Fig. 3.35 *B passes to C. B and E cut near the lane to set a double screen for D. D cuts behind the screen. A cuts when D clears the left side. C passes to D or A.*

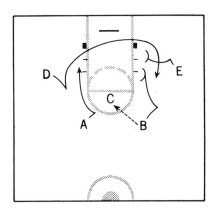

Single Post in a Low Pivot Position (two-three alignment)

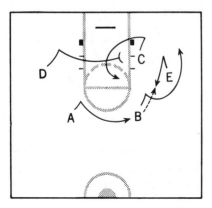

Fig. 3.36 *B passes to E, fakes, and cuts behind E. At the same time D fakes and cuts in to the lane to set a screen. C fakes and cuts behind the screen. E passes to C, B, or D on her roll. The timing of cuts is essential to avoid a lane violation.*

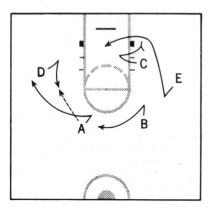

Fig. 3.37 *A passes to D, fakes, and cuts behind her. C fakes in to the lane and sets a screen for E who cuts around it. D may pass to A, E, or C on her roll.*

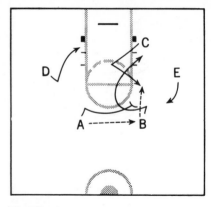

Fig. 3.38 *A passes to B and sets a screen for B. C fakes in to the lane and then cuts for a pass from B. B cuts around the screen to receive a pass from C, or C may pass to A on her roll or out to E.*

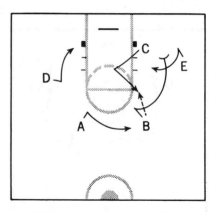

Fig. 3.39 *C fakes and cuts to receive a pass from B. B fakes and cuts down to set a screen for E, who cuts for the baseline and then behind the screen. C may pass to E, B on her roll, or D if she is free.*

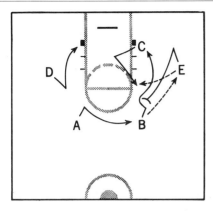

Fig. 3.40 *B passes to E who passes to C. C looks for a reverse cut by D as E screens for B. B fakes and cuts off the screen. C may pass to B or E on her roll.*

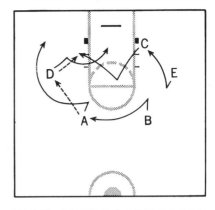

Fig. 3.42 *A passes to D as C fakes and cuts to receive a pass from D. A continues toward the corner as D fakes and cuts around C. C passes to A or D.*

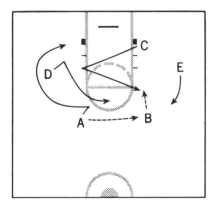

Fig. 3.41 *A fakes a pass to D and C and passes to B. C cuts to receive a pass from B. D fakes and cuts and receives a pass from C. After D clears the side, A tries a reverse cut. D can pass to A or drive, using C as a screen.*

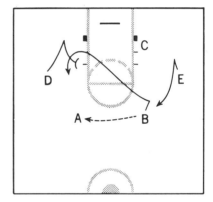

Fig. 3.43 *B passes to A, fakes, and cuts around the screen set by D. A passes to B, D, E, or C as she maneuvers to become free.*

Fig. 3.44 *A passes to B as C and E maneuver to set a double screen for D. B passes to D or A.*

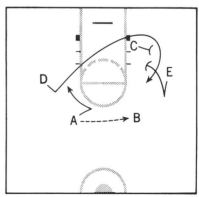

DOUBLE PIVOT OFFENSE

This type of offense is excellent for use with two tall players who can maneuver and shoot within the lane area and three other players who are mobile and able to interchange positions. The post players may play in a tandem position (one high and one low) from a one-three-one or a three-two posture. One of these is generally selected when the post players possess different abilities. The more agile post is assigned the high post position while the other one plays in a low post position. From either of these postures, however, it is possible to design tactics in which the players can exchange positions, if their abilities suggest such action. Nevertheless, if both post players are comparable in ability the parallel high post from a three-two alignment is generally selected.

Use of the double pivot offense places much stress on the defense because two players are always close to a high percentage shooting area. This tends to make the opponents sag and float and to provide opportunities for medium range shots for the other three attack players. It is also a good posture from which to operate when the opponents are playing a zone defense.

Double Post in Tandem Position (one-three-one alignment)

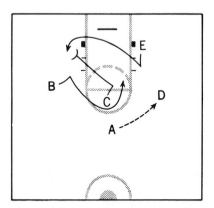

Fig. 3.45 *A passes to D. B fakes and cuts around C. C moves outside the lane to screen for E as she clears the right side and cuts behind the screen. D passes to B or E.*

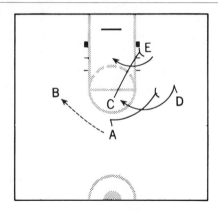

Fig. 3.46 *A passes to B, fakes, and sets a screen for D. C moves down the lane and sets a screen for E. B may pass to D or E.*

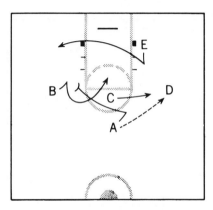

Fig. 3.47 *A passes to D, fakes, and sets a screen for B as C moves outside the circle. E clears to the other side. B cuts around the screen for a pass from D.*

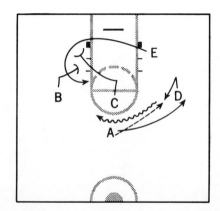

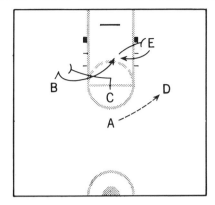

Fig. 3.49 *A passes to D. C fakes and screens for B. B cuts around the screen. If B does not receive a pass, she continues on and screens for E. D passes to E or back to A.*

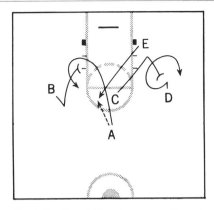

Fig. 3.51 *E and C exchange positions. A passes to E and cuts around E. D cuts, and E may pass to A or D. If neither is open, B and C provide screens behind which A and D may cut. E passes to either one.*

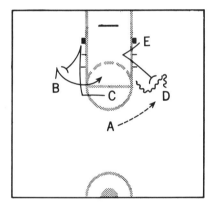

Fig. 3.50 *A passes to D as E fakes and screens for D. C clears outside and down the lane. D drives around the screen. C moves up to screen B, who fakes and cuts around the screen. D can pass to B.*

Double Post in Tandem Position (three-two alignment)

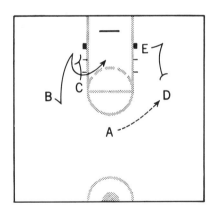

Fig. 3.52 *A passes to D. E screens for D, who may drive. C slides down the lane and sets a screen for B. D may pass to B or back out to A.*

◀**Fig. 3.48** *A passes to D and cuts behind D. Meanwhile B and C form a double screen. E cuts behind it as D dribbles to the top of the circle. D passes to E or A.*

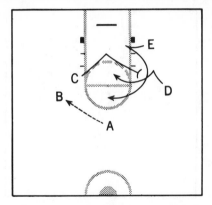

Fig. 3.53 *A passes to B as C clears and sets a screen. B may work one-on-one or pass to D as she cuts off the screen or to E who follows D's cut.*

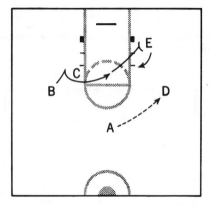

Fig. 3.54 *A passes to D as B uses C's screen. D passes to B if she is open. If not, B continues through the lane and screens for E. D passes to E or back to A.*

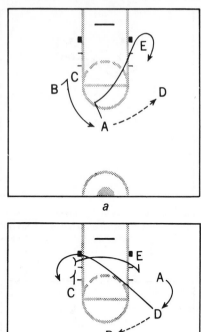

a

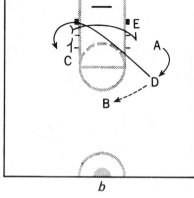

b

Fig. 3.55 *A passes to D, fakes, and cuts around E as B moves to the top of the circle (a). If A is not free, D passes to B and cuts around the double screen set by C and E (b). B passes to D as A moves back.*

Fig. 3.56 *A passes to D and cuts around E for a pass. C fakes into the lane and cuts to the free throw line. B cuts around C. D passes to either A or B.*

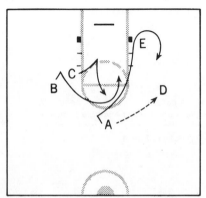

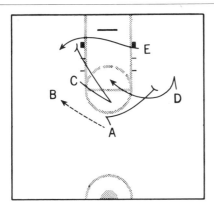

Fig. 3.57 *A passes to B as C screens for E. A screens for D. B passes to E or D.*

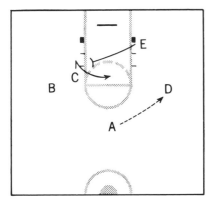

Fig. 3.58 *A passes to D as E cuts across the lane to screen for C. C fakes and cuts to receive a pass.*

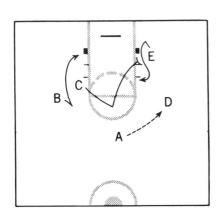

Double Post in High Parallel Position (three-two alignment)

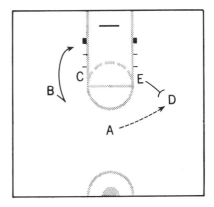

Fig. 3.60 *A passes to D as E screens. D is allowed to work one-on-one.*

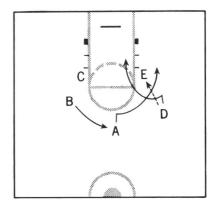

Fig. 3.61 *D passes to E and cuts around E, followed by A. E uses any of the options available.*

Fig. 3.59 *A fakes to C and passes to D. C cuts across the lane and screens for E. D passes to E or to B if she is open on a reverse cut.*

121

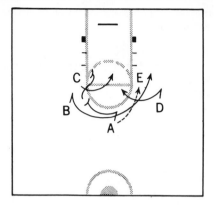

Fig. 3.62 *A passes to E and screens for B. D cuts off E, followed by B who was freed by A's screen. After B's cut, A screens for C. E passes to D, B, or C.*

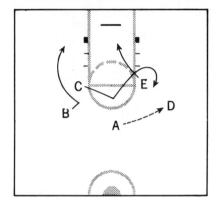

Fig. 3.64 *A passes to D as C fakes to the free throw line and cuts around E. D passes to C or E on her roll. D may also pass to B on a reverse cut.*

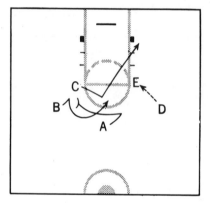

Fig. 3.63 *D passes to E as A screens for B. At the same time, C fakes to the free throw line. B cuts around the screen as C cuts across the lane—E to C or B.*

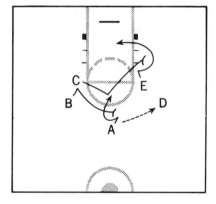

Fig. 3.65 *A passes to D as C cuts to the free throw line. B moves to screen for A as C screens for E. D passes to A or E.*

Fig. 3.66 *A passes to D. E fakes and screens for C. D to C or E on her roll or to B.*

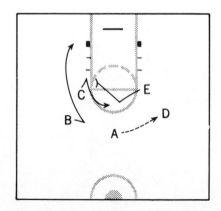

OFFENSE WITHOUT A POST IN A THREE-TWO ALIGNMENT

To assume an alignment of this nature a team should have five players who maneuver well and who are good passers and ball handlers in general. The purpose of playing without a pivot is to keep the lane area open for cuts and screening action. This alignment is often chosen by a team without an exceptionally tall player who can shoot and rebound well within a short distance of the basket. If a team has five players who

are quick and approximately the same height and who have the same general abilities, this offense may be advantageous.

A weave type offense may be developed from this formation. It can be a simple three-player weave out front (at the top of the circle) or a four- or five-player weave involving one or both forwards. Most often a four-player weave involves two forwards and two guards, with a pivot player who moves independently of the weave. A basic three-player weave is shown in Fig. 3.67. A five-player weave is shown in Fig. 3.68.

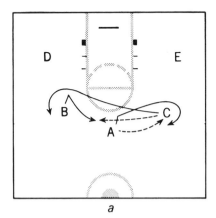
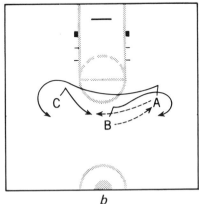

a

b

Fig. 3.67 *Three-Player Weave. A passes to C, fakes, and cuts around C* (a). *B fakes and cuts to receive the pass from C. C cuts around B. B passes to A and A passes to C as the weave continues* (b).

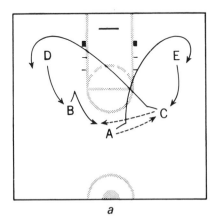
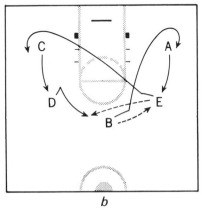

a

b

Fig. 3.68 *Five-Player Weave. A passes to C, then fakes and cuts to the corner; B fakes and cuts to receive the pass from C; C fakes and cuts to the other corner as E replaces C and D replaces B* (a). *The weave continues as B passes to E and B cuts to the corner; E passes to D and E cuts to the corner; A replaces E and C replaces D* (b).

123

A team may also use this alignment to employ screening maneuvers with two, three, or more players involved. The basic two- and three-player maneuvers are described in Chapter 2, and these can be elaborated to include four or five players as one player may screen for two different teammates. In this offense, it is important that players stay wide and that only one player at a time cuts into the primary receiving area. Players must shoot only when in a good position to do so and only when they are unhurried. Short shots may be obtained from this alignment, and players should try to obtain as many from the 15-ft. area as possible. This formation does not provide the most beneficial rebounding positions; therefore, only "good" shots should be attempted. Examples of some of the possibilities from this formation follow in Figs. 3.69–3.76.

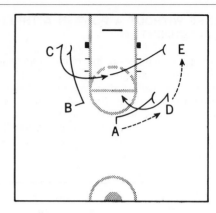

Fig. 3.71 *A passes to D and screens for D. D passes to E as B screens for C. C cuts for a pass. If she does not receive it, she screens for E. Meanwhile D cuts around A's screen for a possible pass.*

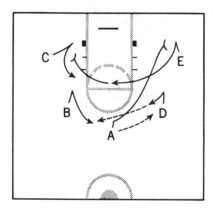

Fig. 3.69 *A passes to D and screens for E. D passes to E or B. If E does not receive the pass, she screens for C to give D another option.*

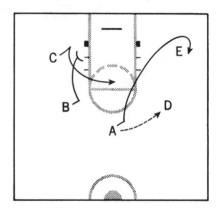

Fig. 3.72 *A passes to D and A cuts around E. B screens for C for another possible pass.*

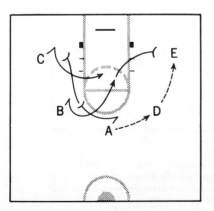

Fig. 3.70 *A passes to D and A screens for B. D passes to E, who passes to B if she is free. If not, B continues and screens for E. After B's cut, A screens for C. E passes to C or back to D.*

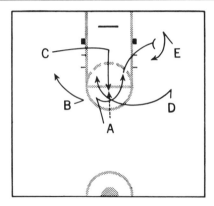

Fig. 3.73 *A passes to C in a high post position. A and D scissor off C for a possible pass. A may continue over to screen for E. C may hand off to A or D, or pass to E or to B who may work one-on-one.*

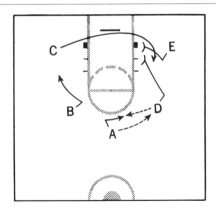

Fig. 3.75 *A passes to D, who returns it to A. D and E set a double screen for C to cut behind. A to C or to B who may work one-on-one.*

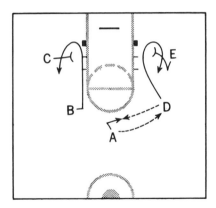

Fig. 3.74 *A passes to D, who returns it to A as C screens for B. A to B if she is free. Meanwhile E screens for D. A may pass to D.*

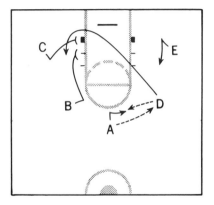

Fig. 3.76 *A passes to D, who returns it to A. B and C establish a double screen for D. A passes to D or E, who may work one-on-one.*

STACK OFFENSE

This offense, popularized by Bob Cousy while at Boston College, has been adopted by numerous college and professional teams, usually as a secondary offense. It has not been as widely used by women's teams but may gain in popularity during the 1970's. It is an excellent offense when a team has two tall players who are not particularly maneuverable and when a team has players who shoot well within 15 ft. of the basket but not as well from greater distances. In order to use this offense, however, a team must have one player who is an excellent dribbler and ball handler. If a team does not possess a player with this talent, the opponents will double-team the player out front, forcing her to commit errors and neutralizing the effectiveness of this formation.

Cousy[1] suggests that this offense has many advantages:

1. it generally forces the opponents to play man-to-man defense, thus taking advantage of individual defensive weaknesses

125

2. it is easy to learn and does not involve extensive running
3. it places players in excellent rebounding position
4. many options evolve according to the defensive positions assumed by the opponents

In order to be an effective offense, timing of moves must be perfected. There are disadvantages to the formation also. If the ball is intercepted out front, a one-on-one break is likely to occur. A team is also susceptible to a fast break when the opponents clear the backboard quickly.

Basic Positions

The position of the five players is shown in Fig. 3.77. Player A is the floor leader and best ball handler on the team. She keys the moves for all other players. For this reason, she must possess much poise and game sense to recognize the defensive positions and initiate a movement to exploit them. Because of her position, player A must also be able to recover quickly on defense.

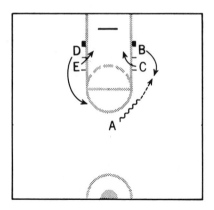

Fig. 3.77 *Basic Position and Maneuver. B cuts out and receives a pass from A. At the same time, D cuts behind E. C pivots into the low pivot position as E cuts toward the basket. B has the option of shooting and passing to C or D. B, C, and E rebound if B shoots. D stays in the intermediate rebound position and A in the deep position. If C or D shoot, C, D, and E rebound and B moves to the intermediate position.*

Basically the offense is geared to operate toward the right side. Therefore, the tall player with the best moves from the medium and low post positions is placed in C position. Her position in Fig. 3.77 may

be adjusted higher if she wishes to be further from the basket. The other players adjust accordingly.

Player E is the other tall player who should be able to rebound well. She should also look for open spaces when her opponent floats away from her to help a teammate.

Player B should be the best shooter on the team. She may be either a forward or guard. She is one who is isolated frequently to maneuver one-on-one or to team up with player C in two-on-two maneuvers.

Player D is the fifth player and is normally either a forward or guard. She is not as good a shooter as player B and is frequently deployed to the top of the circle after the play is initiated.

Basic Options

The following diagrams show options from the basic alignment. The reader is referred to Cousy's[2] work for a more detailed explanation of the stack offense.

ZONE OFFENSE

A team on offense must determine why the opponents have chosen to play a zone defense. The primary reason for its selection is that the offensive team does not have an accurate outside shooter. Other reasons include a player in foul trouble, one or more players with individual defensive weaknesses, or a desire simply to protect a lead or to disrupt the offensive style of attack. If possible, once the reason for the zone's use is identified, the offensive team should exploit the opponent's vulnerable positions.

Basic Principles to Follow Against a Zone Defense

1. The easiest way to defeat the effectiveness of the zone is to beat it downcourt. As soon as possession of the ball is obtained either from an interception or an out-of-bounds play, the ball should be advanced as rapidly as possible downcourt, and a scoring thrust must be attempted before the zone can be established. A long pass to a player in the corner is effective if the defenders are not alert as they recover downcourt.

2. The offensive team must be able to penetrate the zone. This can be accomplished by means of passing to a player in the zone or by having a player dribble into the zone. Once the zone is penetrated, other defense players are drawn toward the ball; this opens a passing lane behind them. By successfully entering the zone, players on the perimeter of the zone may shoot with less pressure and generally from a shorter distance.

3. A team must possess at least one player who can successfully shoot from the 21-ft. range. By

a

b

Fig. 3.78 *Stack Offense. The basic positions: No. 1 is the best ball handler; No. 2 is the best shooter; No. 3 is the best rebounder; No. 5 is a rebounder, and No. 4 should shoot well from medium ranges* (a). *No. 2 has faked and cut behind No. 3, and at the same time No. 4 cuts toward the top of the lane on the other side* (b). *No. 2 is free for her shot* (c–e).

127

c

d

Fig. 3.78 *continued*

e

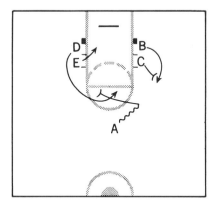

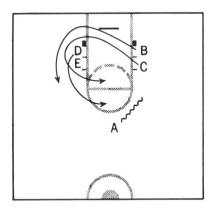

Fig. 3.79 *The play initiates similar to the basic pattern. However, C moves out so that B can use the screen, and A cuts back so that D can break around the screen. In addition to driving around the screen, B has the same options as in Fig. 3.77. Rebounding assignments are also identical.*

Fig. 3.80 *On a signal from A or B, B and C both clear the lane and move behind E. B continues out into a deep position while C delays and then cuts into the lower half of the restraining circle. D makes her usual cut. A may work one-on-one or pass to C or back to D.*

129

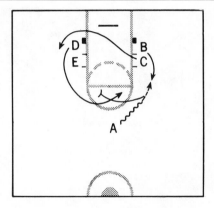

Fig. 3.81 *After B cuts out, C clears to the outer side of the lane to allow B to work one-on-one. B has the option of passing to D cutting around the screen by A.*

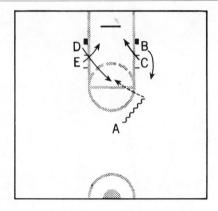

Fig. 3.84 *When D's defender is lured into thinking that D always cuts behind E, A gives a signal and D quickly cuts to the lower half of the restraining circle for a pass and immediate jump shot.*

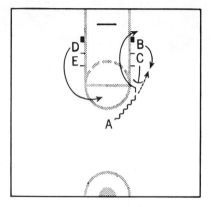

Fig. 3.82 *The play starts in the usual manner, only C moves up to allow A to cut either side of the rear screen. B passes to A if she is free or to C on her roll or back to D.*

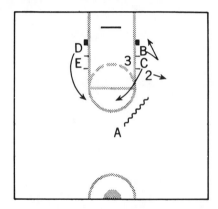

Fig. 3.85 *If the defender guarding B (No. 2) plays in front anticipating the usual cut by B, B starts her cut but then reverses. C clears the area for a pass by A to B. Players E, C, and B rebound with D in the intermediate position.*

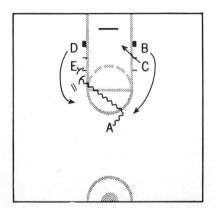

Fig. 3.83 *A reverses her dribble and establishes a double screen with E. A hands off to D. B moves back into safety position as C moves into a low post position.*

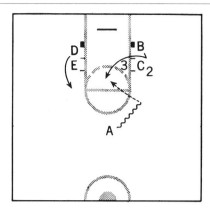

Fig. 3.86 *If the defender guarding B plays in front, B may fake out and cut into the lane. If C's opponent moves to guard B, C is free.*

demonstrating an ability to score from this range the defense is forced to spread their zone to a greater degree which, in turn, opens the zone for greater penetration.

4. Because the defense is basically playing the ball, the zone can be penetrated from the weak side and with cuts from behind the zone (from the baseline). This type of cut can be particularly effective.

5. It is extremely important that all players, with the exception of a pivot player, face the basket when they receive a pass. This allows them to spot a free teammate quickly and pass to her before the zone has time to readjust their positions.

6. It must be remembered that a zone moves primarily with ball movement. Therefore, if the offense can move the ball quickly, the defense should be slightly behind the position of the ball since they cannot slide as fast as the ball can be passed. This advantage is lost any time a player holds the ball, fumbles a pass, or dribbles without penetrating the zone because the defense has adequate time to reposition. This means that players must pass quickly after receiving the ball, but their passes cannot be stereotyped. A player may have a preconceived idea as to where she would like to pass, but the pass cannot be made automatically until it is determined that the passing lane to that position is open. It also means that all passes must be accurate so that the ball is not fumbled; and, it means that dribbling would be eliminated except to drive toward the goal or to move the ball away from excessive defensive pressure.

7. The offense should be patient in maneuvering for a good scoring opportunity and not shoot hurriedly unless the 30-sec. clock is due to sound. The offense should make every effort to enter the zone for a high percentage shot and shoot long shots only when absolutely necessary or in a desire to demonstrate effectiveness from this range in an attempt to spread the defense to a greater extent.

8. Definite rebounding assignments should be made on each scoring thrust. The defensive players are frequently drawn away from desirable rebounding positions, and the offense should take advantage of this. Furthermore, the defense is often not in a position to block out the opponents even temporarily so that the offensive player often is able to move into rebound position uncontained by the opposition.

9. Any offense against a zone must utilize cuts. Maneuvers that utilize diagonal cuts through the lane should be developed, as well as the following: parallel cuts to the ball, vertical cuts toward the basket outside the lane and vertical cuts away from the basket through or along the lane, and lateral cuts across the lane (often behind the defenders).

10. Screens should be employed against a zone defense. These may include running screens, particularly outside screens and also screens set at a seam in a zone so that a defender is temporarily delayed in moving to her new position as the ball is passed. This is an excellent technique, and greater use should be made of it.

11. The overload principle may be applied to attacking a zone. One area is flooded with more offensive players than defensive players assigned to that part of the zone. The temporary advantage in numbers (for the zone will react to the overload) may free a player for a shot, or one of these players may screen a defensive player to allow a pass, cut, or drive.

12. There must be both ball movement and player movement against any type of zone defense. A zone attack that involves ball movement only is an easy one against which to defend.

Selecting an Offensive Alignment to Attack a Zone

The reader knows that every zone has one or more weakness. Because it depends upon the manner in which each is played, one can only generalize about the areas of weaknesses in each type of zone. The most vulnerable areas in most zones are either from the corners or in the area at the top or to the side of the circle. Some zones also have weaknesses in the medium pivot range. The offensive team must recognize where these areas are and take measures to exploit them. In order to do this the teacher/coach must devise scoring thrusts at the places where the zone is most vulnerable, or devise scoring efforts at defenders who are in foul difficulty or who have particularly weak individual defensive skills. To gain the greatest advantage against a specific zone alignment, some coaches select an offensive formation with an odd front line if the opponents are using an even front line or a formation with an even front line if the defense has an odd front line. Table 3.1 shows possible offensive alignments against various zones and the general weaknesses of each zone and, therefore, where they should be attacked if the individuals in the zone have no identifiable weaknesses.

As stated previously the one-four stack alignment may be used to defeat almost any of the zones.

Another factor that should be considered in the decision for choice of an offensive alignment against a zone is the alignment used for the primary offense. The closer the zone offensive alignment comes to the one generally used, the easier it is for the players to learn. It should also be understood that an offensive alignment will not in itself defeat a zone. Player movement must be designed to take advantage of the original positions in the formation to exploit the weaknesses of the defense movements. Formations other than the

Table 3.1   Zone Alignments, Their Weaknesses and Suggested Alignments for Attacking the Zones

Zone Alignment	Area of Weakness	Offensive Alignment to Attack the Zone
2–1–2	at the top of the circle; in the corners	1–3–1; 2–3
2–3	at the free throw line; medium pivot position outside the lane	1–3–1; 3–2; 2–3
3–2	medium pivot outside of lane; after front line is penetrated	2–3
2–2–1	top of the circle; in the corners	1–3–1; 3–2
1–2–2	top of the circle as a player moves away from the point position	2–3
1–3–1	top of the circle; in the corners	1–3–1; 2–3

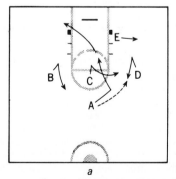
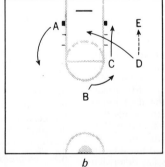
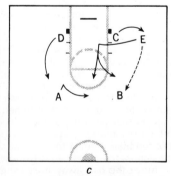

a   b   c

Fig. 3.87 *One-Three-One Continuity Zone Offense. As A passes to D, C fakes and cuts to the edge of the free throw line; A fakes and cuts through the lane as B replaces her and E cuts toward the corner (a). D passes to E in the corner and cuts through the lane; A clears the lane and returns to a wing position as B slides over; C cuts down the side of the lane (b). E passes back to B and D clears to a wing position and A moves to the top of the circle. After passing, E cuts to a high post position off C and then C replaces E in the corner (c).*

ones suggested above may provide equally good results against any zone if appropriate player movement is devised.

One other factor should be considered. Few teams are able to perfect offensive tactics from a number of alignments, and few teams can perfect a different offense to cope with every zone defense. Therefore, it may be wise for a team to develop one zone offense that can exploit the weaknesses of several different zones. Devising a series of options is one way to accomplish this purpose. A continuity offense with options is another. If the latter technique is selected, the player movement should exploit the weaknesses

in any zone.

One-Three-One Zone Offense

This alignment is one of the most popular in use today. Player A should be the best ball handler on the team, while players B and D should be good cutters and good shooters. Players C and E are the tallest players and remain close to the lane most of the time. Players C and E are interchangeable in positions, as are players A, B, and D. Fig. 3.87 shows a basic continuity offense, whereas Figs. 3.88–3.94 show options from that alignment.

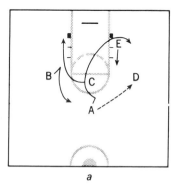
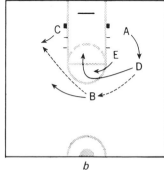
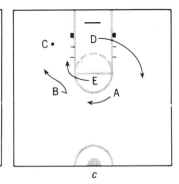

a b c

Fig. 3.88 *A passes to D; E slides up along the lane as A cuts around C's screen; D passes to E or A. If neither player is open, D may dribble to the top of the circle and A replaces her in the wing position (a). If B is free, D passes to her; B passes to C and B cuts away from the lane; E cuts to the high post position and D cuts around E; A moves to the wing position as D cuts (b). If D is not free, she moves back to her wing position and A moves to the top of the circle; E slides across to the other side of the lane and C passes back to B or A (c).*

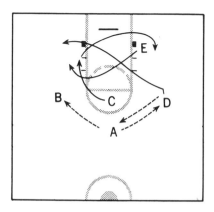

Fig. 3.89 *A passes to D, who returns it to A. As A passes to B, D cuts across the lane and C slides down the lane. B passes to C, D, or back to A. If C does not receive the pass, she cuts across the lane and E replaces her.*

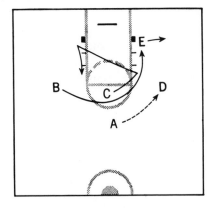

Fig. 3.90 *As A passes to D, C cuts to the edge of the free throw line and then clears to the outer side of the lane. Meanwhile B cuts and E cuts away from the lane. D passes to B or to E. If B does not get the pass, she circles back to her starting position and C returns to the free throw line.*

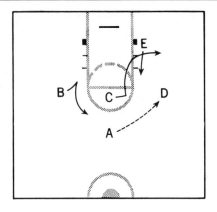

Fig. 3.92 *The passing options in this sequence are the same as those in Fig. 3.91, except players C and E exchange cutting responsibilities.*

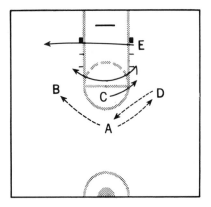

Fig. 3.91 *A passes to D as C cuts to the edge of the lane. D returns the pass to A as E cuts across the lane. C slides down the lane and cuts across the lane. B passes to E, C, or back to A.*

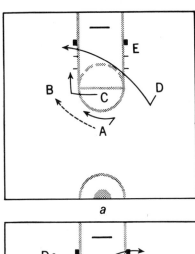

a

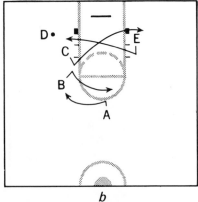

b

Fig. 3.93 *A passes to B as C slides down the lane; D fakes and cuts to the opposite corner; B passes to C or to D (a). If D gets the ball in the corner and is not in position to shoot, she passes to C on her cut into the lane or to E as she cuts off C; B and A exchange positions and D passes out to A if necessary (b).*

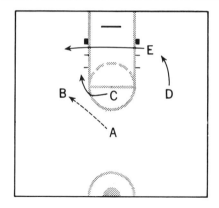

Fig. 3.94 *The passing sequence is basically the same as that shown in Fig. 3.93, except E cuts to the corner and D slides down to replace E. Their responsibilities are then exchanged.*

Two-Three Zone Offense

This alignment is also popular, using a single pivot player who maneuvers from the low post to high post position. The guard and forward positions are somewhat interchangeable, but the forwards return to the corner and wing positions as soon as possible. Player A should be the best ball handler and player B is generally the other guard. Players D and E are the forwards while player C is the post player. A continuity offense is shown from this posture in Fig. 3.95. Options are shown in Figs. 3.96–3.98.

BUILDING A PATTERN

The author has structured only a very limited number of pattern offenses. Anyone can devise others either for an offense against a man-to-man or zone defense. The value of devising a pattern lies in the continuity of motion of the players as one move leads into the

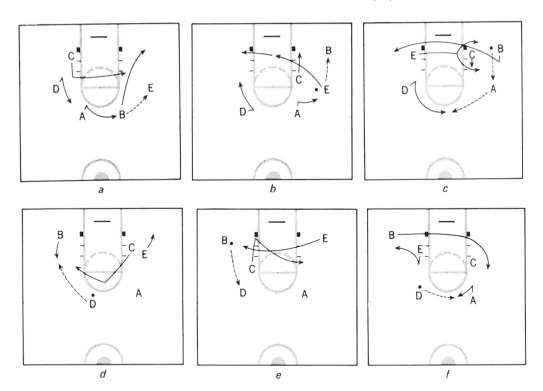

Fig. 3.95 *Two-Three Continuity Zone Offenses. B passes to E and cuts for the corner. A replaces B; D replaces A and C fakes and cuts across the lane (a). E passes to B in the corner, and E cuts through the lane; A replaces E as D cuts in the opposite direction; C slides down the lane (b). B passes back to A as E makes a return cut across the key using C as a screen; A passes to D and B cuts across the lane (c). D passes to B as E moves toward the baseline, and C fakes to the free throw line and then cuts to the edge of the lane (d). C slides down the lane and then clears to the opposite side as E cuts off her; B returns a pass to D (e). D passes back to A as B cuts around C; If nothing has materialized during this sequence, A may dribble the ball while all players return to their starting positions (f).*

135

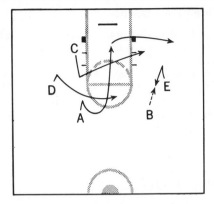

Fig. 3.96 *B passes to E, and A fakes and cuts. C slides up the lane and cuts across. A clears to the corner. D fakes and cuts to the free throw line. If none of these players are open, E passes back to B.*

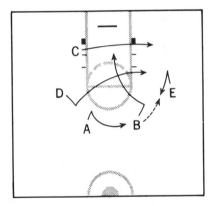

Fig. 3.97 *B passes to E and B cuts as A slides over to replace B. D cuts off B and C cuts to the corner. E passes to B, D, C, or back to A.*

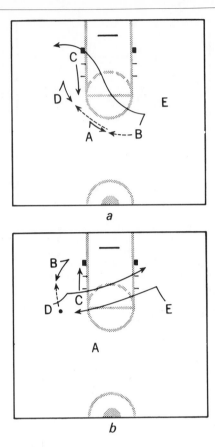

a

b

Fig. 3.98 *B passes to A as C slides up the lane; A passes to C or D (a). If D receives the pass, she passes to B as C slides down the lane; D cuts through the lane as E fakes and cuts to the edge of the free throw lane (b).*

next. Players know their exact responsibilities on every maneuver and recognize that if a scoring opportunity does not develop on one move it will on another. The continuity offense has an inherent disadvantage in that the opponents can identify the basic pattern and structure their defense to limit its effectiveness. However, if the attack utilizes options from the continuity, defensive modifications to overcome the pattern should be nullified.

In the construction of any pattern, certain principles should be followed:

1. There should always be defensive balance. This may necessitate a forward moving back to the top of the circle on a cutting maneuver by a guard.
2. A scoring thrust should be made on the initial maneuver—i.e., there should be immediate player movement to free a player for a shot after two or three passes.
3. Opportunities should be provided for both long and short shots. The best shooters on the team should be freed for these scoring attempts.
4. Player movements should include diagonal and

vertical cuts and should take advantage of the individual assets of various players. Ball movement should include the potential for passing into the lane area and reverse movement.

5. Rebounding strength should be provided at all times. Care must be exercised to assure that all of the best rebounders are not pulled away from the basket at the same time.

Teaching a Pattern

When the instructor/coach is ready to present a pattern to a class or team, she should be thoroughly familiar with all involved movements and should be particularly aware of the desirable timing of the sequential moves. She should be able to visualize the pattern in operation from both the right and left sides, although all patterns are devised to circulate predominantly in one direction to take advantage of player strengths.

It is desirable to circulate diagrams of the movements to the players so that they can follow them while the teacher describes them either on the blackboard or with an overhead projector. Each diagram should contain only one or two movements by each player so that the student can easily follow the drawing. Subsequent action can be included in other diagrams, and players can take the diagrams home for additional study.

Once the pattern has been reviewed orally and diagrammatically, players should be placed on the court in their proper positions and allowed to walk through the movements. This should be followed by running through the pattern, with careful attention given to the timing of the moves both toward and away from the ball. Defense players should be added and instructed to be passive and not interfere either with ball or player movement. They maintain proper position but do not play at all aggressively. At this time particular emphasis should be placed on the players' sequential movements. The pattern should be broken down into its parts whenever necessary to obtain the desirable moves and timing by the players involved. As soon as parts have been learned the whole pattern should be reviewed once again. Defense players can then be instructed to defend in their usual manner.

It is important that attack players be successful with the pattern as they are learning it. They must develop confidence in its ability to penetrate the defense and see evidence that many natural scoring opportunities can arise through its normal movement. By instructing the defense to remain stationary or passive, the attack can gain confidence in its use. Following this initial learning period, the attack must work the pattern against a more normal defense so that they can adjust to whatever defensive feints or moves they may encounter during a game situation.

When the teacher is satisfied that the players have acquired the desirable level of competency with the pattern, options should be learned. The same progression the players experienced while learning the pattern itself should be used while learning the various options. After a period of time, a different style of defense should be employed to provide the players with an opportunity to gain poise in coping with it.

Although far more experience can be gained in learning the pattern by playing five-on-five, it is important during the learning stages that the players play full court also so that they must advance the ball downcourt and set up the offense. The instructor may initially suggest that the ball be advanced to the front court in a controlled manner so that each time ball possession is gained, the pattern or one of its options may be worked. Later, the team may fast break whenever the opportunity arises and slow down to the pattern offense when the fast break does not materialize.

OFFENSE AGAINST A PRESSING DEFENSE

Both teacher/coach and players must understand why an opposing team chooses to use a pressing defense. The common reason is to disconcert the attacking team, cause them to lose their poise, and force them to make a ball handling error. Basically, this is done by overplaying those players close to the ball and trying to double-team the player with the ball. Players should recognize that this is a very weak defense since one player should always be free if the opponents are double-teaming the ball handler. Therefore, after a team passes the ball through the double-team, it has a player advantage and should be able to maneuver quickly for an easy shot. If a team lacks poise or experience against a press however, it may be in for a long afternoon! Through practice, players learn to attack the press—rather than being attacked by it!

Because a press takes time to set up, it can be beaten immediately by a quick pass in bounds. (Most presses are organized after a score has been made.) Although this is true, there is a difference of opinion among coaches as to which player should in-bound the ball. There are those who believe that it is absolutely essential to in-bound the ball as rapidly as possible. Therefore, the player closest to the ball retrieves the ball and passes it in-bounds. Other coaches believe that this may be dangerous because the player who in-bounds the ball may not be a good ball handler and may cause an intercepted pass. These coaches believe that the best ball handler should always put the ball in play even though the pass in may be delayed temporarily as she moves behind the end line. This is caused because the best ball handler is usually playing in the position of guard and may be 15–20 ft. from the end line at the time the goal is scored. The choice of which player is to in-bound the ball must be left to the discretion of the teacher/coach.

It is important that the players stay scattered against any type of pressing defense. They should avoid weaves, any type of lateral crosses, and lateral screens which bring the defenders close and aid them in double-teaming. There should be extensive player movement to cause the defense to adjust their positions. Pass and cut techniques are helpful in beating the press. Competitive teams should practice against both man-to-man and zone type presses so that they become acclimated to the various moves and can attack the press with ease and confidence.

Offense Against a Man-to-Man Press

The primary means of advancing the ball downcourt against a man-to-man press is to give the ball to the best dribbler and let her outmaneuver her opponent. The rest of the players clear the middle of the court as soon as the dribbler receives the ball and the dribbler is allowed to feint and drive her opponent out of position.

When in-bounding the ball, a team generally tries to rely on only one player to receive the pass. Fig. 3.99 shows typical positioning of players for the in-bounds pass. If this is not successful, a team sends another player into the back court. (Positioning is shown in Fig. 3.100.) If the in-bounds passer is the

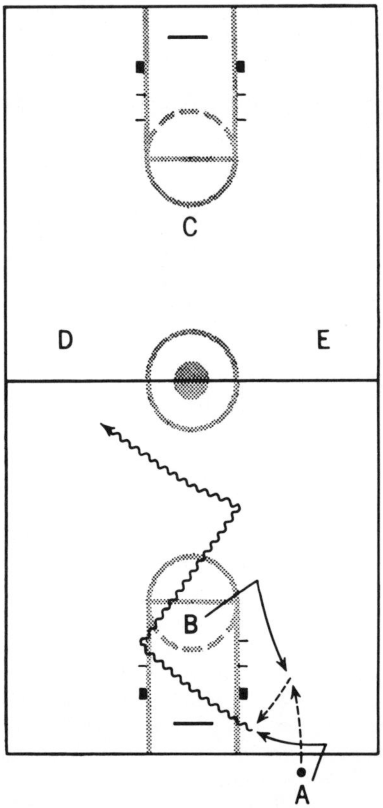

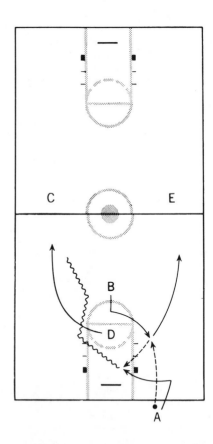

Fig. 3.99 *A One-One-Two-One Alignment Against a Man-to-Man Press. A, the best ball handler, in-bounds the ball. B, the other guard, fakes and receives the pass. B returns the ball to A and clears toward the sideline to allow A as much space as needed to dribble down court.*

Fig. 3.100 *A One-One-One-Two alignment is used against a man-to-man press when A has difficulty in-bounding the ball. B fakes and cuts off D to receive the pass. B returns it to A, and both B and D clear toward the sideline to allow A to dribble downcourt.*

best ball handler, the receiver returns a pass to her so that she may dribble downcourt. Possible moves are shown in Figs. 3.99–3.101.

If a team does not have an exceptional dribbler to advance the ball, a forward or center who is guarded by a weak opponent may be given the responsibility of dribbling the ball into the front court. Other techniques used against a man-to-man press include the use of short passes in which the receiver moves toward the ball. Pass and cut tactics are effective. Occasionally a long pass into the front court may be successful, but the passer must be completely aware of the position of all opponents and be certain that her pass will be successful.

Offense Against a Zone Press

All zone presses are predicated on employing a double-team. Therefore, an attacking team should take measures so that trapping tactics by the defense will be unsuccessful. Since traps are easier to set at a sideline or in a corner (because the sideline serves as another defender) the attack should try to advance the ball down the middle of the court. Any time a trap is about to be set the ball handler should dribble between the two defense players (Fig. 3.102) or pass to a teammate cutting behind the trappers (Fig. 3.103). This method continues to advance the ball up the court and provides an escape to the trap.

When playing against a zone press, an attacking team should also always have a trailer behind the ball handler. The defenders guard the areas in front of the ball and cannot defend well against a trailer. There-

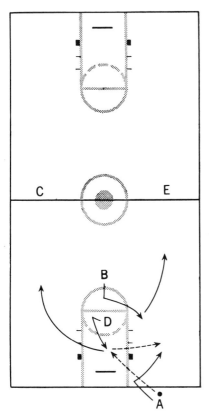

Fig. 3.101 *An Alternate Pattern for a One-One-One-Two Alignment. Both B and D cut for a pass. D receives it and returns it to A. The same principles are followed as previously described.*

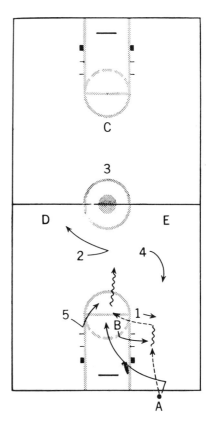

Fig. 3.102 *Dribbling to Beat a Trap Against a Two-Two-One Zone Press. A passes to B, and A cuts up the middle. B commences to dribble to draw defenders Nos. 1 and 4 for the trap. Before they can set it, B returns a pass to A who drives between Nos. 5 and 1 before they can double-team.*

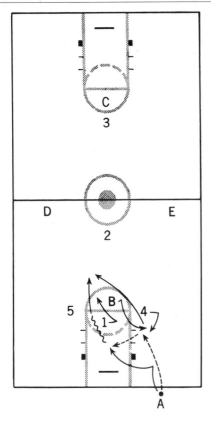

Fig. 3.103 *Passing to Beat a Trap Against a Three-One-One Zone Press. A passes in to B, and B returns the pass to A. A dribbles toward the trap as B cuts behind No. 1 to receive the pass from A.*

the ball handler, the attack players should not pass and cut toward the ball to draw the opponent in their area nearer the ball handler. It is a much better procedure to pass and cut away from the ball. This allows players from another zone to cut toward the ball to receive a pass. All receivers should cut toward the ball.

The zone press should be attacked at its weakest point. Basically this is in the middle of the court. Also, players are freest after the defense has moved to establish a double-team. As this occurs the ball handler must recognize where her teammates will be and find a free player to whom she can pass. She must always face her front court so that she can see the action of both her teammates and the opponents; but, she should understand that she will have a trailer to whom she may pass if no one in front of her is really free.

Players should practice against the most common zone press defenses employed in their region so that they can "attack" the press rather than go on the defensive. It is better to plan to move into a trap and pass off before it is set than to move in an uncontrolled manner and either throw the ball away or cause a tie ball when the trap occurs. Most coaches agree, however, that they would prefer to have a tie ball rather than a poorly thrown pass that ends up in an easy score for the opponents. If the attacking team can pass the ball beyond the front line of the zone press once, they are in an excellent position to move further downcourt with a player advantage. If it results in several easy scores, the opponents will soon resort to a different means of defense.

Different offensive alignments are possible for use against zone presses. Figs. 3.99 and 3.102 show only slightly different positions in a one-one-two-one alignment. Fig. 3.100 shows a one-one-one-two alignment that can also be used against a zone press—although usually against the zone press the back players (C and E) move into the back court just across the division line (as shown by players D and E in Fig. 3.102). Fig. 3.104 shows a one-two-two alignment that is often used against a two-two-one zone press. Fig. 3.105 shows a passing pattern against a two-two-one zone press, and Fig. 3.106 shows a passing pattern against a three-one-one zone press.

Drills

The same practice techniques used to develop skill in operating against either a man-to-man or zone defense should be utilized in learning an attack against a press. The development of this attack takes considerable practice time and patience on behalf of both player and coach.

fore, the trailer serves as a safety valve and should be free when needed for a pass.

In planning an attack against a zone press, it is wise to dribble only when necessary or for some predetermined reason. After a player is forced to pick up the ball following a dribble, she is far easier to trap. Therefore, a pass receiver should attempt to pass immediately upon receiving the ball or plan a controlled dribble to draw two defenders so that a pass to a teammate allows her to escape a trap and advance beyond the front line of the defense. These are the two keys to success in beating a zone press.

It is important that players do not attempt any kind of screening maneuvers except possibly a back screen against a zone press. Since the defense desires to trap

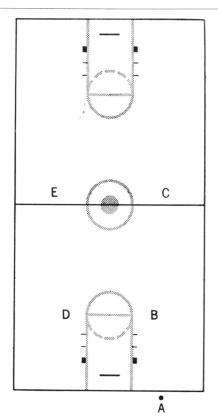

Fig. 3.104 *A one-two-two alignment that may be used effectively against a zone press, particularly against an even front (two-two-one zone press).*

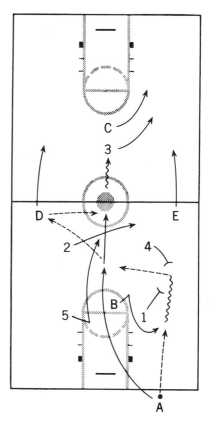

Fig. 3.105 *Use of a One-One-Two-One Alignment Against a Two-Two-One Zone Press. A passes in to B, who dribbles to the right to draw a trap. A cuts up the middle to receive a return pass and immediately passes to D who should be free before No. 2 can recover to that side. D passes back to A for a fast break attempt. D and E cut down the outside lanes. C clears to the side, and B is the trailer.*

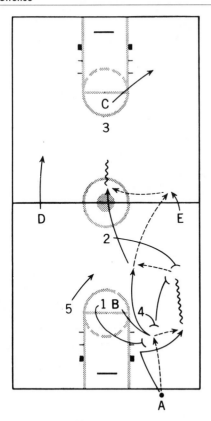

Fig. 3.106 *Using a One-One-Two-One Alignment Against a Three-One-One Zone Press. A passes in to B, who immediately returns a pass to A before the trap is effective. A dribbles up the sideline, drawing another trap and passes to B. B passes to E before No. 2 can recover. B cuts down the middle for a return pass to fill the lanes on the fast break. C clears, and A is the trailer.*

REFERENCES

1. Cousy, Bob, and Powers, Frank G., Jr. *Basketball Concepts and Techniques.* Boston: Allyn and Bacon, 1970.
2. *Ibid.*

II

Defense

4

Individual Defense

High scoring games provide great interest and entertainment, and most players and fans enjoy a fast-moving contest with many goals scored. Most spectators focus their attention on the ball and the offensive players in the immediate area; only a few focus their attention on the defensive players. Because of this, youngsters learn very early in life that offensive skills attract the attention of teammates and adults as well, and therefore concentrate their attention on learning those skills. If one watches children playing without supervision, one observes that they practice shooting skills and other offensive techniques such as dribbling and faking. One can hardly blame them when sports writers and fans give the greatest acclaim to the fancy ball handlers and high scorers. Sports writers and fans rarely pay tribute to the defensive wizard.

The teacher/coach, however, is extremely aware of the vital role that defense plays for any team's success. The teacher/coach often must sell players on the importance of defense because players frequently have directed most of their attention to offensive skills. During this process the teacher must help players develop a keen sense of pride in their defensive ability. They must learn to be so determined, so unrelenting, and so motivated in their efforts that they want to prevent their opponent from ever receiving the ball. Should the opponent receive a pass, they are keen to prevent her from penetrating the defense. This defensive attitude must be inculcated so that players like to play defense as well as they like to play offense.

A teacher will probably find that students learn defensive skills quicker and easier than they learn offensive skills, because timing of moves with the ball is not as difficult. This does not indicate that less time should be spent on defense. To build a sound team, an equal amount of time probably needs to be devoted to both aspects of the game.

The concepts of aggressiveness, determination, and prevention must be developed by defensive players. At all times, their attention must be focused on positioning themselves in such a way that their opponent cannot get possession of the ball. If she does, great pressure must be exerted to make any maneuvering by her most difficult. There is a difference between a defense player who is in the proper place at the proper time and one who is in the proper place at the proper time and who also displays tenacity in her movements.

It is the task of the defense to force the offense to work hard to get the ball into scoring position and to force them to make their movements to places other than where they would like to cut. The teacher must assist *all* players in developing the attitude and skills necessary for defensive success. If one player is weak or loses alertness, the whole defensive structure is weakened. A strong defense places an immediate burden on the opposing team and forces them to make certain adjustments. Any time they are forced to alter their usual strategy, their efforts are weakened.

A well-coached defensive team will always be more consistent than a team that concentrates on offense. "Off nights" seldom occur on defense, although players do have off nights in shooting. These usually occur because of tension. This may be due to the importance of the game or a pressure defense played by the opponents. It may also be due to

1. lighting or backboard structure which causes the ball to rebound differently
2. size of the gymnasium
3. a difference in space between the edge of the court surface and spectators
4. the size of the facility itself

All of these factors may interfere with offensive capacity, whereas none of them should interfere with the defense. As a result, a well-coached team should always maintain stability in their defense.

When teaching defense to players, the principles of man-to-man defense are basic regardless of the defensive system that ultimately will be played. Each player must learn the techniques of guarding a player either with or without the ball and must learn how to guard a dribbler. These situations will be encountered and must be counteracted whether a team is playing man-to-man defense or any of the numerous zones.

Once the basic principles of man-to-man defense are acquired, players may increase their defensive vocabulary by learning to press or employ one or more of the zone defenses to further frustrate the opposition. A variety of defenses, however, does not automatically insure success. A team's ability to apply the principles involved in each is the real test. The number and type of defenses that players can perform well are dependent upon their individual abilities, experience, and practice time available. It is by far better for a team to master one defense than to attempt several with little degree of proficiency in any.

BODY POSITION

Proper body position is the most important fundamental in learning defense. This is basic to all other defensive techniques to be learned. Without proper body position, a player becomes a weak link in the defensive structure. She is subject to fakes, changes of direction, and other evasive techniques employed by an opponent. Any player can learn correct body position and must practice it frequently so that she can maintain the correct position throughout a game.

Foot Position

Feet should be approximately shoulder width apart and in a forward-backward stride. The inside foot (the one closer to the midline of the court) should be forward. The foot closer to the sideline becomes the rear foot. A defensive player playing to her left of the defensive goal should have her right foot forward and left foot back. The staggered position of the feet should never be closer than 5 or 6 in., but a wider base provides better balance. Weight should be divided evenly between the two feet, never on the forward foot. If weight is not evenly distributed, it should be closer to the rear foot to enable the player to retreat to the basket more quickly.

Some coaches prefer the foot position reversed — outside foot forward and inside foot to the rear. The choice of the staggered foot position is dependent upon the coach's philosophy of whether she wants to force the opponents toward the inside (middle) of the court or toward the sideline. When forward, the inside foot tends to force the opponents toward the middle. If this seems desirable, then a coach should adopt this technique. The coach who prefers to force the opponents away from the middle or toward the sideline should encourage the outside foot forward. Proponents of the method described initially subscribe to the theory that it is better to force the opponents toward the middle where other defense players can help. Advocates of the other theory believe that opponents should be forced away from the middle and toward the outside of the court where shooting angles are poorer.

Position of the Knees

Knees should always be flexed, the degree depending upon the player's body build. To attain the correct degree of flexion the player rests her hands comfortably just above her knees. During the early learning stages, the proper degree of flexion should be checked frequently by this method. Players tend to extend their kness and assume a more upright position. This must be checked early, and drills should be used frequently to help players attain the leg strength necessary for maintaining this position over a prolonged period of time.

Hips and Back

If a player has assumed the correct foot and knee position, her hips and back should automatically be in proper position. Hips should be flexed and the back should be relatively straight. As long as proper knee position is maintained, the back and hips should be in proper alignment.

Arms and Hands

The forearms are flexed to approximately 80 degrees, and the hands are almost fully extended, fingers only slightly flexed. Arms and hands are supinated (palms

a   b

Fig. 4.1 *Basic Defensive Position. Light No. 5 has her hips and knees flexed and her weight is centered over her base, allowing her to move in any direction (a). She makes upward jabbing motion at the ball (b). The motion should never be made downward.*

up). This position tends to keep the body in better balance than the technique in which one arm is raised overhead and the other arm is to the side. This latter technique tends to raise the center of gravity and makes the player more susceptible to fakes by the opponent. With arms and hands low, the center of gravity is lowered and the player can maintain balance to a better degree and therefore react more quickly to her opponent's moves. Any movement made by the hands to harass an opponent should be in an upward rather than downward direction. Hitting or tapping downward often produces unnecessary fouls.

Head and Eyes

The head is held in its usual position, but eyes are focused on the waistline or hips of the opponent if she has the ball. Eyes should never focus on the ball itself nor on the opponent's eyes or head because she uses them to fake the defensive player out of position. Since the hips move only when a player moves, a defense player is more likely to maintain a good defensive position if she watches this area.

If the opponent does not have the ball, the defensive player should position herself so that she can see both the ball and her opponent without turning her head. This means that as an opponent moves further from the ball, the defense player is further from her so that this correct position can be maintained.

In summary, the defensive body position places the feet in a forward stride position; knees are flexed; back is straight; arms are flexed; fingers are almost extended; arms and hands are supinated; head is in a comfortable position; eyes are focused on the hips if the opponent has the ball; eyes focus on both ball and opponent if she does not have the ball. By assuming and maintaining this position, the defensive player will be well-balanced and ready to react to any movement by her opponent (Fig. 4.1). This should be her observable position any time a player is on defense. At no time should a defensive player be standing erect with arms at her side.

Foot Movement on Defense

There are very few occasions when a defense player is stationary. If either her opponent or the ball moves,

a

b

c

d

Fig. 4.2 *Defensive Footwork. As light No. 5 cuts, dark No. 3 slides to keep in good defensive position.*

it is likely that the defensive player will have to re-adjust her position. A defense player should never run in making these adjustments. She always slides. To move laterally across the court, a player simply uses a side step. To move to her left she steps left with her left foot sliding her right foot across to it, stepping left with the left foot again, then sliding the right foot to it. This procedure continues until the player wishes to change direction (Fig. 4.2). Movement in a forward or backward direction is done in basically the same

fashion. To move forward, the front foot steps forward as the back foot slides up to it. To move in a backward direction, the back foot steps first with the forward foot sliding to it. At no time should the feet be crossed. When moving forward, care must be taken to insure that the player does not retain her weight for any length of time on her forward foot. The balanced position with weight distributed evenly over the base must be maintained most of the time.

In all cases, sliding steps are made with short quick steps and feet stay as close to the floor as possible. Only one foot should be in the air at any time. The player can change her direction with greatest acceleration by keeping one foot in contact with the floor at all times and by keeping feet very close to the floor.

Although generally the feet should never cross, there is one exception. This occurs when a player is guarding an opponent who has just passed the ball. After the ball leaves the opponent's hands, the defense player must retreat immediately to prevent the possible pass and cut situation. To gain as much distance as possible on the initial step, a crossover step may be used—but for the initial step only (Fig. 4.3).

Defensive players should rarely be in a position where they are forced to run to stay with their opponent. In her own back court, running by a defensive player is a sign of weakness. It is a clear indication that the defensive player has been beaten by her opponent. It may also indicate that further attention should be devoted to proper footwork by that particular player. However, during the course of a game such a situation may arise and a defense player must

a

b

Fig. 4.3 *Defensive Crossover Step. After No. 5 passes (a) and cuts for a return pass (b), the defender uses a crossover step to gain as much distance as possible on her first step. Following the initial step, the defender slides as usual. The only time the crossover step is recommended is during a pass-and-cut maneuver.*

DRILLS FOR BASIC DEFENSIVE BODY POSITION AND FOOT MOVEMENT

1. All players stand with their backs to one basket. They assume the basic defensive position while the teacher/coach checks the position of the feet, knee flexion, and arm position. During the early stages of learning, the teacher may place tape down the midline of the court to distinguish the left side from the right side of the court. This will assist the players in determining which foot should be forward.

2. Same as drill 1 above, except the players move forward and back, to their left and right. For ease in observing correct footwork, the teacher may request that the group on each side of the midline stay on their half of the court. Later, the groups should move across the dividing line so that the players must change the forward foot. Still later, the tape should be removed so that the visual cue is eliminated and players must recognize by other means when they have crossed the midline of the court.

3. All players with their backs to one basket move left, right, forward, and back down the court on command from the teacher. One of the purposes of this drill is to gain endurance and leg strength so that players can continue this drill up to fifteen or twenty times without coming to a standing or resting position.

4. All players have their backs to one basket and a leader faces them, serving as a common opponent for all. The leader moves forward, backward, left, and right with changes of pace and the defense players react to her by moving in the corresponding direction. Emphasis should be placed on the basic defensive body position and sliding step. No player should use a crossover step.

5. One attack player and one defense player. No ball. The attack player moves downcourt by changing direction frequently, and the defense player tries to maintain a good defensive position. Players should remain at the opposite end of the court until all individuals have reached that end. Alternate positions.

6. One attack and one defense player, with the defense player tied to the attack player with a 5-ft. string (not a rope). The string is tied to a pinnie or belt worn by each player. The offensive player moves downcourt, using stops, starts, and changes of direction. The defense player must move correspondingly so that the string is not broken. As soon as defense players maintain good body position the length of the string can be decreased to 4 ft. and then 3 ft., if desired.

---

have some means of guarding her opponent as she is cutting free toward the basket. When this occurs, the defensive player pivots and runs toward her opponent with the arm closer to the basket raised overhead and the other one extended to the side. In this position the defensive player has a chance to deflect either a lob or bounce pass. She watches her opponent's eyes, which may indicate the direction from which the pass is coming (Fig. 4.4).

DEFENSIVE PRINCIPLES

As soon as players lose possession of the ball in their offensive court or following a field goal, they must return as rapidly as possible to their own back court unless, of course, they are utilizing a full court press. As the defense players retreat, it is desirable for them to run back in to position. If they prefer, they may run backward or use a backward skip so that they can keep their eyes on the ball as they retreat downcourt. The aim of the defense is to be waiting in the back court when the offensive players approach the center line.

Once players reach their back court area, there are certain principles that each player should follow under normal circumstances. These principles apply to any style of defense that a team is playing—man-to-man or zone.

Fig. 4.4 *Guarding a Free Player Cutting Through the Lane. Dark No. 5 has allowed her opponent to become free. The defender must turn and run toward her opponent with one arm extended and the other one to the side to deflect a pass to her opponent. After light No. 5 clears the lane, dark No. 5 can move to regain proper defensive position.*

1. At all times, the defensive player must maintain the proper defensive body position previously described.
2. The defense player must always be in position so that she can see both the ball and her opponent. Players should try to improve their peripheral vision.
3. The defense player must never cross her feet when she moves in any direction (except when retreating to prevent the give-and-go play). A sliding step must always be used.
4. The defense player must force the ball toward the middle of the court. She must take a position that will cause this action by the offense.
5. The defense player should always stay ball side of her opponent and generally basket side as well. This simply means that the player is closer to the ball than her opponent. If the ball is to the left of

150

her opponent, the defense player is also to the left of her opponent.

6. The defense player should face the ball; her back should never be turned to the ball.

7. The defense player should position herself so that her opponent can never drive by her toward the sideline. It is perhaps more important that the opponent cannot drive the baseline.

8. The defense player should play in front of an opponent who cuts across the lane under the basket. She should never permit the offense player to be between her and the ball in this dangerous area (Fig. 4.5).

9. The defense player should be ready to assist any teammate if necessary when her opponent does not have the ball. She should be ready to help defend against a dribbler who is free or a cutter who has evaded her opponent.

GUARDING A PLAYER WITHOUT THE BALL

Once players have retreated to their defensive end, they can wait for the opponents to bring the ball downcourt where they can meet them as they move into scoring territory (within 20–25 ft. of the basket). Pressure should be exerted against the ball handler at this time. Other players should obtain proper defensive position against their opponent, who may maneuver for a pass or attempt to keep the defender away from the scoring thrust so that she cannot assist her teammates in the prevention of a score.

Defending against a player without the ball is difficult and demands a great deal of attention. This is *not* the time for a player to rest either physically or mentally. For some reason defense players guarding an opponent without the ball tend to lose alertness both physically and mentally. A good defensive team, however, does not allow this to happen. Much attention must be given to the position of these players in practice. They must understand that their position and actions are equally important as those of the defender guarding the player with the ball. No defense can be sound unless all players are "with it." They must recognize that the responsibility for team defense lies with each and every player, regardless of the position of the ball or the type of defense being played. On every ball movement (dribble, pass, or shot), each defense player must readjust her position in relation to the new position of the ball. This must be done quickly so that passing lanes are blocked to the nearest receivers. Players guarding opponents some distance from the ball can move further from them to be of assistance to teammates if needed.

Defense players should be alert for possible screen situations. When a screening player is approaching,

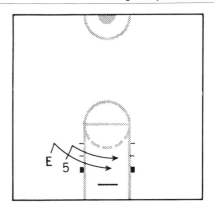

Fig. 4.5 *Defensive Positioning When a Player Cuts Across the Lane Near the Basket. The defender fronts her as she moves across the lane, making it more difficult for her to receive a pass. She does not allow the attack player to cut in front of her this close to the basket.*

a defender can assist her teammate by calling "Screen" so that the defensive player can make the proper adjustment and not be surprised by the screen. When playing man-to-man it is important that players do not rely on switching whenever screens are set. Nevertheless, during the course of the game it is likely that a switch in defensive assignments will be necessary. When this occurs it is the responsibility of the back player to call the switch—not the defensive player being screened. Following the switch in defensive assignments the defense players involved should stay with their new opponent until they can return safely to their original opponent. If the offensive team gains a distinct height advantage, this should be done at the earliest possible time. If no height advantage is gained by the offense, there is no need in hurrying the change in respective defensive assignments.

Every effort should be made on the part of defense players to prevent the attack from receiving the ball within 15 ft. of the basket. In order to accomplish this task it seems helpful to think of the correct defensive position in terms of the opponent's position in relation to the ball. It is necessary to differentiate the defensive responsibilities when a player is guarding an opponent who is one or two passes away from the player with the ball. No player is ever more than two passes away from the ball if the ball is passed to the pivot player. The position of defense players opposing forwards and guards will be discussed in the following section. Positioning for guarding a post player will be discussed later in the chapter.

One Pass Away from the Player with the Ball

An attack player is "one pass away" when she is near the player with the ball and is a logical receiver of the next pass. The ball need not be relayed to her by another attack player. When defending against a player who is one pass away, the defender's position depends upon whether she is defending against a guard, forward, or pivot player. Her positioning and tactics can also be determined by which player has the ball at that particular instant.

Defense Against a Guard Who Is One Pass Away

When the other guard has the ball, the defender drops back to a position slightly ball side of a line between her opponent and the basket, where she can see both her opponent and the ball. From this position she can defend against a cut by her opponent following a pass to the other guard. Anticipating and preventing the guard cut is one of her major responsibilities. From this position she can also prevent a pass into a high pivot position, thus limiting the extent to which the opponents can use the scissor maneuvers. She must also anticipate lateral moves by the two guards and be prepared to reduce their effectiveness.

If the defensive team is pressing, the defensive player does not drop back so far and plays a step closer to the ball handler. In this way she can more effectively harass her opponent by closing the direct passing lane and forcing (to a greater degree) her opponent to maneuver to become free for a pass. This overplay position invites a reverse cut for which the weak side defensive forward must be alert.

If the near side forward (the forward close to the guard without the ball) has the ball, the defensive player drops back, opens her stance, and has three responsibilities.

1. She protects against the forward passing the ball into the medium or high pivot and assists her teammate if the forward drives toward the medium or high post position.
2. She must anticipate any two player maneuvers by her opponent and the forward with the ball and attempt to beat her opponent in her desired cut.
3. If the guard moves away from the forward with the ball, the defense player adjusts her position as necessary so that she can continue to see the ball and her opponent.

This allows her to sag off her teammate so that, if necessary, she is able to assist her teammates. The further away the guard moves from the ball, the further the defensive player positions herself from her opponent.

If the pivot player has the ball in a high or medium post position, the defensive player drops back and at-

tempts to harass the pivot player to limit her maneuverability. She must continue to face her own opponent but reaches backward toward the pivot player to limit movement in her direction. At the same time she must anticipate a scissor maneuver by her own opponent as soon as the pivot player receives the ball, and she must know the type of team defense to use against this tactic. When the pivot has the ball, she must be ready to return quickly toward her opponent if the ball is passed to her. She must also be alert for any cut that her opponent may make (Fig. 4.6).

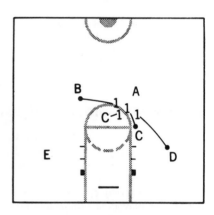

Fig. 4.6 *Defensive Position Against a Guard Who Is One Pass Away. Player No. 1 is guarding A. The diagram shows the position of No. 1 if B, C, or D has the ball. (C is shown in the medium and high post position.)*

Defense Against a Forward Who Is One Pass Away

When the near side guard has the ball, the defensive player takes her stance so that she is in line with the forward and the basket. This means that her forward foot is approximately opposite the midline of the forward's body and that her rear foot is closer to the end line than either of her opponent's feet. This is the basic position to assume if the forward cuts and maneuvers well to receive a pass. If the forward neither cuts well nor is a good ball handler, the defense player may guard her more aggressively—i.e., her stance may be even with that of her opponent. This means that the defensive player's forward foot is directly opposite the forward foot of her opponent. She can also extend her arm to further block the passing lane. If the defensive player can operate effectively from this position, she forces her opponent to move wider and further from the basket to receive a pass which may cause her to be beyond her shooting range. It should

a

b

c

Fig. 4.7 *Defensive Fake. Light No. 2 fakes a pass to the forward* (a). *Dark No. 5 moves to cover her opponent more closely* (b), *but anticipates the reverse cut by the forward* (c). *Having reversed direction quickly, the defender is able to acquire good position and make the interception* (d and e).

153

d

e

be recognized, however, that from this position the defender is more vulnerable to the reverse cut; and, her teammates must be alert for this cut. If the forward does try a reverse cut, the defender must turn toward the ball and run toward the basket, staying between the ball and her opponent for a possible interception. Against a forward who uses the reverse cut well, the defender can fake this aggressive position and immediately retreat to be in position to intercept the pass (Fig. 4.7).

If the pivot player has the ball in the low or medium post position, the defensive player must drop off her opponent to help her teammate defend against pivot maneuvers. The defensive player must be alert for a scissor maneuver or any other type of cut by her opponent when the pivot has the ball. She also must be ready to return quickly to her opponent if the ball is passed to her (Fig. 4.8).

Two Passes Away from the Player with the Ball

There are only a few occasions when a defense player is guarding an opponent who is two passes away from

the ball. For this situation to occur the ball must be on the far side of the court; and, the only way the defender's opponent could receive a pass would be by means of a relay pass from another teammate or a high lob pass. Basically, when a defense player is guarding an opponent two passes away, the defense player's primary task is to help out on team defense. She drops off her opponent further than usual so that she can help double-team an opponent or guard a player who has evaded her opponent. Obviously, she must be aware of the ball's movement and of her opponent so that she may return to a better defensive posture as the ball moves to a position only one pass away from her opponent.

Defense Against a Guard Who Is Two Passes Away

Either the forward or a low or medium pivot player or the far side of the court has the ball. When this occurs, the defensive player drops back into the free throw area and opens her stance toward the ball. She is in a position to observe her opponent and the movement

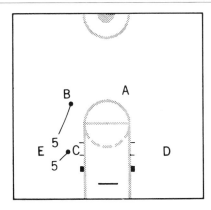

Fig. 4.8 *Defensive Position Against a Forward Who Is One Pass Away. Player No. 5 is guarding E. The diagram shows the position of No. 5 if B or C has the ball.*

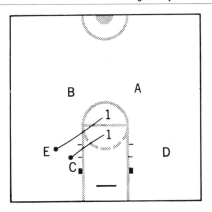

Fig. 4.9 *Defensive Position Against a Guard Who Is Two Passes Away from the Ball. Player No. 1 is guarding A. The position of No. 1 is shown if C or E has the ball.*

of the ball. She tries to beat her opponent on any cut toward the ball and, from her position in the free throw area, tries to intercept or deflect passes into this area (Fig. 4.9).

Defense Against a Forward Who Is Two Passes Away

This situation occurs when either the guard or forward on the far side of the court has the ball. When this occurs she drops off her opponent toward the lane area ready to assist any teammate if necessary (Fig. 4.10). She is particularly alert for reverse cuts by the far side guard or forward who does not have the ball. If she moves quickly and can get into position, she may force a charging foul by an unalert cutter. She must also be alert for a lob pass to her own opponent. If this occurs, she must return to her opponent; but, her approach must be made with her weight back so that the forward cannot fake a shot and drive around her for an easy layup.

The defense player must also be particularly alert for any cuts made by her opponent through the lane. When the opponent cuts in this manner, the defender must front her when she is within 10 ft. of the basket. This means that she must anticipate her cut, beat her to the cutting lane she desires, and remain in front of her as she goes across the lane (Fig. 4.5). This places her in position to intercept the ball. If the forward receives a pass in this area, she is likely to score regardless of the efforts of the defense player. If the forward continues to cut up toward the free throw line rather than going behind the defender, the defense player has successfully defended against that move.

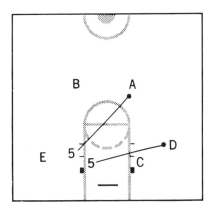

Fig. 4.10 *Defensive Position Against a Forward Who Is Two Passes Away from the Ball. Player No. 5 is guarding E. The position of No. 5 is shown if A or D has the ball.*

Beyond the 10-ft. range, the defender should stay behind her opponent (closer to the basket). The defense player's teammates must warn her of a potential double screen that her opponent may use. She must also be alert for a cut around a low or medium post when the ball is on the weak side.

GUARDING A PLAYER WITH THE BALL

Each player should recognize that she has three alternatives when her opponent has the ball: She may dribble, pass, or shoot. It is each defense player's

---

DRILLS FOR DEFENSE AGAINST A PLAYER WHO IS TWO PASSES AWAY FROM THE BALL

1. Groups of five — two guards and their opponents, and one forward without an opponent. The guard on the same side of the court as the forward starts with the ball. The guard may pass either to the other guard or to the forward, with the defense players moving accordingly. At first the three offensive players should remain stationary while the defender two passes away from the ball becomes accustomed to her move as the ball is passed to the forward. Later, the guard two passes away should attempt to cut through the lane toward the ball for a pass while the defense player tries to check the path of her opponent. After repeating the drill a few times, move the forward to the other side of the court so that the other defense player is able to adjust her position when the ball is two passes away from her opponent.

2. Same as drill 1 above, only replace the forward without an opponent with a low or medium pivot.

3. Same as drill 1, only the guard on the far side does not have an opponent, and a defense player guards the forward. Now the emphasis is on the position of the defender guarding the forward.

4. Same as drill 1, only substitute two forwards and a pivot player with one of the forwards without an opponent. Emphasis is on the position of the defender against the other forward. The forward without an opponent should occasionally try a cross court pass to her other forward and a pass into the pivot who relays it to the forward being guarded. Emphasis is on the defender preventing the desired cut by the forward. Later, the post player moves into a low or medium position on the side away from the ball and the defender tries to prevent the forward from cutting over the post for a pass from the forward on the other side.

5. Five defense and five offense players. Any attack player may start with the ball and the teacher/coach calls out when a pass may be made. Emphasis is on the defensive position of the player(s) who is (are) two passes away from the ball.

---

responsibility to analyze the strengths and weaknesses of her opponent in relation to these possibilities. She should learn very quickly if her opponent is a good ball handler and can maintain poise under pressure. She should learn in what direction her opponent prefers to dribble and whether she can dribble equally well with both hands. She should learn the type of shot that her opponent prefers and from what location on the court her shots are usually attempted. The defense player must ascertain whether the player cuts after she passes or whether she tends to play in one position. The defense player must also determine whether her opponent is a play maker. If so, she will need help from her defensive teammates in preventing her opponent from getting the ball. They should attempt to block the passing lanes to the play maker as much as possible. Whenever the play maker gets the ball her opponent should exert extreme pressure against her so that she will have difficulty in giving an accurate pass.

Body Position

Once her opponent obtains the ball, pressure should be placed on her so that she is harassed immediately. The defense player moves close enough to the opponent so that she can touch the ball. She assumes the normal defensive body position, except that arm position is changed. The arm closer to the sideline is extended in that direction and the other arm reaches toward the player with the ball. Both arms and hands are supinated so that upward jabbing motions may be made at the ball. The hands should be moving constantly so that the opponent is harassed at all times.

The defense player takes her stance so that she forces her opponent toward the middle of the court. (If the reader prefers to force the opposition toward the sideline, the following descriptions for overplaying should be reversed so that the defender is inside her opponent.) Overplaying is accomplished by playing half a player to the outside of her opponent. This

Fig. 4.11 *Overplaying Half a Player. The ball handler prefers to drive to her right. The defender takes her stance half a player in that direction—i.e., her right foot is midway between her opponent's feet, and her left foot is to the left of her opponent's feet.*

Fig. 4.12 *Overplaying a Full Player. The defender places her right foot opposite the right foot of her opponent and her left foot outside either of her opponent's feet to encourage the dribble to drive toward the sideline or her nonpreferred direction.*

means that the defensive player is slightly outside of her opponent and closer to the sideline instead of being directly in line between opponent and basket. The defensive player should have her inside foot approximately in the middle of the opponent's stance and her outside foot outside of her opponent's outside foot (Fig. 4.11). If it is found that the opponent prefers to cut toward the sideline or to drive toward the sideline, it may be more desirable for the defensive player to play a full position outside of her opponent. This means that her inside foot is opposite her opponent's outside foot (Fig. 4.12). This technique of overplaying the offensive player dictates the manner in which the offense must be developed. It forces the opposing players to pass toward the center of the court and also to drive in that direction.

The overplaying position described in the above paragraph is a basic one. It is one that should be used under most circumstances. For reasons of team defense it may not be used by all players at all times. If a team wishes to trap the offensive players at the sideline, they would overplay to the inside. When a defender is guarding a weak shooter, she may drop off her to close passing lanes to other more dangerous players. A team may believe that it must close off the passing lane into a pivot player, in which case the defender guarding the player with the ball may take exception to the outside overplaying position. All of these decisions are matters of team defense, however, and will be discussed more fully in another chapter.

From her basic defensive stance the defender keeps her eyes focused on her opponent's hips. She makes

Fig. 4.13 *Poor Defensive Position. The defender has her weight forward as she reaches for the ball, which makes her susceptible to a fake and drive.*

upward jabbing motions at the ball to disconcert her opponent. In so doing, though, she must not overcommit herself and allow her weight to move onto the balls of her feet (Fig. 4.13). As she makes the jabbing motions, her weight must remain back so that she can retreat quickly. At no time in her effort to contact the ball should she move so that she is no longer between her opponent and the basket (Fig. 4.14). This is often done by beginners and permits the ball handler to pivot and drive for the basket. Emphasis must also be

157

a   b   c

Fig. 4.14 *Poor Defensive Action. The defender is in a good position (a). The ball handler pivots away from the basket, and the defender moves with her in an attempt to tie the ball (b). The defender places herself in an extremely poor position, as dark No. 3 can continue pivoting toward the lane and be free for a drive or shot (c).*

placed on the proper weight distribution described previously (page 146). Beginners often let their weight advance to their forward foot, and this is exactly what a ball handler hopes for. A simple fake and she is able to leave the defender behind. By keeping weight back, knees flexed, and hips low the defender can prevent this action by the ball handler. The defense player must also be aware of the possible fakes that an opponent might use. She should not be de-

ceived by the jab, crossover, or rocker steps, and must not become susceptible to head fakes. Keeping her eyes on the hips of her opponent helps her distinguish between a ruse or an intended move by the opponent.

The position of the defense player and the constant upward jabbing motion at the ball should cause the opponent some concern. The defender wants to harass her to such a degree that it is difficult for her to make an accurate pass. Once the offensive player releases

---

DRILLS FOR GUARDING AN OPPONENT WITH THE BALL

1. Two offensive players (guard and forward, guard and pivot, or forward and pivot) and their two opponents. No dribbling is permitted. The attack players pass back and forth while the defense players maintain proper defensive position. Change offensive and defensive players.

2. Two attack players in any of the positions described above and one defense player guarding the ball handler. The defender harasses her opponent, trying to make it difficult to pass accurately, and immediately slides back to prevent the give-and-go pass. Emphasis is placed on the quick movement backward. Alternate positions.

3. Two attack players opposed by two defense players in any of the positions described in drill 1. This drill is identical to drill 2, except that the give-and-go play is attempted by the attack players. Following the pass to her teammate, the player immediately cuts for the basket to receive a return pass. Emphasis is on the defensive player retreating as soon as her opponent makes the initial pass and preventing or intercepting the return pass to her.

the pass, the defense player must quickly move several steps backward and in the direction toward the ball (Fig. 4.15). This will place the defender in a good position to guard against the give-and-go play. If the offensive player makes no effort to cut toward the basket, then the defense player can be ready to assist her teammates if necessary.

Opponent Shoots

If an opponent is obviously going to attempt a shot, the defensive player moves in slightly, keeping her weight back, places one hand over the ball, and tries to prevent the opponent from raising the ball overhead. A shot is impossible if the offensive player cannot get the ball to that position. However, if the offensive player succeeds in getting the ball high, the defense player should again make an upward jabbing motion at the ball, trying to prevent a good shot.

When attempting to block a shot the defender should never leave her feet until she sees that the ball has left the hand of the shooter. Her jump should be made vertically and not forward into the opponent causing a foul and a possible three-point play. As she jumps she should attempt to block the shot with an upward motion made by her right hand if the shooter has released the ball from her right hand (Fig. 4.16). This action will save many fouls, as the defender turns partially in the air and lands facing the basket. A downward motion to block the ball should never be made because of the danger of fouling.

DEFENSE AGAINST THE DRIBBLER

Defending against a dribbler might have been included under the discussion of defense against a

| a | b | c |
| d | e | f |

Fig. 4.15 *Defensive Footwork. On a pass-and-cut tactic by the ball handler, the defender has used the crossover step* (b) *and the slide thereafter.*

Fig. 4.16 *Attempt to Block a Shot. The defender is evaded (a–c). She tries to block the right-hand shot with her right hand (d and e). This causes her to turn slightly to avoid a foul and places her in position to rebound.*

player with the ball, but it is considered of such importance that it is discussed separately. Every player on the court must be able to stop the advance of a dribbler. When an offensive player can constantly drive against her opponent, the defense is placed in an untenable position. It means that there can be no effective harassment of the player prior to a pass or shot, and it places extreme pressure on the other defenders to assist in the defense against the dribbler. It means that the defense is porous and susceptible to many varied attacks. Because of this, players must be determined in their efforts to halt the dribbler and practice religiously until they acquire the skill to do so.

Body Position

Body position in defending against the dribbler is identical to that of defending against a player with the ball. The defense player has her lead arm extended toward the sideline and her other arm toward the player with the ball. Her hands and arms are supinated, and she constantly makes upward jabbing motions at the ball—but not in a manner to overcommit herself so that the dribbler can easily change direction and evade her. Again, her weight must be evenly balanced so that the defense player can change direction with the dribbler. The body position in relation to the opponent should be one in which the defender overplays her toward the sideline either half a player or full player and forces her toward the center of the court.

If a dribbler begins to drive toward the defense player's forward foot, the defender should use a drop step to regain proper defensive position. This is done by pivoting on the rear foot and dropping the front foot back to the rear and sliding. This technique must be done quickly so that the dribbler does not gain a full step advantage (Fig. 4.17).

If an opponent is considerably faster, the defensive player may have to play her slightly loose. This means that the defense is weakened to that extent, but it is better to keep the dribbler under control in this fashion rather than permitting her to constantly evade a slower defense player.

It is difficult to keep an exceptional dribbler checked all of the time. If a dribbler starts to gain an advantage on the defender, it may be necessary for the defense player to run a few steps to regain her defensive position and then continue with the sliding technique to keep the dribbler under control (Fig. 4.18). If the defense player should lose the dribbler entirely due to a screen, she should immediately retreat to a position in line with the dribbler and the basket. She can recover good body position in this way and slide with her opponent as she approaches. If a teammate moves to guard the free dribbler, the player who was originally assigned to her should retreat toward the basket and help out defensively wherever needed.

Teammates must warn a player who is defending against a dribbler of the development of screens. Some ball handlers are particularly adept at driving their opponent into a lateral or rear screen set some distance from the ball handler. In order to cope with this situation the defender must have verbal help to learn where the screens have been set. It is also important for the defender to know in which direction her opponent prefers to drive. Most often players prefer to dribble to their right because they tend to be better dribblers with the right hand. This conjecture cannot be taken for granted until the action of the opponent bears it out. It should also be recognized by defenders that most players shoot right-handed and are freest when moving to the right. When driving to the right, they may have a half-step advantage on their opponent, which leaves their right hand free during an attempted shot. When they drive to their left and have a half-step advantage on their opponent and shoot with their right hand, they are actually bringing the ball back in range for the defender to block. For this reason defenders should be prepared to defend against the move by the opponent to her right to a greater extent than one to the opponent's left.

a

b

c

d

Fig. 4.17 *Drop Step. The defender slides with the dribbler (a and b). The dribbler does a crossover (c), and the defender drops the forward foot back to prepare for a slide to her right (d).*

161

Fig. 4.18 *Guarding a Dribbler. The defender starts in good position (a). She begins to lose position (b) and (c), runs (d and e), and moves to regain position (f and g).*

The defense player should also know the favorite spots from which the dribbler likes to shoot. She can expect the dribbler to use a variety of fakes or screens —to free herself so that she can dribble to or receive a pass in those positions. If the defender recognizes those favorite spots, she is less susceptible to fakes away from them and can better cope with the offensive players' ruses. She also may guard the dribbler differently if these spots are known. For example, if the dribbler likes to shoot from the top of the circle and starts to dribble toward the sideline to her left, the defense player may overplay her toward the center so that she is unable to change direction and drive to that spot. The defender has violated one of the previously stated principles by undertaking this overplay position toward the inside. In this case, however, such action has merit.

When guarding a dribbler, the defense player must be alert for the opponent to come to a quick stop and execute a jump shot. For this reason, it is important for the defense player to know the positions on the court where the offensive player is likely to attempt her shots. When the dribbler picks up the ball (catches it), the defender should move in closer, keep her weight back, and continue her upward jabbing motions at the ball. This action is taken to prevent the opponent from raising the ball into shooting position or to prevent her from making an easy pass.

When a defender is clearly beaten by a dribbler, an element of surprise may help the defender to disrupt the attack or help her team regain possession of the ball. If a defender is beaten on a change of direction dribble, she may take a step forward (away from the basket) and reach carefully behind the back of the

---

DRILLS FOR GUARDING THE DRIBBLER

1. Pairs. One dribbler and an opposing defense player. The dribbler starts at one end of the court and dribbles toward the opposite basket. She is required to stay within half of the court divided lengthwise. If the offensive player evades the defensive player, she should stop her dribble, permit the defensive player an opportunity to regain good defensive position, and then recommence her dribble. When the players reach the other end of the court they exchange responsibilities.

2. Same as drill 1 above, except the offensive player continues to drive toward the basket for a layup if she evades her opponent. The defense player runs to catch up and slides as good defensive position is attained.

3. Pairs. A dribbler is opposed by a defense player who must keep her hands on her waist or hips. The dribbler starts at one end of the court and uses a change of pace and change of direction as she proceeds down the court. The purpose of this excellent drill is to teach defense players the need for retaining good body position in relation to the dribbler. It is easy to spot those defense players who rely on an extension of their arms to keep a dribbler from penetrating.

4. A dribbler and an opponent in either corner position. The dribbler attempts to drive the baseline. By proper footwork and positioning, the defense player prevents that baseline drive and forces the opponent in toward the lane. Players should alternate positions.

5. A dribbler and opponent anywhere on the court. The dribbler is instructed to change direction several times and to suddenly pick up the ball. The purpose of this drill is to force the defensive player to make several directional changes and to move in quickly toward the dribbler once she picks up the ball. Change positions.

6. Groups of three—two attack players and one defense player guarding the dribbler. The dribbler is instructed to make several directional changes, stop, pick up the ball, pass to her teammate, and cut for the basket. The defensive player maintains good body position as she dribbles; moves in close to her when she picks up the ball; and, following the pass, immediately retreats several steps to prevent the give and go. Exchange positions.

Fig. 4.19 *Stealing a Dribble. The defender is overplaying the dribbler (a) and is clearly beaten as her opponent starts a reverse dribble (b). She moves so that her rear foot is even with the rear foot of her opponent and her other foot is in front of her opponent (c). This allows her to bat the ball toward a teammate without fouling (d).*

dribbler to bat the ball toward a teammate (Fig. 4.19). At another time when an opponent is dribbling downcourt, a defender can approach from the rear and to the side of the dribbler and intercept the dribble or bat the ball to a teammate. Both techniques are effective (Fig. 4.20).

Fast Break

The defense for stopping a dribbler on a fast break or following an interception is slightly different when a lone defender is in position while a single opponent approaches. It is the defense player's responsibility to delay the dribbler as long as possible so that other teammates have time to retreat. To assist in this process the defender overplays the dribbler toward the middle and attempts to force her toward the sideline so that her route to the basket is considerably lengthened. By jabbing at the ball the defender may be successful in causing the dribbler to pick up the ball. In this way the dribbler's forward progress is checked, and she is forced to shoot beyond the layup range or wait for a teammate to come downcourt to pass off.

It should be clearly recognized that a player in possession of the ball is extremely dangerous prior to the time she has dribbled. At this stage the defense player must be leary of the three possibilities previously mentioned (page 155). Once the offensive player has dribbled, one of her alternatives is reduced and the task of guarding her is considerably easier.

GUARDING THE POST PLAYER

Guarding an active post player who maneuvers well and who has a variety of shots is a difficult assignment. The most important task for the defender is to prevent the pivot player from receiving a pass. Since she operates primarily within 15 ft. of the basket, she is in an excellent scoring position should she get the ball. Nevertheless, it is extremely difficult to maintain a good defensive position against a post player who keeps moving.

Defense Against a Player in a High Post Position

An offensive player is in the high post position whenever she is 15 ft. or more from the basket. She usually stands with her back to the basket just beyond the free throw line or its extension. She may also move laterally or forward (away from the basket) to set a screen. Regardless of her exact position, she is considered to be in a high post position whenever she is beyond the free throw line. The ball is usually passed in to a high pivot by a guard.

The defensive player guarding a high post takes her

a

b

c

d

Fig. 4.20 *Stealing a Dribble. A defender approaches from the rear and to the side of the dribbler (a and b). She reaches forward with her inside hand (c) to bat the ball to a teammate and stops quickly to reverse direction (d).*

| a | b | c | d |

Fig. 4.21 *Guarding a Player in the High Post Position. The ball is to the defender's left (a). As the ball is passed to the other side, the defender slides her right foot behind the post player (b), takes a short step with her left foot (c), and slides her right foot even with the pivot's foot (d).*

stance on the ball side of the post player. One foot is even with the post player's foot and the other foot is to the rear of the pivot player. The arm on the ball side is extended in front of the pivot player, and the other arm is to the rear of the pivot. By keeping an arm in front of the pivot, the defender can discourage passes to her or force them to the weak side of the pivot (Fig. 4.21). If a guard passes to the other guard the defensive player slides behind the post player and returns to the same relative defensive position on the other side. On initiating the slide across the first step is always taken with the rear foot.

When a player is in a high post position she is generally used to feed cutters and is often outside her normal shooting range. Therefore, when the high post player receives the ball the defensive player can safely move 1 or 2 ft. behind her. The high post player is permitted to shoot from that position and is encouraged to do so if she lacks success. Of course, if successful on a number of shots the defensive player will be forced to contest each shot. However, if unsuccessful in her shooting attempts, the defender can drop off and assist her teammates as cutters scissor off her.

If a player in a high post position moves away from the free throw line either laterally or forward, she is generally moving in this direction to set a rear screen for a teammate. When this occurs the player guarding the post must warn a teammate of a possible screen and be ready to change opponents if this action is necessitated. If the pivot player is forced to cut toward the outer edge of the restraining circle to receive a pass, the defender has accomplished her purpose extremely well.

Defense Against a Player in the Medium Pivot Position

The medium post area is between 9 and 15 ft. from the basket. This area includes the area from the third lane space mark out to the free throw line and includes the portion of the restraining circle contained within the lane area. Because the medium post player is in an excellent position to shoot and pass off, it is extremely important that the defensive player prevent her from receiving the ball. Other defensive players must help to close the passing lanes into the medium pivot. The ball may be passed to a medium pivot by either a forward or a guard.

The defender must play on the ball side one-half player to the side of the post player. This means that her feet straddle either the rear foot (the one closer to the basket) or the forward foot of the pivot, depending upon the position of the ball. The defender has her front arm extended in front of the post player to deter any passes to her. The other arm is behind her (Fig. 4.22). She is effective in preventing a direct pass into the pivot from this position. This position, however, makes her vulnerable to a lob pass and she must have confidence that a teammate will assist her if this occurs (usually the weak side defending forward).

If the ball is passed around the perimeter to the other side of the court, the defense player must go behind (basket side of) the pivot before she regains her correct defensive position. If she goes in front of the pivot she is too susceptible to the lob pass. And, this is difficult to defend against from the middle of the lane.

Fig. 4.22 *Guarding a Player in the Medium Post Position. The defender straddles the near foot of the opponent (a). As the ball is passed from the guard to forward position, she slides her right foot behind the pivot player (b), slides her left foot toward her right foot (c), slides the right foot forward (d), and regains position (e).*

If the medium post gets the ball despite the efforts of the defender, the defender should move a step behind her and try to force her toward the sideline. By overplaying her, she tries to prevent her from moving into the lane area where the shooting percentage is much higher. This is particularly true when the pivot is to her left of the basket. When she is to her right of the basket and prefers to move to her right, the defender may overplay her toward the baseline and allow her to move toward the lane. In this case this should be more effective defensively.

The defensive player should be aware of any shooting limitations of the pivot. She should know the range from which she can shoot; and, when she is beyond that, the defender should allow her to shoot freely and protect against the post passing off to cutters. She can be extremely effective in this capacity.

Defense Against a Player in the Low Post Position

The low post area is within 9 ft. of the basket. Generally, a player is in this position to maneuver for good shots. She is rarely used as a passer to cutters because the passing lanes usually are closed due to the relatively close position to the basket. In this position the ball is passed in to the pivot from a forward, and when the pivot is unable to shoot she usually returns the ball to a forward.

Because any shooting done from this area generally results in a score, the defense player must prevent her opponent from receiving a pass. This means that the defender plays either in front of her opponent or three-

quarters. If a defender chooses to play in front of her opponent, she may either face the ball or her opponent. By facing the ball she is better able to see the total play and to assist in blocking shots near the basket and getting into position for rebounds. She cannot be as aware of her opponent, however. She can keep her opponent under control by facing her, but will be of little help to team defense. If her teammates can rebound well and it is important to prevent the low post from receiving a pass, this defensive posture may be advisable. Most often though, the defender plays her opponent three-quarters. The defensive player's rear foot is opposite the rear foot of the pivot and her other foot is comfortably advanced. Her arms are extended in the usual manner (Fig. 4.23).

When the opponents cannot pass the ball in to the pivot from one side, they often pass it around the perimeter to the forward on the other side and try to make the entry from there. When the ball is reversed to the other side, the defender must move in front of the pivot player rather than behind her. Lob passes are not as dangerous when the player is in this position because of the player's proximity to the basket. As the pivot player maneuvers to the opposite side of the free throw lane, the defending player steps in front of her by taking the first step with the rear foot. She slides across the free throw lane and then resumes her three-quarter defensive position by stepping back with the opposite foot. In the process of moving across the lane the defense player must not permit the pivot to receive a pass from a guard. The defender must stay ball side (in front) of her opponent as she moves across the lane. Once the low post player gets the ball she should be

a	b	c	d

Fig. 4.23 *Guarding a Player in the Low Post Position. An offensive guard has the ball* (a). *The ball is passed to a forward and light No. 3 pivots on her right foot and fronts her opponent* (b), *pivots on her left foot* (c), *and regains position* (d).

forced toward her weakest shooting side. Generally when the pivot is to her right of the basket, the defender should force her back toward the middle by overplaying her toward the baseline. When the pivot is to her left of the basket, the defender usually should overplay her toward the middle and force her toward the baseline. If the pivot player's actions do not substantiate this action by the defense, the defender should adjust her position to become more effective.

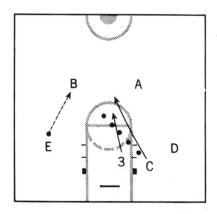

Fig. 4.24 *Defense Against a Pivot to Force Her Wide of Her Desired Cut. The dotted line shows the cut desired by C. By floating away from C, player No. 3 can beat her on her cut and force her higher than the free throw line.*

Other Thoughts About Pivot Defense

Against a pivot player in any position the defender guards her with one arm extended in front of her. The purpose of this posture is to discourage a pass in to the pivot. The pass must be toward the weak side and extremely accurate in order to be successful. This often causes the pivot player to fake and/or cut to another position so that she might be free before the defender can resume this position again. This constant maneuvering becomes frustrating to a pivot who has difficulty getting free.

One of the real advantages of this posture is that it forces the pivot to readjust her position frequently. If she is not trained to accomplish this, she may be rendered ineffective for the game. Of course, the defender cannot hold the pivot in any way as she attempts to maneuver. The defender must lower her arm and allow the pivot to cut. As the pivot moves, however, she is forced away from the basket, which generally reduces her effectiveness. This, of course, is favorable for the defense.

Whenever the ball is on the weak side, the defender should anticipate a cut by the pivot player to receive a pass. The defender should ascertain where the cutting lane exists and beat her opponent to the position where she would like to receive the pass. A pivot should never be allowed to cut where she would like. The defender must contest the cut legally and be one step ahead of the pivot. By floating away from her opponent when the ball is on the weak side, she is able to gain this desirable position (Fig. 4.24). It is almost imperative that the pivot be unable to receive a pass

---

DRILLS FOR GUARDING THE POST PLAYER

1. Two guards and one pivot player in a high post position, each with a defender opposing her. The two guards pass the ball back and forth to one another and attempt to get the ball into the post player. The defender against the post player changes her position as the ball is passed from one guard to another and tries to prevent the ball from being passed into the post player. If the post player receives the pass, the defender moves back a step and allows the post to take a shot from that position. If the pivot player decides not to shoot but rather to drive, the defense player guards her and tries to force her away from her most successful shooting spots. After the shot is taken, the defensive player blocks her opponent out. The two guards are not permitted to cut toward the basket at this stage. The purpose of this drill is to assist the post player's opponent in regaining proper defensive position as the ball is passed from one guard to the other.

2. Five offensive players and five defensive players. No cutting is permitted by the offensive players. Their purpose is to pass the ball around the perimeter in an attempt to find an opening to get the ball into the post player. The post player starts in a high post position and may move to any position she desires in order to receive a pass. The defense player must play her accordingly.

3. Five offensive players against one defensive player guarding the post player. The post player plays only in a medium post position and maneuvers from one side of the free throw lane to the other in order to receive a pass. The purpose of this drill is to assist the defensive player in moving from playing the post player half a player on the left side of the court to playing half a player on the right side of the court. Emphasis must be placed on the defensive player moving behind the post player when she moves across the lane and regaining proper positioning as rapidly as possible. She also must understand that while she is maneuvering behind the post player under normal conditions she will have defensive help from her teammates so that it is not as easy to get a pass into the post player as it appears in this particular drill.

4. Five offensive players and their opponents with the pivot player in the low post position. The offensive players pass the ball around the perimeter in an attempt to get the ball into the post by means of a pass from one of the forwards. The post player maneuvers from one side of the key to the other but tries to stay in a low post position. The defense player moves in front of the pivot in this instance so that she is between the ball and her opponent to prevent a pass from reaching the pivot while she is in the free throw lane. The defense player constantly tries to front the pivot whenever she is in a low post position. If the post player gets the ball in this position, the defender tries to force her in the appropriate direction.

in the lane. Her favorable position almost assures her of scoring.

The defender against the pivot should never leave her opponent to help a teammate unless an opponent is going in for an uncontested shot. In this case she may attempt to harass the opponent or block the shot, but one of her teammates (usually the weak side forward) must block out the pivot player.

DEFENSIVE REBOUNDING

Individual defense players must learn the value of good defensive rebounding. Defense players will often concentrate and work extremely hard to prevent their opponent from receiving a pass or prevent her from taking a high percentage shot. Frequently, however, as soon as a shot is attempted, they relax slightly, per-

a

b

c

Fig. 4.25 *Blocking Out. The defenders face their opponent for an instant after the shot* (a), *pivot to keep their opponent behind them* (b), *and go for the rebound* (c).

mitting the offensive players to maneuver for the rebound. This can be extremely disheartening for a defense that has caused the opponents to work for 20–25 sec. and forced an outside shot, only to find they score a rather easy layup following the rebound.

Blocking Out

It has been said many times and by many people that many games are won or lost "on the boards." Although this statement applies to both offensive and defensive rebounding, the implication for superior defensive rebounding is clear. Regardless of the type of defense being played, the defense players are closer to the basket than their opponents (except a defender against a low or medium pivot) and, therefore, are in a better position to secure the rebound. Whenever a shot is attempted, they must continue to exert pressure so that their opponent cannot move in toward the basket to obtain the rebound. This pressure is established by moving into the path of the opponent, thus preventing her from gaining that advantage. The concentration and effort that rebounding demands can be developed if players acquire the attitude that the opponents should never get more than one shot on offense. They will not always succeed in their effort, but if *every* defense player concentrates on blocking out her opponent on *every* attempted shot, there will be few easy offensive tip-ins or rebounds.

When playing man-to-man defense, rebounding assignments are relatively easy to establish. Each player is responsible for keeping her opponent away from the backboard. This can be accomplished if each defensive player always keeps her eye on the ball. By doing this she can see each time a shot is taken and can turn immediately so that one shoulder is perpendicular to her opponent. From this position she can see in what direction her opponent starts to cut toward the basket. As the offensive player makes her move, the defensive player pivots directly in to her path so that the defensive player is facing the basket with her opponent behind her. The defense player pivots on one foot, swings her other leg across in front of the opponent's path, and assumes a wide stance to cause the opponent to move in a wide arc around her (Fig. 4.25). As the offensive player maneuvers toward the goal, the defender uses sliding steps to retain her favorable position. Once this position is attained the assigned defensive players move toward the basket for the rebound. Some teams assign only three players to obtain the rebound while other teams use four. Regardless of the number who advance toward the basket, the passing lanes should be open so that a pass can be made successfully toward the sideline once the rebound is gained.

Fig. 4.26 *Starting a Fast Break. The defenders are in position for the rebound, and it appears as though it will go to dark No. 1 (a and b). Dark No. 3 cuts for an open space as the rebounder prepares to pass (c). The fast break is underway as dark No. 4 cuts for the next pass (d). Note how dark No. 2 moves to block out her opponent (b–d).*

Each time a player blocks out an opponent who makes no effort to rebound, she remains in her position perpendicular to her opponent no longer than 2 sec. She can estimate that time by counting one thousand and one, one thousand and two, and then pivot to face the basket so that her attention is focused on the ball as it hits the backboard or rim. If she delays longer, she will not be in position to rebound, and a smart offensive player who observes a defender's tardy pivot will continue to maneuver on subsequent shots so that the defensive player does not pivot in time to be of assistance in rebound responsibilities. The 2-sec. period is an arbitrary one that is usually used on long shots for the time it takes the ball in flight to reach the goal. On shorter range shots the time should be reduced to 1 sec., more or less. As players gain experience in playing, they will acquire the timing necessary to be in proper position.

Specific Rebounding Responsibilities

Guards

A team that can rely on its forwards and pivot player to secure the rebound should not require either of its guards to rebound. Their responsibility is to cut to receive the outlet pass and try to start a fast break attack. If a team does not possess strong rebounders, one of the guards may be assigned to cover the area near the free throw line. The offensive team usually keeps one of its guards back for defensive measures in case the ball is lost, so that one defensive guard generally does not move for a rebound.

When either of the offensive forwards or pivot player shoots, the offensive guards usually remain back. In this instance the defensive guards hold their perpendicular position for the 2-sec. period and then

171

pivot to see if either is able to secure a rebound. If so, the player recovers it quickly and attempts a pass to her other guard to start a fast break. If the ball is rebounded by any of their teammates, the appropriate guard cuts to the sideline for the outlet pass.

When one of the offensive guards shoots, she generally rebounds so that her opponent must use correct blocking out techniques. The other offensive guard will remain back and her opponent pivots after 2 sec. and is prepared to cover a wide rebound or move for the outlet pass.

Forwards

Offensive forwards always rebound, and their opponents must block them out on every shot. If a defense player's own forward shoots, or if any other offense player one pass away shoots, the defensive player is close to her opponent and can follow the techniques described to block her out. If the player who shoots is two passes away, the defense player will have sagged off her opponent. Therefore, she takes a step or two toward her opponent so that she meets her sooner than if she waited for her opponent to move toward the basket. As she approaches her opponent, she pivots in to her path and retains her favorable position as she moves toward the basket.

Pivot

The opposing pivot player always rebounds so that her opponent must block her out on every shot. Basically, her opponent is never more than one pass away from the ball; therefore, the defense player has

---

DRILLS FOR DEFENSIVE REBOUNDING

1. Each player does a series of ten short jumps followed by ten high jumps. Repeat this process for a designated number of times or until a predetermined time has elapsed. The purpose of this drill is to develop both leg strength and the explosive power necessary for rebounding.

2. The sargent jump and reach test or other similar test can be used to measure a player's jumping ability or to record progress.

3. Columns of four or five players. The first player in each column has a ball. That player tosses the ball against the backboard and each player in turn moves forward, jumps, tips the ball against the backboard, and tries to keep the ball in play. Continue until the ball can no longer be controlled; restart the drill.

4. A player with the ball near the backboard tosses the ball and, by constantly tapping the ball against the backboard, keeps it in play as long as possible. Allow players to rest while others attempt the same drill. To increase the difficulty of the drill once players acquire success, the player should attempt to tap the ball from the right side of the basket to the left side and continue to alternate sides as long as possible.

5. Two forwards and a pivot player and their opponents. The teacher/coach has the ball. A shot is attempted whereupon the defensive players pivot slightly so that one shoulder is perpendicular to the opponent. They eye their opponent for a split second and then pivot in the direction of their opponent's cut for the rebound. As a defense player gets the rebound, she should return to the floor with her elbows extended outward.

6. Two forwards, a pivot player, and their opponents. One of the attack players has the ball and is permitted to shoot. The defense players immediately block out and move for the rebound.

7. Columns of four to five players standing 8–12 ft. from the basket and behind lines placed on the floor 4–5 ft. in front of the basket on each side of the basket. In turn players run forward to the line, jump for the rebound, and attempt to gain the V

little opportunity to sag off her opponent. Therefore, she utilizes the same technique described previously to block out her opponent. This task is easiest when the opposing pivot is playing in the high post position. Here the defense player is behind her or closer to the basket and in a good position to block out properly. As the offensive pivot player moves down to the middle or low post position, the defender's problems are increased. By playing one-half, three-quarters, or a full player in front of the offensive pivot in these positions the defender no longer is closer to the basket than her opponent and the offensive player has a clear advantage in rebounding.

When the post player is in a medium pivot position and a shot is taken on the far side (side away from the pivot), the post defender should be between her opponent and the ball and able to obtain good rebound-

ing position. When the medium pivot player shoots or the shot comes from the near side (on the same side as the pivot) the defender will be half a step in front of her. She must obtain good rebounding position as best she can. She pivots on her rear foot, swings her other foot across to form a wide stride, and tries to keep her opponent behind her.

When the offensive pivot player is in the low post position, she is always in better rebounding position than her opponent regardless of who shoots since her opponent plays her three-quarters to a full player in front. This means that when a shot is taken, the defender must attempt to neutralize the effectiveness of her opponent's rebounding efforts. At the same time the offensive pivot player is in position to block out the defensive player's moves. Nevertheless, the defender must pivot, preferably toward the middle, and

position. Later a ball is tossed toward the backboard so that the player may time her jump with the descent of the basketball.

8. One forward or pivot player and her opponent. The attack player tries to maneuver one-on-one and follow her shot for the rebound. The defense player blocks her out; after gaining possession of the rebound, she pivots away from the offensive player who attempts to guard her.

9. Two attack players and two defense players playing two-on-two. Any time the offensive players attempt a shot, the defensive players block out and move into position for the rebound. Later, add another attack and defense player.

10. Two defense players, preferably one forward or a pivot player, stationed 5–6 ft. from the basket. A guard is stationed near one of the sidelines. A third player or manager tosses the ball against the backboard while the pivot player (forward) moves in for the rebound. The rebounder attempts to acquire a secure grasp on the ball, turns in the air, and passes to the guard near the sideline. During the early learning stages of this drill, the shooter must insure that the ball rebounds on the same side of the basket, as the guard is located so that poor passing techniques (passing the ball across the basket) are not developed or encouraged.

11. Same as drill 10 above, except the guard starts out in front of the keyhole prior to the time the shot is taken. As it becomes apparent that the pivot player is going to gain possession of the rebound, the guard cuts to the sideline to receive the outlet pass. Later, if desirable, the other guard is added so that she can cut toward the middle of the court to receive the second pass for the start of a fast break.

12. Same as drill 11 above, only add opponents against players involved. Following the shot, defense players must block out prior to their assigned moves.

13. Five attack players and five defensive players. The offensive players run a designated set of offensive plays or maneuvers and attempt shots whenever the opportunity arises. Emphasis is placed on the defensive players blocking out, rebounding properly, and making a quick outlet pass.

attempt to position herself beside her opponent so that she has an equal chance of gaining the rebound. If this cannot be accomplished, she must maneuver to find an opening.

Obtaining the Rebound

Although it is not always possible, ideally, a defense player should be moving forward at the time she goes up for the rebound. This means that as she moves toward the backboard for the rebound she should slow down or stop about 7 ft. from the basket if she has arrived before the ball will descend. She takes a firm side stride position with her knees and hips flexed, arms raised, and elbows at shoulder height. From this position she can jump forward for the rebound. This action prevents a taller opponent from reaching over her head to obtain the rebound or tie it up. The ball will rebound over her head to an opponent if the rebounder is too close to the backboard. As the defense player jumps forward with her arms stretched high and forward, her legs also reach forward so that her body is in more or less a V position with the buttocks forming the point of the V. In this position the ball can be grasped firmly and the rebounder may turn on her descent to make a quick outlet pass toward the sideline before she returns to the floor. Obviously, she must have good body control in order to make the turn in the air and she must be certain that the passing lane is open before passing to a teammate. This type of outlet pass following the rebound is of great value for any team that likes to use a fast break (Fig. 4.26). If the passing lane is not open, or if the rebounder does not have clear possession of the ball, the outlet pass should not be attempted while the rebounder is still in the air. In this case, as she returns to the floor her elbows extend outward so that the ball is better protected. Upon landing, the rebounder immediately looks for a free teammate and an open passing lane. If a pass seems unwise, the rebounder moves as rapidly as possible away from the basket, preferably toward the nearest sideline. If upon landing, the rebounder discovers that she is in a congested area, she should bring the ball close to her chest with elbows extended outward, and she should combine pivots and fakes to give further protection to the ball. However, some coaches prefer that a tall player keep the ball above shoulder level while a short player lower the ball to the floor for greater ball security. Once the opponents move away from the defensive area the player may either dribble or pass to a free teammate.

5

Two-, Three-, and Four-Player Defensive Tactics

Many offensive maneuvers involve two, three, or four players utilizing screens and double cuts (scissors) while attempting to free an attack player momentarily for a good shot. Defense against these maneuvers must be coordinated between the players involved.

There are other occasions when the defense may be placed in a weakened position. This may occur when the opponents move downcourt with a four-on-three, three-on-two, or two-on-one break. The defenders must combine their efforts to prevent the easy layup under these conditions.

DEFENSE AGAINST SCREEN PLAYS

The means of coping with the offensive action is dependent upon the type of screen that is set, and is partially dependent upon the site of the screen. Basically, there are four ways of defending against screens. The defender being screened may

1. move over the top of the screen (stay between her opponent and the screener)
2. slide through (go between the screener and the screener's opponent)
3. slide behind the screen (go behind the screener and the screener's opponent)
4. switch (exchange opponents)

A screening situation may arise any time a player dribbles or cuts toward a teammate. As the reader knows, the player may move toward her teammate to

set a screen for her, or she may move to use her teammate as a screen. The player may move between her teammate and her opponent; she may move behind both her teammate and her teammate's opponent or she may set a side screen for her teammate. She also has the option of going behind her teammate so that her teammate screens for her. As an offensive player moves toward a teammate, the defense players opposing them must anticipate a screen whether or not it actually develops.

As an offensive player moves to set a screen, her opponent is responsible for warning her teammate of the impending screen. She calls out "Screen." Her teammate will know from which side the screen will be set depending on the direction from which her voice comes. Some teams prefer to call "Screen left" or "Screen right" to designate the direction from which the screen is coming. Regardless of the technique used, the defense player guarding the screener is responsible for informing her teammate of the potential screen so that she may take measures to avoid or at least minimize the screen's effectiveness.

At no time should a player who is two passes away from the ball be screened. A successful screen against her indicates that she has a poor defensive position (Fig. 5.1). A defense player who is two passes away from the ball should sag or float away from her opponent and open slightly toward the ball. In this position, the defense player can see any potential screener approaching and should be able to avoid the screen (Fig. 5.2).

175

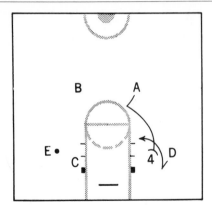

Fig. 5.1 *Poor Defensive Position by Player No. 4, Who Is Guarding D, a Player Two Passes Away from the Ball. Her poor positioning allows player A to set a lateral screen to free player D. This should never occur under these circumstances.*

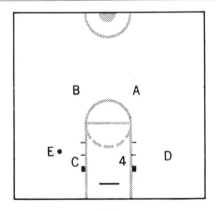

Fig. 5.2 *Proper Positioning by Player No. 4. Her opponent D is two passes away from the ball, so No. 4 has floated toward the ball. If player A attempts to screen No. 4, it will be ineffective, as No. 4 has plenty of space to avoid the screen.*

Defense Against a Side or Lateral Screen

The greatest pressure can be exerted against the side screen when the defense player goes over the top of the screen. This means that she must go between her opponent and the screener. By doing this, she forces the offensive player to protect the ball to a greater degree and may cause her opponent to move slightly wider of the screen. If the offensive player has a good outside shot, this method of dealing with the screen may be necessary. On the other hand, if the offensive player is much quicker than the defensive player, this method may be treacherous. The offensive player may gain a half-step advantage due to the screen and may be beyond the defensive player before she can maneuver into good defensive position.

Over the Top

This may be facilitated by any one of several practices. First, the defensive player to be screened may take a step back from her opponent as she hears her teammate call "Screen." She takes a step forward toward her opponent just before the screen is set. A lateral screen is most effective when the defense player is guarding her opponent tightly; it is much less effective when the defense player is guarding loosely, because there is space into which the defense player can move. By taking the backward step the defense player places herself in a looser defensive position and, therefore, can more easily go over the top of the screen. By

delaying her move over the top until just before the screen is set, she can force the screener to continue in her same predetermined path; thus, the screen will be set behind the movement of the defense player. If the screener changes her path at this stage, she probably will be called for blocking because the defense player has already started to move in a new direction (Fig. 5.3).

The defense player guarding the player to be screened may also move up very close to her opponent as a means of coping with the lateral screen. If this technique is used the defender must have help from her teammate who jumps in front of the offensive player freed by the screen for an instant to delay her progress and then quickly returns to guarding her own player. This action provides the defender who is screened with time to go over the top of the screen to stay with her own opponent (Fig. 5.4). Much practice must be devoted to this method, for the timing of the moves is critical.

Another method that aids the defense player in going over the top is by her moving one-half or whole player to the ball side of her opponent. This forces the screen to be set further from the player for whom it is intended, and forces the offensive player to take more steps before she is around the screen. This provides the defense player with additional time to move over the top to stay with her opponent. This position by the defense player makes her vulnerable to a cut or drive away from the screen, so she must anticipate this action by her opponent.

Fig. 5.3 *Going Over the Top. Dark No. 5 moves to set a lateral screen (a and b). Light No. 3 anticipates it and moves closer to her opponent (c), and is in good defensive position against her opponent (d).*

Behind the Screen

A weaker means of dealing with the side screen occurs when the screened defense player goes behind the screen. This movement permits the offensive player to take an open outside shot. If she is inaccurate from this range, however, nothing is lost. This method may be desirable also, if the defense player is much slower than her opponent.

In order to defend effectively in this manner, the defense player to be screened must move a half to a whole player to the ball side of her opponent before the screen is set. She also opens toward the direction from which the screen is coming so that she can move more quickly behind the screen (Fig. 5.5). By moving toward the screener she forces the offensive player

for whom the screen is set to take additional steps before she can utilize the screen. Once again this allows the defense player time to recover good defensive position, but she must be alert for a cut away from the screen. This is particularly true in this situation, since the defender has opened her stance. This makes her considerably more vulnerable to the cut away from the screen.

The technique of overplaying (moving one-half or a full player) toward the side of the screen is useful when back court players are setting screens for each other. It is less useful and probably undesirable when a back court or pivot player sets a screen for a forward in the corner. Since the screen generally comes from the middle area, it leaves the baseline open for the forward to drive away from the screen. Most

177

Fig. 5.4 *Going Over the Top. Light No. 5 is guarding dark No. 3 (a). Light No. 3 takes a step out in front of the ball handler to force her to go wide around the screen (b and c). This enables light No. 5 to go over the top (d and e) and regain good position (f). In (d–f), note that light No. 3 has moved quickly to front her opponent.*

Fig. 5.5 *Going Behind the Screen. Defender No. 5 has moved half a player toward the direction from which the screen is coming (a and b). As her opponent drives toward the screen, light No. 3 takes a step back which allows light No. 5 to slide through (c and d), and regain position (e).*

179

coaches prefer that the offense be stopped at the baseline and therefore would not encourage or permit their players to utilize this practice in this situation.

Switching

A switching type defense is another means of counteracting a screen's effectiveness. Switching simply implies that the two defensive players exchange opponents following the screen. This technique should be used rarely and then only when absolutely necessary. In other words, it should not be used as the fundamental method for dealing with the screen. A switch should be necessary only when the defense player being screened has not adequately avoided the screen.

It should be apparent that a defensive switch between two guards may not be as dangerous as a switch between a guard and a forward. In the latter instance, one defense player is often left guarding a player much taller than she. If an opposing team knows that a team normally switches on screen maneuvers, they will plan to utilize guard-to-forward screens to effect this height advantage.

Generally, it is the responsibility of the defense player guarding the screener to call for the switch. However, some coaches believe that either player should be given that privilege. In any case, the teammate must react to the switch once it is called, and carry out her new responsibility regardless of whether she thought the switch was necessary. There is no time to question the decision. Once the switch is called, the defense player guarding the screener must move close to the screener so that the other offensive player cannot drive between her and the screener. From this point she must maintain good defensive position against her new opponent. The defense player being screened must move quickly to the rear of the screener immediately after the switch is called so that she will be able to defend against the subsequent roll. At the same time she must also be ready to guard her former opponent if she decides to drive away from the screen (toward the opposite side). As the screener rolls for the basket, the defender must be particularly conscious of preventing a bounce pass to the rolling player, and her teammate must prevent the lob pass. She does this by raising her arms high in the air as soon as the dribbler catches the ball (Fig. 5.6). The two defense players involved may obtain additional help from a weak side defender when the switch is necessary.

Defense Against a Back Screen

As the reader knows, the back screen occurs when an offensive player cuts behind a teammate who has the ball, or when a player dribbles behind her teammate. The method of defending against this action is the same in both instances but will be described in terms of the player cutting behind her teammate with the ball, since this is the way in which it develops most

---

DRILLS FOR A LATERAL SCREEN

The technique for counteracting this type of screen should be clearly presented to the students on a blackboard or magnetic board, in a "live" demonstration, or a combination of these means. Only one method should be introduced and then practiced. Other methods may be presented and practiced later. The following drills provide a progression that is adaptable for any of the methods described.

1. Two offensive guards and their opponents. One guard passes to her teammate and walks over to set a screen. The defender moves over the top of the screen as the dribbler moves slowly. The screener rolls toward the basket and her opponent stays ball side of her. Repeat to the other direction.

2. Repeat drill 1 above, only permit the players to move at normal speed.

3. Repeat drill 2 above, only the dribbler moves away from the screen.

4. Repeat drill 2 above, only allow the dribbler to move in either direction.

5. One offensive guard and one offensive forward and their opponents. Repeat drills 1 and 2 above.

6. Repeat these drills, utilizing a different technique of combatting the screen.

Fig. 5.6 *Switching. Dark No. 3 is guarded by light No. 3 (a and b). Dark No. 5 sets a screen on light No. 3 (c). Light No. 5 switches to guard dark No. 3 (c and d). Light No. 3 moves quickly to front her new opponent, dark No. 5 (e) and makes the interception (f).*

often. The basic defense against the back screen is known as "slide through."

The defense player guarding the player with the ball takes a step back toward the basket to allow her teammate to slide through between her and the player with the ball. As the defense player slides through, she keeps her hands active to discourage the ball handler from shooting. As she slides through she must be alert to a change of direction by her opponent and a cut back toward the side from which she started. This action is not usually taken by the offense; but, if the defense player predetermines where she will move on a specific play, she leaves herself open to the directional change by her opponent. When the player completes her slide through, the defense player guarding the player with the ball returns to her normal defensive position (Fig. 5.7).

Defense Against an Inside Screen

To defend against an inside screen in which a player moves between a teammate and her opponent, the defense has two choices:

1. they may permit the long shot and protect against the drive and roll
2. they can prevent the long shot and recover against the roll

If the defense selects the former method, they must know that the player, who is freed by the screen, does not have an accurate outside shot or that she is beyond her normal shooting range. As the offensive player

moves to set the inside screen, the two defense players move shoulder to shoulder to prevent a cut between them. Once they attain this position they remain there and encourage the player with the ball to take the long shot. If the offensive player chooses not to do so and starts to drive, her own opponent must quickly maneuver to guard her. There is no problem if she cuts away from the direction from which the screen was set. If she moves toward the direction from which the screen was set, her teammate must drop back a step to allow her to slide through between her teammate and the screener. The other defense player moves quickly to get ball side of the screener (her own opponent). For these situations, neither defense player should have difficulty in regaining good defensive position.

If the player for whom the screen is set is a good outside shooter, the problem for the defense is magnified. As the screen is set the two defenders once again must come shoulder to shoulder to prevent the cut between them. Then, one of the defenders must move to guard the outside shooter. If the game plan calls for forcing the attack toward the middle, the outside defender (the one closer to the side line) makes the first move. As this is done, the offensive player with the ball will probably commence her drive in the opposite direction—i.e., toward the middle. The defense player must hustle to attain a good defensive position but needs help at this stage to delay the drive of the player with the ball. The defender's teammate helps by jumping forward, causing the dribbler to slow her progress and make a wider turn than she

---

DRILLS FOR A BACK SCREEN

1. Two offensive guards and their opponents. One guard passes to her teammate and cuts behind her for a hand-off. The screener's defender moves one step back to permit her teammate to slide through. Emphasis should be on the timing of the defender's backward and return step so that she does not leave her opponent with the ball unguarded either before or after her teammate has moved through. Repeat in the other direction.

2. Same as drill 1 above, only permit the player who receives the hand-off to reverse direction so that the defender must adjust.

3. Same as drill 1 above, only let the player receiving the hand-off move in any direction she wishes.

4. Same as drill 1 above, only the player who receives the initial pass fakes the hand-off and retains possession and attempts a shot if she is free or dribbles in any direction.

5. Repeat the same drills with an offensive forward and offensive guard and their opponents.

Fig. 5.7 *Back Screen. Light No. 5 passes to her teammate and starts behind her (a). As her intention becomes clear, dark No. 3 takes a step back (b) to allow her teammate to pass through as the ball is handed to light No. 5 (c). Dark No. 5 has regained defensive position (d).*

desires. This provides the dribbler's opponent with the time necessary to regain good defensive positioning. Following the jump forward, the other defense player quickly retreats and stays ball side of the screener (Fig. 5.8).

There is an alternate method of defending against this situation. The procedure is identical to that already described—up to the point where one guard moves forward to prevent the long shot and her teammate jumps forward to delay the offensive player's drive for the basket. At this stage the defender who jumps forward continues to defend against the dribbler while the other player quickly adjusts her position to get ball side of the screener. This method may or may not result in a switch of defensive

assignments, depending upon which defensive player initially confronts the player with the ball. If it is team practice to force the opponents toward the inside, a switch in assignments will occur with use of this practice.

If a screener dribbles over to set an inside screen and hands off to a teammate behind her, the defense usually switches to counteract this action (Fig. 5.9).

Defense Against an Outside or Rear Screen

The outside or rear screen is generally set by a pivot player or a forward opposite the free throw line at the edge of the lane or approximately 3 ft. outside the lane. The screen is usually set to allow a guard to free

183

Fig. 5.8 *Inside Screen. Light No. 5 moves to set an inside screen (a and b). Dark No. 5 steps forward to cause light No. 3 to make a wider arc on her drive as No. 3 moves around the screen (c and d). Dark No. 3 regains position as her teammate returns to her own opponent (e and f).*

Fig. 5.9 *Inside Screen. Light No. 5 dribbles, hands off, and sets an inside screen for No. 3 (a–c). Dark No. 3 starts to move around the screen (d). Dark No. 5 moves to stop the drive of No. 3 as dark No. 3 moves to get ball side of her opponent (e–f).*

DRILLS FOR AN INSIDE SCREEN

1. Two offensive guards (or one forward and one guard) and their opponents, both of whom are guarding loosely. Neither offense player has a good outside shot, so the defense allows the long shot. One player dribbles over between her teammate and her opponent and hands off to her teammate. Emphasis should be placed on the defender guarding the dribbler to move shoulder to shoulder with her teammate. From this position they allow the long shot. Repeat in the other direction.

2. Same as drill 1 above, only the offensive player recognizes that she has not been successful in shooting from that distance and is instructed to move away from the side from which the screen was set. Emphasis is on her defender moving with her (which should not be difficult) and on her teammate obtaining a position between the screener and the ball.

3. Same as drill 1 above, only the offensive player with the ball moves toward the direction from which the screen was set. Emphasis is placed on the player guarding the screener retreating one step so that her teammate may regain defensive position more quickly. The defender against the screening player must then maintain a fronting position on her opponent.

4. Two offensive guards and their opponents, both guarding loosely. The two attack players are known as good outside shooters; the defenders, therefore, must utilize a different method of defense. The team has decided to force the dribbler toward the middle, so the outside defender moves to guard the player with the ball. Emphasis is on the timing of the moves of the defenders—the move forward by the outside defender, the jump forward by the other defender, and her quick return to her own opponent while her teammate gains good defensive position. Repeat to the other side.

5. Same as drill 4 above, only the inside defender moves forward to guard the player with the ball and the outside defender jumps forward to delay her. Repeat to the other side.

6. Same as drill 4 or 5 above (but stipulate which one), only allow the dribbler to maneuver if she can and reverse direction on her dribble. Repeat on the other side.

7. Two offensive guards (or one forward and one guard) and their opponents, both guarding loosely. This drill is the same as drill 4 above, only the defender who jumps forward to delay the dribbler stays with her while her teammate must front the other attack player. Emphasis is on the timing involved. Repeat on the other side. Repeat also with the other defender jumping forward.

8. Two offensive guards (or one forward and one guard) and their opponents, both guarding loosely. Allow the player with the ball to dribble in any direction and reverse direction if possible. The defender in the better defensive position guards her while the other defender obtains a fronting position on the screener. Repeat on the other side.

herself by cutting or driving around the screen. The offensive team usually prefers to fake toward the outside since there is less congestion in that area. The defense, in contrast, wants to prevent the cut or drive to the outside and wants to overplay if possible to force the guard in toward the middle where there is additional defensive help.

If a guard has the ball and the pivot or forward

cuts up to the extension of the free throw line, there is a potential screening situation and the screener's opponent must warn her teammate. The defender opposing the dribbler must overplay her toward the outside so that she cannot maneuver in that direction. At the same time, she must prevent her from driving to the inside of the screen to the basket and may need help for this task from the far side forward and guard. The pivot player's defender may hedge also (taking one step toward the inside). If the dribbler is cut off on the inside and starts toward the outside, her opponent must go over the top of the screen. As the dribbler makes her move in this direction, the screener's defender may help her teammate by hedging to force the dribbler to go wide of the screen. The hedger, however, must move back immediately to defend against her own player. At the same time, the defensive guard is able to cut close to the screener to regain defensive position against her driving opponent (Fig. 5.10). Should a switch be necessary, the hedger stays with the dribbler on her drive toward the basket. The defensive guard switches to guard the screener and must maintain a fronting position against the screener and be prepared to intercept a bounce pass to her. The switch should be made as a last resort only, since it commits a shorter player against a taller opponent.

The defense against a rear screen when a guard passes to the screener is basically the same. The defender makes every effort to force the cutter in toward the lane area. After the pass goes in to the screener, the defense player must stay between the screener and her opponent so that she is in a position to intercept a pass.

Similar action is taken by the defensive guard when a forward in the corner has the ball and the pivot player sets the rear screen at the extension of the foul line. In this instance the offensive guard usually fakes toward the middle and cuts around the screener toward the outside to receive a pass from the forward with the ball. The defender guarding the screener must warn her teammate at the start of this maneuver, and the teammate must stay between her opponent and the ball throughout the entire cut by the offensive player.

Drills for an Outside or Rear Screen

Each of the possible rear screens involving the guard and a pivot should be practiced. This should include the guard dribbling to use the screen, passing in to the pivot to receive a return pass, and using the pivot as a screen to receive a pass from the forward. Each one should be tried in order with the two or three offensive players involved and their opponents. Emphasis should be placed on hedging by the pivot defender, prevention of the inside cut and the guard's defender going over the top of the screen, and regaining defensive position quickly. It should be recognized that it is difficult to prevent the inside drive completely without additional help from the other defenders who sag and float; therefore, it may be wise to curtail the guard's move in this direction. Repeat on the other side.

Defense Against Double Screens

Double screens can be extremely troublesome to the defense. These are commonly established along the side of the lane by a pivot player and forward, or along the free throw line by a pivot player and either a forward or guard. The double screen set along the lane line provides the greatest difficulty for the defense. The play usually starts with the weak side guard passing to the strong side guard as a double screen is being set. At the same time the weak side forward cuts across the free throw lane under the basket and cuts up close to the double screen to receive the pass.

The defense players guarding the screeners must alert their teammates as the double screen is set. The defender guarding the screener closer to the basket may also hedge slightly toward the baseline to force the cutter to go wide around the screen. The defense player guarding the ball handler helps by pressuring her opponent to delay the pass to the forward cutting behind the screen so that the forward's opponent has time to cut around the screen and prevent an open shot

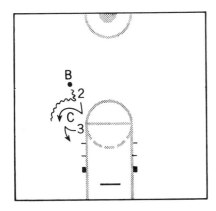

Fig. 5.10 *Defense Against a Rear Screen. Player B dribbles toward the inside of C, but No. 2 prevents her drive in that direction. As B drives to her right, No. 3 hedges to the outside to force B to go wider. This allows No. 2 time to move over the top of the screen and regain good defensive positioning.*

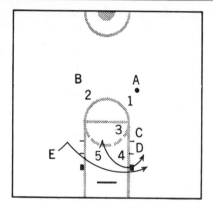

Fig. 5.11 *Defense Against a Double Screen, Along the Lane. As the double screen is set, Nos. 3 and 4 warn their teammates. Player No. 4 hedges to force E to go wide of the screen. Player No. 5 has floated, anticipates E's cut, and forces her wide around the screen. This allows No. 5 space to go over the top of the screen.*

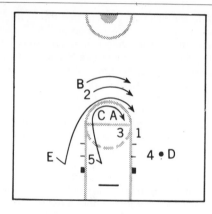

Fig. 5.12 *Defense Against a Double Screen at the Free Throw Line. The defenders guarding the screeners drop off their opponents toward the ball side to congest the passing lane.*

by the forward. The defense player guarding the forward should float away from her opponent when the ball is passed to the strong side. Then she can anticipate the direction of the forward's cut and beat her to the double screen (Fig. 5.11). By taking this action and with the help of her teammates, she may be able to force her opponent to cut to the inside of the screen where she is more easily guarded.

When the double screen is set at the free throw line, a forward or guard on the weak side cuts off the double screen to receive a pass, generally from a forward in the corner or wing position. To defend

---

DRILLS FOR DOUBLE SCREENS

The defense against the two types of double screens should be practiced on each side of the court.

1. Players necessary for a double screen along the lane line and their opponents. Emphasis should be placed on the defender against the ball handler guarding tight and the defender guarding the player to receive the pass anticipating the screen and beating her opponent to it.

2. Same as drill 1 above, but the defender should allow the forward to go behind the screen and maneuver to defend against her.

3. Players necessary for a double screen at the free throw line and their opponents. Emphasis is placed on the screener's defenders sagging off their opponents toward the ball to cover the passing lane to the cutter moving around the screen. Practice on both sides.

4. Same as drill 3 above, but permit the ball handler to pass to either screener if the defender's action leaves them free. Emphasize a quick return to guarding their own opponent.

against this action the defense players guarding the screeners must alert their teammates to the offensive maneuver and also drop back a step from their opponents and slide toward the ball side. This generally congests the area so that the ball handler cannot pass into the cutter (Fig. 5.12).

Jump Switch

A jump switch may be used in defense of a lateral or inside screen executed by two guards. Because the jump switch involves an exchange of opponents, it is not often used when other players are involved in a screen maneuver. The jump switch is used when a teammate is guarding her opponent closely. As the screen is set, the defender guarding the screener jumps forward and places herself in the path of the ball handler for whom the screen was set. This action should stop the forward drive of the ball handler and, as she picks up the ball, her new opponent raises her arms to prevent the overhead pass. Meanwhile the other defender quickly gets ball side of her new opponent (the screener) and anticipates a bounce pass to her (Fig. 5.13).

A more daring jump switch involves double-teaming an opponent. The purpose of the two-player jump switch is to force the ball handler to stop her drive and make it difficult for her to make a subsequent pass. Because of the dangers involved, this tactic is rarely used throughout an entire contest. It is generally designed for use during specific times — at the beginning of a period, after a time out, or at some other predetermined time. It can be extremely effective with the element of surprise.

The jump switch is started in much the same manner as the one previously described, with the exception that the defense player guarding the screener may start her move an instant sooner. She forces the driver to stop her dribble and catch the ball as she jumps into the path of the driver. As this occurs the driver's own opponent has time to approach from the other side, and the two defense players form a V and pressure the ball handler. The timing of the formation of the wedge is critical! While in this position the two defense players make no attempt to tap the ball out of the player's hands. They keep their arms moving and high so that the ball handler's vision is obstructed. This, of course, delays her pass and gives the defense players' teammates time to cover the free player cutting for goal (Fig. 5.14). These players must be alert for a bounce pass because the players forming the wedge should prevent the overhead pass. With anticipation and good timing, a defense player may be able to intercept a pass into the cutter if one should be made. Because of the dangers involved, this maneuver

should be used sparingly and then only when teammates have acquired excellent timing. It is used most often by guards only, although some coaches utilize it with a guard and a forward.

Drills for All Screens

Once players have practiced the defense against a specified screen, there should be time provided for them to defend against a variety of screens. Considerable practice is necessary to develop the timing required for proper execution of screen defense. Therefore, much practice time should be devoted to two-on-two maneuvers so that players have time to acquire the skill. Practice time should be so arranged that the two guards and their opponents can work for a period of time. The forwards and pivot can be practicing simultaneously in another area on forward-pivot maneuvers. Time should also be devoted to the guard and forward on each side of the court who are working together to acquire defensive skills.

Early in the learning stages and for review purposes as well, the instructor can designate the screen to be practiced. Exercise care to see that players practice the ones most likely to occur in their position or against an upcoming opponent. The teacher should also provide time in which the offensive players can maneuver and utilize whatever screen they desire, force the defense to recognize it while it is being set, and react properly to it.

Double-Teaming

A double-team is executed any time two players move in to guard one opponent. The purpose of any double-team tactic is to exert pressure on the ball handler with the intent of causing a poor pass. A double-team can be attempted any time a player dribbles toward the side line or baseline. As the offensive player is forced to stop her dribble, an opponent from her blind side approaches and the double-team is executed.

The purpose of any double-team maneuver is not to tap the ball away from the ball handler or to tie it up, but merely to harass her so that she is likely to make a poor pass. This means that the double-teaming defense players' teammates must be ready to make an interception. It is likely that the ball handler will try to pass to a teammate whose opponent is now guarding her. With this in mind, a defense player close to that opponent may anticipate the pass, intercept it, and possibly have a breakaway downcourt. If the ball handler holds the ball still rather than keeping it moving, the defense players may quite obviously tie it up. However, if they can force the ball handler

Fig. 5.13 *Jump Switch. Light No. 5 sets a lateral screen for No. 3 (a and b). Dark No. 5 jumps out to switch opponents and stop the drive (c and d). Dark No. 3 moves to get ball side of her new opponent, light No. 5 (e and f).*

a

b

Fig. 5.14 *Jump Switch with Double Team. As light No. 1 passes to No. 2 (a), dark No. 1 and 2 move in to guard closely and prevent the drive (b and c). They raise their arms overhead to force a lob pass (d).*

c

d

Fig. 5.14 *continued.*

to hold the ball 5 sec., a jump ball will be called anyway.

Double-teaming is effective against a team that has not practiced against pressure defenses. It is also effective against a poor ball handling team. Used sparingly against better ball handling teams, it may be effective once or twice and could result in two to four points, which might be the difference in the game's final score. It is only useful, however, when the other three defensive players are alert to the situation and move to cover the passing lanes to the opponents closest to the ball handler. If the passing lanes are not cut off, the obvious danger exists for a four-on-three offensive situation to arise.

DEFENSE AGAINST SCISSOR MANEUVERS (DOUBLE CUTS OFF A PIVOT PLAYER)

Scissor maneuvers, if allowed to materialize, can be exceedingly dangerous. They provide opportunities for driving layups and short jump shots for both the cutters as well as the pivot player. Double cuts are always made around a pivot player or a player who has moved into a pivot position. The player may be in a high post or medium post position. Whenever the pivot player is in the high post

position and one of the guards has the ball, the defense players opposing the guards should be alerted to a possible scissor maneuver if the ball is passed into the pivot. Similarly, when the pivot is in the medium post position and the forward has the ball in either the corner or wing position, the forward's opponent and the near side guard's opponent should anticipate a scissor maneuver. The post player's defender is responsible for warning her teammates whenever a double cut starts.

Defense Against the Scissors off a High Post

The best defense against this maneuver is to prevent the pivot player from receiving the ball. Certain precautions may be necessary against a team that uses the double cut effectively. First of all, the player defending against the high pivot plays in her normal defensive position, on the ball side with her arm extended to discourage a pass into the pivot. The defender against the ball handler plays half a player toward the inside and has her inside arm extended to discourage a pass into the pivot. The defender against the other guard sags off her player and opens toward the middle and the pivot player. She has her outside arm reaching toward her opponent and her inside arm toward the pivot player (Fig. 5.15). Hopefully, the

Fig. 5.15 *Defending Against the Scissor. Dark No. 1's opponent has moved back toward the pivot to discourage a pass to her.*

defensive position of these three players will discourage a pass in to the pivot and force the guard to pass to a forward. If, however, the guard chooses to pass to her other guard, the defenders must reverse their position. The danger period occurs while the pivot player's defender moves behind her opponent to the other side. The defender (opposing the guard who just passed) must quickly open and retreat toward the pivot player to partially close the passing lane during this process.

If, despite the efforts of these defense players, the ball is successfully passed into the pivot, the defender against the pivot must quickly move one step back from her opponent in line with her and the basket. She must immediately call out a warning to her teammates if the guards start to cut. The two defensive guards must retain their position half a

player toward the inside of their opponent in an attempt to discourage them from crossing. If the offensive players are able to cross, the defense player guarding the player who passed the ball into the pivot should have no difficulty maintaining defensive position, as she is easily able to go over the top of the screener (the pivot player). The problem for the other defense player is considerably greater. If the scissor maneuver is well timed, she will be cut off from her opponent by the action of her teammate's opponent. Nevertheless she must go over the top of the screen while forcing her opponent as high above the screen as possible. The player guarding the post player hedges to force the second cutter wider of the screen, thus allowing the cutter's opponent to slide closer to the screen and regain good positioning more quickly (Fig. 5.16).

a

Fig. 5.16 *Defense Against the Scissor. Dark No. 2 passes to the pivot and cuts first followed by her teammate, No. 1 (a and b). Light No. 2 maintains good defensive position by staying between her opponent and the ball handler (c–f). Light No. 1 is delayed by the cut of dark No. 2 (c and d). To help her teammate, light No. 3 hedges slightly (d) to cause dark No. 1 to go wide of the pivot, thus allowing light No. 1 to regain the inside position (e and f).*

b

c

d

e

f

Fig. 5.16 *continued.*

An alternate method of dealing with the double cut is for both guards to drop back a full step in front of the pivot player with the ball. With upward jabbing motions at the ball, they attempt to force the pivot to pass back immediately to one of the guards. If this is not successful and the guards start their double cut around the post, the defense players switch opponents as they cross. By being a full step in front of the pivot, their defensive position forces the offensive guards to make a wide cut around the post. This position also allows the two defenders to stay between the ball and their opponent (Fig. 5.17). However, if both

a

b

Fig. 5.17 *Defense Against a Scissor. The ball is passed to the pivot* (a). *Both defensive guards slide back one full step in front of the pivot* (b and c). *As the offensive players cross* (d), *the guards switch opponents and maintain the inside position* (e and f).

c

d

e

f

Fig. 5.17 *continued.*

defenders drop back in front of the pivot, both cutters may choose to go to the same side of the pivot. Therefore, guards who choose this alternate method of defense against the double cut must be aware of this offensive option so that they can move to regain defensive position against this maneuver. When the guards are playing in this fashion, the defender against the far side forward should be cautious of clearing the area. From her position, she can assist her teammates if both guards cut to the same side. If she clears

the area, the second cutter should be relatively free (Fig. 5.18). At no time should the defensive guards cut behind the pivot player. This is extremely weak posture and permits an easy shot from about 18 ft.

Defense Against the Scissors off a Medium Post

The defense must anticipate a double cut by the forward and near guard whenever a forward passes in

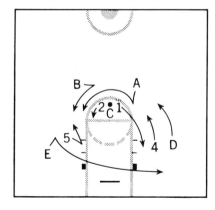

Fig. 5.18 *Defense Against a Scissor When Both Players Cut to the Same Side. Player A passes in to C. When B sees that both defenders drop back in front of C, she fakes her normal cut but cuts to the same side as A. Meanwhile, E clears the area but No. 5 does not follow and remains in position to guard B. At the same time, No. 1 drops back to defend against E.*

DRILLS FOR A SCISSOR (DOUBLE CUT) MANEUVER

1. Two offensive guards and a pivot player and their opponents. The guards pass the ball back and forth between them, making no effort to get the ball into the pivot. Emphasis is on the movement of the pivot's defender as she moves from side to side, and on the defender who sags toward the pivot to close the passing lane.

2. Same as drill 1 above, only the guards pass in to the pivot whenever the opportunity arises. Emphasis is the same as previously described and on the pivot defender taking one step back as soon as her opponent gets the ball.

3. Same as drill 2 above, with the guards executing their double cut. Emphasis is on the pivot player hedging toward the side of the second cutter and both defenders going over the top of the screen.

4. Same as drill 3 above, only the defending guards choose to step back in front of the pivot after she receives the pass. The attack players are instructed to cross. Emphasis is placed on forcing the cutters wide and not permitting them to cut between the defenders and the pivot.

5. Same as drill 4 above, only instruct the attacking guards to cut to the same side (the side of the first cutter) and let the defenders adjust to this action. Emphasis is placed on the guard's ability to anticipate the cut to the same side and to adjust quickly.

6. Same as drill 4 above, only instruct the guards to cross or cut to the same side at their discretion.

7. One forward, guard, and pivot player and their opponents. The guard and forward pass back and forth, making no attempt to pass in to the pivot. Emphasis is on the position of the pivot's defender and the guard's defender during the exchange of passes. The pivot defender moves behind her opponent each time to get one-half a player ball side of her. The guard's defender drops back to help prevent a pass in to the pivot from the forward. The forward's defender does not do this, as the ball is returned to the guard.

8. Proceed as in drills 1 and 2 above to gain confidence in dealing with this tactic between these three players.

to the pivot in this position. Once again the best defense against this action is to prevent the pivot player from receiving the ball. In this position the defender against the pivot player guards her one-half player on the ball side. When the forward has the ball, the defending near side guard drops off her opponent toward the pivot to help close the passing lane into the pivot (Fig. 5.19). Should the pivot receive a pass, the forward usually fakes toward the baseline and cuts around the pivot toward the middle while the guard fakes a move to the corner and cuts off the forward's back. The defender opposing the guard must move over the screen to prevent the easy layup. The far side defensive guard and forward must sag and float off their opponents to help prevent a successful execution of this play.

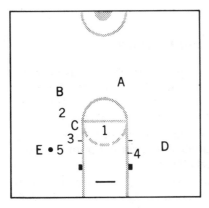

Fig. 5.19 *Defensive Position Against a Medium Pivot When a Forward Has the Ball in the Corner. Player No. 2 sags off her opponent to help close the passing lane into the pivot.*

Cross Block

Figuratively, every defense player should be between her opponent and the basket when her opponent has the ball. This, however, cannot always be achieved. There are times when a lob pass over a defender's head is successful, and there are times also when an offensive player simply beats her opponent in some maneuver. A defensive teammate must leave her opponent to prevent an easy layup shot when this happens. The teammate most often involved in providing assistance is the far side forward's opponent. She attempts to pressure the offensive player so that she cannot obtain an easy shot and, following the shot, she blocks her out from any rebound attempt. This means that her own opponent is left free and can move in for a rebound. The defensive player who is out of position to guard her own player must cross over and block out her teammate's opponent. This is a very simple maneuver but one that is vital in order to prevent an easy layup or second scoring opportunity.

This same technique is also used when a post player receives a pass. If her opponent has been fronting her or playing one-half to three-quarters in front of her, she may not be in position to defend against a shot. The far side forward's opponent moves over to defend against the shot and to block out the pivot player. At the same time the post player's opponent crosses over and blocks out the forward who is left free (Fig. 5.20).

DEFENSE AGAINST AN OFFENSIVE PLAYER ADVANTAGE

It is likely that the opponents will start downcourt with a one- or two-player advantage at some time during

---

DRILLS FOR CROSS BLOCK

1. Two forwards and a guard and their opponents. The guard has the ball and the forward on the near side fakes a cut toward the guard but reverse cuts and receives a pass from the guard. The defender against her accepts the fake so that she is out of position for the subsequent pass. Emphasis is on the far side defensive forward floating away from her opponent, meeting the free forward, and blocking her out, and on the defensive forward who was evaded racing to block out the free opponent. Repeat from the other side.

2. Two forwards and the pivot and their opponents. One forward gives a lob pass to the medium pivot; the defender lets the ball go over her head. Emphasis is on the far side forward floating to guard the pivot and blocking her out, and the pivot's defender hurries to block out the forward's opponent. Repeat from the other side.

a

b

Fig. 5.20 *Cross Block. Dark No. 2 gives a lob pass to post player, No. 3 (a and b). The far side defensive forward, light No. 5, anticipates the pass and moves over to guard dark No. 3 (c–e). At the same time, light No. 3 is hurrying to get in position to block out dark No. 5*

c

d

e

Fig. 5.20 *continued.*

the course of a game. It may happen when the opponents intercept a pass or when a player falls mentally asleep and fails to maintain defensive balance. From an offensive point of view, a team should score whenever it has a one- or two-player advantage. It is the objective of the defending team to delay the offense players and force as many passes as possible before a shot is attempted. The more passes made by the offense, the more time the other defenders have to recover. At the same time, the defense is also trying to force the outside shot and prevent the layup.

There are many situations that may arise—one-on-none, two-on-one, three-on-one, three-on-two, four-on-two, four-on-three, and five-on-four. Some of these occur rather infrequently; therefore, attention will be given only to those that are most likely to occur.

One-on-None

This situation may occur when a player taps the ball away from an opponent or intercepts a pass and makes a clear breakaway downcourt. The defensive player nearest the action must retreat as fast as possible and

attempt to disconcert the shooter. Once the shot is taken, the defense player should attain rebounding position so that the ball does not rebound over her head. In beginning play the shooter and defensive player are often running at such speed that neither can stop after the shot and both continue to run out of bounds. This means that another offensive player hustling downcourt may obtain the rebound and score an easy layup. This should never be permitted. The defense player must slow her forward speed so that she is positioned for the rebound.

Two-on-One

When this happens the lone defensive player must run backward as rapidly as possible to the top of the free throw circle. She should not attempt to harass the dribbler while she maneuvers at midcourt. This can be extremely dangerous for obvious reasons. The defender meets the dribbler at the top of the circle and retreats with her. She may make feinting motions at the ball, but her weight always remains to the rear. She does not commit herself to either player and stays at least 6 ft. from the dribbler until she is within that distance of the basket. By sagging off the dribbler and opening toward the cutter with one arm pointing in her direction she can deter a pass to her. As the cutter is the more dangerous player since she is closer to the basket, the defender wants to cut off the passing lane to her. The defender tries to force the dribbler into catching the ball. If successful, she quickly retreats toward the cutter to encourage an outside shot by the dribbler. As she retreats, she stays in the lane and waits for the cutter to come toward her. Moving out of the lane opens a passing lane closer to the basket. If the defense player succeeds in preventing a layup shot, she has demonstrated excellent defense regardless of whether a long shot is successful.

Three-on-Two

There are two ways of combating a three-on-two advantage. One method calls for an up-and-back system while the other places players parallel. The former method is the one generally preferred. When a three-on-two break occurs, the two defense players must hurry back to the free throw lane. One player stops inside the top of the circle while the other one moves back in the lane about 6 ft. in front of the basket. It is the front defender's task (at the top of the circle) to stop the dribbler by the time she reaches the free throw line and cause her to pass. The more passes that the defenders can force, the more time their teammates have to recover. Usually the offensive advantage is lost after the second pass.

The back player is responsible for guarding whichever player the dribbler passes to. She must not commit herself too soon but wait until she actually sees

the ball released so that she is not susceptible to a fake and pass in the opposite direction. As soon as the dribbler passes, the front player retreats down the middle of the lane about 6 ft. in front of the basket to protect the passing lane to the offensive player cutting toward the basket on the other side. This player is now responsible for guarding whichever player is the receiver of the next pass. These two defenders continue to exchange positions until additional help arrives (Fig. 5.21). The next defender back should hasten down the middle of the court to the free throw area.

The parallel system of defense may be used against a poor fast break team or when a poor ball handler is in the middle position on offense. The two defenders position themselves at the corners of the free throw line and open toward the cutter on their side, but keep their eyes on the player with the ball. They must prevent the dribbler from driving between them. The defender on the ball side of the dribbler makes feinting motions to cause the dribbler to pass. As the pass is made, the defender closer to the receiver prevents the easy layup while the other defender drops back in the lane to cut off the passing lane to the cutter on her side. If the ball is passed back to the former dribbler at the free throw line, the defender who dropped back goes out to guard the dribbler unless a teammate has recovered in time.

Four-on-Three

Zone principles must be applied in this situation also. A triangle zone is established by the defense, with the front player one step beyond the free throw line and

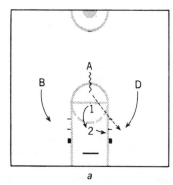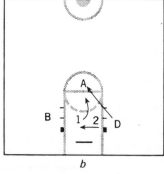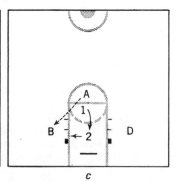

| a | b | c |

Fig. 5.21 *Defense Against a Fast Break. As player A passes to D, No. 2 moves over to defend against D. Player No. 1 drops back to cover the passing lane to B (a). Player D is unable to shoot and passes back to A. Player No. 1 must move out to guard her as No. 2 moves back into the middle of the lane so that she can guard whoever receives the next pass (b). As player A passes to B, No. 2 moves to the edge of the lane to guard her as No. 1 drops back again. After this number of passes, another defender should be retreating. In this instance, No. 4 is moving to cover a return pass to A (c).*

the other two players 6 ft. in front of the basket and at the edge of the lane on their side. The front player must chase between the two outside players if the offense uses a two-two alignment (Fig. 5.22). If they use a one-two-one, the front defender tries to force the dribbler toward the weak side—the side with fewer offense players (Fig. 5.23). All defenders open toward the ball and try to prevent a pass in to a cutter moving across the lane. The defenders must protect against the high percentage shots and allow the long shot.

Five-on-Four

A box zone may be used when defenders are confronted with this situation and when the opponents are in a two-three alignment (Fig. 5.24). The two outside defenders start one step in front of the free throw line on their side while the back players are 6 ft. in front of the basket at the edge of the lane on their side. Again they try to encourage as many passes as possible and prevent the easy shot. If the opponents are in a one-three-one or one-four alignment, the

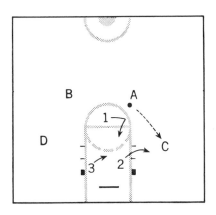

Fig. 5.22 *Defense in Four-on-Three Situation When Opponents Use a Two-Two Alignment. Player No. 1 must guard either player A or B if she has the ball. If A passes to C, No. 1 drops back as No. 2 guards C. Player No. 3 moves into the lane and covers the passing lane to D or B if either cuts into the lane.*

Fig. 5.23 *Defense in a Four-on-Three Situation When the Opponents Are in a One-Two-One Alignment. Player No. 1 overplays to force A to dribble toward the weak side. After A passes, the responsibilities of the defense players are the same as previously described.*

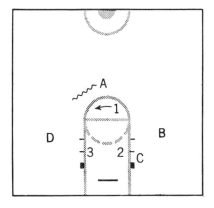

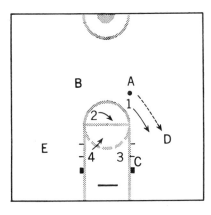

Fig. 5.24 *Defense in a Box Zone in a Five-on-Four Situation with the Offense in a Two-Three Alignment. If player A passes to D, the defenders reposition themselves as shown. Player No. 2 cuts off the passing lane to A or B on a cut through the lane. Player No. 4 cuts off the lane to E.*

diamond zone may be a better posture from which to start (Fig. 5.25). The zones are similar after the initial pass.

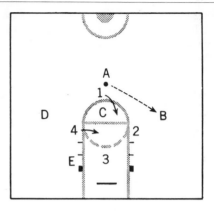

Fig. 5.25 *Defense in a Diamond Zone in a Five-on-Four Situation with the Offense in a One-Three-One Alignment. If player A passes to B, No. 2 moves to guard her; No. 1 drops back and No. 4 floats over. Emphasis is on delaying a shot until the fifth defender recovers.*

DRILLS FOR DEFENDING AGAINST AN OFFENSIVE ADVANTAGE

1. Groups of three—two attack players and one defense player. A defense player starts running backward from the center circle toward the top of her defensive circle. The two attack players pass and dribble downcourt, attempting to score. The defender uses correct techniques to prevent the layup and force the outside shot. Rotate.

2. Groups of five—three attack players and two defense players. The two defense players start at the defensive end in their up-and-back (or parallel) position. The three attack players start at the top of the free throw circle at the other end and bring the ball downcourt with the middle player in possession by the time they reach the offensive circle. The defensive players use correct techniques to cause as many passes as possible.

3. Same as drill 2 above, only the defensive players start at the division line and must hurry back to get in proper position to defend against the approaching attack players.

4. Same as drill 3 above, but add another defense player starting at the free throw line behind the attack players. She is in pursuit and races down the middle of the court to recover at the defensive free throw line. Later, at a sideline or in a corner, start this defensive player from other positions behind the attack players.

5. Groups of seven—four offensive players against three defensive players at one end of the court. The three defense players use a triangle zone and try to force the outside shot and as many passes as possible before a shot is attempted.

6. Same as drill 5 above, only add another defense player starting 6 ft. in front of the basket at the other end. She races downcourt and tries to assist her teammates before a shot is taken.

7. Two teams without a defensive pivot—nine players, all at one end of the court. The defense forms a box zone and tries to force as many passes as possible before a shot is taken. Later, replace a forward with the pivot who has been out of action.

8. Same as drill 7 above, only start the defensive pivot 6 ft. in front of the basket at the opposite end and see if she can recover before a shot is attempted.

6

Team Defense

Team defense requires the active participation of all five players. This is unlike the offense, which requires only two- or three-player involvement at any one time (in most instances). On defense, however, a team is considerably weakened when one or more players is out of position or has a mental lapse. Each player must react to every movement of the ball and her opponent (or the opponent in her zone). The defense is weakened any time a player fails to fulfill her responsibility in this respect.

A team must cultivate pride in its defensive ability. Teammates must recognize and accept their defensive strengths and weaknesses and should be ready to assist those players whose skills are inferior. They must also be ready to help a teammate who has a particularly difficult defensive assignment.

Players must strive to develop the tenacity and aggressiveness that distinguish a truly great defensive player from any other. When playing a man-to-man defense, players must not be permitted to develop the attitude that they are only responsible for "following" a player or guarding her when she has the ball. Often it is more important what a player does when her opponent does not have the ball! When playing a zone defense, players should not move merely from one position to another, but "attack" each position and any player who enters her zone. "Attack" means that no defense player should let the offense run their patterns as they wish. The defense must anticipate where they would like to cut to receive a pass and beat them there (Fig. 6.1). They must learn to disrupt the general offense of their opponents!

Defense players must recognize that causing opponents to commit violations is the easiest way of gaining possession of the ball. Once they develop this concept they will have advanced in their defensive thinking. The next step is to acquire the readiness and anticipation to prevent their opponent or any opponent in their zone from receiving a pass. The cultivation of this concept leads to interceptions and forcing turnovers. As these attitudes are developed along with the necessary skills involved, a team will be on its way toward improving its overall defense.

In competitive play, one type of defense is no longer adequate to confound the offense of the opponents. A highly skilled team should be able to utilize two or three different types of defenses in any one game with equal ability. They should be proficient at some type of man-to-man defense, one or more zones, and a pressure-type defense. Development of skill in a variety of defenses takes considerable practice time; unless this is available, a team probably would perform better by using only one or two defenses well.

The author is a firm believer in the necessity of developing sound individual defensive skills and therefore is a proponent of starting with a man-to-man defense. Beginners must learn the fundamental concepts of this defense before they can successfully use a zone defense or any of the pressure defenses, for in any zone defense a player with the ball must be guarded with man-to-man principles. Once these concepts are acquired they can be incorporated into other types of defenses.

Fig. 6.1 *Aggressive Defensive Position. Light No. 3 anticipates that her opponent wants to cut toward the ball, and she positions herself to force a wider cut.*

BASIC DEFENSIVE PRINCIPLES

1. A team must hinder fast break opportunities and any other offensive advantage. To prevent these from occurring, mental errors must be eliminated on offense. These occur in any of three ways.
   a. Defensive balance must be maintained—i.e., on every offensive thrust, two players should be deployed in the area near the top of the circle to prevent a fast break by the opponents if they should intercept a pass or obtain a rebound.
   b. Players must exercise good judgment in recognizing when a player is free or, more important, when a player is *not* free to receive a pass. Interceptions lead to many instances where the opponents gain an offensive advantage.
   c. When a team loses possession of the ball they must retreat rapidly to a position 6–8 ft. in front of the basket and look for any free opponent (Figs. 6.2 and 6.3). If there is one, a defender moves to guard her while calling to her teammate the number of her own opponent, so that she may guard her. If the team is playing a zone defense the player may return to her own position once the position near the basket is filled. Free and uncovered opponents cannot be permitted to penetrate the area near the basket while a slower defender recovers downcourt.

2. A team must force the opponents to alter their desired offensive maneuvers. They can cut off their normal passing lanes, double-team a high scorer or playmaker, float to the middle to eliminate cuts or drives through the middle of the lane, force the opponents to speed up their play by pressing them if they prefer to use a deliberate passing attack, or slow them down by cutting off the passing lanes if they prefer a fast break style offense. A team should analyze the opponents' strengths and take measures to minimize their effectiveness. It should also analyze their weaknesses and take measures to exploit them.

3. A team must prevent easy baskets. Shots taken within 12–15 ft. of the basket fall within this category. Every possible measure should be taken to prevent a player from dribbling into this area or from receiving a pass within this area. The team should attempt to close the passing lanes into a player in this area and also to force the opponent in that area to alter the path of her cut away from her desired direction. The defense does not want to be penetrated in this area. A team that permits a number of shots from this range will not win many contests.

4. A team must force the opponents to shoot long shots. By congesting the lane and that area within 15–18 ft. of the basket, the opponents should be

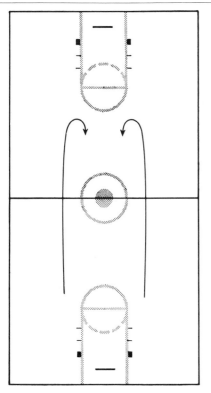

Fig. 6.2 *Poor Defensive Retreat by First Players Back on Defense. Players retreat only to the top of the circle to meet their opponents.*

Fig. 6.3 *Good Defensive Retreat by First Two Players Back on Defense. Players recover downcourt to point within 6 ft. of the basket and then move out to their defensive positions. This technique precludes a long pass downcourt to a free player for a layup.*

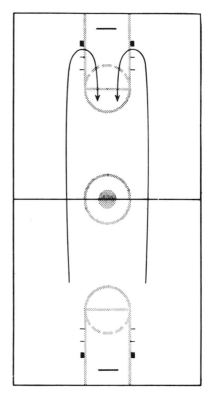

forced to shoot from a distance greater than this. Unless they prove successful in shooting beyond 21 ft., encourage them to shoot from that distance by not moving beyond that distance to guard them. Tactics must be changed if one or more players scores consistently from this distance.

5. A team must rebound well. The defensive aim should be to never allow more than one shot any time the opponents are on offense. A team must block out well and move to the areas where the ball rebounds. They must not allow themselves to get caught too far under the basket, and they must make provisions for blocking out the offensive pivot player who shoots from a low or medium post position.

MAN-TO-MAN DEFENSE

A man-to-man defense is considered the fundamental defense upon which others can be developed. It places the responsibility for an opponent on each player and tends to develop a greater pride in individual defensive ability. It also uncovers those players who have defensive deficiencies.

Fig. 6.4 *Sagging of the Defense. The far side defensive guard sags from her opponent.*

Advantages of Man-to-Man Defense

1. It permits players to be matched with regard to several factors—height, speed, quickness, jumping ability, and defensive skill.
2. It fixes responsibility and encourages a player to improve her defensive fundamentals.
3. It places more pressure on outside shots.
4. It is effective against a stall and is absolutely imperative when a team is behind in score in the last few minutes of a game.
5. It has many variations for which the transition can be made easily.
6. Zone principles may be applied by sagging and floating.

Disadvantages of Man-to-Man Defense

1. It takes time to become proficient in the individual skills and basic principles.
2. It is susceptible to screens and double cuts.
3. Players tend to commit more fouls than when playing a zone defense.
4. More players generally are forced to move greater distances and expend more energy than when playing a zone defense.

There are five ways in which a man-to-man defense may be played:

- normal
- tight or pressing
- loose
- switching
- doubling.

Basic principles apply to all, and they follow.

Basic Principles for Man-to-Man Defense

1. A player is responsible for her opponent first and the ball second.
2. A player is always in a triangle formed by the ball, her opponent, and the basket. Her exact position in this triangle varies according to where her opponent is in relation to the ball and basket. The further her opponent is from the ball, the further she is from her opponent, for she must be able to see the ball and her opponent at all times without turning her head.
3. Basic principles previously discussed in relation to one or two passes away from the ball apply.
4. A player should quickly analyze the strengths and

weaknesses of her opponent and that of the entire offensive team. If her opponent is weak she may concentrate on helping teammates or in double-teaming.

5. Players utilize sagging and floating principles when their opponents are two passes away or when they are beyond scoring range.
   a. Sagging occurs when a player moves away from her opponent toward the basket (Fig. 6.4). Guards use this technique more than other players in order to keep their opponent and ball in sight.
   b. Floating takes place when a player moves laterally across the court toward the basket. This move is made mostly by a forward when the play is on the opposite side of the court (Fig. 6.5). When the ball moves to her opponent she must resume normal guarding position while the other forward floats.
   c. Use of both of these principles allows the defense to congest the area within 15 ft. of the basket, thus preventing the high percentage shots and cutting down the lane. It permits one or more defense players to concentrate on interceptions. It is extremely effective against a team that uses a cutting type offense or has an effective driver.

6. All players must understand and perfect the techniques involved with screens and double cuts. The method of dealing with these two tactics has been discussed previously.

7. Players may influence the direction of the ball. They can influence the offense to pass the ball in a certain direction by overplaying in a designated manner. This may be done for several reasons. Other defense players may be alert for interceptions. It may also be desirable to direct the ball away from a high scorer, toward a poor ball handler, toward a particular side of the court, away from a weaker defensive player, toward a side line, toward the middle, or away from the baseline.

8. Players may also influence the direction of the dribbler by overplaying her (Fig. 6.6). This may be desirable for the reasons stated above.

Normal Man-to-Man Defense

Each player assumes her stance in the triangle between the basket, ball, and opponent. She sags or floats, depending upon the position of the ball; she opens toward the ball if she is two passes away. The defender guarding the player with the ball is 3 ft. from her. A team uses the normal man-to-man positioning when there are outside shooting threats (Fig. 6.7).

Tight or Pressing Man-to-Man Defense

This style is useful when a team wishes to influence the ball in a certain direction. It is also appropriate against a poor ball handling team or when a team is behind in score. It may cause the opponents to lose

Fig. 6.5 *Floating. Note the position of white No. 5, who has floated away from her opponent—dark No. 5.*

a

b

c

d

Fig. 6.6 *Overplaying the Dribbler. White No. 5 overplays the dribbler and maintains good position.*

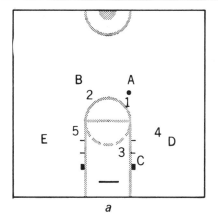
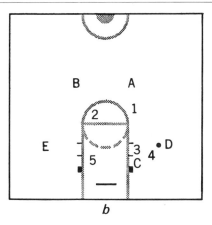

Fig. 6.7 *Normal Man-to-Man Defensive Position. Player A has the ball. Note that No. 4 has cut off the angle of a cut into the lane by D; No. 5 has floated away from E, but is cutting off E's cut in to the lane (a). The ball has been passed to D. Player No. 4 overplays toward the baseline; Nos. 1 and 2 sag to watch their opponent and the ball; No. 5 floats into the lane to be of assistance if necessary (b).*

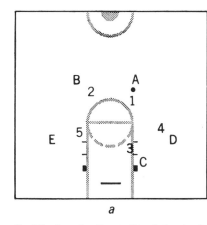
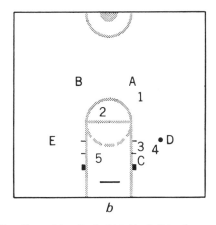

Fig. 6.8 *Pressing Man-to-Man Defensive Position. Player A has the ball (a). The ball has been passed to.D (b).*

their poise and make errors. In order to use this style effectively, all players must be well skilled in individual defensive techniques; they also must be quick and agile. The defender guarding the ball handler guards her close and influences a pass in a predetermined direction. She retreats quickly after her opponent passes so that the opponents cannot execute the pass and cut tactic. All defenders who are one pass away overplay their opponent toward the ball, while those two passes away sag and float to close the openings in the lane (Fig. 6.8). Fig. 6.9 shows dark No. 1 playing her opponent tightly and light No. 1 attempts a reverse cut. Dark No. 4 anticipates the pass and moves over to guard light No. 1. At the same time, dark No. 1 hustles back to intercept the pass to light No. 4.

213

a

b

Fig. 6.9 *Good Defensive Coverage. Dark No. 1 overplays her opponent, who makes a reverse cut (a and b). The near side forward, dark No. 4, anticipates the play and moves over to cover the pass receiver (c). Dark No. 1 hustles back and intercepts the pass (d and e).*

c

d

e

DRILLS FOR MAN-TO-MAN DEFENSE

Players should review the techniques for two-, three-, and four-player offensive tactics. The reader is referred to Chapter 3 for suggested drills. It is the author's contention that the normal man-to-man alignment should be learned before any of the other man-to-man styles. This can be followed by the loose style, although some teachers may prefer to introduce the latter style first. This procedure is probably appropriate in physical education classes where there are likely to be few outside shooters. The double-teaming style should follow the tight man-to-man since it utilizes those techniques. The switching style on lateral crosses may be introduced any time after the normal or loose style has been learned.

1. Four offense players and their opponents; no pivot player or her opponent. The four offense players can take their position on the court with any one having the ball. On signal from the instructor, they pass the ball around the periphery. No offense player may cut, and the ball may not be passed until the signal is given. By using this method each player's move can be observed and corrections made. Focus attention on the player within her triangle and her position in relation to the ball. The teacher checks carefully to see that guards have sagged far enough to see the ball and their opponent and that a forward floats when she is two passes away from the ball.

2. One pivot player and either a guard or forward and their opponents. This drill can be done simultaneously with drill 1 if two separate areas are available. The forward or guard attempts to pass in to the pivot while the defenders try to prevent it. This should be practiced at the high post between the pivot and guard, and at the low and medium post with the pivot working with a forward.

3. Five offensive players and their opponents. The drill is the same as drill 1 above, with the addition of the pivot player who has freedom of movement.

4. Same as drill 3 above, only allow the offense to pass at their own discretion.

5. Same as drill 3 above, only allow all players to maneuver as they wish. At first the instructor may wish to limit the types of screens that can be set and gradually add all of them. For example, it may be wise to permit only back screens at the start; add side screens followed by inside screens and rear screens.

6. Two teams on the court, with offense players attempting double cuts whenever possible. Emphasis is placed on the correct action of the defenders directly involved and the sagging and floating of teammates to help.

7. Two teams—the offensive guard with the ball at the top of the circle and one step inside (closer to the basket than) her opponent. She tries to drive down the lane for a layup. Defensive players sag and float to prevent this action. Practice from both sides.

8. Same as drill 7 above, only a forward has the ball in a wing position and one step inside her defender. Later, place the forward in the corner position and repeat the drill.

9. Two teams with the offense trying to get a lob pass into the medium pivot. Emphasis is on the floating of the far side forward to guard the pivot as she receives the pass, and on the sagging of the far side defending guard to cover the passing lane to the forward.

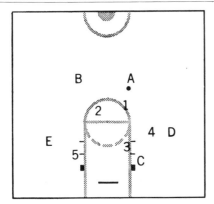

Fig. 6.10 *Loose Man-to-Man Defensive Positions.*

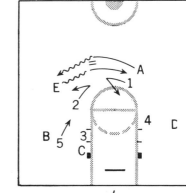

a

Fig. 6.11 *Switching Man-to-Man Defensive Positions. Player B passes to E. No. 2 guards B until E crosses and starts dribbling toward No. 2, at which time No. 2 guards E. At the same time as No. 2 switches opponents, No. 5 guards B (a). With No. 5 guarding B and No. 2 guarding E, A cuts behind B and receives a pass. A dribbles to her right. Player No. 2 starts to guard A as No. 1 guards E (b).*

b

Loose Man-to-Man Defense

This style may be used against a team that cannot shoot from beyond 21 ft. No defender goes beyond 21 ft. and actually encourages any offense player to shoot from beyond that distance. This style provides the greatest protection within good scoring range, and utilizes zone principles by allowing outside shots and preventing close shots and penetration. Because it permits freedom of movement and passing beyond the 21-ft. area, it cannot be used late in a game when a team is behind in score. Fig. 6.10 shows the players' positions.

Switching Man-to-Man Defense

A switching style defense in which the defenders exchange opponents may be used on all lateral crosses by the guards. Due to the usual height disparity, it is not practiced as a basic defense when a forward and guard cross vertically. However, the switching style is effective against a weave style offense (Fig. 6.11).

Double-Teaming Man-to-Man Defense

This is a form of pressure-type defense in which the player guarding a dribbler influences her toward a side line. At the same time a player from the blind side of the dribbler edges off her opponent and double-teams the dribbler when she catches the ball. The closest defender (except the pivot) to the free player moves to cover the passing lane to her. The fourth defender overplays her opponent, and the pivot player zones the passing lane between her opponent and the player furthest from the ball, concentrating on the player closer to the ball (Fig. 6.12). If the opponents do not commit an error on the subsequent play, the defense players involved in the double-team sag off the opponent to encourage a return pass to her. At that time all defense players may return to guarding their own player. With good timing of their moves they are able to resume good positioning by

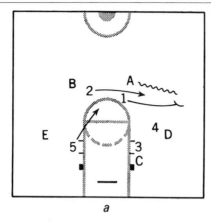 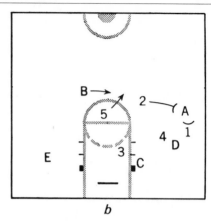

a　　　　　　　　　　　　　　*b*

Fig. 6.12 *Double-Teaming Man-to-Man Defense. Player No. 1 overplays A, forcing her toward the side line. While this is occurring, No. 2 drifts away from B to help double-team A at the side line. At the same time, No. 5 moves up toward B to guard her (a). As A pivots, No. 2 meets her to complete the double-team. No. 5 plays B tight. No. 4 plays D tight. No. 3 is responsible for zoning against both C and E. She is more concerned with C because she is closer to the ball and the basket (b).*

DRILLS FOR LOOSE AND TIGHT MAN-TO-MAN DEFENSE

The same drills listed for Man-to-Man Defense may be used for developing skills in either of these styles.

DRILLS FOR SWITCHING MAN-TO-MAN DEFENSE

1. Two offense players in the guard position and their opponents. The two offensive players combine dribbling and passing as they cross laterally and remain in the back court area. The defenders switch on each cross.
2. Four offensive players execute a weave, and the defenders switch on each cross.

DRILLS FOR DOUBLE-TEAMING MAN-TO-MAN DEFENSE

1. Two teams. An offensive guard has the ball and her opponent overplays her on the inside. The guard dribbles toward the side line and no other attack players are permitted to move. The guard's opponent and nearest other defender double-team the ball handler. The other defense players adjust their position and attempt to intercept the next pass.
2. Same as drill 1 above, only permit the attack players to move as necessary. Emphasize covering the passing lanes and the correct timing of the double-team.
3. Same as drill 2 above. If the subsequent pass is successful, emphasis is on the defenders sagging off the former dribbler and encouraging a pass to her. All players return to guard their own opponent.
4. Same as drill 1 above, only a forward has the ball and is trapped at the side line by the defending forward and guard. Apply the same principles.

the time the ball is one pass away from their opponent. This style may be used whenever a defender overplays a dribbler toward a side line.

ZONE DEFENSE

In a zone defense, players play the ball instead of a specified opponent. Everyone faces the ball and moves in relation to its position on an assigned area of the court. The purpose of a zone defense is to defend from the basket area outward, with emphasis on preventing short shots and permitting long ones, if necessary. A zone defense should be learned only after players acquire skill in individual defensive techniques.

Advantages of a Zone Defense

1. Players can be assigned to a position on the court to utilize their strengths.
2. It is an effective defense to use against a team that dribbles, cuts through the lane, and relies on high percentage shots.
3. Weaker defense players can be ''hidden'' to a greater extent than in a man-to-man defense.
4. It reduces the number of fouls called and protects those in foul trouble.
5. Many zones afford opportunities for a fast break since players are assigned definite positions at the top of the circle.
6. It is easy to make the transition from offense to defense, since players run back to an assigned position on the court rather than look for a particular opponent when they reach the defensive end.
7. In a zone, players in certain positions are required to cover little space and therefore find it less tiring than man-to-man defense.
8. It may provide a psychological barrier to the opposing team.
9. It may help a team secure more interceptions.

Disadvantages of a Zone Defense

1. All zones are vulnerable at certain positions; they tend to be weak against long shots at the top of the circle, shots from the corners, or both.
2. A zone is weak against a fast breaking team because it does not have time to set up.
3. A zone does not place pressure on players outside the perimeter and allows them to pass with little interference.
4. A zone may not encourage players to improve their own defensive skills.
5. A zone may permit players to become complacent as they move from one assigned position to another. Players may lose their aggressiveness.
6. A zone may overcommit itself by being drawn out too far or by sagging too far.

Basic Principles for a Zone Defense

1. Players are responsible for guarding the ball first and an opponent second. They always face the ball and are responsible for covering the passing lanes and intercepting the ball if it is passed within the perimeter of the zone.
2. The zone's configuration should be maintained with the correct spatial relationship. The zone should not be overextended beyond the 21-ft. area. Shots should be permitted from beyond that distance.
3. The stance assumed by players is higher than for man-to-man defense, and the arms are spread in a legal manner to give an impenetrable appearance to the zone.
4. Players should quickly retreat to the defensive end when they lose possession of the ball. Once in their assigned position, they can rest.
5. Defenders guarding a player with the ball move their arms in windmill fashion, trying to deflect the ball or force a high pass.
6. Players moving in a zone must be aware of the position of attack players in their zone. They play an attack player who is one pass away one-half step ball side, and try for an interception if possible, knowing that there is another defender behind.
7. Players should not permit an attack player to receive the ball in the free throw lane. If she does, all players sag and float toward the ball.

SPECIFIC ZONE DEFENSES

Zone defenses are named according to the configuration of the zone starting with players closest to the center line. For example, in a three-two zone, three players form the front line near the free throw line and two players are closer to the basket. Zone defenses are characterized by having an odd front line or an even one. Examples of zones having an odd front line include the three-two, one-two-two, and one-three-one zones. Even front lines include the two-one-two, two-three, and two-two-one zones. Choice of the zone depends on the individual abilities of the defense players, considering both their physical and mental attributes. It also depends on the capability of the opponents.

Each zone has certain strengths and weaknesses depending upon the deployment of the players. A zone is strong where it has the greatest concentration of players and weak where fewer players are positioned. The strengths and weaknesses of the popular zones will be discussed with diagrams presented to show the movement of the players in relation to the ball. The positions for each player shown on the diagrams are basic and should be adjusted slightly depending upon the position of an opponent within that area.

a

b

Fig. 6.13 *Two-One-Two Zone. No.'s 1 and 2 are the front line; 3 is in the middle line, and 4 and 5 are the back line.*

The reader should keep in mind that Nos. 1 and 2 represent guards, 4 and 5 represent forwards, and 3 is the center.

Two–One–Two Zone

This zone is one of the most popular in use today. It combines some of the advantages of the three-two and two-three zone. It is strong near the basket and in the lane and therefore is useful against a pivot of-

fense. It also provides good rebounding strength and opportunities for a fast break to develop as either player No. 1 or 2 is in position to start downcourt following a shot. It is weak from the point position and in the corners. Fig. 6.13 *a–i* show the movements of players and Fig. 6.13 *j–n* diagram the position of players as the ball moves around the perimeter of the zone. Fig. 6.14 shows the movements of the individual players when the ball is in the left corner, left wing, point, right wing, and right corner positions.

c

d

e

f

g

Fig. 6.13 *continued.*

h

i

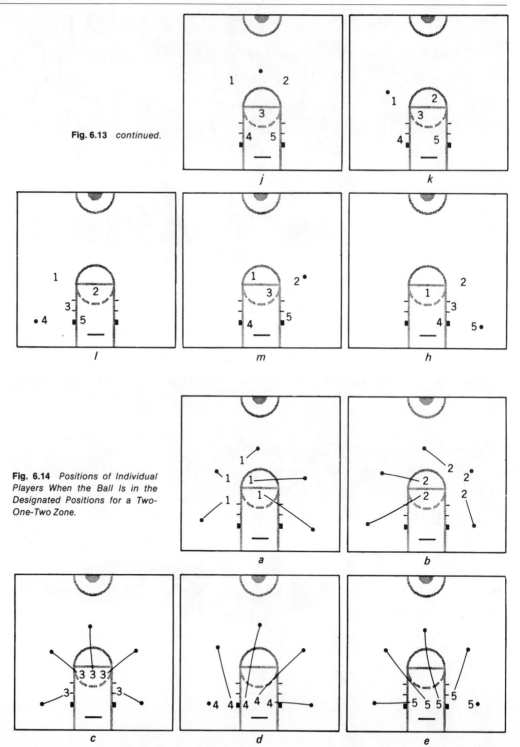

Fig. 6.13 *continued.*

Fig. 6.14 *Positions of Individual Players When the Ball Is in the Designated Positions for a Two-One-Two Zone.*

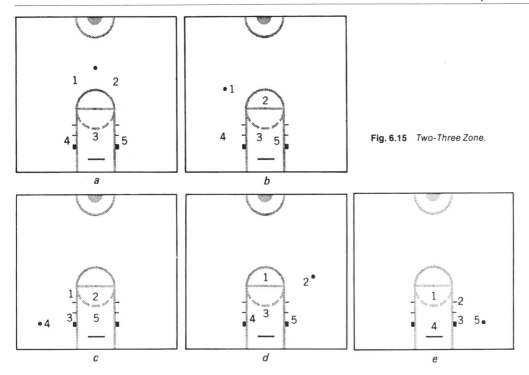

Fig. 6.15 *Two-Three Zone.*

Two-Three Zone

In many respects, the two-three zone is similar to the two-one-two zone. The primary difference between the two zones is that player No. 3 plays closer to the basket in the two-three zone and therefore it is stronger against low or medium pivot moves and weaker at the free throw line. Because player No. 3 is deeper in this zone, Nos. 4 and 5 need not cover as much area. This makes the zone somewhat stronger in the corners than the two-one-two. It has good fast break potential. It is weak to the side of the lane in the medium post area. It has good potential for double-teaming in the corners.

Fig. 6.15 shows the position of the players as the ball moves around the perimeter of the zone. Fig. 6.16 shows a double-team tactic in the left corner. Fig. 6.17 shows the movements of the individual players when the ball is in the left corner, left wing, point, right wing, and right corner positions.

Two-Two-One Zone

This zone resembles the two-three, although it is stronger in the medium pivot area and weaker under the basket. It is a good zone to use when a team has one player whose greatest asset is her rebounding

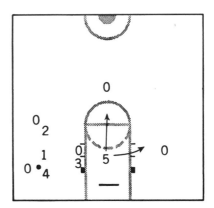

Fig. 6.16 *Two-Three Zone with a Double-Team in the Left Corner. Player No. 1 slides down to help No. 4 double-team; No. 2 slides over to play an opponent in that area aggressively; No. 5 zones against the two players furthest from the ball.*

225

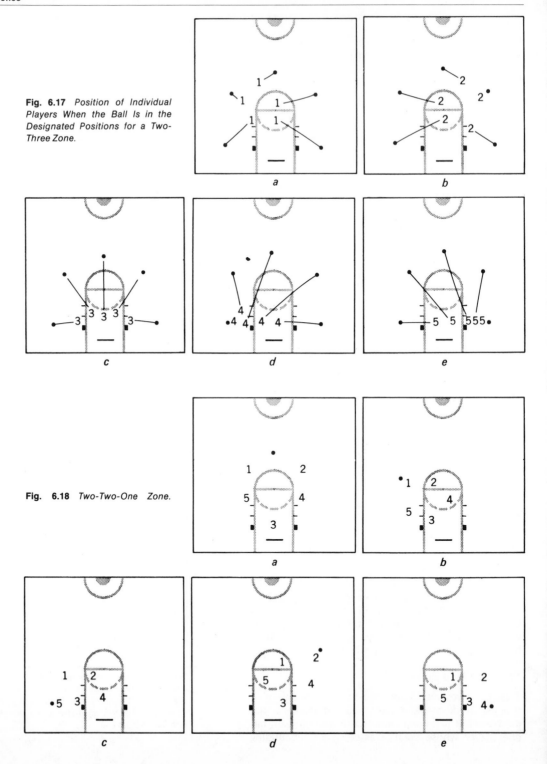

Fig. 6.17 *Position of Individual Players When the Ball Is in the Designated Positions for a Two-Three Zone.*

Fig. 6.18 *Two-Two-One Zone.*

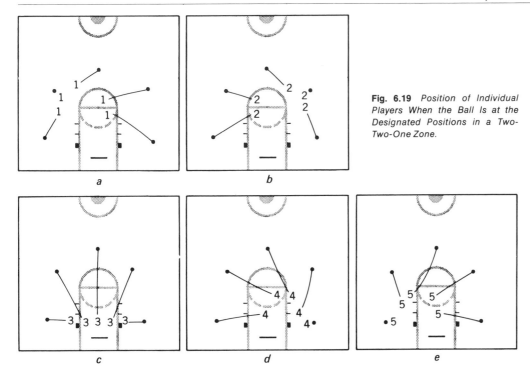

a b c d e

Fig. 6.19 *Position of Individual Players When the Ball Is at the Designated Positions in a Two-Two-One Zone.*

ability. It may also be used by a team that has one tall player and four short, quick ones. It provides opportunities for double-teaming and fast breaking. It is weak beyond 18 ft.

Fig. 6.18 shows the players' positions as the ball moves around the perimeter of the zone. Fig. 6.19 shows the movements of the individual players when the ball is in the left corner, left wing, point, right wing, and right corner positions.

Three-Two Zone

This zone is extremely strong at the free throw line and is excellent to use against a high post player. The three quickest players are assigned to the front line positions; the rebounders are in the back line. If the rebounders are strong, this zone is an excellent one for fast breaking. It is strong against outside shooters from the top of the circle and the free throw line extended. It is weaker once the front line has been penetrated, and is not a particularly strong rebounding defense.

Fig. 6.20 shows the positions of the players as the ball moves around the perimeter of the zone. Fig. 6.21 shows the movements of the individual players when the ball is in the left corner, left wing, point, right wing, and right corner positions.

One-Two-Two Zone

This zone is similar to the three-two zone, but is stronger in the medium post area outside the lane and is weaker beyond the free throw line. It is good against a medium or low pivot. It provides better rebound positioning than the three-two zone and is stronger in the corners. It is weak against outside shooters at the top of the circle, as they move away from the point position.

Fig. 6.22 shows the positions of the players as the ball moves around the perimeter of the zone. Fig. 6.23 shows the movements of the individual players when the ball is in the left corner, left wing, point, right wing, and right corner positions.

One-Three-One Zone

This zone is effective against a high scoring pivot player. It is strong at the free throw line and at the wing positions, but is weak in the corners and at the top of the circle. It is not a strong rebounding or fast breaking alignment.

Fig. 6.24 shows the positions of the players as the ball moves around the perimeter of the zone. Fig. 6.25 shows the movements of the individual players when the ball is in the left corner, left wing, point, right wing, and right corner positions.

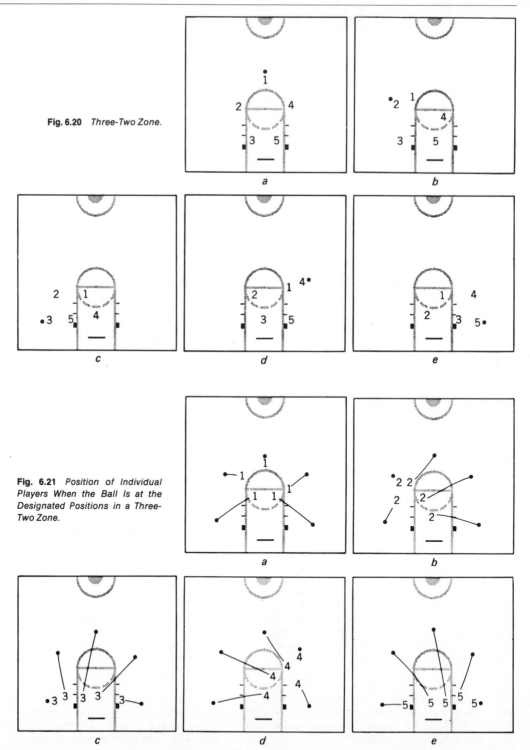

Fig. 6.20 *Three-Two Zone.*

Fig. 6.21 *Position of Individual Players When the Ball Is at the Designated Positions in a Three-Two Zone.*

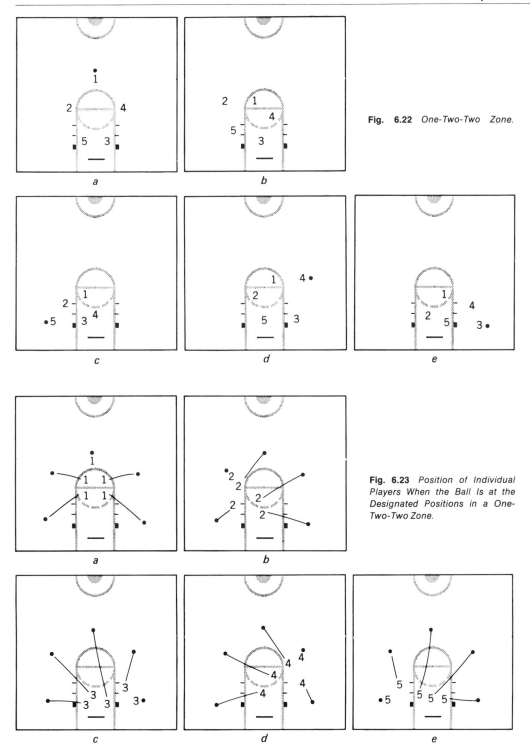

Fig. 6.22 *One-Two-Two Zone.*

Fig. 6.23 *Position of Individual Players When the Ball Is at the Designated Positions in a One-Two-Two Zone.*

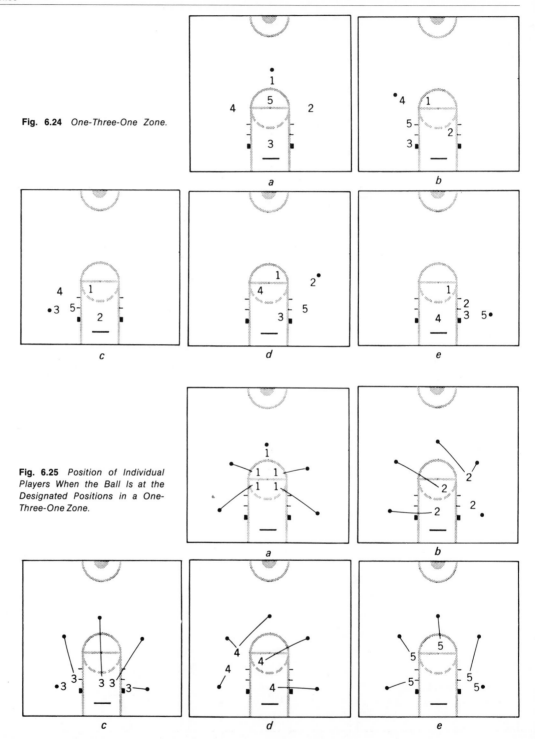

Fig. 6.24 *One-Three-One Zone.*

Fig. 6.25 *Position of Individual Players When the Ball Is at the Designated Positions in a One-Three-One Zone.*

Drills for Any Zone Defense

Prior to presenting a zone defense to a group, the teacher should prepare a mimeographed (or dittoed) diagram of the zone for every student. If this is too costly, each team of five players should have a copy and additional copies might be placed around the gymnasium for easy reference. A series of diagrams show the position of the defensive team in a zone when the ball is in the corners, wings, or at the point position. It should also include diagrams showing the positions of the individual players when the ball moves to each of these positions. Examples of these diagrams have been shown for each of the zones described. The teacher may add other pertinent information.

Before introducing a specific zone, general principles related to all zone defenses should be discussed. Then a specified zone may be introduced to a class. Its advantages, disadvantages, and reasons for selection should be presented. Diagrams for the zone should be distributed to students at this time if not done previously.

Players should then be permitted to get into groups of five, if they have not already done this. The ability necessary for each position should be discussed, and the students should decide on which player should play each position. Time should then be provided for each student to mentally gain a picture of her moves when the ball changes position.

Each team should be assigned to a free throw lane area for practice. If there are not a sufficient number of these, additional ones may be taped on the floor in extra space. If this does not provide enough areas, teams will have to rotate. Once the teams reach their assigned area, all players sit down under the basket behind the end line, with the exception of the player in the No. 1 position. She takes her starting position on the court and the teacher verifies that all players be ready with "arms out." Slowly, and in turn, the teacher calls out "Right wing," "Right corner," "Right wing," "Point," "Left wing," "Left corner," etc. As all No. 1's move to a new position, time is taken to verify that they have moved to the correct position. This is continued until they have moved to each position twice (or more). The signal to move to a new position may be speeded up if they seem ready. Again the calls should be made in order around the perimeter. This process is repeated for No. 2's, 3's, 4's, and 5's.

This technique is repeated, starting with the 1's once more. At first the signal should be to move to the adjacent position in one direction only. After the students have acquired some confidence, however, the teacher may alternate direction—for example, she may call left wing, point, and left wing again. At this time, she should only signal for a move to a position "one pass away."

It is now time for all five players to assume their starting position and, on signal, move to a new position. All players' arms should be outstretched in a legal manner to give the appearance of impenetrability and unity. As players gain confidence, the teacher can change direction frequently and increase the tempo of the signals.

Now half the teams are asked to put on pinnies and move to an adjacent court to be attack players against the zone defense. One player for each attack team gets a ball and the attack players take their places on the court in their usual positions. The attack players are informed that they may not dribble or cut. They must be stationary and pass to an adjacent player only when a signal is given.

When all teams are ready to start the teacher may call, "Pass"; the defense reacts to the ball's new position. A signal is given again and this process is continued. Following each pass, the teacher checks the positioning of as many groups as possible. The tempo of the signals is increased. The teams alternate and the same process is repeated.

Next in the progression is the permission for the attack players to cut as they please. Again, they may only pass on signal. With these directions the process is repeated for both teams. Following this drill, players should be ready to practice on their own with five-on-five, and the teacher moves from group to group to correct positioning when necessary.

COMBINATION DEFENSES

This type of defense combines man-to-man and zone principles. Normally, it is not appropriate for teaching in physical education classes but may prove valuable in competitive play. A teacher with imagination can devise a number of combinations that should prove effective against a particular offense. An example of a combination defense is four defenders playing a box or diamond zone and the fifth defender playing man-to-man against a high scorer or outside shooter.

Advantages of Combination Defenses

1. The advantages of principles for both man-to-man defense and zone defense are realized.
2. A defense can be devised to reduce the effectiveness of one or more particular players.
3. It provides opportunities for double-teaming.
4. It is a special defense for which the opponents may

not be prepared; thus, it may take them time to solve it.

Disadvantages of Combination Defenses

1. It takes special preparation and time to learn.
2. If the opponents can counteract the defensive deployment, an easy basket usually results.
3. If the defense misjudges the potential of each opponent and utilizes an inappropriate defense, an easy basket will result.
4. Disadvantages of man-to-man defenses are apparent for those players utilizing man-to-man tactics.
5. Disadvantages of zone defenses are apparent for those employing zone tactics.

SPECIFIC COMBINATION DEFENSES

Some of the more popular combination defenses are described briefly. For clarification purposes the defenses are named by identifying the zone first followed by the man-to-man coverage.

One and Four

The defensive player assigned to guard the poorest shooter becomes a "rover" and, in a sense, a zone player. She gives the outward appearance of guarding her assigned player when the opponents are setting up on offense. When they start their offensive thrust she sags off her opponent and is free to move wherever she can assist other defenders. Among other things she can help double-team an effective scorer or pivot player, cover the passing lane into the playmaker, or cover a favorite shooting position of one of the opponents. She is given unlimited freedom in her movements; for this reason, the player assigned to this position is usually quick, agile, and has the ability to be in the "right place at the right time."

Two and Three

In this defense three players play man-to-man while two back players in an up-and-back position in the lane play zone. This can be effective against a team that has two players with weak shooting and ball handling techniques. The players using zone principles stay in the lane ready to assist on cuts or drives through the lane. Both players start in the middle of the lane—the front player 12 ft. from the basket (3 ft. behind the free throw line) and the back player 6 ft. in front of the basket. The front player must be agile and the back player should be a strong rebounder (Fig. 6.26). If one of the opposing strong players is a pivot, this defense permits double-teaming her, regardless of her position in the lane.

Triangle and Two

The triangle zone should be familiar to those readers who remember the divided court game with only three players permitted at each end of the court. One player takes her position at the free throw line, and the other two players are 6 ft. in front of the basket; each stands astride the free throw lane on her side. The front player must be quick and possess good game sense.

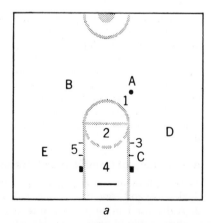 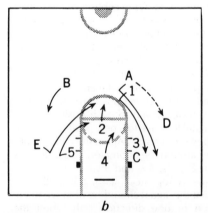

a *b*

Fig. 6.26 *Two- and Three-Combination Defense. Players B and D are considered weak ball handlers or poor shooters as they allow Nos. 2 and 4 to zone in the lane (a). A passes to D, who remains unguarded unless she dribbles in to the lane. Nos. 1 and 5 continue to guard their opponents closely. Note that No. 2 helps No. 5 cut off the passing lane to E (b).*

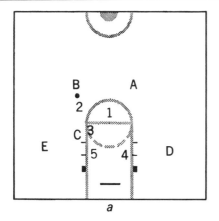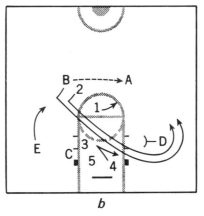

Fig. 6.27 *Triangle and Two-Combination Defense. The two best ball handlers are guarded man-to-man while the others play a triangle zone (a). B passes to A and cuts diagonally through the lane. No. 2 fronts her as No. 4 moves up and follows B's cut through the lane to discourage a lob pass. Player No. 1 moves up to prevent A from dribbling into the lane (b).*

Fig. 6.28 *Box and One-Combination Defense. E is the best shooter and is played man-to-man by No. 5. Note that No. 4 has modified her starting position slightly because of the position of C. After B passes to A, No. 2 retreats (a). As the ball is passed to A, E cuts up, guarded by No. 5 who is assisted by No. 2. Since no player is in the corner, No. 4 can afford to place pressure on C as she makes a cut (b).*

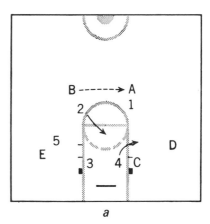

The back players should be the best rebounders. The remaining two defenders play man-to-man against the most dangerous opponents (Fig. 6.27).

Box (or Diamond) and One

The box or diamond zones should be familiar to most readers. In a box zone the front players start a step in front of the free throw line with the inside foot on the lane line on their side. The back players are 6 ft. in front of the basket and have their outside foot on the lane line on their side. The two front players should be quick and aggressive while the two back players should be the best rebounders. The other defender may either be assigned to guard a high scorer and place extra pressure on her or may be free to rove anywhere (Fig. 6.28). If the choice is the latter, the player should be the quickest one on the team with good anticipatory characteristics. When the opponents shoot, she may have the opportunity to cut downcourt for a lead pass and an easy layup.

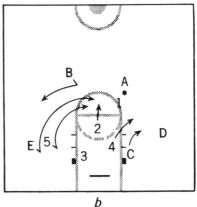

If a team prefers the diamond posture to the box, the front player takes her position halfway between the free throw line and outer circle. The back player is in the center of the lane 6 ft. in front of the basket, and the two middle players are just inside the free throw lane with their outside foot on the lane line on their side (Fig. 6.29).

The diamond zone is strong against shots from the side, but has some weakness in the medium and low post area. It is often used against a three-two offensive alignment. The box is strong under the basket but is weak in the 18 ft.-range to the side of the free throw line.

Drills for Combination Defenses

Because these defenses are extraordinary, sufficient time must be spent in practice so that the players have complete confidence in their ability to apply the principles involved correctly while under stress. As explained previously, in learning any zone it is possible to have the players move individually through their pattern—particularly, with the three- and four-player zones. Then, all zone players should practice moving as a unit before the man-to-man players are added. This should be done next, with attention being given to the defensive positioning of all players as an opponent guarded man-to-man cuts through the lane. Time should be devoted to this phase as well as to any other potential double-teaming opportunities.

The two-player zone can be introduced in the same manner but is somewhat more dependent upon the position of the opponents since two players are covering a larger zone and must position themselves within an area occupied by an opponent. During the early

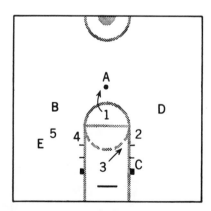

Fig. 6.29 *Diamond and One-Combination Defense. Player E is guarded closely by No. 5. No. 3 has adjusted her position slightly due to the position of C.*

stages, strong emphasis should be placed on the principle that neither player in the zone leaves the lane area regardless of where the other opponents are. If attention is given to the two players involved with the zone alone, soon their actions should be integrated with the other defenders. This is probably the best way to practice the one-and-four combination defense also.

PRESSURE DEFENSES

Although there may not be a need to teach a pressure-style defense in physical education classes, almost all highly competitive teams utilize some type of pressure defense in every game. Some teams use it throughout an entire game while others use it as a surprise measure at different times during a contest. There are two types of pressure defenses—man-to-man and zone. Each may be employed full court, three-quarter-court, or half-court. A full court press is started at the end line in a team's own front court, a three-quarter press is started at the top of the circle in a team's own front court, and a half-court press is initiated at the division line or one step into a team's own front court.

The type of pressure defense employed by a team depends upon the qualifications of the players. Players must possess better individual defensive abilities if they choose a man-to-man press. It is easier to "hide" a weak defensive player in a zone press defense.

Regardless of the type of pressure defense a team chooses to play the further downcourt it can initiate the press successfully (full court rather than half-court), the more effective it is in accomplishing its purpose. It also follows that in order to use a full court press a team must possess better defensive personnel than if they are using a half-court press. Because any pressure-type defense takes time to set up, it is used only after a successful field goal or free throw, a time out, or any other situation causing a temporary suspension of play.

The purpose of any pressure defense is to cause the opponents to use more energy—both physical and mental—before gaining position to shoot. In so doing the defense hopes to cause them to make tactical errors and turn the ball over to them. Although the pressure to get the ball over the division line is not a factor in women's play, because there is no 10-sec. rule, the pressure of shooting within a 30-sec. period is operative. Thus, a pressure defense causes the opponents to consume more time in advancing the ball into their front court.

A team that selects to play a zone press has several alignments from which it may operate. The most popular ones are the two-two-one and the three-one-one, which may be used from the full, three-quarter, or half-court posture. Other possibilities for a half-court press include a two-three and a one-one-three. Therefore a team may choose to use a zone press with an odd or even front line. The choice may be made on the basis of team personnel, the strengths or weaknesses of the zones in question, or the offensive alignment of the opponents. If an opposing team relies on one player to receive the in-bounds pass, the defensive team may attack it with an equal number of front line defenders. Hence their choice would be an even front line. If the offensive team sends two players to help the in-bound passer, the defense might counteract with a three-one-one alignment.

As has been the case throughout the text, in all diagrams which follow, players who normally play in the guard position are Nos. 1 and 2, forwards are Nos. 4 and 5, and the center is No. 3. Their placement in a zone press depends upon their inherent qualifications.

Advantages of Pressure Defenses

1. It is a highly effective defense to use against a weak ball handling team or an inexperienced team. It causes them to commit ball handling errors that lead to easy scoring opportunities for the team using the pressure defense.
2. It is effective against a team that has a height advantage or against a slower team.
3. The team that uses the pressure defense tends to control the tempo of the game.
4. It is a defense that causes the opponents to become both physically and mentally fatigued. They are given no time to rest, relax, or think; this pressure often leads to the demise of all but the most poised teams.
5. The defense often causes the opponents to call a time out to solve the defense. This means that they have one less time out later in the game.
6. It is the most effective defense to use in the last few minutes of a game when a team is behind.
7. It is effective against a team that uses a controlled style offense because it helps to consume part of the 30 sec.
8. It may also be used as an antidote to a team's own lethargic play.

Disadvantages of Pressure Defenses

1. The defense takes time to set up, so it cannot always be used when a team is forced to go on defense.
2. It requires a great deal of endurance and may be inappropriate for a team that has little practice time.
3. When the opponents solve the defense, they may create many offensive advantage situations—four-on-three, three-on-two, etc.
4. When the defensive team makes a mental or physical error, an easy scoring opportunity for the opponents results.

MAN-TO-MAN PRESSURE DEFENSE

In order to use this defense effectively, all players must be well skilled in fundamental defensive techniques. They must be quick and aggressive and possess good body control. Players must be exceptional to play a man-to-man press full court. It is difficult to control from this posture, and players need extraordinary stamina. A team also must have a number of substitutes who can press well so that the starters may be given short periodic rests if necessary.

In whatever posture (full, three-quarter, or half-court) a team establishes its press, defenders must be able to stop a dribbler. If any player is unable to contain her opponent, the pressure defense is useless. If a dribbler should evade her opponent, the defender must retreat quickly and force her opponent toward a side line, which helps curtail the dribbler's forward progress. The defender must then regain good defensive positioning.

An opponent who has not as yet dribbled must be approached cautiously. Once the player starts to dribble, the defender attempts to influence her in a predetermined direction. With a man-to-man press most teams choose to direct the ball toward the middle rather than the side line. With a particular opponent, however, a team may choose to force her to dribble with her weak hand regardless of the direction this influences her. As the dribbler is forced to catch the ball, other defenders play their opponents at an intercepting angle to try to force them to make a reverse cut requiring a lob pass from the ball handler. After the dribbler passes off, her opponent must drop back immediately so that she does not succumb to a give-and-go pattern.

When using the man-to-man defense full court it is extremely vital that the guards are quick, agile, and can stop a dribbler. The forwards must also be quick, but height to match their opponents is not as vital. Due to the press their opponent is forced out further from the basket where the value of their height advantage is reduced. The center should be a good rebounder and possess good reflexes and powers of anticipation, for most likely she will be confronted with several two-on-one situations.

As the opponents put the ball in play, a team using a full court press may choose to guard the passer and make it difficult for her to in-bound the ball and possibly commit a 5-sec. violation; or, the team may choose not to guard the in-bound passer but to double-team the receiver and cause a 5-sec. violation or errant pass.

The half-court man-to-man pressure defense is not as strong against a taller team because it does not draw the offensive players out far enough from the basket to reduce the effectiveness presented by their height advantage.

ZONE PRESSURE DEFENSE

This type of pressure defense may be played by a team that has one weak defense player who is placed in the zone where she can do the least amount of damage. This placement depends upon which of the zone defenses is used. With more than one weak player it is doubtful that a successful zone press can be maintained.

The purpose of a zone press is to double-team the ball handler and zone the rest of the opponents— i.e., to play the intercepting angles to them. Two defenders cover the passing lanes to the two opponents closest to the ball handler. The remaining defender must cover the passing lanes to two opponents, but must play closer to the player in a more dangerous scoring position. By double-teaming the ball handler and closing the passing lanes, the defense hopes that the opponents will be forced to use high passes that are more easily intercepted.

The method used for double-teaming a player depends upon whether the ball handler has dribbled. If an opponent receives a pass and has not dribbled, two defenders approach cautiously and form a wedge in front of her with their inside feet touching and the inside hand low so that the opponent cannot dribble between them. The other arm is held high. If an opponent has dribbled and a defender forces her to catch the ball, a teammate approaches from the blind side. If the ball handler pivots, the approaching defender should try to tap the ball or tie it up. If this is not successful, the two players form a wedge in front of the ball handler, but their inside feet need not be touching (since the ball handler has already completed her dribble). Both players hold their arms high to force a high pass. Because of the double-teaming tactics the zone press uses, it is considered a better pressure defense to use than a man-to-man against a good dribbling team.

Full Court Pressure Zone Defenses

The in-bounds passer is not harassed for any of the zone pressure defenses. The defenders drop back to their starting position and allow the initial pass inbounds and then move to double-team the pass receiver. If a player dribbles, the defenders influence her in a predetermined direction and try to stop the dribble as quickly as possible. The remaining de-

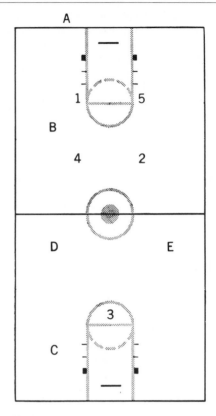

Fig. 6.30 *Poor Positioning by Zone Pressure Defensive Players. Player A can pass the ball over the first line of the press to B or over the second line to D or E.*

fenders play in front of the opponents in their zone and try to intercept the pass. After the ball has cleared one line of the zone, those players retreat quickly in a straight line back toward the basket. At no time should the defense allow the opponents to pass over a zone. In Fig. 6.30 it should be relatively easy for player A to pass over the heads of the front line and/or the second line of defenders. With the offense players in these positions, the defenders should adjust their position as shown in Fig. 6.31. The back player in any of the alignments must protect the goal and prevent any full court passes. She must be particularly skillful in playing a two-on-one situation, for she will be confronted with it when the defense breaks down.

In any zone press, it should be recognized that considerably more energy is expended on the part of all players than in a normal zone defense. Players must have considerable endurance and often must

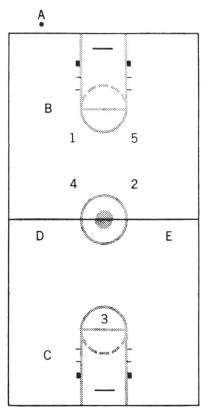

Fig. 6.31 *Modified Positioning of a Zone Pressure Defense So That the Opponents Cannot Pass Over a Line. Nos. 4 and 2 are in position to intercept a lob pass over their heads to D or E. The starting position for any zone press must be modified to prevent the ball from going over a line.*

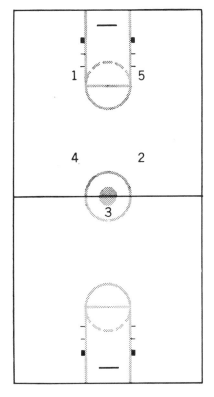

sprint to their new position. Sliding techniques usually employed on defense are too slow. Once an attacking team has penetrated to the top of its offensive circle area, the defenders may continue the press or revert to a normal zone defense.

A team must also understand that permitting the ball to be in-bounded to the defender's right weakens the defensive posture considerably because of the qualifications of players in those positions. If the inbound player starts to the defender's right of the basket, the defensive wing players (and the front line in the two-two-one) can reverse positions to counteract this move.

The two full court zone presses utilized most frequently are the two-two-one and the three-one-one. Each will be discussed separately.

The Two-Two-One Zone Press

As the reader might assume, the two-two-one zone press contains three "lines" of defenders who take their starting positions as shown in Fig. 6.32. Nos. 1 and 5 compose the front line, Nos. 4 and 2 the wing line (or wings), and No. 3 is called the back player. The peculiar numbering system occurs because the

Fig. 6.32 *Basic Positions of Players for a Two-Two-One Zone Press. These positions may be altered, depending upon the positions of the opponents. Nos. 1 and 5 represent the front line, 4 and 2 the wings, and 3 the back player. Nos. 1 and 5 take their position astride the lane line; Nos. 4 and 2 are directly behind Nos. 1 and 5, approximately midway between the top of the circle and the division line; No. 3 is in the back court half of the center circle.*

numbers represent the usual playing position for each player. As the reader recalls, Nos. 1 and 2 are guards, 3 is the center, and 4 and 5 are forwards.

Qualifications For and Responsibilities of Each Position in the Zone Press

Player No. 1

1. She should be the quickest guard.
2. It is her responsibility to direct play up her side of the court. She forces a pass to be received in front and to her left.
3. With the help of No. 5 she does not allow a pass to go between them.
4. She permits the receiver to dribble beyond the free throw line and then moves quickly to help No. 4 with the double-team.
5. If the ball goes downcourt she retreats quickly to the medium post position on the ball side.

Player No. 5

1. She is the taller of the two forwards.
2. With No. 1's assistance she prevents a pass from going between them.
3. She prevents a pass to the in-bounder.
4. She protects the middle while No. 1 double-teams.
5. If the ball is passed in on her side, she double-teams with No. 2 as No. 1 covers the middle area.
6. If the ball is advanced downcourt she retreats quickly straight downcourt to a position about 6 ft. in front of the basket.

Player No. 4

1. She is the quicker and more agile of the two forwards.
2. She prevents a pass from going between them with No. 2's help.
3. She allows the ball to be in-bounded in front of her; if no opponent is in front of her, she drifts back so that the ball cannot be passed over her head.
4. She prevents the receiver from dribbling downcourt between her and the side line. She helps double-team with No. 1.
5. If the subsequent pass is on her side of the court, she double-teams with No. 2.
6. If the ball is advanced downcourt she retreats quickly in a straight line and is prepared to double-team in the corner on her side; if the ball is on the far side, she retreats to the top of the circle and moves down the lane to about 6 ft. in front of the basket.
7. If the ball is in-bounded on the other side of the court, her duties become the same as those of No. 2.

Player No. 2

1. She is the second guard.
2. With the help of No. 4, she prevents a pass from going between them.
3. She moves up near the division line on the ball side to zone any opponent in that area.
4. If no opponent is in her area she adjusts her position to cover any free opponent so that the ball cannot be passed over her head.
5. If an opponent receives a pass in her area, she prevents her from dribbling downcourt between her and the side line. She double-teams with No. 4.
6. If the ball advances downcourt, she retreats to front any player in the medium post position on the ball side.
7. If the ball is in-bounded on her side of the court she assumes the responsibilities of No. 4.

Player No. 3

1. She is both center and safety valve and must protect against any easy field goals. She must be skilled in playing two-on-one.
2. She must prevent any full court passes. If she cannot intercept them she must at least deflect them away from an opponent.
3. When playing in front of her opponent she must not allow a pass to go over her head; if she does, it is almost a sure two points.
4. As the ball crosses the division line she should anticipate a pass into the corner and try to intercept it. Her timing on the interception must be perfect, or the opponents should score easily.
5. She must be a good rebounder.

In Figs. 6.33–6.42, the attack players are also included so that the reader can better visualize the relative positions of a defender to an opponent. In this zone the defenders do not allow the ball to be advanced down the middle of the court, and direct all ball movement toward the side line.

The Three-One-One Zone Press

This press also has three lines of defense, as shown in Fig. 6.43. The player in No. 1 position will be referred to as the top player, Nos. 4 and 5 are the wings, No. 2 is the middle player, and No. 3 is the back player. Although the three-one-one alignment differs from the two-two-one, basically the same zones on the court are covered with this zone as the one previously described. Placement of personnel may make one of the zone presses more desirable and effective than the other. This zone permits the initial trap to be made sooner than does the two-two-one. The two zones resemble each other after the in-bounds pass is made.

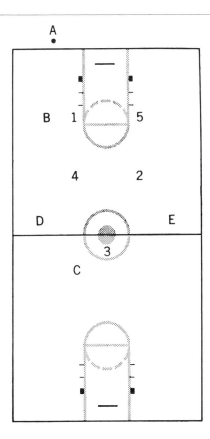

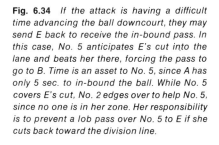

Fig. 6.33 *The defensive team wants the ball to be in-bounded to their left. Therefore, No. 1 allows A to pass to B. Nos. 2 and 5 prevent E from cutting in to the middle; No. 5 also covers the passing lane to E if she cuts down her side of the court toward the end line. No. 4 prevents the pass to D. No. 3 can prevent the full court pass to C.*

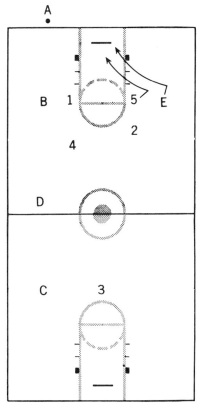

Fig. 6.34 *If the attack is having a difficult time advancing the ball downcourt, they may send E back to receive the in-bound pass. In this case, No. 5 anticipates E's cut into the lane and beats her there, forcing the pass to go to B. Time is an asset to No. 5, since A has only 5 sec. to in-bound the ball. While No. 5 covers E's cut, No. 2 edges over to help No. 5, since no one is in her zone. Her responsibility is to prevent a lob pass over No. 5 to E if she cuts back toward the division line.*

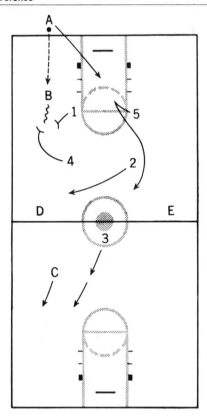

Fig. 6.35 *No. 1 allows B to receive the pass and dribble beyond the free throw line. No. 1 delays her move toward B to discourage a return pass to A. No. 5 moves toward A for the same purpose. As B dribbles, No. 4 moves over to prevent her from driving by; No. 1 moves over to double team. At the same time No. 2 moves over to prevent the pass to D and No. 5 moves to the intercepting angle so that E is not free; Nos. 1 and 4 have arms high trying to force a lob pass.*

Fig. 6.36 *If B in Fig. 6.35 cannot pass to D, she may return a quick pass to A. No. 5 must not permit her to drive down the middle. She must overplay her and force her to the defensive right side. There the double-team and other coverage can be re-established; No. 2 reverses her direction to assist No. 5 with the double team; No. 4 reverses her direction to cover the passing lane to E; No. 1 recovers down the middle.*

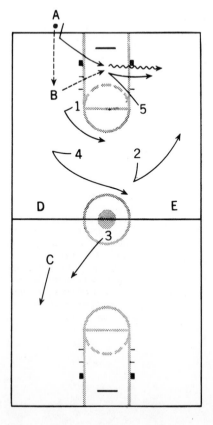

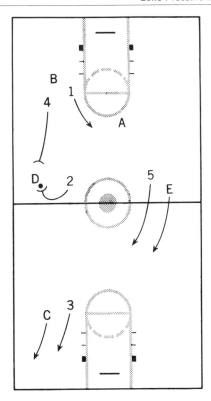

Fig. 6.37 *If B succeeds in passing to D. No. 2 approaches cautiously so that she is not subject to a fake and drive by D. At the same time No. 4 moves up from behind. If D pivots, No. 4 attempts to tie up the ball. If not, both players raise their arms high and try to force a lob pass. Nos. 2 and 4 must not let D dribble between them. At the same time, No. 1 cuts down the center of the court, filling in where needed. Nos. 5 and 3 cover the passing lanes to the opponent in their zone.*

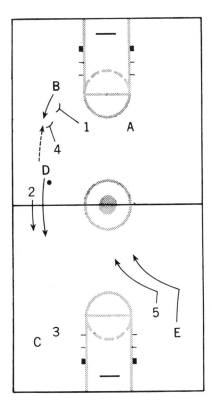

Fig. 6.38 *D is unable to pass to C or E and is forced to pass backward. No. 1 has zoned well against A, so D returns a pass to B. (When D has the ball in this position, No. 1 tries to zone against both B and A, but must be more concerned with A because the defense does not want the ball to be passed in to the middle.) Once D passes to B, Nos. 1 and 4 double-team B while No. 2 zones D. No. 3 cuts off the passing angle to C, and No. 5 cuts off the angle to E. If D succeeds in passing to A, No. 1 forces her toward the defensive right sideline; No. 2 moves over to help No. 1, while No. 4 plays zone between B and D.*

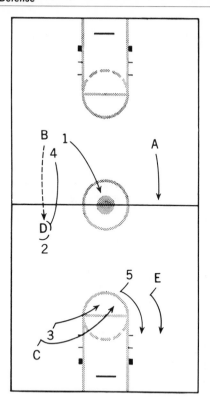

Fig. 6.39 *B returns the pass to D, and players resume their same relative position as described in Fig. 6.37. No. 1 must be ready for a pass back to either B or A.*

Fig. 6.40 *D succeeds in passing to C. Nos. 3 and 2 double-team C while No. 4 cuts ball side of D. No. 5 moves over near the free throw line covering the passing lane to E and is ready to help if C eludes the double-team. No. 1 breaks down the middle to help where necessary.*

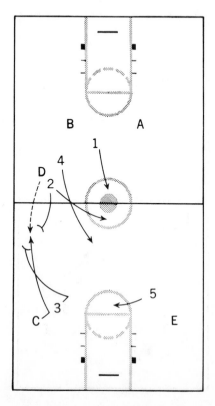

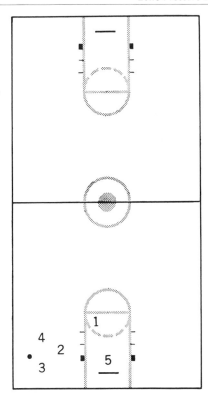

Fig. 6.41 *Position of the Players if the Ball Moves to the Defensive Left Corner. No. 2 fronts any player in the medium post position. No. 1 adjusts her position according to the position of the opponents.*

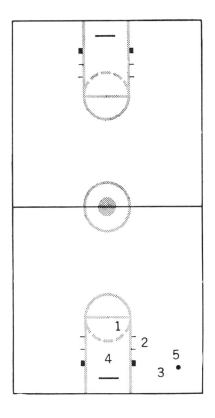

Fig. 6.42 *Position of the players if the ball is in the defensive right corner. When the ball is successfully advanced downcourt, the defense has the option of continuing with the press or reverting to a normal zone defense.*

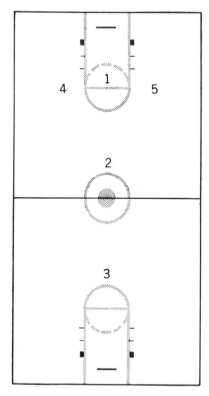

Fig. 6.43 *Basic Positions for a Three-One-One Zone Press. No. 4 is the better defensive forward as the defense tries to force the ball to their left.*

Qualifications For and Responsibilities of Each Position in the Press

Player No. 1

1. She should be the quickest guard.
2. It is her responsibility to direct play to her left, and she forces the in-bound pass to that direction.
3. She prevents an immediate return pass to the in-bounder.
4. She allows the receiver to obtain the pass and double-teams with No. 4.
5. If the ball is returned to the in-bound passer, she forces her to the defender's right and double-teams with No. 5. It takes time to set the trap, so the players involved should not be too hasty in their moves or else the dribbler will escape the trap.
6. She protects the middle area whenever she is not involved in a double-team.

7. When the ball is advanced downcourt she retreats quickly to the medium post position on the ball side.

Player No. 4

1. She is the quicker and more agile of the two forwards.
2. She allows the ball to be in-bounded in front of her; if no opponent is in front of her, she drifts back so that the ball cannot be passed over her head.
3. Once the ball has been in-bounded in front of her she sets a double-team with the help of No. 1. She must be certain that the dribbler does not evade the trap by dribbling between her and the side line.
4. If the subsequent pass is on her side, she double teams with the help of No. 2.
5. If the ball is advanced downcourt on her side, she retreats quickly to help No. 3 double-team in the corner. If the ball is on the far side of the court she retreats to the top of the circle and moves down the lane to about 6 ft. in front of the basket when the ball is in the far corner.
6. If the ball is in-bounded on the other side of the court, her duties become the same as No. 5.

Player No. 5

1. She is the second forward.
2. She prevents a pass from being in-bounded on her side.
3. While Nos. 1 and 4 are double-teaming, she protects the area at the top of the circle.
4. If the ball is returned to her side of the court through a pass to the in-bounder, she prevents the ball handler from dribbling between her and the side line. With the help of No. 1 they double-team the ball handler.
5. When the ball is advanced downcourt on the other side, she retreats quickly to the top of the circle and moves down the key to about 6 ft. in front of the basket as the ball is passed to the far corner. When the ball is on her side, she helps double-team any player who has the ball.
6. If the ball is in-bounded on her side of the court, her duties become the same as No. 4.

Player No. 2

1. She is the quicker of the two guards and should have outstanding anticipation.
2. When the ball is in-bounded to her left, she prevents a subsequent pass up that side of the court. She overplays any opponent in that area.
3. If the opponent receives the ball she prevents her from dribbling downcourt between her and the side line. She helps double-team with No. 4's assistance.

4. If the ball is passed back to the in-bounder and is dribbled up the far side of the court, she crosses to the other side at midcourt to overplay a logical receiver in the area.

5. When the ball is advanced downcourt, she retreats quickly to the ball side and moves down outside of the lane as the ball moves into the corner.

Player No. 3

1. She is the pivot player and the best rebounder.

2. She must protect against any long downcourt pass, but her timing for an interception must be exceptional so that an easy layup does not result.

3. She must anticipate and fake well in a two-on-one situation.

4. She must anticipate a pass into the corner and contain the ball handler until she has help in a double-team effort.

5. She must not let a pass go over her head while she is overplaying a potential receiver.

In Figs. 6.44–6.53 which follow, the defenders' positions are shown as the ball is passed downcourt.

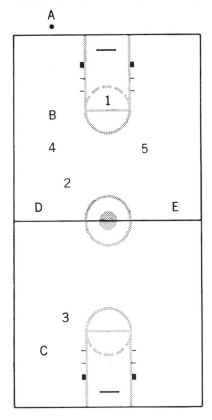

Fig. 6.44 *Modified Starting Position When the Offensive Players Start Behind the Free Throw Line. The defense must not allow a pass to go over a zone, so they drift back to force the pass to be made in front of them. No. 5 prevents a pass to E, and No. 4 forces the in-bounds pass to go to B.*

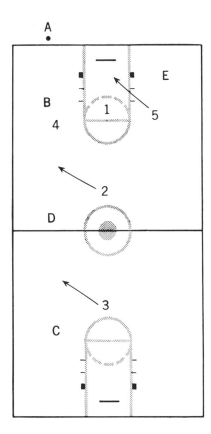

Fig. 6.45 *If the attack is having difficulty advancing the ball downcourt, they may send another player to receive the in-bound pass. The defenders want the ball in-bounded and brought down the court to their left, so No. 5 cuts off the passing lane to E.*

245

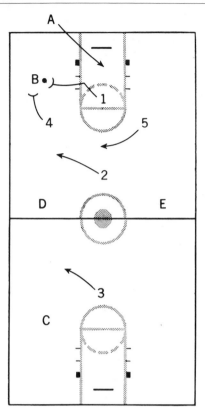

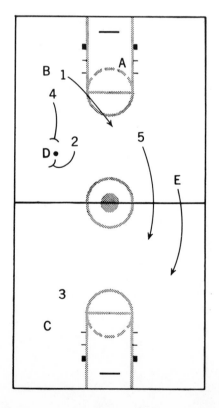

Fig. 6.46 *No. 1 allows the ball to be passed in to B and cuts down the lane to prevent a return pass to A and then helps No. 4 double-team B. As the ball is in-bounded to No. 2's left, she moves over to cover the passing lane to D. No. 5 edges back to cover the passing lane to E. No. 3 moves over to prevent a pass to C.*

Fig. 6.47 *B is able to pass to D. No. 4 joins No. 2 in a double-team. No. 1 cuts to the top of the circle to prevent a pass to A. This leaves B open, but should the ball be returned to her, the players resume the same positions held previously. No. 5 continues to play the intercepting angle to E, while No. 3 does the same to C.*

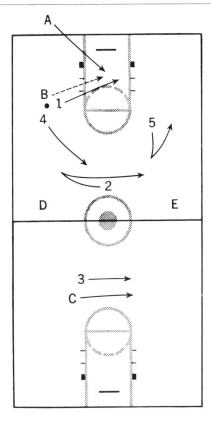

Fig. 6.48 *If B cannot pass to D but is able to return a pass to A, Nos. 1 and 5 must move quickly to double-team her as rapidly as possible. No. 4 moves up to cover the middle while No. 2 moves over to play the intercepting angle to E. As C cuts to the ball side, so does No. 3.*

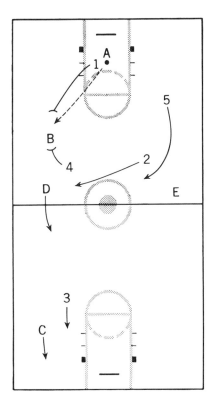

Fig. 6.49 *Player A anticipates the double-team approaching and returns the ball quickly to B. The defense players reverse their actions to cover the intercepting angles. No. 1 returns with No. 4 to double-team B. Nos. 2, 5, and 3 recover as shown.*

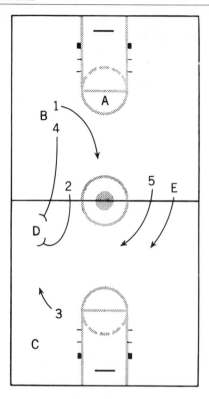

Fig. 6.50 *If B is able to pass to D, the defense players move to the same relative positions they had when D was double-teamed previously (Fig. 6.47). No. 1 must be ready to return to either A or B in case D passes back. If this should occur, the players resume the positions previously described (Fig. 6.49).*

Fig. 6.51 *After D gets the ball in Fig. 6.47, she is able to pass to C. No. 2 helps No. 3 double-team C. No. 4 cuts to the ball side of D, while No. 1 is ready if a pass is returned to B or A. No. 5 covers the passing lane to E.*

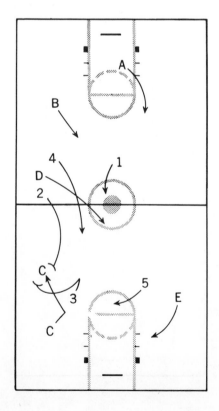

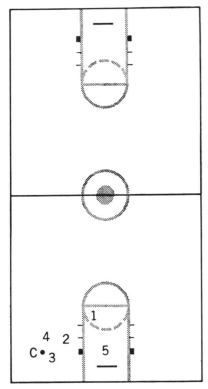

Fig. 6.52 *Position of the Players When the Ball Moves in to the Defense's Left Corner. No. 2 fronts any player in the medium post area. No. 1's position is adjusted according to where the opponents are positioned.*

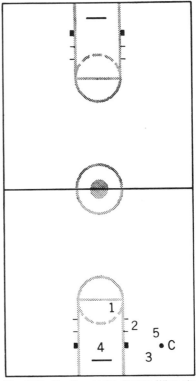

Fig. 6.53 *Position of the Players When the Ball Is in the Defense's Right Corner. No. 2 fronts any player in her area and No. 1 adjusts her position according to the position of the opponents. When the ball is successfully advanced downcourt, the defense has the option of continuing with the press or reverting to a normal zone defense.*

DRILLS FOR FULL COURT PRESSES

1. Two teams in position for the ball to be in-bounded to the defender's left of the basket. The initial pass is made in-bounds on signal from the instructor. The defenders move accordingly. A subsequent pass is made on another signal, and the defenders react accordingly. Attack players must remain stationary at this stage so that the defenders can gain knowledge of intercepting angles. Later, as they acquire this ability, the attack players are permitted to move wherever they choose but must continue to pass on signal. At first also, the instructor designates where the next pass is made; later, the players use their own discretion.

2. Two teams. The team that is practicing the pressing defense possesses the ball in their front court. Any player may shoot, and when the goal is made the team moves quickly into their pressing alignment before the ball can be in-bounded. The instructor must watch carefully to see that the offensive team rebounds properly. Players have a tendency to shoot and run to their position in the press. They must first rebound before they can move to their pressing positions.

Fig. 6.54 *Two-Two-One Half-Court Press.*

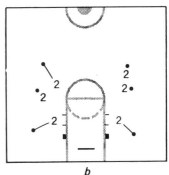

Fig. 6.55 *Position of Individual Players When the Ball Is at the Designated Positions.*

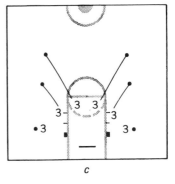

c

Half-Court Zone Presses

If a team does not have the personnel to employ a full court press, it may be able to use a half-court press successfully. Periodically, it may also prove valuable as a surprise tactic if a team does not have confidence in using it throughout a game.

Numerous half-court zone pressure defenses can be established. The most popular ones are the two-two-one, three-one-one, one-one-three, and the two-three. For the odd front zones the front line starts one step across the division line; but for the even front zones, the front line starts on the defensive side of the division line. It should be noted that all of the zones resemble one another after the initial pass.

The Two-Two-One Half-Court Press

Player qualifications for the various positions are the same as those described for the full court press. The reader will recognize that the defense is much stronger to the defender's left than to the right. Every effort should be made to influence the ball in this direction or reverse the positions of the front and wing lines. As the ball moves to the right wing position, player No. 1 (a guard) is in the lane after No. 5 has dropped back from her double-teaming duties near the division line. When the ball goes into the right corner, No. 5 drops down into the lane about 6 ft. in front of the basket to afford better protection against taller opponents under the basket and for better rebounding strength.

The positions of the players as the ball moves around the perimeter of the zone are shown in Fig. 6.54. Fig. 6.55 shows the movements of the individual players as the ball moves to various positions.

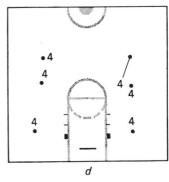

d

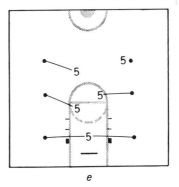

e

251

The Three-One-One Half-Court Press

Player qualifications for the various positions are the same as those described for the full court press. Fig. 6.56a–k show the movements of the players, and Fig. 6.56l–r show the positions of players as the ball moves around the perimeter of the zone. Fig. 6.57 shows the movements of the individual players as the ball moves to various positions.

a

b

Fig. 6.56 *Three-One-One Half-Court Press.*

c

d

e

f

Fig. 6.56 *continued.*

g

h

i

j

Fig. 6.56 *continued.*

k

Fig. 6.56 *continued on following page.*

Fig. 6.56 *continued.*

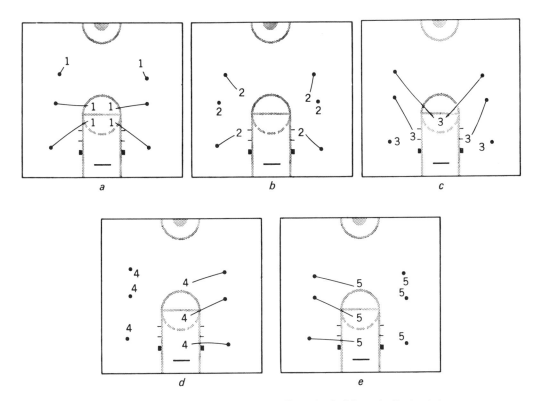

Fig. 6.57 *Position of Individual Players When the Ball Is at the Designated Positions.*

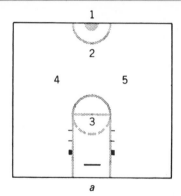

The One-One-Three Half-Court Press

Of the two guards, No. 2 should be the quicker and better skilled defense player. She has considerably more territory to cover than does the other guard. Of the two forwards, No. 4 should be the better defense player if the ball is to be influenced toward her side of the court.

The positions of the players as the ball moves around the perimeter of the zone are shown in Fig. 6.58. Fig. 6.59 shows the movements of the individual players as the ball moves to various positions.

Fig. 6.58   *One-One-Three Half-Court Zone Press.*

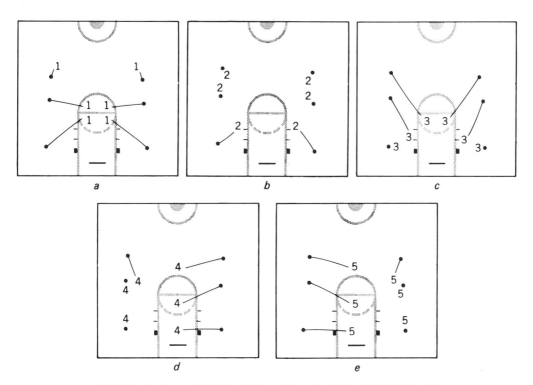

Fig. 6.59 *Positions of Individual Players When the Ball Is at the Designated Positions.*

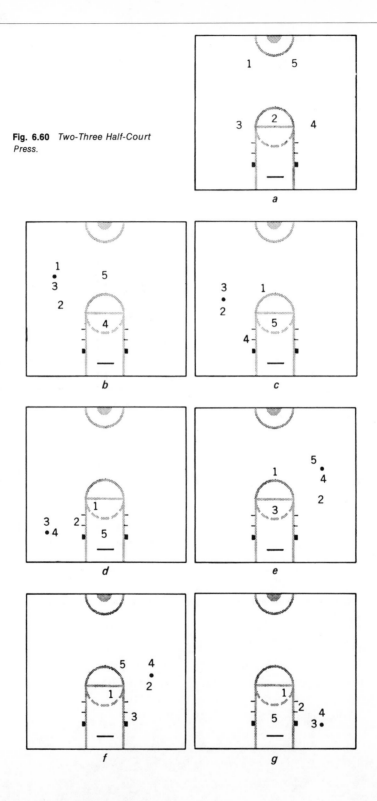

Fig. 6.60 *Two-Three Half-Court Press.*

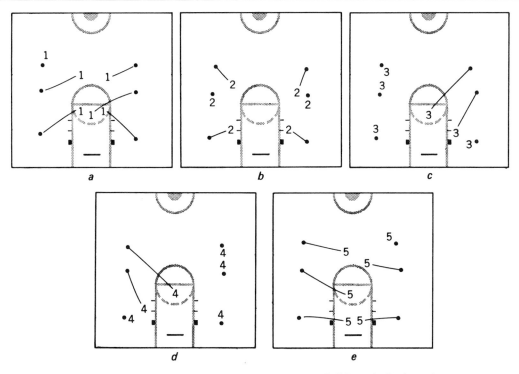

Fig. 6.61 *Position of Individual Players When the Ball Is at the Designated Positions.*

The Two-Three Half-Court Press

The guard assigned to the No. 2 position should be the quickest defender. Because both forwards and the pivot cover a great deal of area with this press, all must be agile. The player assigned to the No. 5 position should be the best rebounder. Player No. 5 must also sprint under the basket when the ball moves from the right wing to the right corner position so that the team does not give away a great height advantage under the basket.

The positions of players as the ball moves around the perimeter of the zone are shown in Fig. 6.60. Fig. 6.61 shows the movements of the individual players as the ball moves to various positions.

Drills for Half-Court Presses

The drills used for zone defenses can be adapted for instruction in the half-court pressure defenses.

DEFENSE AGAINST A FAST BREAK

Once a fast break has developed, the defense against it is most difficult. The defense must have a little bit of luck to be successful! The best way to defend against a fast break is to prevent it from starting! One of the requirements for this is the maintenance of defensive balance while a team is on offense. On any offensive play two players must remain in the back court area in case ball possession is lost. If a fast break is started the defenders at least have two players to force an outside shot rather than a lone defender.

It may be possible for a team to make certain adjustments on offense when it has to contend with a good fast breaking opponent. There are several steps that may be taken to cause certain key players on the opposing team to be out of position to start the fast break. A team may play its pivot in a high post position to lure the opposing player away from the backboard and out of good rebounding position, thus reducing the opportunity for that team to start a fast break. This tactic may prove successful if a team has forwards who are equal or better rebounders than the opponents. If this tactic also pulls its best rebounder away from the basket, thus reducing its own rebounding strength, it may not be worthwhile. A team may also try to maneuver the opposing guards into the corners so that they are not in a favorable position

263

to receive an outlet pass to start a fast break when their team rebounds. This tactic may be effective against a man-to-man defense; against a zone, of course, players are not that maneuverable.

Utilizing methods such as those described may limit the number of fast breaks the opponents start, but it may also reduce the effectiveness of the offense of the team employing them. Such maneuvering may necessitate special offensive plays, the timing of which may not be fully developed. It may also maneuver some of the better offensive players out of position and psychologically affect their offensive contributions. Many teams find that the values accrued from these measures do not outweigh the problems created in structuring a different offense.

The tactics used most often against the fast break include three measures.

1. The team rebounds strongly. If unable to obtain the rebound, a player or players guard the rebounder aggressively. They do not necessarily attempt to tap the ball or tie it up, but try to stall the rebounder from making her outlet pass.
2. The defenders guard the receivers for the outlet pass. Very soon after a game begins, it should be evident which players are the usual recipients of the outlet pass. Whenever the ball is lost, players are then assigned to guard them closely following a rebound, thus slowing the start of the fast break.
3. Another method of dealing with the outlet receivers may be used. It should be obvious where the opponents generally receive the outlet pass, and players may then be designated to move in to the intercepting angles.

By a combination of the first and either the second or third measures, the fast break effort should be delayed long enough so that the other defenders have ample time to recover downcourt.

Should a team make a mental or physical error resulting in a fast break by the opponents, the defense will be subjected to a situation where the offense has more players than the defense. Examples of these situations and methods of dealing with them are found in Chapter 5.

TEAM REBOUNDING

For most girls the blocking out process is not a natural one and must be cultivated by extensive practice. The procedure and drills for becoming proficient in this vital technique are discussed in Chapter 4 if the reader needs review. Unless a team develops proper blocking out techniques it can never become a good rebounding team.

Generally a team assigns three players as their primary rebounders, while a fourth player moves near the free throw line to recover any shot that rebounds hard off the backboard or rim. The fifth player moves to her assigned position outside of the lane, or cuts to receive an outlet pass. Some teams rely wholly on three rebounders; this is desirable if a team has strong rebounders, for it allows the outlet pass to be made further downcourt. Generally, the two forwards and pivot player are given the primary responsibility for rebounding; but there may be occasions when a guard has cut through the lane and is in better position to rebound than a forward.

Most authorities agree that when playing man-to-man defense all players should block out their opponent immediately after a shot is taken. There are two theories on the tactics that follow, however. One suggests that defenders should block out their opponents, keep them blocked out in that position until the ball rebounds, and then move to obtain the ball. The other proposes that the opponents should be blocked out momentarily and that the rebounders should then move toward the ball. This latter technique seems to be the most desirable since less body contact results. To retain a blocking out position longer than an instant requires body contact. The defender must maintain pressure against the opponent so that she can feel her change of direction. Because of this, this tactic seems objectionable. The author, therefore, recommends that all players be blocked out initially and then the assigned players move toward the basket for the rebound. This method should accomplish the same purpose as the other, since the opponent should continue behind the defender. As soon as a rebounder obtains the ball, she should pass it quickly toward the near side line.

Defensive players must be aware of free opponents in the scoring area and be ready to block them out on any shooting attempts. Players must be ready to cross block under these circumstances.

Because a player is not responsible specifically for any one opponent, zone defense screening responsibilities are more difficult. As a matter of fact, the offense has a better chance of obtaining a rebound against a zone defense than it does against a man-to-man defense. Because defenders are not responsible specifically for any one opponent, it is more difficult to keep the offensive players away from the logical rebounding areas. This is one of the disadvantages of a zone defense, but if player personnel qualifications make the zone defense desirable, this aspect must be overlooked in determining the type of defense to be played overall.

A team using a zone defense may establish its rebounding responsibilities in either of two ways.

1. It may assign its best rebounders to specific positions in a triangle in front of the basket: A fourth player may also be assigned to a position near the free throw line. Those who believe this tactic is

effective maintain the philosophy that if the rebounders position themselves in these vital positions the ball must rebound to one of them.

2. A team may block out the nearest opponent before moving into rebound position. If a zone is overloaded, it may not be possible to block out all players. Nevertheless, blocking out some may be better than none!

It is the author's contention that this second method is better, since it momentarily stalls the forward movement of the attack players and keeps them behind the defenders as they move toward the backboard. It may also prevent complacency from developing and the resulting poor positioning of the defenders.

Regardless of the technique used to block out, rebounders should react immediately. They should operate under the philosophy that no shot will be successful and obtain proper position against an opponent rapidly. There is no time to admire a shot or catch a breath!

III

Special Situations

7

Special Situations

Several situations will be covered in this chapter, and each will be treated from both the offensive and defensive points of view. Included within this discussion are jump ball, out-of-bounds, and free throw situations. Situations that may occur near the end of the game are also discussed. This includes the stall situation and the shot in the last few seconds of the game.

JUMP BALL

Although jump balls may not play a major role in determining the winner of a game, thoughtful and intelligent play is necessary for a team to win their share of the taps. A jump ball situation occurs approximately ten times during a game — four of them occurring at the start of periods.

Regardless of whether a team believes it will win or lose the tap, thoughtful consideration should be given by the jumper and those players positioned around the circle to ensure that some member of her team will acquire the ball. No team should ever assume that they will win the tap and take no measures to assure that they will; similarly, no team should ever assume that they will lose the tap and take no measures to prevent the opponents from gaining it.

Technique for the Jumper

A right-handed jumper should turn her right side to her opponent, with feet in a forward-backward stride. Her right foot should be forward and the stride no wider than her shoulders. Ankles, knees, and hips should be flexed. The degree depends upon her leg strength. A more flexed position allows her to exert force over a greater distance and permits her to jump higher, but also requires more strength to accomplish the greater work (raising her body a greater distance).

Thus, the degree of flexion depends upon the individual's leg strength. Weight should be evenly balanced over her two feet so that the force can be exerted directly upward. The right hand should swing forward and upward as her legs extend. The jump should be timed so that, at the peak of the jump, the ball may be contacted with the arm in an extended position. To acquire the timing for this action, players should practice jumping and have various people tossing the ball. The height of tosses differs, and jumpers must make the necessary timing adjustments. All players should practice jumping against players of different heights. Lack of height is no excuse for not practicing jump ball plays.

When contacting the ball on the tap, jumpers must direct it to a teammate. Simply contacting it is not sufficient! Prior to taking their position in the circle for the jump, each jumper should check the positions of her teammates. She looks to see if her own opponent is covered when her opponent is not one of the jumpers, and she checks for defensive balance in case the tap is lost. She also determines which teammate is in the freest position to receive the tap. The jumper may signal her teammates to notify them to whom she will attempt to tap the ball. This allows them to screen opponents near the receiver so that the player can obtain the tap. Specific plays may also be designated. In all instances the tap should be directed away from the side of the defender (Fig. 7.1). The receiver should be ready for the tap and, upon receiving it, protect the ball if she is closely guarded.

It should also be apparent to the jumper that it is easier to tap the ball accurately to a facing player. In Fig. 7.1, player No. 3 can tap the ball with greatest accuracy to either player No. 1 or 4, but with less ease to player No. 2, as she is not completely within the visual field of the jumper. Since player No. 5 is behind the jumper, she is outside the jumper's vision

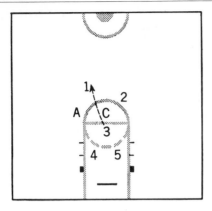

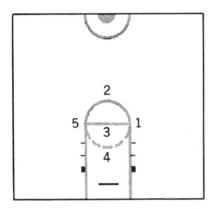

Fig. 7.1 *Box Formation. Player No. 3 is shown tapping the ball to player No. 1 and away from Player A.*

Fig. 7.2 *Diamond Formation.*

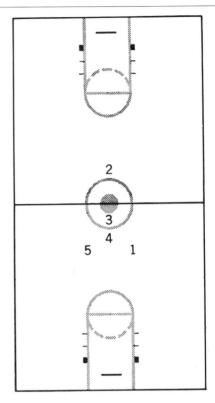

Fig. 7.3 *Y Formation.*

and is, therefore, the least likely player to receive the tap.

Depending upon the situation and abilities of the players, different formations may be used during a jump. Fig. 7.1 shows a box formation by one team. Fig. 7.2 shows a diamond, and Fig. 7.3 shows a Y formation that is used for a defensive position only. A formation may be used for a specific purpose, although players should discern that the configuration may be changed as soon as the ball is tossed by the official. Players may move to new positions at that time so that the original formation is abandoned.

It is wise to assign players to a specific position in a formation. This eliminates the last second shuffling by players to assure that all places in the formation are covered. Each player takes the same

position along the circle every time. If a different player is involved in the jump, the former jumper replaces the new jumper in her assigned position at the circle. This method tends to eliminate confusion during a game. When competing against different opponents, it may be desirable to change the assigned positions for that particular game in order to take advantage of the weaknesses of particular opponents; but, the same positions are assumed by all players throughout the game.

Team Tactics on Jump Balls

Teamwork is just as important on jump balls as at any other time during the game. When a jump ball is called by an official, all players should immediately and carefully size up the situation. They should ascertain whether they will win or lose the jump, or if it is a "toss up." They should also consider whether the jump is taken in the center circle or at the offensive or defensive end. When taking the jump in the defensive end, greater precautions are taken,

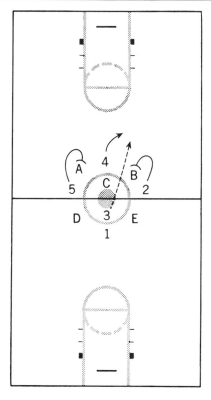

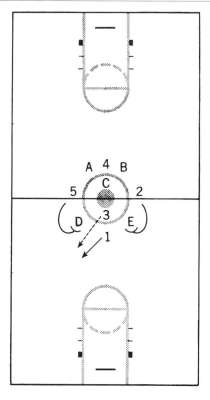

Fig. 7.4 *Expect to Win the Tap—Tap to Front Court. As the ball is tossed, Nos. 2 and 5 cut in front of B and A, respectively, and screen so that the tap can be made successfully to No. 4.*

Fig. 7.5 *Expect to Win the Tap—Tap to Back Court. If the opponents take measures to prevent the tap from going to No. 4, then No. 3 can tap the ball into the back court for No. 1 as players 5 and 2 screen.*

regardless of whether a team believes it should secure the jump.

Tactics When a Team Should Win the Tap

In this situation a team should not become complacent and allow the opponents (who have a height or jumping disadvantage) to outmaneuver them and acquire the tap. The jumper must try to determine if the opponents are taking their positions in such a manner that they may move to double-team or cover an otherwise free player. The jumper should tap to the player most likely to be freest after the opponents have moved because it is extremely important that a team obtain possession of the tap when they have an apparent height advantage. This is not always easy to ascertain. In certain positions on the court, players can assist a teammate in becoming free by screening the opponents. Figs. 7.4 and 7.5 show screens set at

the center circle. (*Note:* The screeners move to the outside of the circle to establish their screen so that they can move sooner (when the ball is tossed).) This also permits them to move into the defender's cutting lane, which is not possible if the screeners cut into the circle.

Either the diamond or box formation may be used if the jump is taken at the offensive end of the court. A diamond formation is shown in Fig. 7.6. Player D is a dangerous scorer and the opponents have double-teamed her. This is rather common procedure with this formation. The tap should go back to A. If the defense takes their positions as shown in Fig. 7.7, the tap may go to either D or A. If both teams line up in a box formation, possibilities for the tap are shown in Fig. 7.8.

If the jump is taken at the defensive end, the team must take defensive precautions in case of a poor tap or an unexpected successful tap by the opposing

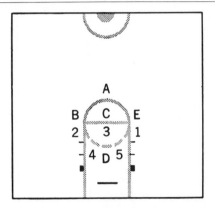

Fig. 7.6 *Expect to Win the Tap—Offensive End. Player D is a dangerous scorer and is double-teamed. Other offensive players are covered goal side by a defender. Player A is free at the top of the circle in the least dangerous position to shoot. Player No. 3 should tap the ball between players 2 and 4, unless other move has been pre-arranged.*

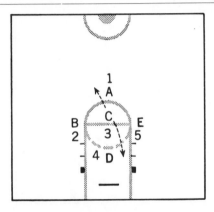

Fig. 7.7 *Expect to Win the Tap—Offensive End. Player D is free on her right side. The tap may be made there, but C and D should be aware of any movement by No. 5, who may slide down to help No. 4. If this occurs and D receives the tap, she should immediately pass to E, who will be free. If player C anticipates the move of No. 5, she may tap back between A and B.*

jumper. The position of the players is shown in Fig. 7.9. Player C must tap accurately to player A or B.

Tactics When a Team May Lose the Tap

In this situation a team should never concede the tap to the opposing team. They must take measures to prevent them from receiving the tap or at least force

them to tap the ball backward. By thoughtful positioning the team may deceive their opponents into thinking a player is open; but this may not be so after the ball is tapped, as a player moves to a new position. Fig. 7.10 shows the team expecting to lose the tap in a diamond formation and the moves of the players. Figs. 7.11 and 7.12 show the team expecting to lose the tap in a box formation. Fig. 7.11 shows how a

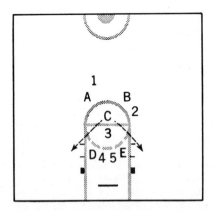

Fig. 7.8 *Expect to Win the Tap—Offensive End. Using a box formation and the defending team responding with the same, C should be able to tap to D or back to A.*

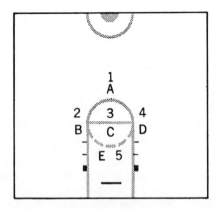

Fig. 7.9 *Expect to Win—Defensive End. Player C must tap accurately to A or B. A poor tap may result in an easy score for the opponents.*

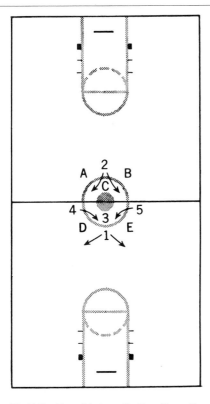

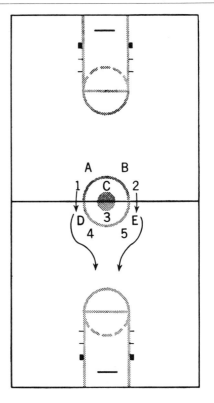

Fig. 7.10 *Expect to Lose the Tap. Player No. 1 is ready to retreat quickly in either direction, depending on the direction of the tap. As the ball is tapped, players 4 and 5 move inside the circle to intercept a tap to D or E or deflect it backward to No. 1. Player No. 2 is ready to move to cover either A or B, but is particularly aware of B because it is easier for C to tap in her direction.*

Fig. 7.11 *Expect to Lose the Tap. Players 1 and 2 leave their opponents when the ball is tossed to help double-team D and E. If the ball is not intercepted, players 1 and 2 retreat and meet their opponents as they move into the front court.*

team may double-team the likely receivers. Fig. 7.12 shows a more daring type of tactic.

If the jump is taken at the offensive end of the court and the attacking team expects to lose the tap, Fig. 7.13 shows possible tactics for use.

When the jump is taken at the defensive end and a team expects to lose the tap, certain measures may be taken. Figs. 7.14 and 7.15 demonstrate these tactics.

DRILLS FOR JUMP BALL SITUATIONS

1. Groups of three (all approximately the same height). One player tosses the ball while the other two practice jumping and tapping the ball to a predetermined target. Rotate.

2. Two teams. Tactics should be practiced for situations when it appears as though a team will win a tap or lose a tap at each of the three restraining circles.

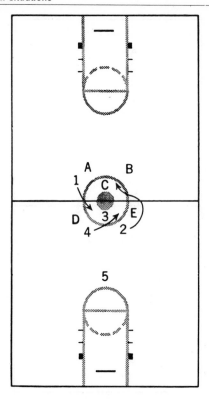

Fig. 7.12 *Expect to Lose the Tap. Player No. 5 retreats to be in a defensive position in case the attack gets the ball. The other defensive players rotate counterclockwise to attempt to intercept or deflect the tap. Note that No. 2 moves to the outside, while the others go in to the circle. This is necessary because she has a greater distance to cover; by taking this route she may move as soon as the official tosses the ball.*

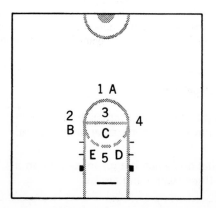

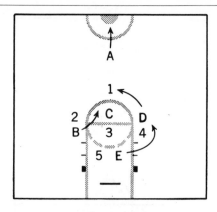

Fig. 7.13 *Expect to Lose—Offensive End. Player No. 3 has a height advantage on player C. Player No. 3 usually is reluctant to tap the ball backward in this position. Therefore, E may leave her position as the ball is tossed and move up to cover No. 4. Meanwhile D has moved up near No. 1. When the ball is tapped, B moves in to the circle to cut off the tap in that direction. Player A retreats to prevent the long tap.*

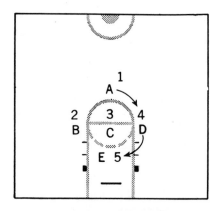

Fig. 7.15 *Expect to Lose—Defensive End. As the ball is tossed, players D and A rotate clockwise. If the ball is secured by their opponents, they return to guarding them.*

Fig. 7.14 *Expect to Lose—Defensive End. Player 5 is considered to be a dangerous scorer and is double-teamed. Player B is goal side of her opponent. If the tap goes to No. 4, D moves back to guard her own player.*

OUT-OF-BOUNDS SITUATIONS

During the course of a game, the ball will be put in play from the defensive end line and from the side line at both the defensive and offensive ends of the court. Different formations and tactics are used for in-bounding the ball in each of these situations. Under most circumstances special measures need not be taken to in-bounds the ball in the defensive end, as the ball usually can be passed in-bounds with little difficulty. The reader is referred to Chapter 3 to review means of combating a pressing defense, and to Chapter 6 to initiate a pressing defense in the back court, if desired.

When putting the ball in play from the side line in the defensive end, little defensive pressure generally occurs. If pressure does occur, the pass is usually made backward to a player who cuts quickly in that direction.

When in-bounding the ball from the side line in the offensive end of the court, a team generally uses quick moves to outwit the defense or uses a pre-determined play to free a particular player for a shot. In either case a good passer should be assigned to put the ball in play. Some teams assign their best passer to in-bound the ball, while others assign either a forward or a guard—depending upon the spot from which the ball is put in play. The teacher/coach must determine which choice is more suitable for her player personnel. Regardless of which system is selected, the same player or her substitute should always put the ball in play. The player who is to in-bound the ball should take her time while getting into position along the side line so that she may analyze the positioning of the defense and allow her teammates

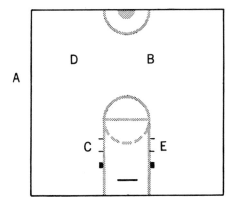

Fig. 7.16 *Out of Bounds—Box Formation.*

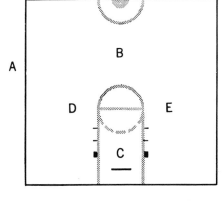

Fig. 7.17 *Out of Bounds—Diamond Formation.*

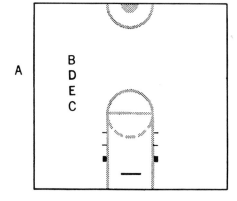

Fig. 7.18 *Out of Bounds—Vertical Formation.*

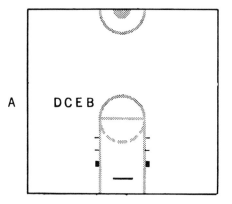

Fig. 7.19 *Out of Bounds—Parallel Formation.*

275

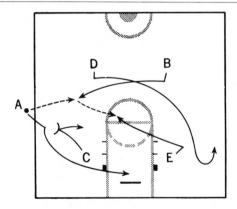

Fig. 7.20 *Out of Bounds. On signal, D fakes and screens for B, who fakes and cuts for the pass from A. C moves up to screen for A as E cuts for a pass from B. A cuts off the screen and C rolls. E has the option of shooting or passing to A or C. A, C, and E have rebounding responsibilities.*

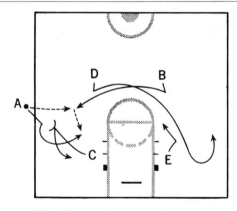

Fig. 7.21 *Out of Bounds. The moves start as in Fig. 7.20. A passes to B. C cuts to screen for A. A fakes and cuts to receive the pass from B. C rolls, and E clears to the free throw line. A can drive, shoot, or pass to C, E, or D.*

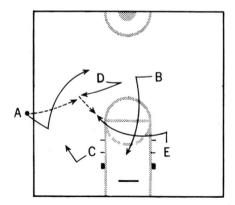

Fig. 7.22 *Out of Bounds. D fakes and cuts back to receive the pass from A. C fakes as E cuts for a pass from D. B fakes and cuts down the lane for a pass from E. C, B, and E rebound.*

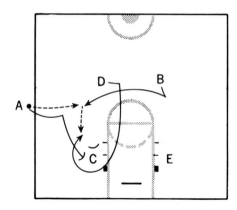

Fig. 7.23 *Out of Bounds. D fakes and B cuts off her to receive a pass from A. D cuts down the lane and behind the double screen formed by C and A. B passes to D, who may shoot or use any of the double screen options. C, D, and E rebound.*

time to move into the desired positions. Meanwhile her teammates hustle to get into position.

Several formations can be used to confuse the opponents and vary the out-of-bounds maneuvers. These are shown in Figs. 7.16–7.19. The box formation is probably the most popular because it lends itself to more options. The vertical and parallel

formations are more commonly used in men's play from out-of-bounds situations at the end line, and their names are derived from setting the formation for an end line play. Nevertheless they may be used occasionally with success from a side line position. However, definite precautions must be devised when utilizing the vertical formation from a side line be-

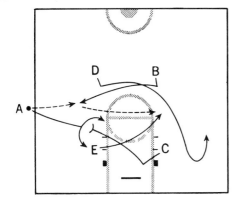

Fig. 7.24 *Out of Bounds. D moves over and screens for B. B cuts for the pass from A. E cuts and C cuts. B passes to E as A cuts either side of C. E may shoot, pass to A or C who rolls.*

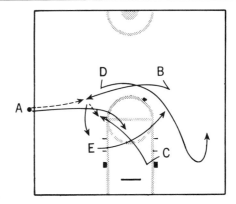

Fig. 7.25 *Out of Bounds. D and B make their usual moves. C cuts after E to receive the pass from B. B cuts around C followed by A. All of the options on a scissor play are available.*

cause of the obvious defensive dangers involved.

When installing any of the formations, the teacher may exchange the positions of individual players if desired. The pivot is usually assigned a position near the basket in either the box or diamond formation. Her position is obvious in the diamond formation, but the pivot may be placed either on the ball side or the far side in the box formation. Figs. 7.20–7.23 show her on the near side, while Figs. 7.24–7.26 show her on the far side.

The player putting the ball in play should take her position about 3 ft. from the side line. This allows her enough space to step forward or to move slightly without committing a line violation. She usually gives a signal of some kind to initiate the moves of her teammates. The signal may occur when the official hands the ball to her; or, the out-of-bounds player may slap the ball or call the name of a play.

The plays devised for use from out of bounds should be simple. They should all look similar with one or two changes so that the defense must make different adjustments. Figs. 7.20–7.26 provide some examples of tactics that can be used from the side line.

Whenever the opposing team is ready to put the ball in play from the side line the defending team takes measures to force them to pass the ball backward or away from the offensive basket. The defender guarding the in-bound player should stand on a diagonal between her opponent and the basket. She should never stand directly opposite her, for she is extremely vulnerable to a pass-and-cut tactic. Fig. 7.27 shows both the correct and incorrect methods of

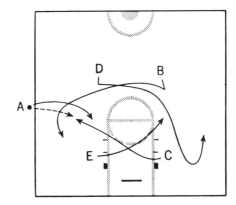

Fig. 7.26 *Out of Bounds. D and B make their usual moves. A fakes to B. E and C make their usual moves, and A passes to C. B and A cut around C and the scissor options are available.*

guarding the out-of-bounds player. The other defenders exert pressure on the basket side to encourage the pass backward. These tactics are particularly important when the ball is being put in play in the defensive team's back court. The defense should be particularly aware of the possibility of a return pass to the out-of-bounds player, and cut off the passing lane to her. Her own opponent should assist in this process by taking a few steps back toward the basket as soon as the ball is in-bounded.

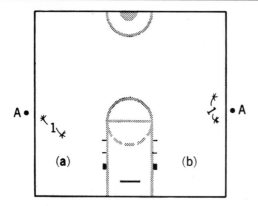

Fig. 7.27 *Player No. 1 stands between her opponent and the basket with her arms extended toward her opponent and the basket. As soon as the ball is inbounded, she takes a few steps back toward the basket to prevent a pass and cut maneuver* (a). *Poor defensive position by No. 1* (b).

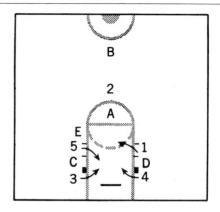

Fig. 7.28 *Free Throw Situation. Player C has a height advantage, so Nos. 3 and 5 attempt to reduce her rebounding effectiveness. Player No. 1 moves in to the middle of the lane to prevent a rebound or tip from going to A. As No. 3 or 4 obtains the rebound, No. 2 cuts to the near side for the outlet pass. Player B is in a safety position.*

When the opponents are behind in score in the last few seconds of the game and are putting the ball in play from the end line in their back court, the defenders must prevent a long pass downcourt. They must closely guard players in the midcourt and front court area and allow a player to remain free near the in-bounder. They encourage the short pass and then double-team the player, taking all precautions to prevent fouling. As a matter of fact, all players must be careful to avoid fouling since all fouls result in two shots in the last 2 min. The pivot defender must not be lured away from the lane area so that she remains in position to intimidate any opponent trying to shoot from that position and maintains good rebounding position.

When the opponents are behind in score in the last few seconds of the game and are in-bounding the ball from the side line in the front court, the defense desires to force them to pass backward toward the division line or into their back court. Therefore, the player guarding the in-bounder plays between her and the basket, and the other defenders guard their opponent closely on the basket side to force the pass backward. Once the ball is in-bounded, players should guard their opponent closely, not allowing a free shot. If a team has not used a press during the game and is competent in executing it, the new defense may surprise the opponents and delay them in attempting a shot. Otherwise the standard defense employed by a team should be used. Every effort must be made, however, to prevent the opponents from obtaining an unguarded or unchallenged shot. Players within 15 ft. of the basket should be guarded extremely close so that it is difficult to pass in to them. If the opposing team has one or more weak shooters, it may be desirable to allow them to receive passes freely and encourage them to shoot anywhere beyond their range.

Basically, there are four things the defense is trying to prevent:

1. any unchallenged shot
2. any player receiving the ball within 15 ft. of the basket
3. a layup shot or offensive rebound shot
4. a foul of any type by any defense player

A player should never foul an opponent when she is attempting a shot under these circumstances. Defenders must play it carefully.

Drills for Out-of-Bounds Plays

When they are being pressed, players should practice putting the ball in play from the end line and side line in the defensive end. They should also practice each option in the front court repeatedly until the timing of the moves is perfected. These should be practiced first with players in position for the ball to be in-bounded and later during a scrimmage situation. At this time the teacher can frequently blow her whistle to signal an out-of-bounds play so that players can practice moving into the proper position for the prescribed in-bounds play. The offense should practice against both a man-to-man defense and zone defenses. The out-of-bounds plays should be practiced from both sides of the court.

FREE THROW SITUATIONS

When a team is awarded a free throw, both teams must have at least two players line up along the lane lines, although all of the players may line up if this seems desirable. The defensive team should place its two strongest rebounders in the spaces nearest the basket. The best rebounder should be on the same side as the best rebounder from the offensive team. If the defensive team has a distinct height disadvantage, it may choose to have two other players line up also. This alignment is shown in Fig. 7.28. The team's third best rebounder lines up on the same side where the height disparity exists. With defensive players on both sides of the taller opponent, some of the advantage she has should be overcome by reducing the space in which she can maneuver.

If the defensive team believes that it can control the rebound without double-teaming one player, it may line up as shown in Fig. 7.29. This provides for a defensive player in the corner on each side and as a rebounder obtains the ball, she can immediately turn to the outside and make her outlet pass. If one of the offensive players should shun her rebounding responsibilities and move to press one of the defender's in the corner, that player should notify her teammate that she is covered so that she will not make her pass while still in the air or make an automatic pass in the direction of her teammate.

If the defensive team is certain that it will obtain the rebound, or if an extremely accurate free throw shooter is at the line, it may choose to line up in a manner to start a fast break very quickly and, as a result, place a great deal of pressure on the team taking the free throw. This alignment and a modification of it are shown in Figs. 7.30 and 7.31. The latter is a dangerous formation if there is a chance of losing the ball, for it should automatically give the opposing team a player advantage. The team must be certain that it will obtain the rebound and also that accurate passes can be made to get the ball into the front court. On the other hand, use of either of these formations causes the opponents to think about defense before the free throw is even attempted. This may psychologically affect the free throw shooter in particular, causing her to lose concentration and miss the free throw. The offensive rebounders may

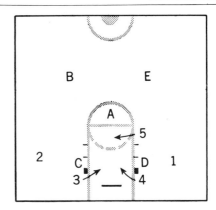

Fig. 7.29 *Alternate Method of Lining Up for a Free Throw.*

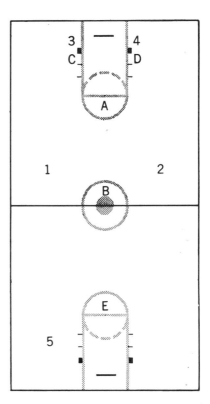

Fig. 7.30 *Free Throw. Defensive positioning. to start a fast break.*

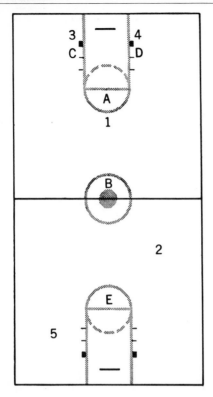

Fig. 7.31 *Free Throw. Extremely aggressive position of the defensive team to start a fast break.*

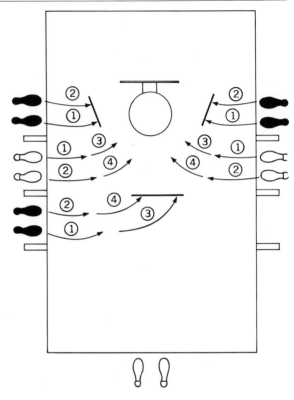

Fig. 7.32 *Basic Footwork for Both Teams in Trying to Obtain a Rebound Following a Free Throw.*

also be more concerned with going back on defense than attempting to maneuver for a missed free throw.

Rebounding Techniques by the Defensive Team

The two defenders closest to the basket stand as close to the lane space mark as possible. When the free throw shooter is ready, the defenders raise their arms partially overhead and lean in toward the center of the lane. (Their arms may not be extended into the adjacent lane space in front of an opponent.) After the ball has been released, each defender takes a step with her outside foot diagonally backward and into the lane in an effort to block out the offensive rebounder. The step should be so timed that the foot strikes the floor at the same time as the ball hits the rim or the backboard. The player assigned to block out the free throw shooter pivots on her inside foot and steps out with her outside foot to that she is parallel to the end line and in front of the shooter. The de-

fender may have to take a shuffle step in order to get into the middle of the lane. The footwork is shown in Fig. 7.32.

Rebounding Techniques by the Offensive Team

The best rebounders are assigned to the second lane spaces. The best rebounder attempts to move to the side opposite the best defensive rebounder. As the ball is in the air during the shot, the offensive players time their moves so that they may take the first step into the lane with their inside foot and land in the lane at the time the ball hits the backboard or rim. A second step is taken into the lane and they may need to use a shuffle step to acquire a position beside the defensive player rather than behind her. These moves are also shown in Fig. 7.32. If the offensive player can obtain the rebound, she should try to catch it and go back up with her shot. Since the area is congested, this is not likely to occur very often. Her next choice should be to tip the ball into the basket. If this is not possible, she may try to tap the ball back over the head of the defender to her teammate at the free throw line or to a teammate who is positioned deeper (Fig. 7.29). If unable to catch or tap the ball, she should try to harass the rebounder at least momentarily to prevent a quick outlet pass to start a fast break.

If the defenders tend to slide into the middle of the lane to keep the offensive rebounders blocked out, the offensive player may choose an alternate method of gaining the rebound. She may fake into the lane with her outside foot, push hard off it, and step with her inside foot behind the defensive player. The offensive player continues moving toward the outside to get in front of the defensive player. From this position she may be able to deflect the ball if she is unable to catch it.

This move is selected prior to any action taken by a defense player because the initial step is taken with a different foot. Since a defender almost automatically moves into the lane in the manner previously described, this technique may be effective occasionally. The player must be quick in her move however, or the ball will rebound before she can reach her destination.

Fast Break Options by the Defensive Team

The defensive team may attempt a fast break after both a successful and unsuccessful free throw. Because the defensive rebounders have the inside position, they should acquire the rebound if the shot is missed. The rebounder turns toward the outside and executes her outlet pass as quickly as possible. If the defenders are lined up as shown in Fig. 7.28, player No. 2 cuts toward the ball side for the pass. Player No. 1 cuts up the middle, and No. 5 fills the lane on the right. If defenders are situated in the corners, the rebounder passes to the near side player. If the defenders have only two defenders lined up along the lane (Figs. 7.30 and 7.31), the rebounder passes to the near side player at the division line. Obvious fast break opportunities develop from this situation. The player who receives the pass dribbles down the center as the other potential receiver cuts down the unoccupied lane. With two players in the front court (Fig. 7.31), it may be possible to pass the ball to one of them quickly for a two-on-one situation to develop.

When the free throw is successful, one player should always recover the ball, run out of bounds with it, and in-bound it as fast as possible. The player on the side opposite from which the ball is to be in-bounded should be the player assigned to this task, for she is facing the ball and the side from which it will be in-bounded and can race more quickly

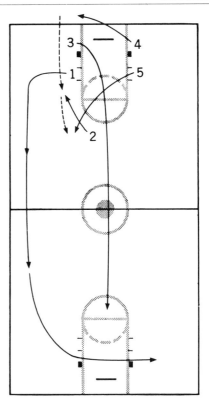

Fig. 7.33 *Fast Break After a Free Throw. Player No. 4 quickly recovers the ball. No. 1 clears to the side line and cuts downcourt. No. 3 clears down the middle of the lane. No. 4 passes in to No. 2, who passes to No. 5 who has cut off No. 3. Player No. 5 may pass to 1 or 3, or work one-on-one if a pass is not open to either of them. If No. 1 does not receive a pass, she clears to the opposite side to allow No. 5 more space in which to maneuver.*

into position. Fig. 7.33 shows one possibility for a fast break. Others may be devised.

THE CONTROL GAME

The purpose of a controlled style of offense is to change the pace of the offense, to maintain possession of the ball for a longer period of time than normal, and to protect or increase a lead already gained. A spectator watching men's basketball is aware that the men commonly employ two types of control offenses—one basically used to "stall," the other to "freeze." The stall type offense is appropriate in women's basketball only. Because the freeze style offense is generally devised to consume 1, 2, or more minutes, it cannot be employed in the women's game due to the 30-sec. clock rule. Therefore, as a control type offense is discussed for women's play, it is of the stall variety. Perhaps this term is a poor choice, for one cannot stall very long in a 30-sec. time period!

There are times when a control style of offense may seem desirable either very briefly or through a series of offensive opportunities. For example, the team that has gained possession of the ball within the last 30 sec. of each quarter may desire to maintain possession as long as possible, to acquire the "last shot," thus precluding the opponents from gaining another offensive opportunity.

When a team has a slim lead near the end of the game, it may wish to abandon the fast break style of play it has used and adopt a more controlled style of offense. This accomplishes two purposes.

1. It consumes more time, thus forcing the opponents who are behind in score to gamble somewhat more. This, in turn, opens scoring opportunities for the offense.
2. A controlled style of play keeps ball handling errors at a minimum and fewer turnovers should result.

During the game, there may be times when it seems desirable just to change the pace of the offense. By consuming close to 30 sec. on each possession, a team develops discipline in its offense and recognizes that it has the poise and capacity for controlling the ball as long as they are permitted to do so by the rules. Psychologically, this may also affect the defensive team adversely and cause them to take unnecessary chances or become a little careless or sluggish in meeting a control pattern.

Basic Principles to Use on Offense

In selecting an offense to use in a control style, a coach may choose to use the basic pattern that has proved most effective during the contest, or she may prefer to devise a special offense for controlled play. In either case the offense should be constructed so that a ball handler cannot be trapped at a boundary line or in a corner. The ball should stay in the central portion of the court as much as possible so that double-teaming is less likely and so that the ball may be passed in all directions. Crossing in front of or behind a player with the ball should be avoided so that the opponents may not double-team. Crossing is still appropriate for players without the ball, however.

Players should eliminate all dribbling or keep it to a minimum. The ball should be passed constantly so that there is extensive ball movement and little

chance for double-teaming. Occasionally, an exceptional dribbler can consume a great deal of time, but even then there is difficulty in preventing a double-team unless she has excellent timing and good peripheral vision so that she can entice a double-team and pass off to a free player. Often, however, the dribbler is forced to turn her back to the basket and cannot see her teammates before she is trapped by two opponents. If a dribbler is about to be tied or called for a jump, she can call time out so that her team is sure to maintain possession of the ball. (Some time outs should always be saved for the last few minutes of a contest.)

Cross court passes should be avoided. These are long and high and easily intercepted. During controlled play, all players should be encouraged to go to meet the ball, even more so than usual. Actually, the offensive pattern used should force the players to cut toward the ball so that there are fewer chances for interceptions by the defense.

When a controlled style of play is to be followed for a series of possessions, the best ball handlers should be in the game. This may mean that a third guard replaces one of the forwards. This may be done only, however, if a great height disparity is not created when the offensive team goes on defense.

Only sure shots should be attempted during a stall offense. The offensive team should continue to make scoring thrusts, but take only those shots that are of a high percentage nature. If the offensive team fails to look for scoring opportunities while they run the clock, the defense can afford to take more chances in an effort to get an interception. As the opponents press, the offensive team can look for backdoor cuts. Other options should be devised from the basic pattern so that an advantage can be taken of any defensive carelessness.

When a team starts to use a stall offense, it may also begin to press the opponents when they secure the ball as a surprise tactic. This tends to delay the opponents from getting the ball downcourt, which in turn consumes more time. Often it is also a psychological barrier to the team behind in score, since they recognize they must hurry and are being slowed in their own back court. They also may be surprised by the tactic at this time and make careless passes that result in easy baskets for the team leading in score.

One more consideration should be given when a team is using the stall during the last few minutes of the game. Because the opponents are likely to guard closely under these circumstances, they also are likely to commit more fouls. For this reason the offensive team should have good free throw shooters on the court at this time.

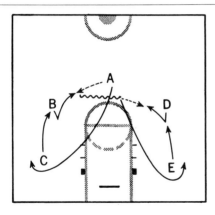

Fig. 7.34 *Control Pattern. A passes to B and cuts to the corner. B dribbles, passes to D, and cuts to the corner. The pattern continues as C replaces B and E replaces D.*

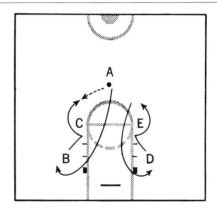

Fig. 7.35 *Miller's Control Pattern. B fakes and cuts around C to receive a pass from A. A cuts down to replace B. D times her cut so that she is moving toward the ball to receive a pass from B. The pattern continues, with A and B interchanging positions and D staying on her side of the court.*

Stall Patterns

There are several stall patterns. Fig. 7.34 shows one that is commonly used. The reader will note that the players remain spread throughout the pattern, that no player crosses another one with the ball, that the ball is always passed from the middle of the court, and that the lane area is kept open for cuts on options. This is a very simple pattern to learn and can be used effectively.

At the University of Iowa, Ralph Miller used a stall offense with a high double post around which the other players cut. Fig. 7.35 shows this pattern. Two players cut around one of the posts, while only one player cuts around the other one. Timing of the cut around the post is an important part of this pattern, as receivers are always moving to meet the pass. Passes may be made to other players who become free momentarily for a shot.

Defense Against the Control Game

When the stall is employed at the end of the quarter for a last shot or for a change of pace, the defensive team is wise to continue to use its normal defense. There is no need at this time to press the opponents. Instead, the defensive team should sag off their opponents slightly and cut off the passing lanes into the free throw lane and other high percentage shooting areas. At this time the defensive team must remain patient and force the offensive team to come to them. They desire to prevent a short shot and force a

long shot. However, they must remain alert and not become lackadaisical in their defense or the offense will make a premature scoring effort at the defensive weakness. During the last 12–15 sec. that the offensive team has before they must shoot, the defense should tighten up slightly and press the opponents more in an effort to force them to take a shot beyond the range from which they would like. Or, the defense should force them to take an off-balanced shot, a shot from an undesirable spot on the court, or cause a weak shooter to make the attempt.

When a team is behind in score and time seems to be running out, they must employ a pressing defense, at least in the front court. At this stage they can ill afford to sit back and wait for the opponents to consume close to 30 sec. before shooting. If they have any hope for winning, they must get the ball. As they operate their press, however, they must be careful not to allow an easy shot. Nevertheless, if it comes down to the last possession before time expires and they are behind by one or two points, they must take chances to get the ball. It makes little difference whether a team loses by two or four points.

Last Shot

In the closing seconds of a quarter (other than the fourth quarter) the defensive team may delay their shot so that they do not allow the opponents another offensive opportunity. Usually a team attempts to maneuver for its last shot with approximately 8 sec.

remaining. This gives the team time to pass the ball to the desired shooter, allow her to attempt her shot, and provide time for a rebound shot if the original attempt is unsuccessful. Yet it does not allow time for the opponents to recover the rebound and pass it downcourt for an unrushed shot for goal.

In making an attempt for the last shot in any of the first three quarters, a team generally does not call a time out to decide what action should be taken. Instead, a specific maneuver is predetermined, or a signal for a play is given as the ball is advanced downcourt. The play may have been successful previously, or may have been devised specifically for this situation. A team may also choose to spread four of its players wide and give the ball to the best one-on-one player and let her maneuver in the last few seconds for a shot.

Last Shot in the Game

Concern over the last shot in the game occurs when the game is tied or when the team in possession of the ball is behind by one, two, or three points. If the game is tied, the offensive team wants to run down the clock to the last few seconds so that it obtains the last shot. If a team is behind by more than three points during the last seconds of the game it must take and make shots very soon after it acquires possession of the ball. Then it must press and regain the ball so that it may score quickly again. Basically the same tactic must be used when a team is behind by three points, as a defensive team should never foul under these conditions to provide the opportunity for a three-point play.

Before attempting the last shot in the final quarter, a team usually calls a time out and establishes exactly what tactic should be followed. In this way all players should be aware of their exact responsibilities, including rebounding. Since the ball is put in play from out of bounds, a specific play may be devised for use at this time, or common out-of-bounds tactics may be used to get the ball to the desired shooter. If a specific play is not to be used, a primary shooter should be designated and the player who receives the ball inbounds should try to get the ball to her. If she is guarded too closely, the ball should be passed to the secondary shooter who also was designated during the time out. One of these two players should attempt the last shot. If both are so well guarded that the ball cannot be passed to either of them, then some other player must make an attempt preferably with at least 5 sec. remaining so that a rebound attempt may be made if the shot is unsuccessful.

Defense Against the Last Shot in the Game

The team that is ahead in the last minute or two can afford to sag off their opponents slightly and cut off the desirable passing lanes. If they are ahead by four points or more, they should encourage the outside shot—particularly by players who have not demonstrated much success heretofore. Good outside shooters should be guarded more closely. The defensive team encourages numerous passes by the offense so that more time is consumed.

If the defensive team is ahead by only three points, it continues to encourage the opponents to consume as much time as possible. Great defensive care should be exercised so that the opponents do not secure an easy shot. They should attempt to score quickly, but the defense should not be flustered and foul when they attempt a shot even if it appears to be an easy field goal. They do not want to give the opponents a chance for a three-point play. It is better by far to allow the easy basket, get the ball out of bounds, and then control it for the rest of the game. This way they win by one point. This is far smarter than to risk a tie game.

If the defensive team is ahead by two points, the players know they can do no worse than a tie unless of course, they foul a player in the act of shooting. They must not do this! Again it is better to allow the easy basket causing a tie game than to foul a player in the act of shooting. If she makes the shot she can win the game with a free throw. Although the team must think DON'T FOUL, they must also force the opponents to work hard for a desirable shot. The defensive team should be able to ascertain those players likely to be designated as shooters. Although they do not wish to leave any opponent open for an easy shot, they can direct more of their attention to the more likely shooters and the spots from which they like to shoot.

If the defensive team is ahead by one point or the game is tied, they should recognize that the game is about over if the opponents score. As the players take their positions for the in-bounds pass, the defenders should press their opponents slightly to force the in-bounds pass to go backwards. Under no circumstances should they allow the ball to be passed toward the basket. By forcing the pass backward, time is consumed before another pass can be made forward into shooting position. The player guarding the player who passes the ball in-bounds must retreat quickly so that a pass and cut maneuver is not possible. Players on the near side should guard their opponents tight and on the ball side. Teammates on the far side can sag or float to clutter the free throw lane. The defense must make it difficult for the opponents to shoot and force them to take an undesirable shot. Again the defense cannot afford to foul!

Drills for the Control Game

Offensively, players should learn whatever pattern they intend to use in this situation and then practice it frequently with a 30-sec. clock operating. They must become aware that 30 sec. is a long time when they are controlling the ball. By frequent practice with opponents pressing, they can gain the poise necessary to use a controlled offense. At the proper time the offensive thrust should be made to allow time for rebounding efforts. During practice sessions, various individuals should be assigned as the primary or secondary shooter so that it can be ascertained who is most successful under stress.

While one group is practicing offensive measures for the last seconds, the defensive team can simultaneously acquire poise in the way in which they meet the offensive tactics. They must learn to recognize when it is better to allow an unmolested shot rather than risking a foul and possibly the game. They must also become aware of when to sag and when to guard closely.

IV

Teaching and Coaching

8

Teaching Beginners

Teaching beginning players any team sport is a challenging and demanding task—and basketball is no exception! Like field hockey, lacrosse, and soccer, basketball is difficult to teach (and learn) because the ball moves almost constantly, and the players must adjust not only to the moves of their teammates but also to those of their opponents. This means that players must make continual adjustments during even a very elementary maneuver. Not only must they acquire an understanding of the way in which tactics are performed, but they also must acquire the skill to execute them properly. All of this takes time, practice, and patience!

PROBLEMS OF BEGINNERS

If one were to observe beginning players in the early stages of learning the game, certain incompetencies would be clearly evident regardless of the players' ages or grade levels.

1. No organization for play. Players are grouped near the ball or under the basket. When the opponents obtain possession of the ball, a long pass downcourt usually accounts for a goal.
2. Players on offense stand (often because they do not know where to move or when to move), often very close together, which cuts off the passing lanes.
3. Ineffective dribbling—frequent dribbling, often while standing still without benefit of forward or lateral movement. Beginners often develop "bouncitis," the act of bouncing the ball each time it is

received. This is a most difficult habit to break later and one that should never be developed.

4. Poor passing is usually the result of not pivoting to look to see if a teammate is free. Often an unorthodox pass is used because the player has not pivoted to face her teammate. Passes may be made automatically in a predetermined direction regardless of whether the teammate is well guarded. Passes are made to players standing still, with a resultant interception by an alert defense player.
5. Players have little confidence in their ability to score. As a result most players always consider passing as the primary choice of action. Those who desire to shoot often are inaccurate because the ball is released from a very low height (waist or shoulder level). Frequently, these players are off-balance.
6. Defensively, players maintain poor position. Their weight is too high and too far forward. They generally fail to take a step back from their opponent after the ball is passed, and thus cannot stay in a proper defensive position as the opponent cuts.
7. Defensive players often lack judgment in trying for an interception. Therefore, when they miss the interception their opponent is free to dribble toward the goal.
8. Defensive players often guard too closely and make every effort to get their hands on the ball. This generally brings their weight on to their toes and often causes them to move to the side of their opponent when she pivots. Thus, the opponent is left free to drive or cut toward the basket after she passes.

These problems are witnessed most frequently. Perhaps the reader has observed others. The problems that are known to exist for beginning players must be curtailed, if not eliminated, as rapidly as possible. This requires careful planning and critical analysis of individual skills throughout the learning process. The teacher must understand and recognize correct performance so that she may lead each student through a natural progression and assist her in realizing her own potential.

It is advisable to help students learn a few skills well rather than many skills ineffectively. Therefore, considerable attention should be devoted to drills of a game-like nature in order that skills and elementary tactics are overlearned so that they may be applied and executed properly under conditions of duress in a game. It seems questionable that the concept that a great variety of drills is necessary to motivate the students. Looking through a book of drills and coming up with one that looks "interesting" is an antiquated concept. It makes far more sense to ascertain what the student needs to learn to apply in the game, and then construct a drill that will accomplish that purpose. If a player in a guard position has difficulty in passing a chest pass to her teammate in a guard position, practicing a chest pass in a shuttle formation will not help this player! Instead, place the two players on line with one another and, facing the basket, encourage them to pivot toward one another before passing! The shuttle formation would help a guard pass to a forward and vice versa, but why not have the two players in their proper position on the court with the guard passing to the forward, then cutting for the basket to receive a return pass, thus learning to pass and cut. This is one of the elementary offensive tactics! In this way, proper passing techniques are acquired and a useful game tactic is learned as well.

CLASS ORGANIZATION

As a teacher observes her class, she is likely to become aware that she does not have a very homogeneous group. She is likely to have some students who have never used a basketball, others who may have played with one occasionally, and other students who have played frequently with brothers or other friends. In this case, the teacher cannot teach at one level and keep all of the students interested and motivated, but must prepare her lessons to treat groups at different levels of achievement. In this day and age, no one can any longer advocate teaching to the "average" student! One must be concerned with helping each student achieve her maximum potential.

In order to meet the needs of all of the students in her class, the teacher may choose (at times with suggestions from the students) either of two techniques.

She may prepare entirely different lessons for the various skill levels, or she may have all students practicing the same skills or tactics but at different levels of execution. Probably she will use both techniques.

When practicing any skill or tactic it is desirable to establish goals toward which the students may work. For example, in shooting layups the goal for inexperienced players might be three successful shots out of ten; for those with some experience, five out of ten; and for those who have had even greater experience, seven out of ten. These goals may be adjusted upward or downward, depending upon the students' ability. The goal selected, however, should be attainable by the majority within that group. Later, the success level for each group may be increased so that it continues to be motivating.

Throughout the entire learning process, but particularly during the early learning stages, it is important to have the class working in small groups. A ball for every two players is desirable. A ratio of one ball to more than four players is impractical from a learning point of view. Students are unable to secure sufficient practice with an inadequate supply of balls. Basketballs, however, may be supplemented with soccer balls, volleyballs, and playground balls although students using these supplementary balls should be allowed to exchange frequently with students using basketballs.

The small group technique can be used even with large classes. For practicing individual skills, players can take those positions on the court they choose to play; and, with proper directions, they can work individually or in pairs on the skills required for that particular position. For example, basic faking techniques can be learned by all, and then each player can apply what she has learned effectively to her own position. Forwards can practice faking toward the end line and cutting out to receive a pass from a guard, or faking out and cutting across the lane for a pass from the other forward or pivot. Guards can practice faking right and cutting left or vice versa, or faking to the side and cutting for the basket. A pivot can fake to the side and cut out to the free throw line, or fake out and cut across the lane. These are specific moves that can be used in a game and seem more appropriate than spending considerable time on moves that will not be used except in a drill.

From the previous discussion, it would seem obvious that the author encourages students to choose a position—forward, guard, or pivot—early during the unit after the characteristics and qualifications for each position have been discussed. Basketball is too complicated a game to expect any student, let alone a beginner, to become proficient in the moves necessary for every (or several) position on the court. It is impossible and unrealistic to request such competency from any player. Opportunity, however, should be provided for students to change positions if the one that was originally selected does not prove satisfying. Players should be encouraged to make such changes early in the unit.

In addition to practicing individual skills in small groups, it is also advisable to introduce and practice elementary team tactics in small groups. Practicing with two offensive players against two defensive players provides all players with the opportunity to react to the movement of the ball and facilitates learning. Acquiring skill in passing, receiving, faking, changing direction, starting and stopping, and defensive skills all are enhanced by this method. Becoming familiar with the pass and cut technique, setting screens, and the defense for these is also facilitated by working in small groups. Extensive practice can be gained by this method, as all players in the group are involved in every move. Later the players must have the opportunity to attempt their newly acquired skills with other team members. In some instances, it may be desirable to wean beginning players slowly from a two-player team to the regulation five-player team. This may be accomplished by adding only one player to form a team of three (usually two guards and one forward); or, that stage may be omitted by adding two players to form teams of four (two guards and two forwards). Finally, another player can be added to form a team of five.

While working in groups of four the court size can be modified so that many groups can be practicing at the same time. It is not always necessary for small groups to have access to a basket, so a court may be divided into four parts, accommodating sixteen players simultaneously. If the gymnasium is lined for two courts, thirty-two players may be involved at the same time. With players working in groups of eight—four per team—additional space is necessary. It is necessary to provide a wider area in which the players may operate; otherwise negative transfer is introduced as the players practice in a very cramped space. The length of the space in which students practice is not as important as the width. 18–20 ft. in length is ample for beginners to practice, but if four players per team are practicing, the minimum regulation width is needed for proper learning.

When court space and/or number of baskets is limited, adjustments can be made. Tape can be used to mark extra keyholes if additional space of this kind is needed. These are particularly useful when teaching a pattern offense or zone defense. Each team (or most of them) may practice the necessary movements

without waiting for a "turn." If there are not enough baskets for all groups, players can go through the offensive pattern of making shots at a nonexistent basket. The pattern or moves involved can be inculcated so that players understand the concepts. Teams should be rotated to baskets frequently.

While utilizing the small group technique, it seems advantageous to retain the same groups for every class period with minor changes made as necessary. Each group can be assigned to a specific area, and little time is wasted at the beginning of the class period for organizational purposes. This not only facilitates class organization, but also improves learning. Students have the opportunity to play with the same individuals for a period of time and can become acquainted with the type of cuts they prefer, the speed with which they move, and their defensive and offensive strengths and weaknesses. In this way they do not have to readjust constantly to new teammates daily.

When players are learning specific offensive or defensive tactics, they may change their role in either of two ways.

1. One team may be designated as the offensive team for a designated length of time. At the end of that time interval the teams exchange responsibilities for a similar period of time.
2. The role may change each time the defensive team gains possession of the ball.

Some teachers using the latter method also request that the change take place after each field goal; others allow the scoring team to continue on offense. (Some smart players will miss a shot purposely so that they may remain on offense!) Both methods of exchange seem to have merit, but the first one is preferred during the beginning stages; the latter is preferable during the later stages.

As indicated previously, all players in the class need not practice the same skill or tactic. As a matter of fact, there may be as many different activities in progress as there are groups. The primary consideration is that the task be relevant and that it be based on previously learned material. There are times when the students should be given the prerogative of selecting their own activity, at least for a portion of the period if not all of it. Some will select individual skills to improve, while others may be more interested in either offensive or defensive team play. As a result, in some areas of the gymnasium, one may observe players working individually or in groups of two, three, four, six, eight, or ten. Some may be playing half-court while others are playing full court. During this time the teacher can move freely to all groups and provide whatever assistance is necessary.

When players have attained a level of achievement sufficient to enjoy and have success in a game with four or five players per team, it is wise to teach them a very basic pattern to follow for their moves. If this is not done, all players tend to congregate under the basket. The pattern simply gives them direction. It helps them to know where and when to cut so that all players do not end up in the same place at the same time. It helps them by letting them know their responsibilities at a specific time. Generally, a pattern encourages the use of all players in the ball movement. Otherwise one or two skilled or knowledgeable players may dominate play.

Rules should be taught concurrently as skills or tactics are learned. Players can become familiar with traveling violations when they are learning to start, stop, change direction, and receive passes. Dribbling violations are introduced as players learn how to dribble. Lecture, discussion, or demonstration of rules without immediate application seem questionable.

OFFENSE vs. DEFENSE

Teaching defense in any team game is considered easier than teaching offense by most experts. The timing of moves is important but not quite as vital; the coordination of action with teammates is less crucial; and, of course, they are not involved with the ball. For these reasons one generally attempts to develop offensive tactics first. Defensive measures are then taught to counteract the offense, and the cycle is repeated many times over.

Depending upon the tactic being taught, it may be desirable initially to allow the attack players to attempt the maneuver without hindrance by any defense players. Once the concept is gained, one defense player may be added. Assuming that only two attack players are involved, the defense player is assigned to guard the player with the ball — she is not permitted at this stage to try to defend against both attack players. Later, a second defender is added. This progression might be used in learning the pass and cut tactic, for example.

For teaching other offensive tactics (screens, scissor), the defense players should be passive initially and follow the stipulated method of guarding (stay man-to-man; play switching man-to-man, etc.) so that the offense can gain confidence in the tactic and the timing involved. Then the defense can be instructed to guard as usual, but the manner should be designated again. After the offense begins to have some degree of success with their newly acquired skills, then time should be devoted to the defense and the means of counteracting the offensive moves. When this has

been learned, new options should be learned by the attack and the process is repeated. Both attack and defense players must be sympathetic with one another, as they are trying to learn new tactics. Each should help one another by using the techniques that will make the opposite group successful. By progressing slowly and competently from one stage to the next, both skill and confidence will be acquired.

MAN-TO-MAN vs. ZONE DEFENSE

Almost all authorities agree that man-to-man defense should be learned prior to zone defense. Although a player's primary responsibility in a zone is to guard an area, once a player enters that area her actions are predicated on her ability to use individual defensive techniques according to whether the player has the ball or is moving to receive it. The basis for all guarding must be man-to-man defense, and students who are not given the opportunity to become proficient in its use will never become skillful zone defenders.

There is also another very practical reason for teaching man-to-man defense first: Beginning defense players often "lose" their opponents and allow them to become free near the basket. Since team defense has not been introduced at this time, the player should be free for a pass and a relatively easy shot. This gives the offensive team some sense of accomplishment and achievement, and encourages more players to try shooting. Beginning players find it very difficult to penetrate a zone defense. When they get the ball by one defender, another one moves into position. For this reason it is hard for beginners to acquire as many close shots and they often become discouraged. Teaching man-to-man defense first seems to provide a better balance between attack and defense.

The author recommends teaching man-to-man defense first to all players, except possibly those who may never have instruction in basketball again. These players include seniors in high school who elect basketball for the first time or students in college. Often their purpose in choosing the activity is simply to learn something about the sport so that they might enjoy it to a greater extent in intramurals or a park league. These students can acquire success more quickly with a zone defense and, because of this, may enjoy defense to a greater extent. Nevertheless, it may not be as satisfying to play against because of the inability to penetrate it consistently.

TEACHING AIDS

Various aids may be used for beginning players to help them acquire skill more quickly, or to help them with their understanding of the game and specific tactics. Some are included below, but the reader is encouraged to devise others to meet the needs in her own situation.

1. Use junior size balls with young children—junior high school age or younger. Lower the height of the baskets and decrease the size of the playing area for youngsters.

2. If glass backboards are not available, place markings on the backboard to identify a point of aim for layups or other shots.

3. Through discussion, help students to recognize that shooting is nothing more than accurate passing. Show them that two balls will fit in the basket at the same time, thus demonstrating that there is space for error and that there is more than one entry into the basket.

4. Place tape or another substance on the floor to show the angle of a cut from a specific position or a designated pattern to follow. This is extremely helpful when first teaching the layup shot, as players tend to make the angle of approach to the basket much wider than desired.

5. Footprints can be placed on the floor (rugs with rubber backing or footprints drawn on the floor) to help students follow the desired cutting path or to help them to learn to change direction.

6. A percussion instrument may be used to help students acquire the rhythm of a two-step stop. The same technique can be used in teaching the footwork for a layup shot.

7. Groups of four or five may be formed to aid players in cutting and timing their move for a cut. Players are positioned informally on approximately one-half of a court. Player No. 1 starts with the ball and passes to No. 2 as she cuts. Player No. 3 times her move and cuts for the next pass. This continues with the last player passing to No. 1 to repeat the process. Only the receiver of the pass cuts, and at first she should cut in a direction that makes passing easy. Later, she may cut anywhere so that a pivot may be required of the ball handler before she can pass to the cutter. If desirable, players may be positioned in their normal playing positions and make their cuts accordingly.

8. When players are practicing in small groups and without benefit of a basket, targets may be placed on the walls to give students playing offense an objective to hit. It also provides defensive players with a target so that they can refer to it for maintaining good defensive position. If targets on walls are impractical, wastebaskets, boxes, or other objects may be placed behind the playing space (far enough back so they are not hazardous) to serve the same purpose. Both offensive and defensive skills can be learned by using this technique. A game such as "Keep Away" teaches only rules and offensive skills, and for this reason its

use seems questionable when additional skills can be learned by other means.

9. If players tend to be very slow in passing, they may be instructed to "pass on the whistle." Each time a player receives a pass, the teacher whistles to signal time for the next pass. The speed with which the whistle is sounded should depend on the players' skill level. The purpose is to hasten the speed with which they look for a receiver and execute the pass.

10. A magnetic board is a valuable tool for demonstrating player positions and moves for numerous offensive and defensive situations. It generally is more useful than a blackboard for showing concepts concerning player movement, since students can see more readily the new positions of players without interference of numerous chalk lines.

11. Use of films, loop films, and film strips can be valuable in demonstrating various skills or offensive and defensive maneuvers. Video tape is an excellent tool for reviewing skills or game action by players so that they can become aware of their strengths and deficiencies. Observing college and professional games on television can also be a learning experience, particularly in demonstrating skill techniques. It also has some value in showing team offense or team defense, although this is limited to the court coverage visible to the viewer. The "instant replay" has provided the viewer with a new dimension in witnessing superior play.

12. Evaluative measures should be used throughout the unit. This may be done by means of progression charts, incidence charts, rating scales, and other devices. Students should recognize the progress they have made throughout a unit. They should also be aware of areas in which they have weaknesses so that they may be motivated to improve them.

TEACHING PROGRESSION

It is really very unrealistic to propose a teaching progression for any activity, because each situation is unique and demands a progression that is suitable for the students involved. Each class varies in age, skill level, and previous student experience, among other factors. The choice of activities also depends on the individual teacher's beliefs with regard to those aspects of play she considers most essential. There are probably no two circumstances under which the same unit would be taught identically to different groups. Therefore, it is with considerable hesitation that the following units are presented as guidelines for those teachers who would like some assistance in structuring a sequential progression.

The activities in the units are merely listed. Drills

and the progression for teaching each skill or tactic are presented in the chapter in which each is described. During the development of each unit, considerable attention is devoted to one-half court play. The author firmly believes that more time should be devoted to this method of practice than use of the full court. Other than the fun of participating in a regulation type game, little is gained by advancing the ball from the defensive court to the front court. Furthermore, twice as many players can be accommodated on one court by playing half-court. Periodically, in all units the players should experience the true game form. And, probably the amount of time devoted to this should increase as the players become more competent.

An attempt has been made to formulate six units—each based on previously learned materials. The starting point for teaching any class should be based on where the students are at the current time. In many instances the starting point should not be at the beginning of one of the units, but part way through it. Learning may continue into the following unit. In one class, it is entirely possible that some students will be learning activities suggested in Unit 1 while others may be practicing those in Units III or IV.

No attempt has been made to identify the units' length. The units' length will vary according to the students involved and also on the level of achievement desired. It is relatively safe to assay each of these units, however, and anticipate that a unit of more than ten or twelve lessons is necessary to complete it. Longer units must be prepared for students to gain a reasonable degree of competency in an activity.

Unit I

1. Chest and overhead passes. Practice catching.
2. Two-step stop. Rules on traveling.
3. Pivot, with emphasis on facing the player to whom the pass is made. Review the rules on traveling related to the pivot foot.
4. Passing to a moving receiver, with emphasis on 1–3 (Unit I).
5. Dribbling. Rules related to number of bounces, changing hands, and "carrying" the ball, with emphasis on only using the dribble to gain distance or to draw a defender.
6. Play two-on-two using half-court and a target as a goal. Rules on boundaries, putting ball in play, with emphasis on defense players choosing one opponent and staying with her (No. 1 guards A when A is on offense; player A guards No. 1 when No. 1 is on offense).
7. Individual defense. Position when guarding a player with the ball and guarding one without the ball. Introduce the fact that there may be no

body contact (no need to distinguish between fouls at this stage—award ball out of bounds rather than taking free throws).

8. Play two-on-two, with emphasis on individual defense—players sliding and correct position.
9. Layup shot, with emphasis on footwork and releasing ball high overhead.
10. Two-on-two, with emphasis on shooting layups whenever free. Rules on scoring.
11. Starts and changing direction.
12. Pass and cut by attack players.
13. Two-on-two, with emphasis on pass and cut and shooting layups. Keep score.
14. Defense for pass and cut.
15. Two-on-two, with emphasis on defense positioning for pass and cut.
16. Feints.
17. Three-on-three half-court. Play with two guards and one forward. Feint before each pass. Feint before shooting if necessary. Emphasize that one offensive guard must always be back—both may not cut under the basket; if one guard cuts under the basket and does not receive the ball, she clears back out to her position and does not stay under the basket. Use pass and cut. Defense players pivot toward the outside when they obtain a rebound and pass toward the side line—never across the basket.
18. Short one-hand shots. Practice within 6–8 ft. of the basket. This is the area from which they will shoot—no point shooting from 15–20 ft. at this time.
19. Three-on-three, emphasizing Nos. 16–18 (Unit I).
20. Four-on-four (use of three-on-three may be omitted if desired and go immediately to four-on-four). Two groups of two may combine to form a team of four players. Emphasize all of the above points (not in the same lesson though) as they practice. Use a simple weave pattern (Fig. 8.1) so that players know when and where to cut. Let them formulate their own options from the pattern, but insist that at least one player is back for defensive balance.
21. Continue using four-on-four, with emphasis on whatever tactics need improvement.
22. Five-on-five. Use the same pattern and add the pivot player moving independently trying to acquire position for a pass. Rule on 3 sec. in the key.
23. Play full court. Rules, strategy, and positioning for center jump. As players pair off, they guard each other (No. 1 guards A when A is on offense; player A guards No. 1 when No. 1 is on offense). Players stay on the same side of the court for offense and defense (a player on defense in the right guard position becomes the offensive right guard). Allow no defense player to interfere with play until the ball crosses the division line. The

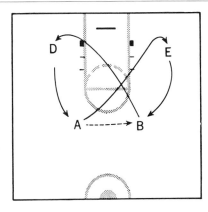

Fig. 8.1 *Four-Player Weave. A passes to B and cuts for the corner. D replaces A and receives the pass from B. B cuts to the corner and E replaces her. Continue.*

best ball handler is instructed to dribble the ball downcourt, while the other players move to the opposite end of the court and get into position. Shoot free throws after fouls are called. Study rules for free throws and scoring.

Throughout Unit I, time is taken periodically and when necessary to review previously learned skills or tactics. Progress in the unit may be interrupted at any time to assure that overlearning is acquired.

Unit II

1. Players review passing, catching, feinting, individual defense, shooting layups and other short shots, stops, starts, changes of direction, and pass and cut. Review the pattern used previously when playing four-on-four and five-on-five, with emphasis on performance improvement in all skills. Distance from the basket should be increased for shooting.

2. Putting the ball in play from out of bounds. Guard in-bounds the ball in the back court and either a guard or a forward in-bounds it in the front court. Emphasis is placed on the positioning of players on the court and the timing of their cuts so that all players do not cut to the same place at the same time; use an elementary play.

3. Lateral screens. Players practice in a two-on-two situation. Two guards practice together, and a pivot and forward practice together. Later, a guard and forward work together. Defense players are instructed to play man-to-man. No switching.

4. Five-on-five, with emphasis on lateral screens intermixed with pass and cut. As a screen is set,

other players clear the area to allow space for the drive.

5. Defense against the lateral screen. Players go over the top. Practice two-on-two.

6. Five-on-five, with emphasis on both the offense and defense with lateral screens. Sagging and floating by defenders.

7. Defense players are instructed to start their moves too soon, and the attack cuts away from the screen. Practice two-on-two.

8. Five-on-five, with emphasis on attack cutting away from the screen whenever the defense moves too soon. Emphasis is on correct moves by all.

9. Screen switch. Defenders switch players as a screen is set. Two-on-two.

10. Screen and roll. As the defense switches, the attack player passes to the one who is rolling. Defense players are instructed to switch. Practice two-on-two.

11. Five-on-five. Defense players are instructed to switch on all screens. Emphasis is on correct timing and moves by the attack.

12. Two-on-two. Defense players are instructed to either stay man-to-man or switch—their choice. The attack adjusts to the actions of the defenders.

13. Five-on-five. Same emphasis as 12 above.

14. Three-player lateral screens if time permits.

Review basic skills throughout as necessary. Allow time for improving shooting techniques, and warm up with one-on-one moves at the beginning of the period. Allow students to incorporate pass and cut techniques with the screens. Let them use their own initiative, and insist that at least one player is back for defensive balance.

Unit III

1. Review previously learned skills, with emphasis on passing, cutting, individual defense, shooting, and lateral screens. Practice one-on-one, two-on-two, and five-on-five.

2. Back screen and defense against it. Practice two-on-two (two guards, one guard, and one forward). Pivot players can work in another area on pivot moves and defense.

3. Five-on-five. Emphasis is on use of back screen. Fake a lateral screen and use a back screen, or fake the back screen and move for a lateral screen.

4. Five-on-five. Encourage players to use all screens and offensive tactics learned to date.

5. Front screens. Two-on-two.

6. Defense against front screens.

7. Five-on-five. Emphasis is on front screens and use of all types of screens. Attack must adjust to

actions of defense. Defense changes tactics to confuse the offense.

8. Play full court as desired. Allow the defense players to defend in the back court if they desire. Guards bring the ball downcourt and use screens if necessary.

Unit IV

1. Improve competency in passing, fakes, shooting, screens, and defense. Play five-on-five, improving positioning and timing of moves on offense.
2. Introduce the jump shot for those who are ready.
3. Blocking out on rebounds defensively; offensive rebounding.
4. Five-on-five, incorporating 2 and 3 (Unit IV).
5. Scissor maneuver. Two guards and the pivot. Three-on-three while the forwards practice shooting in another area. Defense players are instructed to stay man-to-man.
6. Five-on-five, using scissor tactics whenever possible. Forwards are instructed to clear the area and move to the top of the key as the scissor starts.
7. Three-on-three, with emphasis on defensive moves against the scissor.
8. Five-on-five, with emphasis on both attack and defense.
9. Three-on-three with the pivot, one guard, and one forward; repeat 5–8 (Unit IV).
10. Three-on-three. Two guards and the pivot. Defense players are instructed to switch. As the attack sees that the scissor does not work as well, both attack players cut to the same side. Defenders continue to switch.
11. Five-on-five. Defenders are instructed to change their tactics at their discretion—stay man-to-man or switch. Attack players use the scissor and adjust to the defense's action.
12. Three-on-three. The pivot, one guard, and one forward. Repeat 10 and 11 above.

13. Five-on-five. Players utilize all of the tactics and skills they know, and work to improve competency.

During Unit IV, allow time for shooting and practicing one-on-one. Provide time for full court play and administering free throws. Differentiate between pushing, charging, and blocking.

Unit V

1. Improve skills and tactics learned to date.
2. Introduce the hook shot for those who are ready.
3. Fast break.
4. Defense against the fast break.
5. Five-on-five full court, with emphasis on fast breaking whenever possible.
6. Five-on-five incorporating screens, pass and cut, and scissor maneuvers. Defense players improve in defensive positioning for man-to-man and switching when necessary.
7. Two-one-two zone (or any other zone desired).
8. One-three-one offensive alignment utilizing tactics already known.
9. Five-on-five, both half- and full court. Improve competency in all areas. Rule related to fouls during the last 2 min. of the game.

Unit VI

1. Improve skills and tactics learned to date.
2. One-three-one zone (or other).
3. Two-three offensive alignment as used previously.
4. Allow the teams to choose their own offensive and defensive alignments. Let them test their choices against the opponent's choice. Five-on-five both half- and full court.

9

Coaching Advanced Players

Coaching advanced players is not unlike teaching beginning players. The primary difference is that the players start at a higher level of skill and understanding. The same techniques used with beginners are continued in developing greater proficiency with higher skilled players. Drills for improving individual competencies and drills for two-, three-, and four-player tactics are used frequently. Scrimmaging or playing half-court are also common means of improving teamwork.

While working with highly skilled athletes, a coach must remind herself (if necessary) that the educational benefits which accrue from competition are the primary purpose of an athletic program. The experiences provided for the athlete should be educationally sound and should supplement other educational experiences provided by the institution. The benefits to the individual athlete should remain uppermost in the mind of the coach as she makes any decisions bearing on the player's welfare. The coach must recognize that the purpose of the interscholastic or intercollegiate program is not for promoting her own self-vested interests or for the notoriety which a successful program brings to a school.

QUALITIES OF A COACH

The characteristics of a coach in women's competition may be of greater significance than in men's programs. Male high school and college players have reasons for participating in a competitive program which differ from those of women athletes. Since women athletes are not bound by scholarship programs, they can drop membership on the squad whenever the sport no longer remains enjoyable. This may be due to a personality conflict with the coach, practice sessions becoming too demanding, disagreement with the philosophy or practices of the coach, or for innumerable other reasons. Usually the reason can be attributed either directly or indirectly to one or more characteristics of the coach.

Anyone who has coached women athletes recognizes their high motivation. Those who participate in the program do so because they want to. They recognize that the competitive program is demanding upon their time and that they must make value judgments of what is most important to them. If they choose basketball, they usually are sincerely interested in playing and becoming a better player. No coach could ask for any more!

Respect

The coach can gain her players' respect by demonstrating her knowledge of the game. Depth of knowledge in terms of correction of errors, rules, and their interpretation, and strategy of an offensive and defensive nature are necessary. She must not only possess this knowledge, but must also help the players gain an understanding of these aspects and become proficient in applying them during game play.

She must treat all players with equal respect. She cannot afford to show favoritism to any player or group of players. To avoid giving the impression that she is closer to some players than others, she must give equal attention to all. Praise and criticism should be given to all—in the proper manner and at the proper time.

All practice sessions must be well planned, as often women's teams have limited time available in the gymnasium for practice. Every minute must be well spent. Plans for each practice should be drawn carefully, with time allotments established so that no time is wasted. Managers should be notified before practice of any drills that require special equipment so that this can be readied in advance.

Attitude

The coach's attitude is often reflected in her mannerisms and language. Both should be exemplary. The coach must consider that she is a female first and associated with basketball second. She should be cordial, pleasant, and be a lady at all times. Players should follow the same code. Boisterous talking or laughter is unnecessary. There also is no need for players to draw attention to themselves either by their conversation or wearing apparel. People in the community should be unable to distinguish a group of basketball players from any other representative group of the school.

Emotional Control

The coach must learn to keep complete control over her emotions. In any conversation or discussion with players, she should remain calm and keep her voice in its normal tone. Under the stress of a game situation, emotional coaches may have more difficulty in keeping their "cool." At this time, outbursts are particularly inappropriate. Generally when a coach displays her emotions, players on her team exhibit the same type of action. Players question officials' decisions; begin to pull opponents off-balance on tie balls; and retaliate against good play by elbowing, pushing, or other more subtle means. None of these actions should be condoned or permitted.

It is well recognized that the coach is the key influence in the conduct of players and spectators toward officials. Any questioning of calls by officials should be done quietly and during a time out. There should be no outbursts against an official while the game is in progress. If the coach can conduct herself in a quiet orderly manner, players and spectators will usually follow a similar behavioral pattern.

Guidance

The coach is in an excellent position to guide her players in making numerous judgments. In order to aid players in this fashion the coach must have an open door policy, and players must believe that the coach is interested in their welfare. The coach must demonstrate faith in their actions and an understanding of their problems.

Throughout the season the coach should be concerned about the scholastic standing of her players. If a player's academic work is suffering because of the rigors of a season's schedule, the coach should help guide the player to drop basketball so that her academic average does not decline. She can also suggest tutorial help for students having trouble in a particular subject area. Players should be encouraged to make up their work for missed classes *before* they leave for away contests or tournament play so that it does not accumulate.

PREPARATIONS DURING THE OFF-SEASON

Budget

A tentative budget should be prepared to give a detailed account of anticipated income and expenses for the season. It should be itemized by category and designed in accordance with budget policy of the department or institution.

Income provided by the institution should be listed separately from income anticipated from other sources—clinics, workshops, gate receipts, etc.

Anticipated expenses might fall under the following categories:

1. Equipment—backboards, goals, electric scoring-time devices
   a. Purchase
   b. Repair
2. Supplies—basketballs, scorebook, timer's clock, and timer's horn (if electric device not available), air pump, etc.
3. Laundry—uniforms and warmup suits (if provided)
4. Travel
   a. Transportation—bus, car, air; number of miles per vehicle and cost per mile
   b. Lodging—number in group, number per room, cost per room, number of nights
   c. Meals—number in group, allowance per meal, number of meals
5. Officials—number of games, cost per official
6. Entry fees—for tournaments
7. Home game—oranges, other
8. Miscellaneous—rule book, other
9. Contingency—regional, national tournaments (college level)

Care of Equipment

Leather basketballs should be cleaned and a leather conditioner applied. They should be partially deflated and stored in a cool, dry place. Rubber basketballs should be washed, partially deflated, and stored with the leather basketballs.

Uniforms and warmup suits should be repaired, washed or cleaned, folded or hung on hangers, and stored in plastic bags in a cool, dry area.

Other items used during the season should be cleaned, repaired, and stored in an appropriate place. New equipment or uniforms should be marked and stored.

Facilities

During the spring, facilities for practices and games should be scheduled for the following season. In many situations the girls' teams may use the facilities only when they are not used by the men's team so that scheduling in those situations must be delayed until the men's scheduling is completed. Nevertheless, it is wise to schedule as early as possible. Precautions should also be taken so see that the proper authorities have the scheduling of facilities on written record.

When coaches find that it is difficult to obtain a gymnasium for practice, they should investigate the feasibility of other rooms in the school that are reasonably large and open. For example, rooms used for dance, fencing, or wrestling might be available. The stage in the auditorium, the cafeteria, the music room, or any other room with moveable chairs might be suitable. Many phases of the game can be learned in this type of facility—screens, scissors, zones, sagging and floating, pattern offenses, and others. About the only restriction in this type of facility is inability to shoot, block out, and rebound. There is no substitute for a gymnasium, but much learning can be acquired in other facilities.

Scheduling

The formulation of a schedule should be done carefully. An effort should be made to schedule teams that traditionally are comparable in skill or slightly better. Little is gained by either team when one wins by twenty points or more. For this reason, scheduling teams that are traditionally weak seems questionable. In order for a team to continue to improve, it must meet competent opponents who challenge their skills and knowledges.

When arranging a schedule, the coach should view her talent for the following year and determine how strong she expects them to be. If it appears that the team will be inexperienced, it may be wise to schedule the easiest opponents first so that the team has time to mature before meeting more difficult opponents. If the team is composed of veteran players it may be wiser to schedule a few games against difficult opponents first so that the players are challenged early in the season and see the need for continued learning. Games against traditional opponents should be scheduled near the end of the season.

Games scheduled at home and away should be equally spaced throughout the schedule. Each season a similar number of games should be scheduled at home and away; if possible, distances for travel each year should be comparable. (It may be difficult for an administrator to understand why the budget requires considerable more money one year than another year with no apparent additional benefits.) In all cases, travel should be held to a minimum. Travel is tiring and takes time. Games that require students to miss classes should be few in number. Long trips should be scheduled on weekends when travel will not interfere with classes.

Some games may be scheduled over the telephone, but should be confirmed later by written communication. Use of game contracts may be desirable under some circumstances. For all games the site, time, number of games, and responsibility for furnishing officials should be confirmed in writing.

An information sheet may be prepared to forward to visiting coaches to give them additional information. This might include directions to the site of the game, parking facilities for cars or buses, entrance for players, restaurants in the area with types of food and average price, motel and/or dormitory accommodations and prices.

When the scheduling has been completed for the following season, copies should be dittoed and made available. Copies should be forwarded to the department head and other administrative authorities.

Officials

Following the completion of the schedule, arrangements should be made to secure the most qualified officials. Engaging a competent official is an asset to a highly skilled team, as her standards and interpretation of rules are likely to be similar. Games officiated by less competent officials often become rough and induce injuries as a result.

It is recommended that women officials be secured whenever possible. Although the women's game resembles the men's to a much greater extent now, there remains a difference in the way in which men officials tend to interpret certain rules. Men officials tend to be much more lenient with body contact —particularly in the free throw lane and during rebounding situations. In addition, their interpretation of blocking and charging often differs from the accepted interpretation of the women's rules. It should be noted, however, that the men's rules as written on changing and blocking differ very little from the women's. Nevertheless, possibly due to the televised broadcasts and the more liberal interpretation of rules in the men's professional game, the appearance of considerably more body contact has become evident at the high school level in boys' contests. This permissiveness is undesirable in women's play and provides an obvious reason for hiring women officials providing they are as competent as available men officials.

Travel

Tentative travel arrangements should be made for all away games. This includes reserving cars or buses and making reservations when overnight accommodations are required.

File on Opposing Teams

A file on each opponent may be made and supplemented annually. The file should contain general information on the site and facility and specific information on team play. Basically it should include

1. General information
   a. Directions to the playing site
   b. Parking facilities for cars and buses
   c. Motels and cost per room; any special accommodations
   d. Restaurants—type of food served and average cost
   e. Dressing facilities and meeting room
   f. Playing facility—court size, type of backboard, space around court, ceiling height
   g. Opponents' uniform color
2. Characteristics of team
   a. Individual characteristics
      1) Name, number, and class of each player
      2) Is she right- or left-handed?
      3) Does she dribble in both directions? Does she favor one side?
      4) What are her pet moves?
      5) Is she a playmaker?
      6) What type of shots does she attempt? From where does she like to shoot?
      7) Is she a good defensive player?
      8) Does she rebound—offensively or defensively?
      9) Is she a good ball handler? Does she have poise? Can she be pressed?
      10) Other?
   b. Team offense
      1) Do they fast break? Who is the ball handler?

How is it started? How do they tend to finish it?
      2) What is their offensive alignment?
      3) Who do they attempt to free for shots? How is this done?
      4) Where is the pivot positioned? How is she used? What are her assets? Weaknesses?
      5) What alignments are used on out of bounds? Jump balls? What are the pet plays?
      6) Can they be pressed?
      7) Who is the weakest player? Strongest player?
   c. Team defense
      1) Do they play man-to-man? Switching? Are they tight or loose?
      2) What kind of a zone do they use? How far is it extended?
      3) Do they press? Where? Man-to-man or zone?
      4) Are they susceptible to fakes?
      5) How do they rebound?
      6) Who is the weakest player? Strongest player?

A file of this nature reminds a coach of the strengths and weaknesses and general pattern of play for each opponent. Although it is based on a previous season, basic team tactics are not often changed drastically from year to year unless a new coach is appointed. Comments can be added as new information is gained; information that no longer is correct is deleted. Names of players who graduated or who are no longer members of the squad are eliminated, and names and information about new players are added when they become known.

Notes of this nature are not as valuable as a current scouting report, but few women have the time and/or budget to permit them to scout even a portion of their rivals. If more complete or current information is desired, it may be possible to have alumnae or former players who live near the school in question to scout one or more of their games. If this can be arranged, they should be given a scouting sheet so that they know the specific information desired. One word of caution must be raised about reports by non-trained friends. Often they fail to depict exactly what formation and moves the players are following. Wrong information about a team is probably worse than no information at all. To have prepared for one type of offense or defense and have the opponents play something entirely different is psychologically deflating to players.

Preparation of Player Handbooks

Some coaches find it helpful to devise a "play book" for their players for their review and digestion. Often given to players in the fall, it rekindles their interest and establishes a good mental set to start the new season. Because players have time to become mentally prepared, it takes less practice time for learning positioning or patterns. All of this can be learned beforehand. Usually a handbook of this nature contains the following information:

1. An introduction by the coach stating her philosophy and expectations for the season.
2. Game schedule — indicating time of game, home or away, and whether one or two games (varsity and junior varsity) will be played
3. Pre-season conditioning suggestions
4. Date and time for first practice; practice schedule throughout the season
5. Offensive alignments, patterns, plays, options
6. Defensive alignments; zones, press
7. Special plays

The coach should make some provision for checking the handbook out to players at the beginning of the season and having them returned at the conclusion of the season so that revisions may be made. The handbook should also be turned in by any player who drops from the squad during the course of the season. Care must be taken to guard the security of the information within the handbook. No coach wants the plays to be public information.

Miscellaneous Arrangements

Well in advance of the start of the season, arrangements should be made with the school doctor (or health service) for medical examinations of the athletes. No athlete should be permitted to play in a contest until she has been given medical approval for competition.

Health insurance should be checked annually to ascertain whether players are covered by a school policy or should be advised to secure their own insurance. It should be noted that recent court litigation in some states has declared illegal the purchase of insurance for athletes by public funds.

High school coaches should arrange for accessibility of a school nurse or school doctor during practice periods and home games. If the medical staff has other responsibilities at the time, arrangements should be made for contacting one of them or an alternate in case of an emergency. The coach should be certain that she has access to a nonpay telephone with emergency numbers listed near it. The coach should have immediate access to the name of the parents, their address, telephone number (business and home), and the family physician in case of emergency.

At the college level, the coach should check the

hours that the student health service is open and make arrangements for emergencies at other times. She also should have access to a nonpay telephone with emergency numbers listed nearby. She should advise the trainer of the time and dates for home games and make arrangements for treatment of injuries during the season.

College coaches would also be wise to send the Dean of Women (or supervisor of dormitories) a schedule for the season and a list of all players and their dormitory. If, due to an emergency, players will be out beyond scheduled hours, house mothers can be notified easily. The coach should also check on special arrangements that may be made for players who miss the scheduled meal hour because of practices or games. In some instances it is possible to make arrangements for box lunches or meals to be served later or earlier than usual. The coach should also check the policy regarding the housing of opposing teams. In some situations this is considerably cheaper than motels; in other instances it is more expensive.

The method for dispensing uniforms should be determined. Provision should be made for recording the number of each item issued to a player so that the responsibility for its return is placed on each player.

PREPARATIONS DURING THE SEASON

As all coaches are aware once practices start, the season becomes very busy. Teaching classes and preparing for daily practices and games take a considerable amount of time. Good organization is a necessity at this time.

First Day of Practice

Either the first day of practice or some time prior to the time practices are scheduled to begin, a meeting is called for all prospective candidates. At this time the coach welcomes the candidates and reveals her expectations for the season. If rules and regulations are also discussed at this time, this may serve as one of the most important meetings held all season. From the beginning the players will understand any regulations that the coach wishes to impose. This should eliminate problems which foreseeably could develop later if new rules were added. When regulations are publicized at the start of the season, they generally are accepted by the group. When imposed later, they are assumed to be directed toward a particular individual or group and resentment may develop. Rules concerning tardiness, absences, dress code, etc., should be discussed.

In addition the coach may remind the players of

the importance of proper conditioning. If the meeting is held during pre-season, she may comment on how "conditioned" they should be by the first day of practice and offer suggestions for attaining this level. She may review the season's schedule at this time to demonstrate the need for proper conditioning.

She should encourage players to retain or improve their grade point averages during the season, and to request help as soon as they encounter any difficulty. She may remind players that their education is the most important factor and that basketball is secondary. She may also remind them of the current eligibility rules.

The importance of punctuality should be stressed. It should also be made clear that the coach expects 100 percent effort on the part of all players and that the season should bring a great deal of fun and satisfaction. However, these do not develop as a result of clowning or horseplay during practice. A team that practices in this manner is likely to play in this manner. Above all the coach should make it known (and demonstrate it thereafter) that teamwork is the most important factor in any team's success. Players must be selfless and undertake any role that will help improve the play of the team.

Players should be reminded of the importance of immediate care to any injury and the damage that may result from unattended blisters, cuts, floor burns, sprains, etc. The availability of medical staff and a trainer should be cited.

Careful attention should be given to the method of selecting the squad. Players should know on what basis selection will be made, the number of cuts that will be made, the dates for each of those cuts, the general conduct of practices until that time, and the number of candidates who ultimately will comprise the squad.

Managers

One of the most valuable assets to a coach is dependable, resourceful, and loyal managers. They can be responsible for numerous items that ease the load of the coach. Depending upon the number of responsibilities she wishes to assign to them, she may choose to have one or more managers. It seems desirable to have at least three to carry out all of the responsibilities, but some coaches may not see a need for this number; others will desire more.

It is recommended that each manager be assigned specific duties for daily practice sessions, home games, and away games. These assignments may be made by the coach or by mutual agreement of the managers involved. Below is a list of responsibilities that may be assigned to managers.

Practices

1. A list of equipment is compiled and checked off daily as it is taken to the gym. The list should include a designated number of balls; pinnies, preferably the color of the uniform of the next opponent; timing devices; score sheets; shot charts; other devices for collecting data; and a first-aid kit.
2. Other equipment or materials are taken to the gymnasium on specific occasions as designated by the coach.
3. During practice, balls not in use are collected and placed in bags or other receptacles. Data are collected, and other duties are performed as requested.
4. Towels are made available for showers after practice.
5. All equipment is counted and returned to the equipment room. Items left by players are collected.

Home Games

1. The gymnasium is prepared for the game (if the custodians are not responsible for this). The scoring table with at least five chairs is readied. Chairs are set out for both teams on either side of the scoring table. Timing devices are checked.
2. Uniforms are dispensed (if not assigned for the entire season).
3. Equipment is taken to the gym: a designated number of practice balls, a game ball, scorebook, timing devices, shot charts, other charts, first aid kit.
4. The visiting team is greeted as it arrives, and is escorted to the dressing room. When ready, these players are taken to the gymnasium.
5. The officials are greeted upon their arrival and shown to their dressing room.
6. Oranges and other refreshments are prepared.
7. Towels are made available for both teams.
8. A manager serves as a scorer, timer, 30-sec. clock operator, or statistician.
9. Balls are collected after pre-game and half-time practice; all equipment is counted and returned after completion of the game.
10. Uniforms are collected.
11. Refreshments are served.

Away Games

1. Uniforms are dispensed.
2. Equipment is collected for travel: a designated number of practice balls (if not provided by the home team), scorebook, timing device, shot chart, other charts, first-aid kit.
3. A manager serves as a timer, scorer, or statistician.

4. Practice balls are collected after pre-game and half-time practice (if team's own balls are used).
5. Equipment is counted and collected after the game and returned to the gymnasium upon return.
6. Uniforms are collected.

Miscellaneous

1. Balls are cleaned and inflated periodically.
2. A card file of information on each player is prepared. Data collected might include name, address (dormitory), telephone, parents names, parents address, parents business and home telephone, family physician, uniform number, locker assigned, lock combination (in high school it is usually owned by the school), and other desired information which may be useful if an emergency occurs.

If dependable managers are secured, they relieve the coach of attending to all of these items and save the coach considerable time. It makes little difference who is selected to serve as managers, so long as they have the desirable qualities. Those selected may be players who were cut from the squad, students with a physical disability which prohibits them from participating otherwise, or interested students who would simply like to have some part in the athletic program.

Team Selection

A sufficient length of time should be devoted to tryouts so that a careful analysis can be made of the strengths and weaknesses of all candidates. The time that is necessary varies with the group, but two to three weeks should be ample for making wise judgments. Longer than that seriously cuts in to the amount of practice time for the squad prior to their first game, and less time probably does not give all candidates a fair chance for observation.

During tryouts it seems desirable to use specific drills that utilize all basic skills involved in the game. By observing players performing in small groups, the coach can analyze their ability in performing individual skills and their potential for improvement. Drills should include passing, stopping, pivoting, faking, shooting, individual defense, blocking out, and rebounding.

Scrimmages should also be a vital part of the tryout program. During the tryout period each player should play with and against players who are better than she, poorer than she, and players who are of equal ability. This may be done by formulating teams to compete in a round robin tournament each day. On different occasions every player should be assigned to play on a relatively strong team, a weak team, and an average team. Through this means each player has an opportunity to demonstrate her skill against all levels of ability. The coach is also able to see how well she can adjust to playing with different individuals. And, perhaps more enlightening, she can see each player's mental attitude under various conditions.

Since a basketball team is comprised of individuals who play various positions, each with their own qualifications, the coach must determine prior to tryouts exactly what she is looking for. How many players does she want to carry on her squad? Is she selecting enough players for one team or for two teams? If she plans to play only one team all season, she probably should select a squad of fifteen players, or three teams. If she plans to have varsity and junior varsity games, she may choose to select four teams or twenty players. The point is that she wants a balanced squad. She does not want a team composed of all players with qualifications to play guard and none with qualifications for a forward position. In choosing twenty players, she should look for eight forwards, four pivots, and eight guards.

While observing players during tryouts (as well as during the season), it is wise to use data-collecting devices in order to appraise the players as objectively as possible. These may be in the form of Shot Charts, in which shooting range, types of shots, location of most shots, and accuracy can be detected; Incidence Charts, which identify the number of assists, rebounds, turnovers, fouls, violations, tie balls, and interceptions gained; and other devices favored by the coach. Reference to performance records eliminates the halo effect and provides a more vivid picture of the attributes and deficiencies of individual players. The coach may then compare abilities of individual players and determine which players will complement the others to the greatest degree.

Conditioning

One of the most important facets in any sports program is that of proper conditioning. Physicians support the theory that 60 percent of all injuries incurred in basketball are the result of improper conditioning — both physical and mental. This means that not only must cardiovascular and muscular endurance be increased, but also that the player must be mentally prepared for practice and game situations.

To attain top physical condition a player must continue to increase her workload until the desired level is achieved. Continued activity will maintain that level. The workload can be increased basically in either of two ways:

1. increase the extent or amount of work
2. increase the intensity of the work (the amount done in a given time)

Related specifically to basketball, periods for half-court play or scrimmaging are increased throughout the early practice sessions. With unconditioned players it may be wise to start with 5-min. playing periods. This is increased to 8-, 10-, 12-, 15-, and perhaps 20-min. periods with rest periods shorter and less frequent. To increase the intensity of the activity, the same time period may be used but the workload within that time period is increased. For example, early in the season drills in a practice session may be alternated so that there is one that requires considerable running, followed by one that is less demanding. As endurance increases, running is included in all drills.

To improve cardiovascular endurance, the legs must be involved in the activity. Jumping, hopping, running, and sliding are the usual activities chosen for basketball players. Some coaches suggest that their players undertake a pre-season conditioning program, while others wait for practices to start. Although each coach usually has pet drills for conditioning her players, some suggestions follow.

1. Players run up and down stairs at the gymnasium, in the dormitory, or at the football stadium. Increase the length of time in which the task is continued, or increase the number of stairs climbed in the same time period.

2. Harvard step test variation. A bench 16–18 in. high is needed. The player steps up on to the bench with one foot, then steps up with the other foot to an erect position; she steps down with the lead foot and steps down with the other foot to the starting position. The player may change her lead foot, if desired. This is continued as long as possible; increase the number of cycles periodically. Or, the player may complete a designated number of cycles in a specific time period; increase the number of cycles within that time period periodically.

3. Jumping in place. The player takes ten short jumps followed by ten high jumps. Continue. During the short jumps the player's feet just rise above the surface by a few inches. During the high jumps, the player jumps as high as possible on each jump. The number of cycles must be increased periodically.

4. Individually or as a group. Sprints. The player starts at one end line and sprints to the opposite end line, then jogs back to her starting position. Continue. Increase the number of cycles.

5. Individually or as a group. The player assumes a proper defensive position at one end line. She maintains that position as she slides to the other end, turns, and slides back to the starting position without rising to a standing position. Increase the number of cycles.

6. All players line up along the end or side line and move around the court counterclockwise. As they come to a side line, they sprint to the other end; across the end lines they slide with their hands touching the floor. Increase the time performed or the number of cycles.

7. All players line up along the end or side line and move around the court counterclockwise. They run, slide, hop on one foot, hop on the other foot, or hop on both feet (not for very long; balance is lost) on signal from the coach. During this drill, the run may be a jog rather than a sprint. The players should touch the floor with their hands whenever they are sliding. Increase the time or the number of cycles.

8. Russian layup. Preferably no more than twelve players. Two lines are formed for layups at the end baskets. One ball is in play at each basket as layups are taken from the right side (or left side) at both ends. Players move to both ends of the court. They move from the shooting line at one end, to the rebounding line at the same end, to the shooting line at the *opposite* end, to the rebounding line at the opposite end, and back to the shooting line from which they started. This cycle is continued. With only twelve players involved, it should force the players to run continually if, after shooting, they run out to the division line before falling into the rebound line. If more players are added to the drill, players run in place while waiting to shoot or rebound. The drill is continued as long as possible. Increase the time periodically.

9. Russian layup variation. Proceed as described above, but continue until a designated number of layups have been made consecutively—fifteen, twenty, twenty-five, or fifty. Count layups at both ends of the court. Increase the number of consecutive layups periodically.

10. Informally or as a group. Cross-country running. Preferably players run on a grass surface in a somewhat hilly area. Golf courses, city parks, or county roads provide pleasant surroundings to enjoy a run of 1, 2, 3, 4, or 5 miles. Increase the distance periodically or decrease the time to run a designated distance.

Injuries

Early in the season two of the most common injuries which occur are blisters and shin splints. Blisters usually can be prevented early in the season by wearing two pairs of wool socks and by using a commercial skin toughener. Cotton socks do not provide the same type of cushion as woolen socks. Shin splints are an inflamation of the muscle between the shin and the foot and usually occur due to unaccustomed activity on a hard surface. Early season running on grassy surfaces should be encouraged for those who have had little activity recently. Running on a hard surface track is little better than the gymnasium floor. Prevention of this injury is considerably easier than the treatment.

Injuries to the ankle, knee, and fingers are also common in basketball. All of these can be treated immediately by elevating the extremity and applying pressure and ice. The limb is elevated to decrease arterial flow and increase venous flow. Pressure is applied to decrease arterial flow (it also decreases venous flow), and the ice is applied to keep swelling at a minimum. If ice is to be applied for a long period, a thin towel should be placed over the skin surface. Ice is applied on top of the towel to prevent possible frost bite. In all cases following any type of an injury the player should be referred to the school nurse or doctor or to the health center. No player should be permitted to resume practice following a serious injury until a medical release is given.

The scope of this book does not permit a full discussion of injuries and their treatment, but a coach should prepare herself in this area through appropriate courses or workshops.

Practice Sessions

During the early part of the season, emphasis should be placed on the improvement of individual skills. Later, emphasis should be changed to improving teamwork, although individual improvement should not be neglected. It is probably true that few women's teams devote a long enough period of time to practice prior to their first game. A three-week period is not uncommon; if a sufficient period of time has been devoted to tryouts, little time, if any, remains for practice with the selected squad. This means that in all probability the squad selection is done within a few days in order to prepare the squad for its first game. With this short practice time it is difficult to improve indi-

vidual skills to any great extent if teamwork is to be developed.

It is during this early practice period that the coach should prepare the team with a basic offense and variations, a secondary offense, a primary and secondary defense and a pressing defense, and plays for special situations. If enough time is not allowed, only a portion of these may be learned prior to the start of the season. Once the season starts, there may not be time to learn many more of them.

Throughout the season ample time should be devoted to shooting practice. Players need time in which to learn new shooting techniques. They need to develop confidence with and without an opponent under all types of defensive circumstances. Players should also be encouraged to develop new moves prior to attempting shots. This, too, takes time to learn. Many players need to increase the range in their shooting as well as to improve accuracy at all distances.

Time should also be devoted to the improvement of other individual skills, as needed. As a matter of fact, a list of activities for the start of practice can be posted at the entrance to the gymnasium. For example, two pivot players may be assigned to work on pivot moves and defense against the pivot; another player may work on shooting quickly from the corner; two others on blocking out and rebounding; another on free throw shooting; four others to work on two player moves and the defense against it; another player on guarding a dribbler, etc. At this stage, some portion of the practice should be individualized.

During the early stages of the season, the coach needs to learn which combination of players consistently brings the best results. She also should assay which offense provides the greatest number of shots and the shooting accuracy attained from each. This usually indicates which offense frees players to the greatest degree and allows them unhurried shots from a distance within their shooting range. For example:

Alignment	Time Played	Opponent's Defense	Number of Possessions	FGA	FGM	%
Fast break	—	—	5	4	3	75
2–3	8	M-M tight	13	11	6	55
1–3–1	8	M-M tight	10	9	4	44

In order to assess data such as this accurately, the same defense must be used against each of the offensive alignments and each must be played for the same length of time. The above data were gathered

from two quarters of full court scrimmage. In this situation the fast break resulted in the highest shooting percentage as one would expect. The two-three alignment produced a higher shooting accuracy and more goals scored than the one-three-one alignment. Data may be collected for half-court play under game-like conditions, which would produce considerably more possessions and shooting opportunities—but no fast break attempts.

To make these data most useful, the coach should try various combinations working together under the same conditions. Also, defensive changes should be made to learn if results differ under these conditions. For example, these offensive alignments should be used against a loose man-to-man defense and against one or more zones.

Up to the time when games are played, the activities scheduled for the daily practice session may increase in intensity until players have attained the desirable level of conditioning. This means that attention should be given to longer periods of continuous play than normal (15–20 min.) in scrimmages of a half-court nature or full court. (For high school students or players not in good condition, the time allotment should be adjusted.) Once the season starts and games are played once or twice a week, little full court scrimmaging is necessary except for those who do not play in these contests. These players should engage in a full court scrimmage at the practice following the game. For the other players the workout may be moderate in intensity unless a weekend has interceded; in this case, a more strenuous session may be planned. Prior to all games, activities should be scheduled that are relatively light and not exhausting.

Publicity

Arrangements should be made to have a team photograph taken after the squad has been selected. Players often wish to purchase copies, and a copy should be kept in the coach's files for reference at a later date. The photograph can also be used for publicity purposes to accompany articles in the school or community newspaper, for bulletin board display, for use in the school yearbook, among others.

News releases should be prepared throughout the season for the school and local papers. Names of veteran players returning to tryout and a resume of the preceding season provide interesting reading when notification for this year's tryouts is given. This may be followed up by an announcement of the candidates who made the squad. Later highlights and results of each game should be submitted.

It is true that most women can attest to the difficulty of getting information on women's sports printed either in the school or local paper. However, continued efforts should be made to keep the public informed and provide the players with the recognition

they deserve. Other means of publicity can also be used to a greater extent. Attractive copies of the schedule can be printed (dittoed) and distributed around campus or on bulletin boards in high schools. The physical education department may publish handbooks which list the schedule of intramurals and all sports for the forthcoming year. These may be distributed to all women students. A departmental newspaper may be published weekly, biweekly, or monthly to report on intramural and team results. This also may be distributed to women students and administrative authorities.

PREPARATION FOR TRAVEL

Attention to detail is necessary so that trips are uninterrupted by delay due to incomplete directions, improper or incomplete motel accommodations, or poor service.

Arrangements for Travel and Meals

Communication is made with the motel to verify or alter the tentative arrangements previously made. Arrival and departure time should be stated as well as any special accommodations that are desired. A list of the players and their room assignment can be forwarded so that keys for each room may be placed in an envelope and ready for distribution on arrival. This eliminates a large group from congregating in the lobby and permits players to settle in their rooms more quickly.

Restaurants should be alerted to an arrival time so that they may be prepared to serve a large group. They should also be notified if one large table to accommodate all players is desired. If a special menu is desired, the management should be informed so that the food may be prepared and served more quickly. This information also permits them to have sufficient waitresses on duty to assure good service to all diners.

Itinerary and Trip Directions

A complete itinerary for each trip should be formulated. It should include the time and place of departure, mode of transportation, name(s) of the driver(s), destination, estimated time of arrival, time of game, motel, restaurant(s) listed for different meals, time of departure, and anticipated return arrival time. A telephone number for the host school and the name of the home team coach should be included. A copy of the itinerary should be given to the department chairman and other administrators as desired. A copy may also be given to each player, particularly if the trip extends for more than one day. Additional copies should be available for parents and other interested parties.

When more than one vehicle is used, travel directions should be given *in writing* to each driver. The information should include maximum speed limit, routes to follow, in-town directions for turns on specific streets to reach the gymnasium, estimated time of arrival, parking accommodations, procedures for vehicle breakdowns and additional fuel, and a name and telephone number to call in case of emergency. If stops are to be made en route, the location of each and approximate arrival time should be noted. If an overnight stay is involved, directions to and from the motel to the gymnasium should be included. Each driver should also receive a copy of the itinerary.

Player Conduct

At the practice prior to departure on the first trip each year it is wise for the coach to review the dress code and conduct that she expects during the trip. Briefly, this discussion might include such items as

1. wearing apparel to and from the game
2. the need for promptness at all times
3. the desire to bring respect to themselves as well as to the institution
4. their actions should not differentiate them from any other group representing the school
5. they are the guests of the school (and a motel as well) which has invited them and their actions should reflect this; they should care for their property as though it were their own and not "borrow" souvenirs.
6. their actions following the game should be the same whether they win or lose

Departure and Arrival at Destination

Each player is given the responsibility for taking her own uniform. The coach makes a final check to be sure the managers have all necessary equipment, data sheets, and first-aid kit. Before departure the coach counts the number of players in the vehicles to determine whether all are accounted for. The same procedure is followed before departing from the host school.

Although it is not always possible to arrive in time for rest prior to the start of the game, a team should make plans to arrive in time for players to become mentally prepared to play the game. There should be ample time for them to dress, have a team meeting, and warm up before the contest is scheduled to begin. If a game is scheduled in the afternoon following classes, the players should be warned against eating pre-game snacks. If an early evening contest is sched-

uled, a light meal may be ingested during early afternoon; no meal should be eaten within four hours of game time. If desired, a meal or snack may be enjoyed following the game.

If a team is participating in a tournament, it is desirable for them to follow a normal routine as much as possible. This means that they should arise at a near normal hour and have breakfast together. If they are scheduled for an afternoon game, breakfast should be ingested four hours before game time and then the players should return to their room for rest until time to leave for the gymnasium. If they are scheduled for an evening contest, they may be placed on their own during the remaining portion of the morning. However, they must always be with at least one other player. By early afternoon they should be in their rooms resting. The pre-game meal should be eaten four hours before game time.

PREPARATION FOR A GAME

The coach should prepare her team to meet any eventuality during practice sessions prior to the first game of the season. They should be prepared

1. to face various zone defenses
2. to deal with pressing defenses and man-to-man defenses; also to deal with different offensive alignments
3. to put the ball in play from out of bounds against various defenses and to defend against various offensive alignments chosen by the opponents
4. for jump ball situations at each of the restraining circles under conditions when they may win or lose the tap
5. to follow a specific plan of action if they are ahead or behind, or if the score is tied in the last few minutes of the game
6. to use warmup drills with which they are familiar so that they may proceed in an organized fashion

In order for the team to demonstrate poise and confidence in all of these, they must have practiced each of them many times and under game conditions as well.

Two or three practice sessions before the first game is scheduled the team should experience a regulation intra-squad game in which uniforms are worn, regular warmup procedures are followed, and officials conduct the game using all regulation procedures. At this time the coach can identify the weaknesses under game conditions and conduct additional practice sessions for correction before the initial game. With high school players in particular, the coach is able to ascertain whether all players can follow correct substitution procedures. She can also check to see if the designated players look at the bench for signals for a specific offensive maneuver or a change in tactic. Players also can demonstrate their understanding of the responsibility for calling time outs.

After each game is played the coach analyzes what areas appear to be the weakest and takes measures to correct or improve them as much as possible before the next contest. If possible, practices should be conducted in surroundings similar to those in which the next game will be played. If it is an away game and the court is much smaller than the home team court, it may be wise to place chairs or other objects on the court to reduce it to a similar size. If possible, lighting and other conditions should be made similar.

Game Plan

In addition the coach should establish a game plan of measures to take against the upcoming opponent. This should be based on known information about the opponents' play. If the coach has no information about the opponent, she must simply prepare the team to do whatever it does best and anticipate as much as possible what the opponents might do (based on knowledge of tactics from previous years) and prepare the team to meet those situations.

Against a team:

1. that is slow, tall, or prefers to play a pattern system of offense, the team should prepare to press them. A press should also be used against a poor ball handling team.
2. whose best offense is a fast break, the team should prepare to slow them and prevent a fast break from starting.
3. that likes to drive through the lane, the defense should sag and float.
4. that relies on a high scoring pivot, the defenders should sag and float to prevent the pass in to the pivot.
5. that cannot shoot from the outside, the defense should play loose and not extend beyond the opponents' shooting range.
6. that has only one good shooter, the defense should play her man-to-man and use a four-player zone against the others.

Against a team that is tall or slow, a fast break should be used as much as possible. Against a team that has one or more poor defensive players, the attack should be aimed at them. If a player is in foul trouble the attack should be aimed toward her because she must be somewhat cautious. If the defense is playing a tight man-to-man the attack should use screens. If the attack has a great height advantage, they may use a low double post.

Once the coach has established a game plan, she should discuss it with her players. During the next few practice sessions the players practice the execution of the game plan. Usually the second team is asked to play the defense the opponents play so that the starters can gain experience opposing it. Similarly, the second team is taught the opponents' offense as much as possible so that the defense can become prepared. If any idiosyncrasies or pet moves of opposing individual players are known, the second team players try to use them so that the starters become familiar with them.

GAME PROCEDURES

Players should report approximately one hour or more before the game is scheduled to start. Players who need taping should report earlier. This provides players with ample time to get dressed, be taped, and ready for a team meeting approximately 30–45 min. before game time.

Team Meeting

During the team meeting the coach reviews with her squad the game plan for the day. She points out specifically how each player must contain her opponent. The team defense is also outlined: how to stop their fast break; what measures are to be taken against their ball handler; how to play the pivot player, etc. She then reviews the offensive tactics she wants her team to use. She identifies under what conditions she wants them to try to fast break; who should bring the ball downcourt; what offensive alignment they are to start with and which moves are likely to be most successful. She also indicates what moves should be made on the tap at the start of the game, what alignment should be used on the first out-of-bounds play, and what moves should be made. She may desire to draw both of these on a blackboard for thorough review for the players. She indicates whether or not they are to start with a pressing defense. She provides time for questions by the players. She announces the starting line-up and reviews warmup procedures before sending them to the court approximately 20 min. before game time.

Pre-Game Warmup

Players should move onto the court in an organized fashion. They usually move from the squad meeting to the gymnasium and trot out onto the court led by their captain or someone appointed as captain for the day. This system gives them a feeling of *espirit de corps* and should replace the unorganized system of players moving onto the court when they are ready.

The purpose of the warmup period is to provide the players with time to capture the feel of the ball and gain the rhythm of their shots and timing for passes and cutting. It may also serve to intimidate the opponents if a team moves from one drill to another crisply and executes each with proficiency.

Often the warmup is started by running a simple layup drill. This is followed by several other drills before players informally practice the shots they are most likely to use in the game. All players should shoot free throws as well. While players are shooting, there should be a ball for every two players. When more than six balls are used, however, it becomes somewhat difficult. Most coaches prefer to have those players who are most likely to see action enjoy most of the shooting time. All players may shoot for a designated length of time and then those players who will not see much action may return to the bench or stand near the division line and observe both teams shooting. Those players who are shooting usually pair off, and one player takes several shots before giving the ball to her partner.

Many coaches prefer to end the pre-game session with the shooting activity. Others prefer to return to the dressing room for last minute instructions, but the author prefers to spend the last few minutes to play three-on-three. All players line up at the division line in three columns, with the first three players stepping out on defense. The next three put the ball in play and attempt to score, after which they become the defensive group against the next threesome. After completing their turn on defense, the players return to the end of one of the offensive lines. Defensive practice is the primary purpose of this drill.

Examples of other common warmup drills are shown in Figs. 9.1–9.3.

Substitutions

The substitutes who usually see action sit close to the coach so that she can convey any necessary information to them. Players least likely to see action sit near the end of the bench. While the game is in progress the substitutes encourage their teammates by cheering and shouting words of instruction. These players should watch particularly the player for whom they may substitute and her opponent. Often the substitute can detect a flaw in the opponent's skill and relay that information to her teammate. Also, by watching the opponent she should be better prepared to defend against her when she enters the game.

It is important that the coach helps the substitutes to feel that they are an important part of the team. Often there are a few who rarely get into a game, and special effort should be made to help them under-

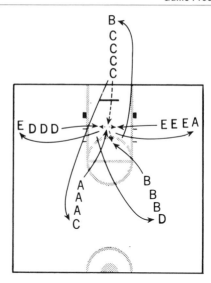

Fig. 9.1 *Passing Drill. Players start in columns as shown. Player C starts with the ball and passes to A who passes to E to D to B and to C and the pattern is repeated. The cuts are timed so that each player may hand off the pass to the next cutter. After passing, each player goes to the right and end of the line to which she passed. The drill can be modified so that players in line B shoot and C recovers the rebound before starting a new sequence.*

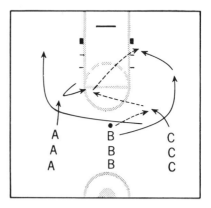

Fig. 9.2 *Figure Eight Passing Drill. Three columns are formed with each player in line B with a ball. B passes to C and goes behind C. C passes to A and goes behind A. A passes to B and goes behind her. B shoots. No dribbling is allowed.*

309

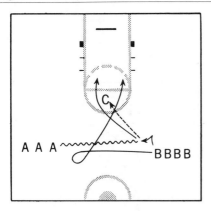

Fig. 9.3 *Pivot and Shooting Drill. Players line up in a shuttle formation as shown with one or two pivot players alternating at the high pivot position. Two balls are used. Player A dribbles across as player B cuts to the opposite side. Both players pivot (on the inside foot) and A passes to C. A cuts around C, followed by B. C hands off to either one for a layup. As the ball is rebounded, the next players start.*

the game, she may be "cooled" off—both physically and mentally—and not perform up to capacity.

4. Put aggressive players into action. If a team has fallen behind in score and appears to be playing somewhat sluggishly, the insertion of an aggressive player may bring them out of their doldrums and "fire" them up.

5. Insert players with special abilities. If a team wants to be sure to recover a rebound, good jumpers may be inserted. Good ball handlers may be inserted when the team wants to control the ball as long as possible. A player who is particularly good defensively may be inserted to guard a high scoring opponent.

6. Allow players who often see little game action to gain some playing experience. Insertion of players when a team has gained a good lead should be made extremely judiciously. Once momentum is lost, it is sometimes difficult to regain. Therefore, when a team has moved to a rather large lead in the first half it may be wise to only substitute for one or two players at most. In the second half, when it appears as though a large enough lead has been attained, starters should be replaced by others. Not only does it give the substitutes game experience which may prove beneficial in years to come, but it also helps to improve team morale.

In order to substitute wisely the coach must also know the temperament of her players and how they react under different circumstances. For example, some may play far better in a game situation than any time in practice. Sometimes the roar of the crowd encourages a player to play a little harder and a little better. Other players may react the opposite and play considerably better when there is not a large audience. Some players seem to be at their best when they enter the game as a substitute rather than as a starter. Some players react favorably to the home crowd cheers while others may perform better away from home and their friends in the audience.

Team Time Outs

Since there are a limited number of time outs permitted in a game, they should be used judiciously and for a particular purpose. Usually only the captain or another designated player is permitted to call a time out other than those which the coach signals. Some coaches do not allow their players the freedom of calling a time out at all and permit only those which she signals.

At least two time outs should be saved for use late in the game, if they are needed. Before calling any time out, the coach should check the official game clock to be certain that there is enough time left in

stand the important role they play. A feeling for "togetherness" or unity must be developed for a team to become highly successful.

For the greatest part of the game the coach should play her starters whom she acknowledges to be the five best players on the squad. Nevertheless, at times substitution is necessary. The following reasons are cited for substituting:

1. Replace a tired player. The coach and substitutes should keep a wary eye for any player who appears to be tiring. Players themselves should be encouraged to signal for a substitute and many will if they know they will be reinserted into the contest after a brief rest.

2. Replace a player who is not playing with her usual vim or ability. The player may not be concentrating completely on the game or she may be having an "off" night. Often temporarily removing her from the game will have the desired effect.

3. Remove a player in foul trouble. It is common practice to remove a player who acquires two quick fouls. Often the third one follows very shortly. If a player is charged with her second foul near the end of the first half, the coach may remove her so that she does not acquire a third foul before the end of the first half. When a player is charged with her fourth foul, she often is removed to save her for the final few minutes of play. At times this practice has merit, but if a player is forced to sit on the bench for a long period of time before re-entering

the period to warrant taking a time out. Time outs are usually taken to

1. slow the momentum the opponents have gained, particularly if they have scored five or six consecutive points
2. change strategy on offense or defense
3. run a specific offensive play
4. rest or make a substitution
5. prevent a tie ball from occurring when a player is double-teamed (called by the player involved)

When a time out is called the players gather near the bench. Some coaches prefer to have them remain standing while others let them sit down on chairs vacated by the substitutes. Whichever system is used, the substitutes gather behind the players and all are quiet. The coach allows them to catch their breath for a few seconds as a manager distributes towels and water. The coach then proceeds with instructions.

When a time out is called by the opposing team a coach may institute a change in defensive tactics or alter the offensive alignment so that instructions given to the opposing team may be useless.

Intermissions Between Quarters

The team gathers at the bench in a fashion similar to team time outs. Players are permitted to rest 15–30 sec. before instructions are given. Comments are made to individuals about trying to fake better, passing the ball in to the pivot, overplaying an opponent more, etc. Suggestions for team play are also given. For example, they may be instructed to change to a two-three offense or to go into a two-one-two zone and start a press after their first score. The first out-of-bounds play and the moves on the jump ball also are determined. During the intermission, players are supplied with towels, water, and orange slices if desired.

Half-Time Procedures

Although many women's teams remain in the gymnasium during half-time, the home team should make provisions for both teams to meet in separate rooms that are suitable for rest, discussion, and instruction. These rooms should be close to the gymnasium and equipped with a blackboard.

During half-time intermission, the players should be allowed to rest for 2 or 3 min. Orange slices can be served and injuries checked. Towels and water should be distributed. During the time that the players are resting, the managers summarize the statistic charts and the coach studies the data from those and the scorebook. She quickly reviews the strengths and weaknesses that they have demonstrated, and makes suggestions for improvement. She informs them of any changes that should be made in the offensive or defensive alignments and indicates the play to be used on the opening tap. She reviews for them the number of fouls they have committed and the number of fouls charged to their opponents. Comments are made to individuals, the starting line-up is given, and the players are permitted time to warm up for a few minutes.

Although the length of the intermission at half-time is considerably longer than at the end of the first and third quarters, there really is very little time to offer suggestions. By the time they rest for a few minutes and a few minutes are allotted for warmup, only about 5 min. remain. The coach must be prepared to use it to the greatest advantage.

Post-Game Procedures

Immediately following the game the captain thanks the officials, and all players return to the dressing room for showers. The two coaches meet to offer condolences or congratulations as the case may be and thank the officials before leaving for the dressing room and their respective teams. If the team has won, the coach may offer her congratulations and, if necessary, quiet their enthusiasm. If the team has lost, the coach should be sympathetic. In either case congratulations should be offered to those players who played well. Particular attention should be given to those who play a subordinate role and do not normally receive the acclaim given to the high scorers and "flashy" ball handlers.

TEAM STATISTICS

Team statistics reveal vital information by which a coach and her players can analyze individual strengths and weaknesses. In order to accomplish this purpose, statistics must be accurately recorded. Managers or other individuals must be trained to use the charts if any faith is to be placed in their accuracy. The same individuals should be assigned to record data for a specific chart for all games. The information is not easy to collect, and only individuals who are dependable and give attention to detail should be appointed to these positions.

Almost all coaches collect data on field goals attempted, field goals made, free throws attempted, free throws made, and the number of fouls charged to individual players. All of this information, except field goals attempted, can be gained from the scorebook. If this is the only information desired beyond what is contained in the scorebook, a manager (without other obligations) can be assigned to tally the number of shots taken by each player. Following the game a profile of each player's actions can be prepared. This information should be collected for individual games, and data accumulated from all games should be summarized.

Shot Chart

Coaches who wish to know where shots are attempted use what is commonly called a Shot Chart. Shots attempted at the basket to the charter's left are recorded on the left side of the diagram. The number of each player who attempts a field goal is recorded where the shot is attempted; if successful, a circle is placed around the number. If the coach desires additional information about the type of shot taken and how it was derived, other symbols may be used. In this way it can be determined how many shots resulted from a fast break and drives and whether the shot was a layup, tip-in, hook, or jump shot.

The diagram shows only a portion of the entire shot chart. Preferably on one sheet, there should be four diagrams for recording data for each quarter. Following the second diagram, in addition to the totals for that quarter, space should also be provided for totals for the first half. This should also be included following the fourth quarter for totals for the second half only, and an additional line for totals for the entire game.

In a game that is likely to be a high scoring affair or that may result in many layups, it is wise to record those shots at the end line so that the diagram does not become cluttered and numbers indistinguishable. This is absolutely necessary if the type of shot is also recorded because of the additional space it requires.

The Shot Chart shows that Team A attempted thirteen shots and made six. They made three out of five layups and attempted six other shots within 15 ft. of the basket and made three of them. Two long set shots were missed. They had two fast break attempts and scored on both of them. In one instance, player No. 3 stopped to shoot a jump shot. Player No. 5 had the only jump shot she attempted, blocked. The team attempted no hook shots or tip-ins. Players 5 and 12 were both fouled on attempted shots. Both made the shots, and No. 12 converted hers into a three-point play.

In analyzing the data, the team was successful in penetrating the opponent's defense for many shots within good shooting range. They should continue to maneuver in the same manner, and players 12 and 3 should be discouraged from any further attempts at long shots and encouraged to pass the ball into better scoring position. In viewing this chart, the opponents must change their defense so that they do not allow the extensive penetration into the lane. Since one opponent has not attempted any shots, they should loosen their defense against her and allow that defense player to help her teammates when necessary.

Team B attempted ten shots and was successful on only three of them. All three were from close range— one, a result of a fast break and the other a hook shot by No. 42. They attempted four long shots and were not successful on any of them. Player No. 41 was fouled on one of her attempted layup shots. All players attempted a shot, but only three scored and no one scored more than one field goal. There were no tip-in attempts.

Team B was successful on two out of three of their driving attempts, so they should attempt to score in this fashion more often. They must adjust their offense so that they can secure better percentage shots. They must also attempt to score more from the left side unless that defender is particularly strong and the right side defender is weak. Team A should continue to use the same defensive tactics, but should question why more shots have been taken from the right side than the left side. Nevertheless, they should not extend their defense to the right until player No. 31 or others begin to score.

At the end of each period the coach makes a similar analysis before offering suggestions to her players. At the end of the game the data should be totaled so that there is an individual record for each player by game and totals for the season. This analysis should include the type of shot attempted (if desired), whether the shot was successful or not, from what range, the number of shots that were blocked, the times she was fouled, and the number of three-point plays that resulted (if desired).

Rebound Chart

To be successful, every team must have good rebounding strength at both the defensive and offensive backboard. A Rebound Chart is used to determine which players are most successful in recovering rebounds. The coach may learn that her players rebound well defensively but that they secure very few offensive rebounds. She may also learn that some players rebound better at one end of the court than at the other. Emphasis in practice sessions can correct whatever weakness exists.

A Rebound Chart consists of the names of the players and columns for tallying the number of rebounds secured by each player. The names of the best rebounders are listed at the top. It is also helpful if the names are listed in the same order for all games.

Space is provided to record offensive and defensive

SHOT CHART

First Quarter __Team A__ vs. __Team B__ At: __Team B__ Date: __Feb. 8__

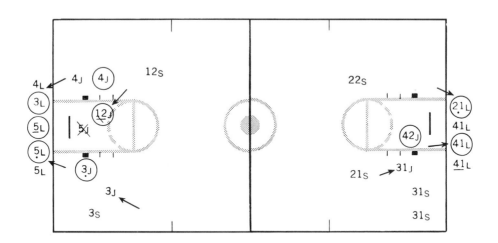

FGA __13__ FGM __6__ % __46__

Offense Used __2-3__

Opponent's Defense __M-M__

FGA __10__ FGM __3__ % __30__

Offense Used __2-3__

Opponent's Defense __2-1-2 zone__

H	hook shot
J	jump shot
L	layup
S	set shot
T	tip-in
←	drive
•	shot completing a fast break
X	blocked shot
4	shot missed
④	shot made
—	fouled
+	fouled; made the free throw

REBOUND CHART

Team A vs. Team B At: Team A Date: Feb. 18

Name	No.	Offensive 1	2	3	4	T	Defensive 1	2	3	4	T	TT	Name	No.	Offensive 1	2	3	4	T	Defensive 1	2	3	4	T	TT
Brown	33	//	/		/	4	/	//	/	///	7	11	Jones	21											
Smith	24		//	/	/	4		/	//	/	4	8	Martin	32											
Propst	55	/		/		2		/			1	3	Lyon	43											
Pohlman	12	/		/		2	/		/		2	4	Young	52											
Towle	14		/			1						1	Hunt	34											
McNally	23												Black	15											
Team		/		/		2		/	/	/	3	5	Team												
Team Total		5	3	3	4	15	2	5	5	5	17	32	Team Total												
First Half		8				15	7				17	32	First Half												
Second Half			7					10					Second Half												

rebounds by quarter. The *T* columns total the offensive and defensive rebounds. The *TT* column indicates the total number of rebounds secured by each player— both offensive and defensive. Team rebounds are recorded at the bottom of the chart. Because a rebound must be recorded for every missed shot, any time a player cannot be credited with a rebound, a team must. This includes the following situations:

- a violation is called after a free throw is attempted
- a foul is called after a field goal is attempted
- either a free throw or field goal goes out of bounds before it is touched by any player
- a shot is blocked and goes out of bounds (if it remains in play, whoever recovers it is credited with the rebound)
- a team gains possession of the ball after a tap on a held ball that results from a rebound.

The rebounds are totaled for each quarter and for the entire game. On this chart, Brown secured four offensive rebounds and seven defensive rebounds. Smith had four offensive and four defensive to give her a total of eight rebounds. Propst secured three rebounds, Pohlman had four, and Towle had one. The team was credited with a total of five rebounds. In the first half, Team A secured eight offensive rebounds and seven defensive rebounds; in the second half they had seven offensive rebounds and ten defensive rebounds. This gave Team A a total of fifteen offensive rebounds and seventeen defensive rebounds for a total of thirty-two rebounds. The total rebounds for each team should equal the total number of shots missed by the opponents.

The same tabulation should be made for Team B. By viewing the chart, players can ascertain which team is obtaining the greater number of rebounds at each basket. The most dangerous rebounders on the opposing team can also be determined so that players can give greater attention to blocking them out.

Turnover Chart

A Turnover Chart is a valuable tool because it clearly identifies which players cause their team to lose possession of the ball and which players help their team gain the ball. This instrument should be used, however, only by an alert recorder who has had considerable practice in using the device. It is difficult to be exact, particularly with teams other than the very highly skilled, because of the large number of violations and poor passes generally made in those contests. Some coaches find it advisable for two people to work together—one as an observer, the other as the recorder. This may be unnecessary in games where there are not too many turnovers.

Space is provided on the chart for the names of all players on both teams. This particular chart permits the recording of both possessions lost and possessions gained. Some coaches may prefer to eliminate the latter part to simplify the chart. Or, a coach may make two separate charts if she desires—one for loses and one for gains of possession. This would simplify the task, but experts are still required for recording. Recording data for the opposing team may be omitted.

The Turnover Chart shows only some of the players on Team B. Normally, all of them would be included. Any time a player causes her team to lose possession of the ball, a tally is made in one of the columns under Possession Lost. Any time a player causes the opponents to lose possession of the ball and thereby gains it for her team, a tally is recorded in one of the columns under Possession Gained.

When a player causes an opponent to commit a violation, the violation is recorded on the chart for both teams—one as a possession lost and the other as a possession gained. For example, by good defensive positioning, Jones forced Propst into committing a traveling violation. Looking at the chart the reader will see a *T* under possession lost violation for Propst and a *T* under possession gained violation for Jones. The reader should recognize that someone does not always "cause" a violation to occur; therefore, tallies are not often made for both teams. However, in the case of an offensive foul, a tally is always made for both teams. The chart shows that Pohlman is given credit for causing an offensive foul to occur while Martin is charged with committing the foul. Similarly, Martin caused Pohlman to foul. Each player, therefore, has a tally under committing and causing a foul. It can be seen that Brown made a poor pass that was intercepted by Jones. A *P* is recorded under possession lost pass for Brown, and a *P* is recorded under possession gained interception. Similarly, Towle had her dribble stolen by Jones, and an *S* is recorded for each player in the same columns. During a jump ball, Brown entered the circle too soon as her team gained possession of the ball, so a *J* appears under violations. Smith entered the lane too soon on a free throw while her team was shooting and caused a loss of possession. Smith also was tied up by Martin, but the team Smith is on gained the tap. Smith is charged with a possession lost due to being tied, but is credited with a gain in possession when her team secured the ball. Martin also is credited with a gain in possession for causing the tie ball. The chart also shows that Team A lost the ball twice due to a 30-sec. violation.

It is possible to ascertain the number of turnovers that occur in each half by using the upper portion of each space to record turnovers in the first half and the lower portion in the second half. For example, one

TURNOVER CHART

Team: **Team A** vs. **Team B** At: **Team A** Date: **Feb. 8**

Team A

Name	No.	Possession Lost					Possession Gained					
		Pass	Commit a Violation	Commit an Offensive Foul	Is Tied (Jump)	Total	Interception	Cause a Violation	Cause an Offensive Foul	Ties an Opponent (Jump)	Gains the Tap	Total
Brown	33	P	J			1 ②1						
Smith	24		F	1		1 ②1				1		1 ①0
Propst	55		T			1 ①0				1		1 ①0
Pohlman	12			1		1 ①0		1				0 ①1
Towle	14	S				1 ①0						
McNally	23	R				1 ①0						
Team (30 sec.)			1 / 1			1 ②1						
Team Total		3 ③0	2 ⑤3	1 ①0	1 ①0	7 ⑩3				1	1	2 ③1

Team B

Name	No.	Pass	Commit a Violation	Commit an Offensive Foul	Is Tied (Jump)	Total	Interception	Cause a Violation	Cause an Offensive Foul	Ties an Opponent (Jump)	Gains the Tap	Total
Jones	21		DT / 3		1	3 ④1	SP	T			1	4 ④0
Martin	32		L / DD	1	1	1 ④3			1	1		2 ②0

Passes
P poor pass
R poor reception
S lose ball on dribble

Interceptions
P pass
S steal a dribble

Violations
3 3 sec.
5 5 sec.
D illegal dribble
F free throw
J jump ball
K kicking
L boundary line
T traveling

30-sec. violation was committed in each half. The totals for each half are shown, and the sum of both halves is centered and circled.

Season Totals

Statistics such as those described should be collected for every game. Following each game on a master sheet the accumulated data should also be recorded so that a coach or players can see the statistics per game and those per season. Accumulated team statistics generally include only general information such as field goals attempted, field goals made, field goal percentage; free throws attempted, free throws made, free throw percentage; rebounds, turnovers, and fouls.

A clear picture of each player's strengths and weaknesses can be ascertained from the accumulated data from all of the charts. By recording detailed informa-tion from the shot, rebound, and turnover charts, it becomes apparent in what areas each player needs improvement. These prove to be excellent references for a player who really desires to become better.

POST-SEASON PROCEDURES

The first thing a coach probably wants to do at the end of the season is to emit a large sigh and then enjoy her first weekend at home in several months! After that she should check to see that her managers have completed the team and player accumulated statistics and that equipment is checked in, cleaned, and properly stored.

Often a team enjoys scheduling a banquet, picnic, supper, or other get-together to complete their season. This should be encouraged.

Glossary

Alive. A term used to denote an offensive player who has not yet dribbled.

Assist. Credit awarded a player who passes to a teammate if the pass results in an immediate score.

Attack. Offense. An act by which a team attempts to score.

Attack Players. Players on the team in possession of the ball who are attempting to score.

Back Court. That half of a court which a team defends; that half of the court which the opponents attack.

Backdoor Cut (play). A reverse cut—one in which a player cuts behind her defender in an attempt to become free to receive a pass.

Ball Control. That type of offensive system in which a team moves slowly downcourt and passes carefully until an opportunity arises for a high percentage shot; it is the opposite of a fast break style of play.

Blocking Out. A tactic employed by the defensive team to keep the offensive players behind them and prevent them from gaining good rebounding position.

Corner. That area of the court that is approximately 5 ft. in from the intersection of the endline and each of the side lines at both ends of the court.

Cover a Passing Lane. A tactic used by a defense player in which she plays in front of her opponent or at an intercepting angle between her opponent and the passer.

Cross Block. A tactic in which a defender first moves over to guard a free opponent who is prepared to shoot and then blocks her out from the rebound. Meanwhile the defense player assigned to guard the free opponent moves over to block out her teammate's opponent.

Cut. An offensive technique in which a player runs to a clear space on the court either to get free for a pass or to clear a space for a teammate.

Deep Rebound Position. The position taken by one of the defenders at the top of the circle when a shot is attempted.

Defense. The act by which a team attempts to prevent the opponents from scoring.

Defensive Balance. A tactic used by the offensive team while in their front court. One or more players are assigned to be in the free throw area or at the top of the circle in a position to defend if the opponents gain possession of the ball.

Defensive Players. Players on the team which does not have possession of the ball.

Defensive Team. The team that is not in possession of the ball.

Double Team. An act by a defensive team in which two players guard one opponent; utilized especially when employing a zone press.

Drive. A tactic used by an offensive player in which she dribbles toward the basket.

Far Side Forward. The forward on the side away from the ball.

Far Side Guard. The guard on the side away from the ball.

Fast Break. An act by the offensive team to move rapidly from their back court to their front court in an attempt to gain a player advantage — particularly, in a two-on-one or three-on-two situation.

Five on Five. Five attack players maneuvering against five defense players.

Float. Floating — a defensive tactic in which a player moves laterally toward the basket when an opponent is two passes away from the player with the ball.

Four on Four. Four attack players maneuvering against four defense players.

Free Lance. A type of offense in which players are given freedom in their moves to take advantage of defensive weaknesses.

Front. Fronting — a defensive tactic in which a player (usually a pivot defender) stands between her opponent and the ball in an effort to prevent her opponent from receiving a pass.

Front Court. The half-court that contains the goal for which a team is shooting.

Give and Go. An offensive play in which a player passes to a teammate and cuts for the basket.

Hedge. A tactic used by a defense player to help a teammate who is screened. It is executed by taking a step toward the side of the driving opponent to force her to go wide around the screen and allow the screened defender time to regain good defensive positioning; the player hedging then returns to guarding her own opponent.

High Post. A player who positions herself 15 ft. or more from the basket with her back to the basket for the primary purpose of passing to cutters.

Inbounder. The player who puts the ball in play from out of bounds.

Inside Screen. An offensive tactic in which a player cuts to a position between a teammate and her opponent. The player may stop in front of her teammate or continue running beyond her teammate.

Lateral Cross. A term usually applied to two guards moving laterally. The guard on the right side of the court moves to the left side, and the guard on the left side moves to the right side. They usually cross close together with an inside or back screen.

Low Post. A player who maneuvers through the free throw lane or stands outside the lane within 9 ft. of the basket for the primary purpose of scoring; when outside the lane she stands with her back to the basket.

Medium Post. A player who cuts through the free throw lane or positions herself to the side of the lane 9–15 ft. from the basket. She has her back to the basket and attempts to score or pass off from this position.

Middle Rebound Position. The position taken by a member of the defensive team near the free throw line to secure a long rebound away from the basket.

Near Side Forward. The forward on the side on which the ball is being played.

Near Side Guard. The guard on the side on which the ball is being played.

Offense. The act by which a team attempts to score.

Offensive Players. Players on the team in possession of the ball who are trying to score.

One on One. One attack player maneuvering against one defense player.

Open Stance. A position taken by a defense player in which she places her inside foot back so that she is partially facing the ball.

Outlet Pass. The initial pass made following a rebound usually toward one of the side lines.

Outside Screen. An offensive tactic in which a player cuts to a position basket side of a teammate and her opponent. In this position the player may stop or continue running beyond.

Overplay. A defensive tactic used while guarding a player with the ball to force her in a predetermined direction. The defender plays either with one foot opposite the midline of her opponent and the other foot to the side, or she plays with one foot opposite one foot of her opponent and the other foot to the side.

Passing Lane. The term used to denote the path through which the ball must go; usually used to refer to the direct path between the passer and a receiver.

Penetrate. A term used to indicate the need for the attack to get the ball within the area covered by a zone defense. Passing the ball within the perimeter of the defense. Sometimes used in reference to man-to-man defense.

Percentage Shot. A shot, taken near the goal, which has a good chance of being successful.

Shots taken closer to the basket have a higher percentage of success.

Perimeter. A term usually used in connection with the position of the defense players; it is the area outside (away from the basket) all of the defenders.

Pivot. Post. A player who maneuvers close to the basket, usually through the free throw lane or just outside of it, for the purpose of shooting or passing to cutters; also, a means of turning while keeping one foot stationary.

Point Position. That area on the court that is roughly 5 sq. ft. located just outside the top of the restraining circle at each end of the court.

Post. Pivot. A player who maneuvers close to the basket, usually through the free throw lane or just outside of it, for the purpose of shooting or passing to cutters.

Press. A defensive tactic attempted to force the opponents to make errors. It may be executed using man-to-man or zone defense and can be applied full, three-quarter, or half-court; it often involves double-teaming tactics.

Pressing Defense. Tight defense. An aggressive defense in which the defenders play close to their opponents and usually cover the direct passing lane. It may involve a single player, several players, or a whole team. It may be used full court or in the defensive end only. If played by the whole team, it usually involves double-teaming and some zone principles.

Rear Screen. An offensive tactic in which a player cuts away from the basket to an open space and stands while a teammate drives or cuts around her.

Reverse Cut. A backdoor cut. A player cuts behind her defender in an attempt to become free to receive a pass.

Roll. An offensive technique in which a player cuts for the basket after having set a screen. The roll is an effective technique when the opponents play a switching man-to-man defense.

Sag. Sagging—a defensive tactic in which a player drops back toward the basket and away from her opponent.

Sagging Defense. A tactic in which defensive players slide away from their opponent back toward the basket. This tactic may be used by an entire team when the opponents are beyond

shooting distance, or it may be used by guards who drop back when the ball has been passed in to the pivot, to the wing position, or to the corner to permit them to see the ball and their opponent at the same time.

Screen. An offensive technique designed to temporarily delay the progress of an opponent or to force her to move in a path other than that which she desires.

Strong Side. A term used to refer to a portion of the offensive alignment. It refers to the side of the court in which there are three or more offensive players; it does not refer to the position of the ball or the abilities of the players involved.

Three on Three. Three attack players maneuvering against three defense players.

Tight Defense. Pressing defense. An aggressive defense in which the defenders play close to their opponents and usually cover the direct passing lane. It may involve a single player, several players, or a whole team; it may be used full court or in the defensive end only. If played by the whole team, it usually involves double-teaming and some zone principles.

Top of the Circle. That area outside the restraining circle at each end of the court, approximately 21–25 ft. from the basket.

Trap. A defensive tactic in which two players double-team an opponent. Often used when the double-team takes place near a side line or in the corner.

Turnover. An act by the offensive team in which they lose possession of the ball before they can attempt a shot; caused by a violation, interception, or poor pass out of bounds.

Two on Two. Two attack players maneuvering against two defense players.

Weak Side. A term used to refer to a portion of the offensive alignment. It refers to the side of the court in which only two offensive players are positioned. It does not refer at all to the position of the ball or the abilities of the players involved.

Wing. Position—a term used to denote a place on the court approximately 10 ft. on each side of the free throw line and opposite it.

Zone. A method used by the defense in which they guard from the goal outward. Players are responsible for a particular area on the court rather than a specific player.

Index